THE

✤

GOLDEN

✤

LONGING

✤

THE GOLDEN LONGING

by

FRANCIS LEARY

Charles Scribner's Sons

New York

Acknowledgments

✢

APPRECIATION is due to the following persons and institutions for cordial and valuable aid:

The Trustees and Staff of the British Museum; Mademoiselle Diane Canivet of the Bibliothèque Nationale in Paris; M. Armand Grunzweig of the Royal Archives in Brussels; the Archives of the Department of Namur and the Municipal Archives in Bruges; M. Georges Bataille and Madame Hélène Cadou of the Bibliothèque Municipale in Orléans; Mademoiselle Emilienne Fournier of the Archives of the Department of the Loire; M. Jacques Levron of the Bibliothèque Municipale in Angers; Mr. T. C. Benfield and Staff of the Town Clerk's office in York; the Trustees of the School for the Blind, formerly King's Manor, in York; Mr. W. Leech, Curate, of Tewkesbury Abbey.

Dr. William Shepherd Dix and Staff of Firestone Library, Princeton University; the British Council Library in Paris; Mr. Harry Goldberg and the Directors of the American Library in Paris.

Also, Miss Isolde Wigram of the Fellowship of the Whyte Boar, in London; and Mr. Alexander Clark of the Friends of Richard III, in New York.

To Mr. Burroughs Mitchell, editor, Scribners, for his rare perception and unfailing support throughout; and to Osyth Leeston, editor, John Murray's, for helpful suggestions at various points.

To my mother, Eve Woodburn, for her constant interest and aid.

And lastly to my wife, Simone Marguerite, whose courage and belief have greatly contributed.

CONTENTS

❖

INTRODUCTION   xiii

JEANNE LA PUCELLE: *saint in armour*   3

RENE AND MARGUERITE D'ANJOU: *the tragic geste*   115

RICHARD THE THIRD   203

BIBLIOGRAPHY   319

APPENDICES

   A–E: Saint in Armour   325

     F: The Stricken Lute   338

     G: "The Wicked Uncle"   344

INDEX   353

LIST OF ILLUSTRATIONS

❖

FACING

I.   JEANNE LA PUCELLE, AS DRAWN BY CLEMENT DE FAU-
QUEMBERGUES, CLERK OF THE PARLEMENT OF PARIS   102

II.   MINIATURE OF JEANNE, FROM A FIFTEENTH CENTURY
MANUSCRIPT   103

III.   SIGNATURE OF JEANNE   103

IV.   JEANNE DRIVING THE DAUGHTERS OF JOY OUT OF THE
       FRENCH CAMP   103

V.   MARGUERITE D'ANJOU KNEELING IN PRAYER   134

VI.   RENE D'ANJOU IN HIS STUDY   134

VII.   RENE D'ANJOU   135

VIII.   HENRY THE SIXTH   135

IX.   TALBOT EARL OF SHREWSBURY PRESENTING A BOOK TO
       HENRY VI AND QUEEN MARGUERITE D'ANJOU   230

X.   COURT OF EDWARD THE FOURTH   230

XI.   RICHARD THE THIRD   231

XII.   EDWARD THE FOURTH   231

XIII.   RICHARD THE THIRD   262

XIV.   ELIZABETH OF YORK   263

XV.   HENRY THE SEVENTH   263

CHART A. HOUSE OF LANCASTER   194–195

CHART B. HOUSE OF YORK   310–311

ENDPAPER MAP OF THE SIEGE OF ORLÉANS, COURTESY OF
THE BIBLIOTHÈQUE NATIONALE

TO THE MEMORY OF MY GRANDFATHER:

HIRAM H. WOODBURN

NOVEMBER 12, 1867—JANUARY 24, 1941

in whose library the past was first discovered . . .

"*Then, play us a tune on the unbroken spinet, let time be as the road to London and we a traveler on it; and let us enter London and find out what year it is there in the Mile End Road; let it be dark, and let us see if we could understand them; and then let us find out what year it is, a lodging for the night, and see if they read mystery on us, or would fly from us . . .*"

THOMAS WOLFE

INTRODUCTION

✣

I T WAS a time of splendour and agony, when Christendom had never been so prosperous and so tormented, and the glowing praise of life as seen through radiant windows of Fra Angelico and Giotto had given place to the Jungian monsters of Hieronymous Bosch. It was a time of terror, when fire and steel devastated the Kingdom of France, when throughout England thousands were spaded into huge grave pits on desolate battlefields, when the richest realm of the West, the Duchy of Burgundy, was wrecked by war. It was a time of treachery and murder, when Princes were stabbed, hacked, throttled by hired killers. It was a time of wolves: great grey Curtaut, "Short-tail," and his fellows slavering at the gates of Paris; of the pack that howled on the frozen plain of Wakefield; of the snarling scavengers of Nancy.

It was a time of witches and wizards, from the charms and waxen images of Eleanor Cobham, Duchess of Gloucester, to the mighty horror of Gilles de Rais. The fissures in the idealized world of Thomas Aquinas had let in the Night. A darkness both ancient and new; the outward reflection of the soul's Dantean landscape. Doom was no longer a simple childish elaboration of the torments of an earthly rackmaster; doom had become a fearful perversion of life itself. The terrible *danse macabre* on the charnel house of the Paris Church of the Innocents. The unbearably haunting naked sufferer crucified upon an enormous gilded harp in Bosch's *Garden of Earthly Pleasures*.

For this Fifteenth Century Christ has nothing in common with the grace of Calvary. This is not God, but man crucified; crucified upon the image of his dearest visions, his ruined dreams. . . .

As the soul of Man emerges naked and tormented from the broken chrysalis of the Christian Middle Ages, there occurs a frantic effort to clothe and to adorn this nakedness; to formulate elaborate rules to mask the desperation and loneliness within. The Fifteenth Century is the Age of formal chivalry; of knightly Orders such as the Garter and the Golden Fleece, empty of true religious fervor, dedicated to martial pride, to royal or ducal glory, to an intense sexuality in which the pleasing of women is all-important to the champions in the lists. The finest literary and poetic evocation of this formal chivalry is Sir Thomas Malory's *Morte d'Artur;* a work conceived in a spirit utterly foreign to such iron priesthoods as the Knights Templar or the Knights of St. John.

Malory is the appropriate troubadour of this hollow chivalry. In and out of jail half a score of times on charges of rape, burglary, felonious assault, disturbing the peace, vagrancy, and that favourite dodge of Master François Villon—robbing the collection boxes of the poor— Malory was only saved from a lifetime behind bars by a pardon from King Edward the Fourth. But Tom Malory—oh supreme redemption! —writes well. He has a good story, most of which he filched from French romances, and he knows how to tell it. It is a pagan story, a Grendel world of scaly dragons, black and green champions, lovely mournful blondes and long adulterous nights—and the Fifteenth Century loved it.

The elaboration, the outward vanity, was most evident in armour and in dress. Plate armour became suicidally ponderous. The ninety-pound suits with complicated straps and buckles were in part a clumsy defense against crossbolts and "hand-gonnes"; in part, a vain show. Perilous vanity; again and again knights fell down and smothered. Dress took fantastic forms; the great flaring wings of the "butterfly" head-dress; the slashed and dagged doublets; the trailing velvet and damask gowns glittering with sequins; the shoes or "shoon" with absurd curling toes linked to the knees by tiny gold chains; the jeweled doeskin gloves. Ladies shaved their eyebrows and the fore part of their heads; no trace of hair should appear from under the three-foot steeple known as the "henniquin." Men shaved their beards and wore their hair in a bowl-shaped cut, to accommodate the helmet. The medieval notion that a peculiar virtue lurked in dirt and masses of hair—much as certain teenage cults affect today—had given way to the pre-Christian practice of regular shaving and baths.

Civilization, that is the strictly material side, had improved in other aspects. Westminster Hall, rebuilt by Henry Yvele, architect or "master-builder" for the gorgeous Richard the Second, supped thousands. Forks came in from Italy; and the noble lords learned to eat from individual silver bowls instead of digging with greasy fingers into a common vessel. Richard made a valiant effort to teach table manners to the Irish during a royal tour of that snakeless Eden. Richard's Queen, Anne of Bohemia, brought the side-saddle to England; while Richard himself is credited with inventing the "handcouvrechef" or handkerchief, to supplant the good oldfashioned way of blowing the nose through the fingers onto the rushes.

But if lords began to shave and bathe regularly, to sleep in a clean bed, to observe amenities at table; if the ravages of the Black Plague receded; if homosexuality and other deviations diminished, still did the familiar human values of cruelty, greed and treachery stamp the Age.

In France, the Court presented a scene of Bosch-like degradation and hellish night. The roars and whispers of that royal madman, squatting in his own ordure, swarming with vermin, hideous with sores from his frenzied nails—was there no pity, no grace for God's Anointed, the heir of Saint Louis, the Most Christian Majesty Charles the Sixth? No pity, not even that shown to a scrawny mongrel—save perhaps the charity of a humble mistress-nurse, the young Odette Champdevilliers?

It seemed not.

Roars and whispers . . . But if God had abandoned Charles, might He be sought in that bedchamber of the Hotel St. Paul, in Paris, where Queen Ysabeau de Baviere gave her blonde German body to Louis, duc d'Orléans, the royal madman's exquisite brother? The Queen of France was a German Messalina; Orléans plotted to poison his brother and usurp the throne . . . so ran the rumours about the Rue St. Jacques and the Place des Vosges.

True or false, the tale suited the sinister purpose of John the Fearless, second Duke of Burgundy in the Valois line and first cousin of both the madman and the dandy; this long-nosed humourless politician, this totally unsympathetic being—even today one can hardly endure to read about him or to gaze upon his dreary portrait—the very arch-type of the pious hypocrite, it was enough for him, the mere suspicion of plot and poison.

And this memory of the Rue Vieille-du-Temple silvered in November moonlight, the hour eight of the clock, on Wednesday the twenty-third, the year 1407, and a gallant in black damask came riding on a richly trapped mule—oh corrupt and joyous duke!—tossing up a pearl-sewn glove and singing; beside him, two pages with flaring torches. Orléans had reason to sing. He came from the Hotel St. Paul, from the lavish bed of the German woman. Their passion had perhaps produced a tainted child of France, the future Charles the Seventh. One day this Charles will be royaled by a girl yet unborn—Jeanne of Lorraine. . . .

At the carrefour of the Rue des Francs-Bourgeois and the Rue Vieille-du-Temple, near the Porte Barbette, the black and silver night was split by murder. Twenty masked men hurled from the shadows, led by a tall varlet in a red chaperon.* Daggers flashed; belt axes gleamed. The pearl-gloved left hand was hacked off; the right arm hung by a shred; the skull was crushed, brains spilling onto the cobbles . . .

God was made an accomplice by the murderer, who saw nothing strange in the partnership. God had lost His wonder, His mystical flame. The God of John the Fearless was a magnificent and eternal Duke and Heaven a gorgeous ultimate Burgundy. And as one prosperous Duke to another the transaction had a solid business aspect, gilded by ceremonious avowals. Duke John contributed handsomely to the funeral of his victim, quite in the floral tradition of modern gangland. He then hired a popular preacher, the Cordelier Friar Jean Petit, to justify his deed to the people of Paris. But John's partner, God, failed the Duke; and twelve years after, despite further expenditures on tombs and chantries, John himself was suddenly cut down at a peace conference between Burgundians and Armagnacs on the bridge of Montereau.

"The hole," as Francis the First acutely remarked, weighing the battered relic of the splendid Duke in one palm, "by which the English entered France." Meaning that the slaying of John the Fearless had driven Burgundy into the English camp for almost thirty years and had made possible an English regime in the major cities and provinces of the kingdom of Philip Augustus and Saint Louis.

But the notion of doing business with God was entirely typical. On his deathbed, the immensely rich Cardinal Henry Beaufort (who also had a murder—that of Humphrey of Gloucester—in his score with Heaven) had tried to bribe another year or so out of God by pledging a huge sum to devotional purposes. God turned down the offer. The "deals" that Louis the Eleventh made with God, or thought he was making, which is the same thing, were the worldly transactions of two calculating monarchs. And that very glittering paranoiac, Charles the Rash, spent vastly to convince God that he—Charles—ought to have Christendom at his spur.

---

* Raoul d'Anquetonville, who had recently been fired from some minor post in the Household of Orleans; Burgundy snapped up his services.

In contrast, Gilles de Rais preferred to make his bargains with the Devil. He was a kind of monstrous flower, an incredible night-bloom of the time. A Marshal of France, Chevalier of the Breton Order of the Ermine, guardian of the sacred ampulla at the Coronation of Charles the Victorious, Gilles de Rais was both a valourous knight and a man of learning and exquisite taste. But all this charm and valour were bartered to the Devil. Passing from one black rite to another, Gilles de Rais ended in horror. He raped and mutilated hundreds of Breton children; victims gathered from every corner of Brittany by the crimson and silver stewards of de Retz to sing in their master's justly renowned choir. His most acute disappointment was the Pope's refusal to recognize the lavish cathedral chapter at Tiffauges, with a 'bishop,' 'canons,' and 'chaplains'—all 'consecrated' by Gilles himself. The Devil's liegeman was marvelous pious.

The Breton Bluebeard was burned in the Place de la Madeleine at Nantes; but in consideration of his exalted rank, he was first strangled, a mercy not granted to Jeanne la Pucelle. But there was more room in the Fifteenth Century for Gilles de Rais than for Jeanne. Today, the mossy ruins of the chateau of Machecoul, near Pornic, seem yet to guard unspeakable memories and one does not care to linger in the Keep's single remaining vault.

There is a hint of the Breton diabolist in John Tiptoft, Earl of Worcester and High Constable of England under Edward the Fourth. Graduate of Padua, noted Latinist, revered patron of editor-printer William Caxton, Worcester was one of the most cruel and accomplished men of his time. His torments were as famous as his sonnets; and Caxton's fulsome eulogies to his noble benefactor recall those other dedications—to terror—set along the Hampshire dunes: the twenty impaled sailors. Even in the Fifteenth Century, impalement created shock. It consisted of severing heads and limbs, setting up the trunks reversed on a row of stakes, driving a smaller stake into the upturned anus and impaling the head thereon.

These impaled sailors had served Richard Neville, Earl of Warwick, and when in 1470 Warwick came again to power the 'butcher'—as the less classically minded termed Edward's Constable—was found hiding in a tree and shortened by a head.

The character of the clergy betrayed the temper of the time. In England, the mighty Evangelical effort of the Lollards had guttered out in witch hunts, burnings, abject recantations. The mouldering corpse of John Wycliffe, spiritual legator of the Lollards and the first man to translate the Bible into English, had been dug up and thrown into the river Avon. Reginald Peacock, Bishop of Chichester, suspected of original thought on Church doctrine, had been menaced with death. Peacock recanted; was condemned to perpetual retirement and his books thrown to the flames. Burnings for heresy were frequent during the reigns of Henry the Fourth and Henry the Fifth, the valiant 'Prince Hal' personally assisting at several conflagrations.*

After the death of the victor of Agincourt, the burnings decreased, partly because the Protector of England and of Henry the Sixth in his young age, Humphrey Duke of Gloucester, was a wise and ironic man, skeptical of the clergy, and partly because the spirit of religious inquiry was dead in England. Not for a hundred years and the Pilgrimage of Grace would there be again a religious movement.

Humphrey Duke of Gloucester and Lord Protector, his jokes, his library, his women. What was he—this Eighteenth Century *philosophe* —doing in this Age? Adventuring . . . and his life, too, had a detached quality of wit and observation. Like most philosophers, Humphrey was happy; he enjoyed the spectacle.

The people of England had a name for him: the 'Good Duke Humphrey,' they called him. But the 'Good Duke' failed to bring the war in France to a successful end or to sponsor an effective peace. It was the vulnerable redoubt in his policy. Twenty-five years of bickering with the Beauforts ended in the plot of Bury St. Edmunds. Humphrey had not credited the deadly passions of his foes (how else explain the fatal carelessness of the last hours?); too late, he discovered that philosophy could not dispute with thugs.

Typical clerics of the time were Cardinal Henry Beaufort, already noticed, who operated whorehouses in Southwark and dealt in usury at rates undreamed of by Jewish money-lenders; George Neville, Archbishop of York, cold, suave, unscrupulous, who accumulated a fortune; John Morton, Bishop of Ely, afterward Cardinal, who master-minded the Tudor plot against Richard the Third and specialized in tax-gathering under several monarchs. Morton's confidential operatives were men of the robe: Richard Fox, Bishop of Winchester, Dr. Reginald Bray,

---

* I am indebted to my friend Alfred Duggan for pointing out that the insistence of Lollards on grace in both rulers and ruled made them anathema to the secular power. This seems a sound theoretical point, but was not the savagery by which the early Lancastrians extirpated heresy partly owing to the fact that their own title was tainted by usurpation and by blood?

and Christopher Urswicke, Chaplain to Lady Margaret Beaufort. Cardinal Morton died at ninety, rich and execrated.

Eternity annexed, men arrayed in a ferocious struggle for the world. Wars were incessant: England against France; Burgundy against France; York against Lancaster. Burnished armour rather than a flickering altar illumined the Age. There was beauty in the glint of steel; a prayer in the dawn trumpet; God in the loneliness of the bootless dead. War was the obsession of the century, the wasting lust, the consecrated passion. Fighting flared; Heaven stormed with anguish; and upon his gilded harp Man was crucified.

The Wars of the Roses. . . .

The Roses were the bloodiest, the most desperate and merciless of all conflicts fought in England. In thirteen major battles between 1455 and 1485, it is probable that more than 100,000 combatants perished. During the first five years, from First St. Albans to Wakefield, quarter was regularly granted; but after the vengeful slaughter of Wakefield, in which Queen Marguerite d'Anjou's northern army of 20,000 overwhelmed a Yorkist force of 5000, the battles became "war to the knife, and the knife to the hilt."

Edward the Fourth told his literary friend, Philippe de Commines, historian and adviser of Charles the Rash, that he ever ordered the knights slain and the commons spared. But the record hardly bears this out. Of the four major battles in which Edward was involved—Mortimer's Cross, Towton, Barnet, Tewkesbury—each was fought to a finish, the opposing Lancastrian army wiped out and fugitives butchered. Towton, fought on Palm Sunday, March 29, 1461, was a freezing horror where the Heralds "counted 28,000 dead" amid the red snow. Towton: the cruelest fight ever known in England. Crimson and white, the colours of the accursed House of Plantagenet—red the blood of Lancaster, white the death pallor of York.

Fifteenth Century warfare had little in common with the courtly staves of Sir Thomas Malory. Henry the Fifth and Charles the Rash, those paragons of the knightly ideal, were ruthless in refusing quarter. When granted, quarter had the economic motive of gouging a substantial ransom out of the prisoner. But in a civil war no such motive might exist, for each side considered the worldly goods of the opposing faction as already forfeit under the law of treason and attainder.

The notion that the savagery and deep national wounds of the Roses have been exaggerated arises from a failure to understand the changing nature of warfare. Fire-power in the form of cannon, introduced to an English battlefield at Duppelin Moor in 1337, had greatly increased in effectiveness and tactical value. For all the inspired captaincy of Jeanne la Pucelle, it was the artillery of the brothers Bureau, Jean and Gaspard, that ultimately blew the 'God-damns' out of France.

It was massed fire-power, toads and serpentines linked cradle to cradle, hurling twenty-pound iron balls or murderous chain-shot, that broke the Yorkist assault at Northampton and seemed to ensure victory until treachery tore open the Lancastrian line. And it was cannon, the skillfully employed great brazen 'gonnes'—*Dijon, Newcastle, London, Edward* and *Richard Bombartell*—that in a matter of days reduced the hitherto impregnable Percy strongholds of Alnwick and Bamborough, with red-hot shot screaming through Sir Ralph Grey's privy chamber at Bamborough.

It is not to be wondered at that no medieval town stood a siege during the Roses. For all of that, the physical and psychological impact of the wars was fearful. An enormous body of fighting men—virtually the whole trained soldiery of the Nation—was spaded into huge grave pits throughout England. Adventures abroad ceased; the Lyon of Edward Longshanks, of the Black Prince, of Harry the Hero-King of Agincourt, was barely able to withstand a Scottish invasion in the early sixteenth century. More: the loss of their liverymen and the waste and confiscation of their property wrecked the semi-royal power of the great lords. Under the Tudors, England became a tyranny; for no collective force existed or would exist for one hundred and fifty years to defy crowned arrogance.

The psychological impact was even more significant. The soldiers who fought for the Roses had learned their trade in France; and the outbreak of violence in England coincided with the return of a horde of jobless veterans. Pension plans had not yet been invented; and the only occupation most of the veterans knew or cared about was soldiering. They flocked in hungry thousands to the Standards of the Roses, Red and White.

The English administration in such towns as Paris, Bordeaux, and Rouen had been better than French rule, as is attested by chronicles of the period.* Even so, the English war in France gave rise to intolerable

---

* See for example the fascinating *Journal of a Bourgeois of Paris,* describing the discipline maintained by John Duke of Bedford among the soldiers of the Occupation. But neither Bedford in the Ile de France nor Talbot in Guyenne might control the wasting of the countryside.

suffering; it was a time of iron, with lurid flashes against a sombre firmament. Armed bands roamed the countryside with torch and axe. The atmosphere seethed.

This moral climate infiltrated England. Oaths were broken, treachery became usual, battle ended in a massacre. At Tewkesbury, May 4, 1471, Edward the Fourth cornered Lancastrian fugitives in the great Norman Abbey. Blood spattered the nave, stained the high altar of Purbeck marble, flowed in gleaming patterns about the immense Norman pillars of the central aisle. The killing lust of the three royal brothers of York was summarily halted by Abbot Trensholm. Abashed, Edward swore to respect the Abbey Sanctuary; an oath violated forty-eight hours later when the Lancastrians, induced to come forth under pledge of safe-conduct, were seized and beheaded. And what was done openly, shamelessly, in the sight of men, was hardly scrupled at in secret, under cover of a great name or office.

Of twelve Princes of the Blood, in lawful succession to the throne between 1400 and 1499, six were murdered; five died on the field of battle; one was beheaded. Four of this number were kings. This bloody swathe through the House of England extinguished the reigning line.*

The four whom we chiefly consider are adventurers of the ideal in an Age of gilded lust. Their lives have the quality of art; even to the magnificent failure of the just-missed masterpiece. Their presumption is enormous, for it is nothing less than to defy time and their own circumstance. Each was rarely gifted; and each burned his gifts warring for an ideal Kingdom, whether of God or of Man. But—forced to deal with the world—these four became trapped in mortal rivalries. Like ruined angels, they fell; driven out of their Heavens by the furies of war, ambition, pride, cruelty, and hate.

The prophet of the Age, the daughter of Jacques d'Arc of Greux and Domremy, was a strange haunted girl who conversed with God. Jeanne astounded the Fifteenth as she might the Twentieth Century. Disconcerted and dismayed her time as well. She served a political purpose to Charles of Valois, not least because in some obscure way she convinced him and then everyone that the Dauphin was really the son and heir of Charles the Mad. But the French politicians were almost as glad to

---

* RICHARD the Second, HUMPHREY Duke of Gloucester, HENRY the Sixth, GEORGE Duke of Clarence, EDWARD the Fifth, RICHARD fifth Duke of York were murdered; THOMAS Duke of Clarence, RICHARD third Duke of York, EDMUND Earl of Rutland, Prince EDWARD of Lancaster, RICHARD the Third were slain in battle; EDWARD Earl of Warwick was beheaded.

be rid of Jeanne as was the enemy. The Burgundians, who captured la Pucelle in a minor military action outside Compiègne, sold her to the English; the English, with the aid of their clerical allies, burned her as a witch and a heretic. Had Charles and his cold-eyed advisers, Georges de la Tremoille and Regnault de Chartres, Archbishop of Reims, wanted to save Jeanne, they might readily have done so by putting the life of Talbot Earl of Shrewsbury, principal English field commander, in the scales for hers.

Jeanne claimed no more than countless saints and visionaries before her, who had adorned the diadem of the Catholic Church, had claimed. But she claimed it at a time when faith was burnt out; when God had left the stable for the palace; when money exerted over men the same wizardry as today. The Twentieth Century is in no position to criticize the Fifteenth; for, while burnings have gone out of style, other and perhaps equally potent dooms await those who exalt their private revelations above the passions of the Age.

Later times, in quest of an inspirational symbol, have over-stressed the immediate effect of Jeanne's martyrdom. At Rouen, in May 1431, during that terrible immolation, no English soldier, wearing the red George Cross on white belted surcoat, cried: "We are lost! We have burned a saint!" (It is possible, however, that a Frenchman did so). A soldier of Warwick did give Jeanne a Cross made of his broken baton; she put it in her bosom next her flesh. The English armies did not suddenly fall apart. They fought on, heroically and desperately, through almost twenty years. The English were finally beaten at Castillon and Formigny by artillery—beginning a long victory-studded tradition of emphasis on ordnance in the French Army.

As a political move, Charles the Seventh—the 'Very Victorious'—had the Rouen judgement quashed by a Trial of Rehabilitation, at Paris in 1455. It would never do that the King of France should seem to owe his crown to a witch. Jeanne, the prophet of the Age, had received much the same doom as was meted out to the diabolist Gilles de Rais. The process of 'rehabilitation' was concluded in July, 1456; and the sentence of the Bishop of Beauvais and his clerical coadjutors formally annulled by Pope Calixtus the Third.

Jeanne had been happy; loved life. Her Voices, Saint Catherine and Saint Margaret, called to her from the dead; and she, who made no distinction between death and life for it was all a part of God's pity, entered into the wasteland of worldly power. She did not foresee how the world would use her; and if she had known, she would have cared no more than Christ. She dwelt in a vision, a joyous Lorraine—full of good things and loving people. That was her dream of France: grace and plentitude.

Jeanne was not a profound teacher, an Augustine, a Benedict. She offered no inspired Rule. But she was tuned to Heaven as those about her were tuned to the world, to the clink of florins and the clash of steel. And this was enough to give her, the visionary, a brief glory and an infinite anguish.

She is wonderfully appealing; wonderfully alone—and if on Heaven's last Day there were but one voice to redeem the whole Century, it would be the voice of Jeanne la Pucelle.

Her direct spiritual legatee was Marguerite d'Anjou, Queen of England. King René d'Anjou had been knight and captain to Jeanne during the march on Paris. The Touraine girlhood of Marguerite was passed in the aura of la Pucelle. In after years, Marguerite evoked Jeanne, the Maid on horseback, leading soldiers to marvelous victory. Marguerite, a being of noble beauty, learning, wit and passion, plunged at fifteen into the hate of the Roses, kept like Jeanne a sense of destiny. Yet, arrogant and Anjou, Marguerite lacked some part of the grace possessed by the girl of Lorraine. Her worst sufferings were visited upon her by pride and the conflicts of her own soul. She went to the stake not once but many times; and she died several deaths before that appalling twilight at Dampierre.

Like King René, her father, Marguerite had this dream of monarchy; a monarchy of the spirit as of the world. Like René, too, she spent her dream in warring. René's Court, at Angers and Tarascon, was the most civilized of the time: sparkling with artists, wits, and learned men; famous for chivalry, liberal and unique. It was the last of the tradition of the South, of golden Aquitaine (the very name of which is like a summons to love!) and the troubadours. That all this splendour should be bartered for the sterile kingship of Jerusalem and the Two Sicilies; for continual expeditions, wasting the treasure of Touraine, killing the noblest and the best, achieving nothing. . . .

And Marguerite, how beautiful she is! how full of grace and Greek . . . until we look closer and perceive that her gown is bright with blood. Her English skies are death-grey; she rides red snow. Her poetry of the South, of Aquitaine, is torn by trumpets. And this is war of the North, winter war, the shock of desperate hordes. War ferocious and wolf-haunted—and with a terrible loneliness at the heart of it.

'Captain Margaret's' war. . . .

With the image of the flamelit Queen arises the shadow of Richard. Deadly foes, yet forever bound the one to the other; neither may be understood without the other. Their hate flares through time; but—each had a vision of radiant monarchy.

This Prince of York, small, shrewd, tormented, blazed into royalty with a 'claim' dubious and dormant for twenty years. The real claim was a passion for kingship; a passion that had already eliminated all Lancastrian obstacles and was now to place the third Richard's Yorkist nephews in a baffling limbo whence they would never emerge. This Richard combined a zest for regality with an impulse to quick effective action. Exactly the manner of Marguerite d'Anjou. But were they not both heir to Melusine, the legendary bride of Anjou and daughter of Satan? They struck swiftly, mortally; and when at last they faced one another the battle continued through death and time.

But unlike Marguerite, who often erred in politics, Richard the Third was an apt and skillful monarch. One searches in vain for his equal among three hundred years of Plantagenets. Perhaps Edward Long-shanks? But even he was far behind Richard in handling the eternal problem of the Scots. If only the English—who ever place 'character' above shrewd government—could have been persuaded to forget about those tender lambs in the Tower and a few other awkward items such as the severed heads of Hastings, Rivers, Grey, and Vaughan, as well as the sudden demise of Henry the Sixth on Ascension Eve.

Shakespeare has Marguerite d'Anjou cry to disdainful Woodevilles: *"oh, but remember this another day, when he shall split thy very heart with sorrow, and say, 'poor Margaret was a prophetess!' "*

And though this be but the Bard's own imaginings, it is a colloquy that might well have taken place sometime between the dark ruin of Tewkesbury and the ransoming of Marguerite in 1475. Years after, Woodevilles and others had cause to recall the wild and grieving Queen. Old enemies rallied to a common cause—Richard's doom. And he, flashing Falcon, was betrayed and undone; overthrown by conflicts within. He left his kingship incomplete, his building projects, his plans for trade, his patronage of books and printing, his religious and heraldic

foundations; and went to a mortal rendezvous with a man that he infinitely scorned—"a beggarly Welsh milksop."

In his extremity, Richard had appealed to his elder sister Margaret,
married at twenty-one to Charles the Rash and now Dowager Duchess
of Burgundy. From the third daughter of a numerous House, Margaret
had become mistress of immense revenues. The girl with big searching
eyes and a long nose would astonish her brothers Edward and Richard
by her mastery of intrigue and learning, in equal parts. Her money
might have saved Richard; but she let him die.

Margaret's life was spent in the service of her House of York. She
had backed Edward and Richard in their marvelous triumph of 1471.
She would back Lambert Simnel and Perkin Warbeck in their ventures.
Always she gloried in her Rose. She hated Henry Tudor worse than
any toad or serpent, but she would not help the man whom she believed to be the murderer of the Princes of York.

The patron of William Caxton, the mistress of French and Latin as
well as of Burgundian prelates, Margaret of York inspired philosophy,
and sonnets, and encouraged the painting of van der Weyden, van
Eyck, Dirk Bouts—the vision of the Madonna to set against the burning night of Brother Hieronymous Bosch.

The tears and grace of Mary, the torment of the naked wanderer in
the *Garden of Earthly Pleasures*—each, seemingly, a disparate view
of the Age. But may not Mary's unquenchable tears be grief for Man,
the frightened Christ of this loveless time?

✠ I ✠

SAINT IN ARMOUR:

Jeanne la Pucelle

"Oh astonishing Virgin, worthy of all glory, of all praise, worthy of all divine honours. You are the honour of the reign, you are the light of the lily, you are the splendour, the glory, not only of Gaul, but of Christianity. Let Troy celebrate Hector, let Greece glorify Alexander, and Africa, Hannibal, and Italy, Caesar and all the Roman captains. France, even if it possesses a great many such heroes, can be content with this Maid alone. . . ."

ALAIN CHARTIER

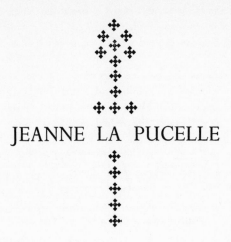

JEANNE LA PUCELLE

IN THE columned Hall, the robing room of Castle Rouen, she stood alone, confronting the black circle of her judges. About her filtered worn Norman light; upon the wall crossed lances, conical helmets, the forked banners of great dead Dukes. In her life she had been always alone, familiar of dreams and forest-wanderings; or in a laughing meadow at blindman's buff or hot cockles, suddenly the vision, the great half-heard shining moment, and she would fall silent.

She wept easily, tears spilling like summer rain. She was possessed by pity. Tales of war and death floated in her sunlit brooding; villages in flames, the blue frozen lips of the dead, a girl's scream. In her father's house, long past curfew, she would awake and glimpse moonlight through the oiled parchment across the narrow casement. She woke and thought of God. Why did He not stop the war? Send the English back to England?

Pierre Cauchon, Bishop of Beauvais and presiding judge in this most dread trial for heresy and sorcery, leaned forward. The Bishop was not a tall man, but with his bulk, his eloquent deepset eyes beneath bushy brows, he made a formidable impression. "When did you first hear these voices?"

"I was thirteen and the first time I was very afraid. And this Voice came about the hour of noon, in the summertime, in my father's garden. I had not eaten since the day before. I heard the Voice on my right

3

hand, toward the Church; and rarely I heard the Voice without light. This light was on the same side whence came the Voice; and usually it was of great brightness. And when I came into France, I often heard this Voice." *

They were dancing in the meadows of the Meuse. Jeanne was there and Hauviette and Michel Lebuin and Pierre her brother and a half-dozen others. Jeanne dashed about so merrily that her red kirtle seemed to fly above the tall grass. She halted breathless, suddenly faint and dazzled (she had fasted since the day before), and in that moment she saw the young man. He appeared abruptly, out of the sun, and for an instant she thought it was her brother Pierre. But then she realized he was not at all like Pierre; she had never seen him before. He smiled at her, saying she was wanted at home. Jeanne left the dance, it was just on noon, and went home. And in the garden the Voice came and she saw the light.

"It was the Voice of an angel or of a saint or directly from God?"

"They were the Voices of Saint Catherine and Saint Margaret. And their heads were crowned with beautiful crowns, most richly and preciously. I have leave from God to tell you this. If you doubt it, send to Poitiers where I have been previously examined."

". . . who came first, Saint Michael or Saint Catherine and Saint Margaret?"

"Saint Michael."

"Was it Saint Michael who came in your father's garden, when you were thirteen?"

"It was Saint Michael with Angels from Heaven. . . ."

"In what form did he appear?"

"I have not leave to tell you."

"What did Saint Michael say the first time?"

"You shall have no other answer." **

Yet elsewhere she had said very quietly that the Voice in the garden told her to be a good girl and to go regularly to Church. Not yet did she experience the thunderbolt of God's will, that she take up arms and drive the English out of France. She was playing with the Bishop, tantalizing him—I know a secret and you don't!—as often she did,

* Session of Thursday, February 22nd 1431. Pierre Champion's French version from the Latin. My English version.
** Fourth Session, Trial in Ordinary, Tuesday, February 27th. Cauchon in the Chair; Master Jean Beaupere leading for the tribunal.

sometimes for tactical reasons, sometimes for sheer pleasure. They were so solemn and crowlike, the sixty assessors, and the purple mitred Bishop high above her, in the mitred monarchy of *ecclesia sanctissima* . . . but it was a deadly game—and the prize? Her own gay and flashing soul.

And this, to them the breath and stuff of sorcery, of heresy, so shocking that in a single session she might condemn herself ten times over, was to her bright with the flame of her love. She knew splendour. She longed to share this light with all the world, even with this Bishop of Beauvais and his sixty assessors. But they would not allow it. La Hire had known more of God than these men. What was it her Gascon captain had prayed? . . . oh God, do Thou for La Hire this day as he would do for Thee, if he were God and Thou La Hire!

Shrewd Gascon prayer!

But once more she was back at the beginning, at Domremy. . . .

"Did you ever speak of these visions, either to your curé or to any other churchman?"

"No; only to Robert de Baudricourt and to my King."

"Did the Voices forbid you?"

"No. I was afraid the Burgundians would find out and would prevent my journey. And especially afraid my father would find out." *

Hardworking faithful Jacques d'Arc! He had become doyen, or sergeant, in his village, dealing in tax matters with Robert de Baudricourt, Sieur de Vaucouleurs and representative of royal authority in the north. Jacques d'Arc owned his own house, had acquired sheep and cattle; recently he had invested in the Château de l'Isle, which was not a real castle but a kind of fortified enclosure on the river Meuse whence the villagers of Domremy and Greux might drive their flocks when the tocsin sounded. Everyone listened to Doyen d'Arc, save his sixteen-year-old daughter.

Jeanne displayed a most unbecoming concern with soldiers and when Jacques d'Arc had gone on tax business to see the Lord of Vaucouleurs, Jeanne had insisted on knowing every detail; how de Baudricourt looked, what he wore, his words. Jacques d'Arc had told her the story at least a dozen times.

Another thing worried the Doyen of Domremy.

He, as everyone else on the march of Lorraine, had heard of the

* Session of Saturday, March 10th.

ancient foresaying of the wizard Merlin that France would be ruined by a wanton woman from another land and would be redeemed by a virgin from Lorraine. The first part of the saying had certainly come true. Since Queen Isabeau had come from Bavaria, more than two-score years ago, at the age of fourteen and a gorgeous cream and gold beauty, to wed King Charles, nothing had gone right in the realm of France. Isabeau had driven the King mad; sold the realm to the English and Burgundians. She had wasted enormous sums of money. Now, the bruit ran, Isabeau was little better than a common whore; everyone around the Court had enjoyed her, as well as the Dukes of Burgundy and Orléans. The Dauphin Charles, down in Bourges, was probably some-one's bastard. Isabeau had said as much.

So the last thing Jacques d'Arc would wish was that any of his children be mixed up in this rotten business of the Kingdom of France. Their Lorraine was not even part of France, but had its own duke and his little court in Nancy. But lately Jacques d'Arc had noticed a strange expression in his daughter's eyes whenever the prophecy of the virgin from Lorraine came into the conversation. Did Jeanne think she was that virgin? God's Nails!

One night the Doyen had dreamed that Jeanne had gone off with a company of routiers, big savage fellows like the Bastard of Vaurus and his brother, an unholy dream if ever there was one. The next morning Jacques d'Arc had said to Jeanne's two brothers, Pierre and Jean, "If I thought she intended such a thing, I would ask you to drown her; and if you would not do it, I would drown her myself!"

But if the Doyen had known what was really going on behind those shining dark eyes, he would have been even more agitated. Jeanne talking with saints and archangels! There had never been, to his knowledge, any madness in the family.

She dare not speak of her Voices; not even to a priest. What if the priest misunderstood? What if he should forbid her to listen to her Voices? She could not take such a chance.

From the beginning, Jeanne had been sure the Voices came from God. She never asked herself: why should God speak to me—poor, obscure, unlettered? Why should the Lord of Heaven send to Jeanne of Domremy His Saint Catherine and Saint Margaret? If God wished to save France, there were so many whom he might call, princes, great captains—but He came to Jeanne.

There had been the prophecy.

Jacques d'Arc was quite right in his suspicion. His daughter was thinking of the wizard's saying. She was a virgin from the march of Lorraine; she had been summoned. Her Voices had said: *go, go, daughter of God, into the realm of France. You must beat the English and bring the King to his Coronation.* Jeanne knew an unusual hesitation (she was sixteen) and replied: "I am but a poor maid and know nothing of war." And the Voices proclaimed: *God will aid thee!*

Then she knew. God had chosen her, Jeanne. She who had never been out of her native village, in a remote corner of the Duchy of Bar, in fief to the Duke of Burgundy, the ally of the English—she was to deliver France.

Jeanne suspected greatness (she was born great); and gave glorious names to what she recked little of—her Voices, the Archangel Michael (occasionally, too, she had talked with Gabriel), Saint Margaret and Saint Catherine. Her mission was that of *chef de guerre,* war chieftain, redeemer of France.

Days passed without exaltation, green willow days, Orléans-coloured days,* when amid those tender islands of the glistening Meuse, she heard the horns of glory faintly blowing. Or Jeanne and her friends Hauviette, who was twelve, and Mengette, who was eighteen and lived next door, with little Michel Lebuin tagging along, would climb to the hill shrine of Our Lady of Bermont, a mile and more through a tangled wood. And at times, with that teasing love of mystery which marked all her life, Jeanne would speak of marvels to come, of veiled matters.

She said to Michel: "There is a young girl between Coussy and Vaucouleurs who before a year is past will have crowned the King of France."

How many misty-eyed young girls, trembling on adolescence, loved to discourse of fabulous secrets! Jeanne of Domremy was no different than the others save in one respect. What she said was as wild and deep as what any young girl might say, but it was nothing more than the plain truth.

In the Bois Chesnu she heard echoes of a kingdom beyond this kingdom, the Merlin-sayings of long ago, the Maiden, the Redeemer. And in the glow and glory of St. John's Day, the listening green, the drooping branches, the utter stillness—they came to the great beech tree,

---

* Since that dread November eve of 1407, outside the Porte Barbette, the House of Orléans had taken as its colour *vert sombre,* in place of *vert gai.*

beautiful and mournful as a lily.* In the kingly tree lived the spirit of
the wood, garlands flaunted on the branches, garlands woven by Jeanne,
Hauviette, Mengette, and sometimes Beatrice de Bourlémont, the young
wife of the local lord of the manor. The daughters of Lorraine formed
a circle about the great tree, dancing.

Jeanne wanted Saint Catherine and the Virgin to have garlands, too.
And when the others had gone and the day burned in the west, she
lingered in the wood to weave a garland for Our Lady.

Her remark to Michel occurred shortly before she went for the first
time to Vaucouleurs. For weeks, she had badgered her father with questions concerning Robert de Baudricourt. Jacques d'Arc had become
weary and suspicious. Often, returning from the wood to the low dim
rush-red room, she would slide into her place at supper and find opposite a dark questioning glance above the fried eels. What was she
up to now?

This contest between them was a result of Jacques d'Arc's love for
his daughter, a love so intense that what happened to her happened
to him; her joy and suffering were his. At the moment of triumph at
Reims, Jacques d'Arc was there. When they destroyed his girl at Rouen,
he perished also in an agony of grief.**

Jeanne's father found little good in the project of a visit to Vaucouleurs and the girl's claim that she had a message for Robert de Baudricourt. Wisely, Jeanne had revealed neither the source nor content of
the message.

He wanted Jeanne to remain at home: to marry; to mother. He was
alarmed by her strangeness. She had no interest in driving flocks to
the common pasture, like other girls of Greux and Domremy. He would
willingly have paid for a course of instruction with the village curé,
but Jeanne was not interested in that either. What was the use of learning to communicate with the minds of men when you had already
talked with God? Sewing she did beautifully, and she helped her
mother around the house, but too often Jacques d'Arc heard of her

---

* This, I regret to say, is not my image; for it is as eloquent and simple and just,
  as one could well wish. It is the description of an old peasant, Gerardin d'Epinal,
  Domremy's sole 'Burgundian.'
** The idea, propagated by writers favouring the theory of Jeanne's noble heritage,
  that she had little in common with her presumed family is absurd. She and
  Jacques d'Arc had a strong emotional bond, to the point where he was actually
  sharing her dreams of soldiers—as Miss Sackville-West points out.

wandering about, talking in that gift of tongues she had of old enchanted things and prophecies long ago.

(had it not been the same in Nazareth, when the son of Joseph, that
honest carpenter, took to preaching instead of sawing, debating on
street corners when he might have been helping his father in the shop?)

Jeanne required someone to present her to Robert de Baudricourt.
Her father was clearly not the man for the purpose, but in the village
of Burey near Vaucouleurs lived Durand Laxart, a relative of Jeanne's.
She called him 'oncle Durand'—though he was really the husband of
Isabelle Romée's first cousin—and apparently was able to get around
him in a way that was quite impossible with her father. In Ascension
week, during May of 1428, Jeanne was at Burey unfolding her project
to 'oncle Durand.'

Though a man of forty, 'oncle Durand' was not keen-witted. He did
not study over the nature of his young cousin's fantastic request. By
the time Durand began to have second thoughts, it was too late . . .
and he and Jeanne were standing in the iron and morning light of
Sieur Robert de Baudricourt.

Jeanne had no doubts. Here she was, at last, in Vaucouleurs before
the captain of France. The light, a strange May green illuminating
the old shabby salle of the royal fortress (and how suddenly, irreparably,
it would all come back at Rouen!), the blunt seasoned faces of the
men-at-arms, the glint of steel, the prowling dogs—and the captain
himself high on a peaked elaborate chair, his face flaming with wine,
his poached light-coloured eyes staring at her.

She perceived that no one had the least notion why she was there;
and being French they were inclined to treat the whole matter as a
joke. It was a feeling that she would know again, in most of the great
moments of her life. 'Oncle Durand' prodded her. Surely the daft girl
did not expect him to do the talking! And vaguely she caught from
that frowning listener a growl or two. *What did she want?*

And she said, with the old beautiful eloquence of hers that had
charmed the children of Lorraine, "I am come, noble sire, with a message for the Lord Dauphin. Let him hold fast and not make war. For
before the middle of Lent, he shall have good help."

It was her first public statement. No one, not Jacques d'Arc nor
Isabelle Romée, not Durand Laxart nor Jeanne his wife, nor their
friends Henry and Catherine Royer, had the least inkling of what

Jeanne d'Arc intended to say. Perhaps she herself did not know—until the moment came.

Her words had an effect. Help of any kind was desperately needed by the young shambling bony Charles, styled Dauphin of France,* who went from one humiliation to another; lord of a steadily shrinking realm and not even lord of that, for Georges de la Tremoille, the royal treasurer, fat gorgeous Georges, was the real master at Bourges. He paid the Dauphin's bills and told Charles what to do. The last counsel necessary was to restrain the young man from fighting. It was almost impossible to rouse a spark of defiance in that spindly frame, the product (everyone thought) of the aging amours of Isabeau of Bavaria.

What did this redkirtled wench propose? Leaning forward, Robert de Baudricourt appraised her breasts.

"The Kingdom," Jeanne said, "belongs not to the Lord Dauphin, but to my Lord. Yet it is the will of my Lord that the Dauphin be made King and have the realm in his command. In spite of his enemies, he will be King. I myself shall conduct him to his crowning."

News indeed. A program that the marshals of France had striven uselessly for seven years to achieve. But: who was behind the wench? She certainly was well-made!

"Who is your Lord?" Sieur Robert inquired.

"The King of Heaven," she replied.

Sieur Robert sat back. She was only a simple goose, after all. He recalled her father, the honest Doyen of Domremy. Jacques d'Arc could not have known of this nonsense. The captain's glance shifted to Durand Laxart, shuffling and panting beside the girl. He had already formed an unfavourable opinion of Master Durand's intelligence, not least because of his role in the present farce.

Sieur Robert stood up. The barracks-note echoed in the salle. Not by chance was Robert de Baudricourt castellan of the most precarious fortress of a precarious realm, the only fount of loyalty in the north

---

* As Charles the Mad slipped into a disastrous grave in 1422, Charles might have called himself King and, in fact, he had gone through a threadbare ceremony of investiture that same year in a rundown little castle where he happened to be staying. But this fooled no one. Kings of France were crowned at Reims and anointed with the holy oil of Clovis. The title of Dauphin came into the Royal House during the reign of Philippe VI; from the death, in tragic circumstances, of the only son of the Dauphin of Vienne, who willed his county to the King on condition that the eldest son of France should bear the title of Dauphin until his succession. The two eldest brothers of Charles, Louis and Jean, had both borne the title. Louis, it has been said, drank himself to death at seventeen!

save Mont Saint-Michel. "Take her home, Durand! See that you warm her bottom. If she hangs around here, my soldiers will have good sport."

Sound advice.

FROM May to February, the starfire of Taureau and Verseau conjoined, in Jeanne, the battle chief and the illuminée; two worlds incarnate, the world without, of fire and steel, the world within, of light. And in the ironblue of Lorraine summer the world without came marching.

Orders in London and in Paris, marshalling of ships and men, a drive to final victory, to crush that wretched frightened being down in Bourges, as one would quash an obscene bug, that soi-disant Dauphin whom Jean Jouvenal des Ursins accused of hiding in his castles, in mean little rooms like closets, to escape the complaints of his poor people.* But retribution was on the road.

Let the great names ring out!

Thomas Montague, Lord Salisbury; John Talbot, Earl of Shrewsbury; William de la Pole, Marquess of Suffolk; Sir John Fastolf; Sir William Glansdale—the captains of Saint George, the armoured hunters who rode to battle with a curse and a prayer.

"And you, Suffort, Classidas, and La Poule!"

And now the great column of 'Godons,' down from Rouen and Harfleur, down from Paris and Calais, up from Bordeaux, conquerors in shirts of mail, in iron salades like inverted soup bowls, wearing the red cross of their George of Cappadocia, choking the roads, clouds of dust steaming in the soft summer air. England passing. The young immortal names of Somerset and Yorkshire, of Kent and Cumberland: John Reid, Bill Martin, Matthew Thornton, Thomas Jolly, Geoffrey Blackwell, Walter Parker, John Burford, William Vaughan, George Ludlow, Patrick Hall, Thomas Sand, John Langham, Dick Hawke, Davy Johnson, Black Henry.

The Army of the Loire. . . .

O little King, six years of age come Saint Nicholas Day, slender fawn-eyed child wandering old Windsor, two crowns upon that pale brow, the Crown of St. Edward, the Crown of St. Louis—a mighty

---

* Not to be confused with his brother, the great Chancellor, Guillaume Jouvenal des Ursins, Jean Jouvenal succeeded Pierre Cauchon as Bishop of Beauvais, later became Archbishop of Reims. He presided at the Trial of Rehabilitation. He wrote: *Vous voulez toujours être caché en chateaux, mechantes places et manières de petites chambrettes, sans vous montrer et ouir les plaintes de votre pauvre peuple.*

weight for such a little lad. Soldiers of Saint George: here is your King!

And waiting now for his uncle of Bedford in Paris to proclaim his Coronation. His uncle would do so as soon as ever the realm was quiet and wicked men ceased disturbing the King's peace; his peace. He longed for France as a child longs for a lost evening country, glimpsed in dreams. In England, he was Henry, sixth of that name; in France, he was Henry, second of that name. He imagined himself riding a white horse through the streets of Paris; he grew impatient, had one of his fits of temper when he heard of troubles in his other kingdom. His nurse had to calm her lord. *Soon, soon*, he was assured. *France loves you. France clamours for Henry.*

Soldiers of Saint George!

In this summer of 1428, the city of Paris contained 200,000 inhabitants. Once the light and inspiration of Christendom, Paris had become in twenty years of savage strife a lean and hungry place, murderous mood, plague-ridden, a raddled Jezebel of a city giving her mortal embrace now to Burgundians, now to Armagnacs. With Charles of Orléans, son of Valentine Visconti and the murdered Louis, captive in London's Tower, the leadership had fallen to Bernard Count of Armagnac, whose daughter Bonne had married the Duke over the water. Bernard had died horribly, flayed alive, in the Paris outbreak of June, 1418. The Maison d'Orléans had no present leader; and the city had been occupied first by Burgundians, then by English.

During periods of Burgundian opulence, the city was run by a cabal of the Butchers' Union and the politicians, chief of whom was John the Fearless. Butchering had got into the hands of about six great families; these controlled the Master Butchers at Châtelet and the Butchers of St. Geneviève, whence they branched out to a grip on lesser butchers and on other trades. The terrible Caboche, virtual dictator of Paris from 1410 to 1413, was a Master Butcher of Châtelet. And when another Master Butcher, Guyot Legois, passed on, Duke John the Fearless walked in the lavish procession of a typical gangster funeral.*

Despite these periods of terror, the Parisians were better off than the villagers without the walls; for these were the prey of dread monsters,

---

* The reader will be struck by the resemblance to the Teamsters of today. The same arrogance, murder, riot, blood-brotherhood with politicians. The importance of the Butchers may be gauged by the yearly figures for consumption of meat in Paris, exclusive of purveyance for the King's table: 30,000 cattle; 188,000 sheep; 30,000 pigs; 19,000 calfs.

human and four-legged. Wolves prowled, huge and slavering, carrying off children, the old and weak. But these beasts, even Short-tail himself, were less ferocious than the *écorcheurs* who ravaged everyone; men who had once been, in another age of time, French, Burgundian, English— it mattered not. They belonged to another nation: pure evil. At Meaux, near Paris, a great elm creaked with the weight of a hundred bodies, hanged from spreading limbs, blackened and slowly turning, many heads festooned with gigantic ants, others torn by crows.* The peasantry of France. France that had been so glorious; France that was dying.

Never let it be said that John Duke of Bedford—Prince John of Lancaster—was not aware of the situation. Regent of France since the death of Henry V at Vincennes in August, 1422, Bedford believed that just one more campaign, one more victory drive, a few thousands more slaughtered and towns burnt, would set all to rights. To despair was not in Bedford's nature; eventually, Frenchmen everywhere would recognize the beneficent sun of English rule. Besides, it was a rule grounded in old right. Henry the Sixth, son of Katherine of Valois, was the sole legitimate descendant of Charles the Mad.

Further, Bedford's realm was founded on the Anglo-Burgundian accord, that rock on which all Armagnacs shattered. Bedford himself had espoused Anne of Burgundy, incredible daughter of John the Fearless. Angel of mercy, visiting the lazar wards, the black holes of the coughing, organizing her charity drives, she humanized the Regency. Friend to Christine de Pisan, who spun amid the dark winter of occupied Paris her praises to Beauty, Woman, and Knighthood; showing pity to Jeanne herself, who had wrecked Bedford's domain. Anne merited the luck of Blanche of Lancaster, a *Boke of the Duchess* by a Geoffrey Chaucer.

But it all faded: felicity, the dream, Lancaster. . . .

Anne was dead at twenty-eight, childless. On this tall big-boned Englishman, the glass and mold of masculinity, had fallen the Lancastrian curse: sterility. And just as his own body in all its glow of armour was cursed and had not the power of the meanest peasant to make a son, so the outward splendour of England's sway hid the im-

---

* Francis Cosby, captain of Wicklow, in good Queen Bess' golden days, had a similar tree at Stradbally. Cosby's tree, a huge Irish oak, was decorated with the bodies of Irish children strangled with their mothers' hair. Cosby jocularly referred to his tree as 'Cosby's Cradle.'

potence within, and a peasant girl possessed more might than the captains of Saint George.*

But now, unmindful of doom, they debated strategy in a chamber of the vast decaying Tournelles, near the Porte St. Antoine. In the town ditches outside, the belled pigs of St. Antoine, privileged scavengers, fought and gobbled; while Bedford's subjects grovelled for garbage. Within, voices rose, querulous in the stained sunlight; they argued amid the vaulted *salle,* the stone corbels above with their leering heads, the dusty trembling tapestry. Bedford's broad face and curving blade of English nose appeared at the head of the oak table; the Regent of France—haute Lancastrian pride!—gazed from a chair of state with scrolled arms terminating in lion claws. (And here, in this same chamber, fifty years later, linked to the old marvelous pride of the Rose, Bishop John Morton would weave a mortal web about King Richard the Third).

There was no argument over the necessity of a campaign. No one even considered that giving the people food and effective government might do more to win their hearts than any number of Agincourts.

But: there were two 'disturbed' areas and a choice had to be made between them.

In Angers, Yolande of Aragon, mother-in-law of the 'King of Bourges,' stirred the political pot, brewing one potent marriage after another for the House of Anjou. (Yet never did Bedford dream of the ultimate audacity that would destroy all his labour—the marriage of Marguerite d'Anjou and Henry the Sixth). In the valley of the Loire wandered the 'King of Bourges'—from Loches to Chinon to Blois, wherever he could find temporary credit. Bedford often spoke of chastising the fellow with a dog whip.

The Regent favoured cleaning out Angers. He rightly judged that whatever fire the soi-distant Dauphin displayed—and it was not much —had been kindled by Yolande. Silence Yolande, and the 'King of Bourges' would fold completely. But Bedford's captains had other ideas. Ignoring the political side, the fact that the House of Anjou, of royal Valois descent, was infinitely more dangerous than that knockkneed

---

* HENRY IV had four sons: HENRY, Prince of Wales; HUMPHREY, Duke of Gloucester; THOMAS, Duke of Clarence; JOHN, Duke of Bedford. Three died childless; HENRY V sired HENRY VI, his sole child. HENRY VI was impotent as well as sterile. The heredity of Lancaster was blighted; some believe by the curse of the murdered RICHARD II, "a vengeful blood-gowned ghost with freezing eyes and hands that shook with curses."

bastard down in Bourges could ever be, Salisbury, Talbot and the others clamoured for an assault on Orléans, the key to the line of the Loire. To Bedford's objections that they had not sufficient men either to storm or to starve so strong a place, Salisbury promised to mine the defenses. He also reminded his chief that one soldier of Saint George could put to rout a dozen French monkeys. Only Fastolf, cautious, grizzled, supported the Regent.

The captains had their way. The Army of the Loire would march against the ducal capital of the House of Orléans. Nor did Bedford, frowning, liverish, overworked, nor yet these others, suspect what Destiny had prepared.

(In a remote village of Lorraine a redkirtled girl with bold dark eyes and splendid breasts said to an acquaintance, "If you were not a Burgundian, I should tell you something that would astonish you.")

If you were not a Burgundian!
What is a Burgundian that God is mindful of him? Yet the meanest creature that crawled beneath God's Heaven—even a Burgundian— may know God's grace.

But not Jeanne's. She remembered those village combats with the young Burgundians of Maxey across the river. She would not have wept if a sword had passed between the head and shoulders of Gerardin d'Epinal, Domremy's sole Burgundian, to whom she had spoken so strangely (he thought she was talking of a local swain she intended to marry!). Now, out of July's gleaming terror surged the Burgundian routier, Antoine de Vergy, former chamberlain to John the Fearless and organizer of the murder of Louis duc d'Orléans; now hatchetman to the sinister one-eyed John of Luxembourg. For a brief hour, this quiet corner of Lorraine knew war, Burgundian war, as Artois, Champagne, and the Ile de France had known it.

Jeanne fled with the others to the walled market town of Neufchâteau, seven miles away, when hoofs struck fire on the road and the dread gold and scarlet banner came out of the sun. A long column with sweating bullocks, waggons piled with the gimcrack hoard of generations of peasant saving, herds of cattle, braying asses, sheep, mongrels yelping in and out of the turning wheels. The peasants fled from the stinking breath of war.

France, that country of the heart—France was dying. The lords were killing France with their war. But among the peasants of Domremy came striding proudly this dark-eyed visionary girl, sturdy body with swinging thighs and thick ankles, generations of black earth in her walk.

With Jacques and Isabelle, Jeanne remained about a week in an auberge kept by a redheaded woman called La Rousse. La Rousse boarded soldiers and her hired girls were plump and amorous. Tooth-less jaws wagged in Neufchâteau. This kitchen-corner gossip was picked up by the ferrets of Pierre Cauchon muckraking into Jeanne's past and distorted into a monstrous accusation. Jeanne, it was insinuated, had not only gone voluntarily into a whorehouse, but had become one of the most prominent flowers of the establishment and a young man in a neighboring village, to whom she was engaged, had broken off their fiançailles and later died of grief. Jeanne, the muckrakers alleged, had summoned the fellow in the district court of Toul to force him to marry her.

Horror and shame.

But was she not accustomed to all the filthiness of which the inquisi-torial mind was capable? Voices, not shining Voices, but the scrape and rustle of clerical voices, rat's feet on naked stone; out of time, out of memory . . . *where many unguarded women stayed and the lodgers were for the most part soldiers. Thus, dwelling at this Inn, she would sometimes stay with the said woman, sometimes would drive the sheep to the fields . . . and there she learned to ride and learned the pro-fession of arms.**

But this idea of picking up soldiering from the boarders of La Rousse (like everyone, the learned examiners were baffled by Jeanne's skill in arms) was as farfetched as the accusation of whoring. With her brothers Pierre and Jean, and the boys of Neufchâteau, Jeanne had bare-backed plough-horses in the fields—as many another country girl. But that this could constitute training in arms only a scholar who had never run a course with a fourteen-foot lance and encased in eighty-pound plate armour could imagine.

As for La Rousse, everyone knew what inn keepers were like. But for sixteen-year-old Jeanne, La Rousse had been an angel of mercy to rescue folk from Pierre Cauchon's Burgundian friends. Jeanne helped La Rousse, as in Domremy she helped Isabelle Romée, sewing, sweep-ing, tidying up. Occasionally, she drove the flocks to communal pasture; she had never cared for sheep, but this was an emergency.

* Articles of Accusation, Article VIII.

But the other element of the charge—that of the young man—touched her more nearly. For it was quite true, her father had arranged a match in a desperate effort to settle his daughter in a normal life. But she, as soon as she heard of the marriage, had flatly refused to go through with the project. She was a virgin vowed to God; nay she was the virgin foretold, from the march of Lorraine.

She explained the matter to Pierre Cauchon and his colleagues. "It was not I that summoned him," she said, of the young man, "but he who summoned me. And I swore before the judge to tell the truth. And never made I a promise to this man."

She appeared three times in the district court of Toul, to answer the summons. Saint Catherine told her she would win her case. Saint Catherine was right. Once more Jacques d'Arc, in this fierce combat for his daughter's soul, had to accept defeat.

Love—marriage—a normal life: what had this to do with Jeanne d'Arc? The love of a young girl and a young man—kisses, moonlit embraces, panting bodies. The girls of Lorraine ripened early. But what of another kind of love? A love crying within Jeanne, tearing at her soul, madness beyond the madness of young bodies—the blazing dream of God. In an armed and cruel summer, her Voices came. About her, glorious light; within, terror and wonder. Afraid, kneeling, and to her the old shining cry, the hour of noon . . . *go, go, Daughter of God. Go into France and beat the English!*

"Do Saint Catherine and Saint Margaret hate the English?"

"They love those whom God loves, and hate whom He hates."

"Does God, then, hate the English?"

"Of God's love or hate for the English, I know not. Or of what may happen to the souls of the English. But I am certain that save for those who are buried here they will be driven out of France." *

And in that Norman dungeon, in that iron light, she gazed at them from her shackles. The Bishop, ponderous yet catlike, eyes cat-glinting in the torches' flare; the Promoter (Prosecutor) Jean d'Estivet, lean and rasping, lusting for scorched flesh; Thomas Courcelles, young Master Courcelles, beacon of the Faculty of Paris, so learned a Thomas—and so cruel. (Master Courcelles was one of two in thirteen who voted to torture Jeanne; the other was Nicholas Loiseleur.)

The sick girl's hands strayed to her sex, huddling there. So did she try to protect herself in sleep from those ravening beasts, her keepers,

* Trial in Ordinary. Session of Saturday, March 17th.

eager to win the secrets of sorcery by sexual relations with the witch herself. But once more, she returned to the beginning—.

In the August morning had fallen the snarling shadow of Burgundy; smoke swirled in the summer haze from blackened ruins; in the corn, rooks squalled and pecked dead men's eyes. Antoine de Vergy rode away; the people of Domremy crept back.

Now: the long hush of this sixteenth summer, Saint Martin in the bronze and yellow leaves. She went to all the old familiar places: the beech tree of the Bois Chesnu, beautiful and mournful as a lily, the fairy fountain of Rains with its miraculous water, from which she drank long and wonderingly, the little hill chapel of Our Lady of Bermont. The sixteenth summer . . . and she would not come this way again. She knew a sudden loneliness, a strange fleeting shadow on her soul. And time passing . . . time like an alouette in the golden sky . . . time like fading tenderness of Vesper bells . . . time in the shadows of the oakwood, in the red-gold apples round and firm as her breasts, in the September sighing of the corn.

She would have so little time!

JEANNE had suffered a setback at Vaucouleurs, but she was not in the least deterred. The prophet was sustained in her mission by the creeping fires of war. She began to receive specific instructions from her Voices to lead an Army to the relief of Orléans, where Salisbury had sat down in October.

She knew no more of Orléans than any other Lorraine peasant girl; no more than the magic name, the *vert sombre,* the capital of the dukedom. At her first interview with de Baudricourt, she had promised the Dauphin help by *mi-carême*—that is, the end of February. She would have to work fast. Conveniently, *tante* Jeanne, wife of *oncle* Durand, was expecting in January.

At the time of Epiphany, her fête, Jeanne set out for Burey and the accouchement of *tante* Jeanne. She went, shouting goodbyes in an icy January dawn and long after folk remembered her striding through the silverfrost of Greux, redkirtled and calling out. "Farewell, Mengette! Farewell, Michel! Farewell. . . ."

She said nothing of her real purpose to Jacques d'Arc or Isabelle. One may imagine the acute humiliation of the Doyen, when he heard about the performance at Vaucouleurs, his rage at that dolt Durand

Laxart. To say that Jacques d'Arc had forbidden further adventures of the sort would be putting it mildly.

She went regretting the evasion; but she went. She was just seventeen. Other girls were stuffing hope chests, walking out in the evening. Jacques d'Arc's one effort to promote such a project had ended in defiance and embarrassment.

What did he say in that January morning when he found her little bed warm and empty? He knew well enough why she had gone; wild horses could not keep her out of Vaucouleurs and the Governor's house. He could have her brought back by force, and no one would have thought the less of him for asserting his paternal right, but he was too proud for that. Besides, short of keeping her under lock and key, there was no way of guaranteeing what she might do in the future.

"Bad cess to her! Let her go." And broke down when he was alone, sobbing for the girl that he loved so much.

And of course he was right.

When she was not helping *tante* Jeanne, the wilful girl was in Vaucouleurs, beseiging the Governor. She had become quite a character. Her story was well known, as was very natural in a little French community, and whenever she appeared curious persons flocked. She now began to say openly that she was the virgin of the ancient prophecy, the redeemer from the march of Lorraine, who would restore the realm of France. She said this to Catherine Royer, a friend of *tante* Jeanne and *oncle* Durand, with whom she stayed in Vaucouleurs, and the good woman was, as she put it, 'stupified.'

One day, in the house of Catherine Royer, Jeanne met a squire of Robert de Baudricourt, a young fellow of thirty named Jean de Metz. He greeted her cordially. "My friend, what do you do here? Is it not necessary that the King be thrown out of his kingdom and that we all become English?"

She had seen him, broadshouldered, blond, about the Governor's *salle*. Perhaps she had already marked him for her own. She was in any case never at a loss for words. "I am come here, to the King's place, to speak with Robert de Baudricourt, that he escort me or give me an escort to the King. But he pays no attention to me or my words. Yet before *mi-carême* I must be with the King, if I wear out my feet to the knees. There is no one in the world, neither king, nor dukes, nor daughter of the King of Scotland, who can recover the realm of France, nor will he have any help save me. Though I would like to stay home with my mother, I must go and I must do this, for my Lord tells me that I should."

As Albert d'Ourches, another of de Baudricourt's men, remarked: "She spoke very well."

And she had made an effort to find out what was going on in the world, for somehow she had contrived to learn that the Dauphin had recently made a treaty with King James of Scotland, providing for the betrothal of his son Louis and the King's daughter Margaret.

As de Baudricourt had done, Jean de Metz asked her: "Who is your Lord?"

And she gave him the same answer she had given his chief, "The Lord of Heaven."

Jean de Metz was impressed. He knelt, put his hands between those of Jeanne. "God permitting, I will escort you to the King." Then, being a man of action, he said: "When would you like to go?"

Jeanne replied: "Rather today than tomorrow. And tomorrow than later."

Jean de Metz glanced at her old red kirtle and black jumper, her braids hanging down. "Shall you go like that?" he wondered.

"I should like men's clothes," she said.

"I'll get them for you," he promised.

Jean de Metz would have done better to have said: "God and Robert de Baudricourt permitting—." For whatever effect the girl's luminous eyes had on his officers, the captain himself was far from conversion. Antoine de Vergy's raid had jarred him, the second such jolt he had had received in four years—the other being the raid of that ferocious condottiere Robert de Sarrebruck, Damoiseau de Commercy. Another such foray might finish the Sieur de Vaucouleurs. He was in no mood for visionaries.

Though he allowed Jeanne to hang around Vaucouleurs, the Governor would not receive her or listen to her petitions. So frustrating did the situation appear that at one point Jeanne, with faithful Durand and one other equally doglike companion, actually started to walk to Chinon —a distance of some three hundred miles through territory infested by gangs of murderers.

Happily, Jeanne's good sense got the better of this mad venture and after a few miles she turned back.

The Governor did try to find out whether or not the strange girl was a witch. He suddenly appeared at the house of Catherine Royer with

Messire Jean Fournier, a priest, who summoned Jeanne: if she were evil, to go far from them; if good, to approach. She was none too pleased with this show, for Father Fournier of Vaucouleurs had already heard her in confession, which he could not well have done had she been a witch. But she played up, fell to her knees and dragged herself toward the two men. . . .

"Oh but I am longing to go!" she exclaimed to Madame Royer, "as a woman in labour longs for her deliverance."

Early in February, the Duke of Lorraine, Charles the Second, sent for Jeanne to Nancy. Robert de Baudricourt was well pleased. This might prove an easy out. The old boy was known for his attentions to young girls. He had already had five children by a vegetable-seller's daughter; and was very likely on the lookout for a successor. The Governor not only gave his blessing to the journey, but provided Jean de Metz to escort Jeanne as far as Toul.

However, in case Jeanne should not prove satisfactory or amenable to the Duke's purpose, de Baudricourt took the precaution of writing to the Dauphin about her.

Whatever the Duke had in mind, he must have seen in the first few moments that this girl could be of no use to him.* When she got back, always with faithful Durand, the Governor was ready for her. A royal messenger, Colet de Vienne, was in Vaucouleurs with word that Jeanne la Pucelle was to proceed at once to Chinon, and the Dauphin.

Who had pleaded for her at that scornful Court? Her most influential supporters were always the lords of the House of Orléans, Jean Bastard of Orléans and Jean duc d'Alençon. It is not unlikely that one or both saw Robert de Baudricourt's letter. The House of Orléans had been fighting for its life since that murderous November evening of 1407.** To such men, willing to accept support from any honest source, Jeanne was worth a try.

Before setting out, Jean de Metz made good on his promise to fit out Jeanne. On her return from Nancy, the virgin redeemer had gone about rigged in the cast-off doublet of Jean de Honnecourt, the lackey of de

---

* This curious interview is described in the opening scene of "Marguerite d'Anjou." See pp. 205–7.
** Louis duc d'Orléans had been savagely assassinated; BERNARD comte d'Armagnac, temporary successor of Louis in the leadership of Orléans, had been flayed alive by the Paris butchers; CHARLES duc d'Orléans, son of Louis, had been a captive in England for fifteen years. The Bastard and d'Alençon fought with prices on their heads; if they fell into enemy hands, it would mean the end of Orléans.

Metz. She must have cut a rather odd figure in the streets, with her cropped black hair and breeches; and though it is not on record that, as with the chained highshouldered apparition of His Majesty King Richard the Third, "the very dogs did bark" as she passed them by, there must have been staring and pointing.

In a laudable effort to impart a little style to the redeemer, the people of Vaucouleurs had made for her a page's habit of black and grey; equipped her with boots of sturdy calf and a set of spurs. *Oncle* Durand and some of his friends had clubbed together and bought a horse for twelve francs. Good old Durand! Her first—and one of her truest. Would that he might have gone the whole way.

Robert de Baudricourt himself mellowed sufficiently to provide the crowning glory: a sword. When Jeanne and her little escort came to say goodbye, he commanded his officers: "Take care of her!"

The Governor embraced Jeanne. "Go," he said, "and let come what may."

When, on that drizzling February afternoon, the little troop rode through the Porte de France into the strangest adventure of the thousand-year-old realm of France, a small group headed by Durand Laxart and the Royers gathered to cheer and cry. Jeanne was one of them, their contribution to the war that the lords of France had fizzled away. She arose out of the rich black earth; she smelled, not of rare perfume, but of the barnyard; she had no longshanked willowy châtelaine's body, pale-haired and sweetly moaning, but a short sturdy frame fit to drive a plough.

She was Jeanne la Pucelle—out of the indestructible passion of the earth, out of the golden rain of God's love for His people, out of blood and tears, not of war, but of life-creating devotion.

With Jeanne rode the squires Jean de Metz, Bernard de Poulengy, and Julien; a man-at-arms called Richard the archer; the King's Messenger Colet de Vienne; and two or three lackeys or varlets. Bernard de Poulengy, who shared command with Jean de Metz, was a man of thirty-six, well acquainted in the environs of Vaucouleurs. He knew Jacques d'Arc and had often passed the time of day at the thatched one-storey cottage in Domremy. Bernard had been present at Jeanne's interviews with Robert de Baudricourt and had decided for la Pucelle.

The first night they slept at the guesthouse of the Benedictine Abbey in St. Urbain-les-Joinville. Then they left the main routes; and struck through field and wood, travelling by night, in armed silence, a wraith-like company. And in the cold moonlight the horses' breath rose in ghostly clouds . . . Across the land of France passed the young hooded face, the dark-glowing eyes. They snatched an hour or two of rest by the wayside, Jeanne lying fully clad between Jean and Bernard. They might have had her any number of times, they were young then and full of blood. But they could not touch her.

Indeed, they were a little afraid of her. Never had they seen a pucelle like this pucelle. Once, to test her, a part of the company pretended to abandon her. "Do not worry," Jeanne said. "They will come back."

The hazards of the road scarcely touched her. But she hungered for her Seigneur; the Blood and Body consumed in rapture, in terrible longing. "If only we could hear Mass," she cried, "we would do well!" But on only two occasions could her escort oblige her, at Auxerre, where Jeanne heard Mass in the cathedral; and at the journey's end, at Fierbois.

They crossed the flooding Loire at Gien; and here it was that the Bastard down in Orléans learned of Jeanne's coming and sent two gentlemen of his household to Chinon, to inquire about her. At Fierbois, on February 21st, they halted; and Jeanne heard three masses in the chapel of Saint Catherine, where an old legend had it that Charles Martel, Charles the Hammer, saviour of France from the Saracens, had buried his sword behind the altar after Poitiers. Jeanne dictated a letter to her 'Gentle Dauphin,' saying he was not to despair, she was on her way, would soon be with him "with many good things for him"; and she would know her Dauphin amongst all his Court. Colet de Vienne spurred on ahead with Jeanne's letter.

On the evening of Wednesday, February 23rd, Jeanne la Pucelle rode into Chinon.

HE was, as his mother said, a wretched case. He was knockneed, shambling, scrawny; his ears stuck out, his nose was bulbous and red, he had thick negroid lips. His blood was low and he wore gloves continually. His nerves were raw. The House of Valois was not renowned for personal beauty; still, no such specimen had been produced in two hundred years.

To increase the almost total insecurity produced by his physical state, his mother had publicly branded him a bastard when he was seventeen.

She had also called him a liar, murderer, and degenerate. Henceforth, he would have no home, no kinsfolk, and almost no friends. He grew into a clown, giggling at what other men revered, hiding in closets from his creditors and angry subjects, playing hooky from his own Councils —incredibly alone.

That this outlandish being did not turn into an irreparable freak was due to a single woman: Yolande of Aragon. She took him in, brought him up, gave him her daughter Marie in marriage. More: Yolande tried to foster in the youth a sense of kingship, to instill in him a tiny portion of her own Spanish pride. When everyone else, even his own Chamberlain, ridiculed his royalty, Yolande addressed him as 'sire'; talked of his Coronation at Reims as if it were the most natural thing in the world.

Curiously, as happened in other matters, Yolande proved to be right and everyone else wrong.

But no one could have predicted ruthless intelligence behind those grey shifty eyes. He spent his time in vast chilly rooms, playing card games with his valet, gossiping with Alain Chartier, laureate who would celebrate the reign (but to date there had been little to celebrate), going over his finances with Georges de la Trémoïlle. Georges had been foisted on him by that bully the Constable de Richemont, to replace poor murdered Pierre de Giac. He hated the constable whose jealousy had doomed his friend Pierre (he couldn't have friends, he was hauled from one set of scheming brigands to another) and he said to that strutting little Breton bully, playing du Guesclin, "You will be sorry for this. I know him better than you do."

And the Constable was sorry. Georges was enormously fat, enormously rich; one by one the crafty Georges got rid of the Constable's friends. Finally the day came when the Constable himself was shown the door and the ugly young man no longer had to put up with lectures. He was grateful to Georges, though he knew his fat friend was feathering his own nest at the expense of what was left of the Kingdom of France. But the King (was he King?) was in no position to make a fuss. There had been the day when the royal treasury held exactly four crowns. There had been another day when a cordwainer of Chinon had refused to deliver a pair of shoes that the King had ordered. The royal credit was no good.

He wore old mended coats that Marie his wife had patched and turned the collars. Poor Marie! She was almost as ugly as he was. He had got three children on her, including sallow scrawny Louis, an un-lovely child, who would one day be King of France or an obscure pen-sioner in a Spanish garret. He had reached the point where he could not bear to go to bed with Marie. If only he could find someone! But he could not afford a mistress. He would have to ask Georges and Georges could hardly be expected to finance a potential rival.

He was trapped.

He could not achieve anything as King and he could not, it seemed, get out. He represented the party of the Armagnacs and the ambitions of the House of Orléans. The whole crowd, the Bastard, d'Alençon, the poet Duke in the Tower of London, his wife Bonne of Armagnac, secretly upheld the claim to royalty of Orléans. The real heir of Saint Louis was Charles duc d'Orléans. They would use Charles de Valois, this miserable sprig of a ruined House (if indeed he was), but when the time came, he would be shoved aside. Make way for Orléans!

The young man shambled with hideous knees up and down the icy *salle,* in an ancient green pourpoint with sleeves out at the elbow, puce-coloured stockings, and black souliers with turned-up toes. And he re-membered Valentine of Milan, Duchess of Orléans. The radiant implor-ing image of Valentine, so much a part of him as if graven on his soul (though he had been but five years of age at her death)—her cries and gasping sobs. *"Rien ne m'est plus; plus ne m'est rien!"*

"Nothing is more to me; more to me is nothing!" . . . And he saw the delicate Italian face framed in mourning violet with white widow's barbe, forever in memory at the lonely midnight street, the bloody splash of torchlight, the echo of a song. And it is always Wednesday, it is always a moonfrosted November evening, and the Duke has just left Queen Isabeau at the Porte Barbette.

Moving now, violet-hooded, through the incommunicable royalty of her grief, Valentine of Milan. And amid the dark tapestry of her chamber the silver cypher of intertwined S's . . . *Soupir, Souci, Soli-tude.*

It had all begun that November evening; the ruin of France, the final darkness of Charles the Mad, the bright horror of the Queen, and this, this quenchless agony—fire, murder, wolves, English . . . that moment when Louis duc d'Orléans rode through the rue vieille du Temple singing and tossing up his glove.

The King of Bourges trembled; the King of Bourges looked down at his turned-up toes. Wildly he dreamed of flight, of disappearing. In his oratory one day, he had prayed that God reveal to him if he were a bastard, as everyone appeared to think; and if he were, to let him go far from France; to Spain or to Scotland, and live out his days. He was still waiting God's answer.

And meantime, to increase his troubles, the captain of Vaucouleurs had sent this peasant, this Jeanne la Pucelle, to Chinon. He wondered at de Baudricourt. Was he trying to make a fool of Charles? A not very difficult thing to do. He imagined the curl of Bedford's lip beneath the fierce blade of English nose—do you know what he has done now, messires? He has taken an illiterate cow girl as his counsellor!

Gentlemen of France: there is your King!

And the girl had the audacity to write to him (or to get someone to take down her words, for of course she knew not one letter from another), saying: "Gentle Dauphin, do not despair. I will soon be with you, bringing many good things for you. I will know you from amongst all your Court." Even the tone of the letter irritated him. Do not despair! As if this girl, or anyone like her, could tell him anything about himself and the ruin of the past.

And now she had actually arrived and was lodged at the Grand Carroi in Chinon. He had done his best to steer clear of the wench, but now he had run out of excuses and after all he had given in to d'Alençon and agreed that Jeanne la Pucelle could come. Would that he listened to Georges and his Chancellor, Regnault de Chartes, Archbishop of Reims! They had advised against her from the first.

But it was too late; besides, he was curious to know what la Pucelle would have to say about the siege of Orléans. Her views, no matter how simple, could not be any more disastrous than the performance of his captains in the field. He himself had given up on Orléans. The battle of Rouvray, 'the day of the Herrings,' had finished the efforts to raise the siege. Let the Bastard get the best terms he could from the English. And for a moment the young man considered what remained after Orléans.

Very little.

A few castles in Touraine, the towns of Bourges and Angers, Mont St-Michel. France—the realization flashed on him, a revelation—France was dying. Was this not more important than what happened to him personally, or to the ambitions of the Maison d'Orléans? This Kingdom, this France, that had endured since Châlons, one thousand years—well, there was nothing in Holy Writ that required France to go on existing.

Kingdoms had foundered ere this. He might well be the last King. He thought of Romulus Augustulus; of Constantine the Seventh.

And through an inner casement came the plaint of a lute, the haunting melody, "l'amour de moy."

Whatever the state of mind of her host, the girl herself knew no doubt. At the auberge of the Grand Carroi, with Jean de Metz and Bernard Poulengy, she hourly awaited a summons to the royal presence. She never questioned that it would come, for did she not bring the finest help that mortal monarch ever had? In that strange poetic style, that exaltation of hers (she was ever on the knife-edge of ecstasy), she had said to Jean de Metz, "There is no one in the world, neither king, nor dukes, nor daughter of the King of Scotland nor anyone else who can recover the Kingdom of France, and it will have no help if not mine."

She was certain.

And indeed the very day that she started for Chinon, February 13th, a disaster to French arms had occurred a few hours before at Rouvray, near Orléans. A large well-equipped Franco-Scottish force under Charles de Bourbon, Comte de Clermont, and John Stuart, Constable of Scotland, had been cut to pieces by a motley array of drovers, sutlers, and crossbowman under Sir John Fastolf. 'The day of the Herrings'—as the battle came to be known from the circumstance that Fastolf was escorting a train of Lenten victuals to the besiegers—seemed to bear out Jeanne's claim: she was the last hope.*

We must think of her as she appeared at the auberge in her black and grey page's outfit given her by the good people of Vaucouleurs, her straight black hair cut *en ronde,* like a boy's, eating her simple repast, eggs, fish, bread soaked in wine. And talking. She had a marvelous eloquence. Within an hour of her arrival at Chinon, she had the old town buzzing. She had a genius for self-promotion unrivaled in history. But it was essential to her mission.

And when she was not talking, she was gazing from the casement; at the great grey battlement riding into a grey rag of sky, above the blue-dark river. Citadel of Henry Curtmantle, of the Lionhearted, of

---

* It is said that Jeanne predicted Rouvray; and when the prediction was fulfilled, de Baudricourt was so impressed that he sent her straight to Chinon. This version of things rests on the view that Jeanne left Vaucouleurs on February 23rd. But Regine Pernoud (*Telle fut Jeanne d'Arc*) has demonstrated the impossibility of this date and that February 13th is correct. De Baudricourt could not have heard of Rouvray the same day the battle was fought. Jeanne's precognition must be rejected.

Philip Augustus and the Holy Order of the Knights of the Temple . . .
old bannered names, half-remembered in the dusk. She had not to fear
the mighty dead. She stood herself at a moment of trumpets; she was
a flare in the huge cruelty of time.

The summons came at eight o'clock in the evening, on Friday, February 25th. Jeanne, with her companions, was to go at once to the
Dauphin. She may have burst into radiant tears and fallen on her knees.
But now was her moment; she must be completely in command of
herself.

Jean and Bernard were nervous enough. As they rode across the pont-
levis of the Tour de l'Horloge and into the purple shadows of the
court, they kept glancing anxiously at their young friend. Was she really
inspired? Or would she prove a delusion, pull some absurd boner before
the Dauphin and ruin their careers? They would become the laughing-
stock of the Army.

A man-at-arms rode up. Drawing rein, he squinted at Jeanne. *"Jarni-
dieu!* Is this la Pucelle?" Turning to Jean and Bernard, he said pleas-
antly, "Just let me have her for a night, messires. I'll give her back in
a different state, I warrant you."

They said nothing, wishing to avoid a fracas on the Dauphin's
threshold. But Jeanne took this badinage of the camp very ill indeed.
She glared at the man, rose in her stirrups, and shouted in a voice of
fury, "What? You deny God and you so near your death!" *

The Great Hall of the Middle Tower blazed. Everyone had turned
out. Three hundred persons jammed the space before the royal dais and
milled about the Norman columns. Many of them were more richly
dressed than the shovelbrimmed Dauphin in one of his old embroidered
surcoats, the cuffs of which Marie had turned. Bets were taken on whom
la Pucelle would hail as the Dauphin. In her letter she had said she
would know him.

But this was not astonishing. Robert de Baudricourt, who had sent
Jeanne, was perfectly familiar with the appearance of Charles. Besides,
he was a hard man to miss. Those ears, that bulbous nose, those knobby
knees.

---

* *"Ha, en nom Dieu, tu le renyes, et tu es si pres de ta mort!"* Jean Pacquerel, Jeanne's
confessor, says that shortly afterward, while Jeanne was closeted with Charles, this
coarse fellow slipped into the moat and was drowned. I doubt this. Pacquerel was
not there; and made his statement long afterward, at the Trial of Rehabilitation, in
1455; when it had become the fashion to lend an air of the marvelous to everything
that transpired about Jeanne la Pucelle.

"What is the Sign that came to the King?"

"It was beautiful, honorable and good. It was the richest that could be."

"Why will you not tell us your Sign? Did you not demand a sign of Catherine de la Rochelle?"

"If the sign of Catherine had been as much seen as mine, by the Count of Clermont, the Archbishop of Reims, the duc d'Alençon, the Sieur de la Trémoïlle, and I do not know what knights and bishops, I should not have asked for Catherine's sign. But this affair is all nonsense."

"Does your Sign still exist?"

"Certainly it exists. It will last a thousand years. It is in the treasury of Milord the King."

"Is it gold, silver, a precious stone? Is it a crown?"

"I will not say further. No goldsmith could make anything so precious. The Sign you need is that God should deliver me out of your hands. It is the most certain that He could send you. My Voices said: 'Go boldly. When you stand before the King, he will have a Sign.'"

"Did the Sign come from God?"

"An angel of God brought the Sign to the King."

"And those of your party saw the Sign?"

"When the King and those with him had seen the Sign and the angel, I asked if he were content. He said that he was. And then I left him and went into a little chapel nearby. And afterward more than three hundred persons saw the Sign." *

In that moment of Recognition, in the flaring Hall, hung with the royal colours of green, white and murrey, amid strange excited voices and torchlit stares, she felt flowing from her that power which her own Voices told her came from God. This vast imponderable force, the glow in her dark eyes, the gift of eloquence, the sudden aspect of the consecrated virgin.

All this: and something more.

For years they had lived amid madness, treachery and blood. For years they had gone terrified to bed and awakened as if to their first morning in Hell. God had abandoned them; rejected France. Oh yes! Once they had known God. But that was in another country and now the dream was dead.

* Session of Saturday, March 10th; in the prison cell of Rouen.

They had heard of old Marie, 'the Gasque of Avignon,' and how Marie had come to the sick Charles, father of this Charles, and had told the King she had dreamed of armour and sword; and of how mad Charles had asked Marie if she put on the armour; and how Marie said no, she had been afraid to do so, and a voice in her dream had told her the armour and the sword were not for her but for a virgin who would come after, to redeem France.

But all this was long ago; and Marie was dead and sick Charles was dead at last, and his kingdom with him, and hardly anyone gave a thought to the old prophecy.

Suddenly here was the virgin-redeemer of Lorraine! It would have been scarcely less strange had Marie herself returned from the dead. . . .

Jeanne, as she had said, knew without hesitation the ugly Charles in his old patched surcoat. She fell on her knees and clasped those short bandy legs. "Gentle Dauphin, I am called Jeanne la Pucelle, and the King of Heaven tells you by me that you will be crowned in the city of Reims, and you will be lieutenant of the King of Heaven, who is King of France."

These perfect opening words set the key for what followed. For now Charles himself was falling under the spell of the Maid. He bade her rise and drew her to one side; and the whole Court might observe him in earnest talk with Jeanne. It was a moment for angels. Jeanne saw an angel bearing a crown of gold not a lance thrust from the Dauphin. This may or may not have been the Archangel Michael, who had taken a special interest in her from the first.

She said to the Dauphin: "You are the son of the King; you are heir to the realm. I am sent by the Lord of Heaven to aid you to recover your kingdom."

Was not this the assurance that Charles had sought from God?

It was.

And yet any of the Dauphin's gentlemen might have told him the same. After all, they had a stake in his future and whatever they thought privately concerning his origins, a façade of legitimacy must be maintained. Still, to hear this assurance from the lips of the miraculously foretold virgin of Lorraine was heartening—but was it enough? Enough to make this dim young man suddenly glow?

Everyone saw how radiant the Dauphin was. He was almost weeping with joy. And when Jeanne spoke of angels, of crowns of gold— he cried that he too saw an angel and that it was she!

Now in the book of the Sieur de Graville, Lord Admiral of France, in the time of King Louis the Twelfth, of blessed memory, it is written that Jeanne la Pucelle said to Charles the Dauphin: "Sire, if I tell you things so secret that they are known only to God and yourself, will you believe that I am sent by God?"

The Dauphin answered yes. The Pucelle then asked: "Sire, do you not remember that last All Saints' Day, when you were in the chapel of the chateau of Loches, alone in your oratory, you made three requests of God?"

The Dauphin replied that he well remembered having made these three requests. The Pucelle asked if he had ever revealed them to his confessor or to anyone at all. The Dauphin said no. "And if I tell you what were the three requests that you made, will you believe in my words?" The Dauphin answered yes.

Then la Pucelle said to him: "Sire, the first request that you made to God was when you prayed that if you were not the true heir of France, it might be His pleasure to take from you the desire for this heritage so that you might no longer be a cause of the war to recover the realm, from which has come so much evil. The second was when you prayed that, if the great adversity and tribulation under which the poor people of France suffer and have suffered so long, come by reason of your sin, that it might be His pleasure to relieve the people, and that you alone might be punished, and bear whatever He might be pleased to inflict, be it death or any other penance. The third was that, if it were the sin of your people that caused these miseries, it should be His pleasure to forgive them and to soften His wrath and free the realm from the tribulation." *

But the Dauphin revealed nothing of what Jeanne had said. Only her effect was wondrously visible. And those looking on agreed that an angel had come amongst them. For the strange bright magic of her had flowed amongst them while she was standing there, beneath the torchlight, talking to the Dauphin. This precious sign of hers, "beautiful, honourable and good" as, weeping, she cried to her judges at Rouen— her power, rarer far than any crown of gold and rubies.

* From the Orléans Ms. Folio 518, Bibliothèque Municipale, Orléans. Translated into English by W. S. Scott and published by Folio Society, London. Orléans Ms. is based on original French Minute of Jeanne's Trial; and first appeared in the reign of Louis douze, edited and transcribed by a gentleman in the service of the Sieur de Graville.

In this moment, she had won by that gift of spirit, the vision and loving wonder which had almost perished from the realm of France.

FOR CHARLES, who could not afford a mistress and who was bored stiff with his make-believe kingship, Jeanne's advent promised a change. Besides, her faith in him made the Dauphin feel good (so few, including his mother, had ever made him feel good). For her, Charles had been chosen by God. He was her 'gentle Dauphin'; her 'very noble Prince.' She was not bothered by his appearance. If God had wanted a handsome Dauphin, He would have sent one. The Dauphin's character was another problem. But even here she was confident. Her Voices told her Charles would listen.

Still, there must inevitably have been constraint in their walks and talks. Jeanne was not a dancing bear or a dwarf, or any kind of simple diversion like that; she was a messenger straight from God. And messengers from God are all very well in life's stained-glass moments, but as a regular routine something more humourous is desired. And Charles, whatever his drawbacks as a fire-eating warrior, was by no means a fool. After all, he had been raised by Yolande of Aragon, one of the shrewdest women of her time. He knew books and painting; his laureate Alain Chartier was to achieve renown as one of the two greatest poets of the century, the other being François Villon. His Court painter, Jean Fouquet, would stand unrivaled in 15th Century France.* Charles himself was not without a wry artistic integrity in that he allowed Fouquet to paint the ugliest and finest of royal portraits—that of himself, Charles the Very Victorious, warts and all. Shifty eyes peer vaguely above the gross nose; a huge hat ridicules the long sallow face. The King is wearing a furred murrey journade and appears against a background of *vert sombre,* between parted white curtains—the royal colours, green, white and murrey.

Jeanne was not only unable to read or write, but throughout her brief career seemed determined to remain unlettered. She had a peas-

* One may instance as well the Master of Moulins, another of Charles's discoveries, who may or may not have been Jean de Paris, but who reveals strong Flemish influence in his wonderful realism combined with the most magical innocence. If, as some think, the Master of Moulins and not Jean Fouquet did paint that exceedingly embraceable Madonna of Melun with the pouting sensual mouth and naked breast of Agnes Sorel, it would contrast strongly with the lost innocence of his Magdalene, a heartbreakingly lovely child without a trace of lust.

ant's scorn of learning. She knew not one painting from another, unless it be some tinted crudity of saints. Music, poetry, philosophy—these mattered not. Yet, in her way, she was the greatest artist of her time. Her life was a marvelous tapestry, an unbearably haunting oratorio, a poem more strange and tragic than any dreamed of by Alain Chartier.

She appealed to men of action. On the day after she had taken up residence in the royal château, lodged in the tower of Coudray, Jean duc d'Alençon broke off his hunting at Saint-Florent to see la Pucelle. For already the girl's fame had blazed: to the Bastard of Orléans, to Duke Philip of Burgundy, to Philip-Maria Visconti, Duke of Milan, son of the great Gian Galeazzo and brother to that grieving shade Valentine Visconti. And if John Duke of Bedford had not heard of la Pucelle, he was shortly to be honoured with a personal message from Jeanne. From the moment that comet-like she flashed on the troubled midnight of France, Jeanne was headline news.

Jean duc d'Alençon was one of the Orléanist crowd whom Charles suspected of designs upon the throne. Descended from King Philippe le hardi, d'Alençon had married Jeanne, daughter of Charles duc d'Orléans. When he arrived at Chinon, he found Charles de Valois and Jeanne together.

Playing hostess, Jeanne greeted the Duke. "You are very welcome," she said. "The more of the royal blood are together, the better it will be."

Joined by Georges de la Trémoïlle, they all dined in the Dauphin's privy chamber. Jeanne, who was progressing very rapidly indeed, from Domremy to Chinon and dining with the Dauphin and the first peer of the realm, regaled the company with her views. Charles (she advised) was to surrender his realm to the King of Heaven; and afterward the King of Heaven would restore the realm to Charles in its original state, as in the time of his forebears. During this discourse, the pouched moon of the Treasurer's countenance alternated from incredulity to dismay.*

After dinner, they adjourned to the meadows near the river Vienne. Still holding the center of the stage, Jeanne put on a riding and tilting exhibition. She displayed a mastery of horse and lance that astonished d'Alençon. For these masculine games, Jeanne had as much aptitude

---

* As Georges made one of the party, it is probable that on this occasion Charles' table afforded a bit more than the sheep's tail and tough chicken which a popular ballad described as the Dauphin's regular fare.

as had belligerent young Bertrand du Guseclin or fiery Harry Hotspur who unfurled his banner at the age of twelve.

She was in fact exactly where she wanted to be. Tilting before the admiring glance of one of the noblest and handsomest lords in France was infinitely preferable to driving flocks in Domremy. She had achieved a frame worthy of her genius. And whatever guardian angel had fostered in her this skill, she was immediately as suited to the profession of arms as if she had been bred to it all her life.

D'Alençon was so delighted with her that he presented Jeanne with a fine horse and spirited her off to Saint-Florent.

It was pleasant being house guest in the old abbaye at Saint-Florent, fussed over by Madame, the mother of d'Alençon and sister of the Duke of Brittany; taking tender walks with Jeanne d'Orléans, daughter of the *vert sombre*. Already the happy guest was calling d'Alençon 'mon beau duc'; and they were calling her 'Jeannette,' the way Hauviette and Mangette used to do. She longed to sleep in Jeanne d'Orléans' bed.

They were merry at Saint-Florent over Georges de la Trémoïlle and Artus Constable de Richemont; and how Georges had outwitted the fierce little Constable and so upset him that in his very next battle he had raised an enormous army of 16,000 men to fight the English in Brittany, which army had been routed in a surprise night attack by a tiny force of 600 English 'with tails.' D'Alençon didn't mind the Constable being taken down a peg; but after all he was the general of the Army, commanding the allegiance of thousands of brave men. Because of Georges, the Army had lost the Constable's services.

Jeanne agreed it was a serious matter. She had taken the measure of Georges at their luncheon; and knew that Georges had been foremost in advising Charles against her.

She learned for the first time the use of forks. At Domremy, they had dipped into the common bowl with fingers and used bonehandled belt knives on their meat. They ate like peasants; they were peasants. At Saint-Florent, each had a silver bowl and was served by pages from a grand sideboard; they drank from sparkling glasses of Venice red. They had napkins and little bowls of rose water for their fingers.

Jeanne d'Arc and Jeanne d'Orléans took their bath together. La Pucelle liked this best. The bathing closet was hung with fragrant herbs, with pine and spruce; hot water was brought in stone vessels and poured into the tiled bath. The satin body of the daughter of the duc d'Orléans splashed with the sturdy muscled peasant girl.

Then they had their collation of spiced wine and ginger; and then they went to bed.

Jeanne showed her hostess how well she could sew; she feared no one in her native village when it came to sewing or housekeeping. And Madame, the sister of Jean V of Brittany, very pious was she, brought out her treasures: a Book of Hours bound in blue velvet and gold, with rich illuminations and the blazon of Brittany on the velvet binding, the black ermine tails on a field of silver with greyhound supporters; silver reliquaries; missals in the flowing Celtic script.

Occasionally, they took long rides in the countryside, dismounting amid the first glinting spring to pluck wildflowers and to weave chaplets. Saint-Florent was one of the happiest times. Too soon, time turned westward, the shadow of Jeanne's days lengthening. . . .

The Dauphin's Council, after much bickering, had decided to send la Pucelle to the relief of Orléans. A new army was mustering at Blois. When Jeanne set out, after a voide or parting cup (she took claret and water), Jeanne d'Orléans came to the gate. She said to la Pucelle: "I fear for my husband, Jeannette. He has been prisoner already, and we had to pay an enormous ransom. I should be very willing that he remained here."

And Jeanne d'Arc said to Jeanne d'Orléans: "Oh lady, fear not! I shall bring him back in the same state or better than he is now."

Nimble as a boy, she swung into the saddle.

Jeanne had to be cleared by the Church. Whatever her status with the Army—and this essential aspect was by no means clear—her past must be gone into, to determine if she were really a blameless Christian maid. While investigators were busy in Domremy and Vaucouleurs, Jeanne went down to Poitiers to face an ecclesiastical tribunal. The real center of the scholastic hierarchy had been Paris; but Paris was occupied by Bedford and many black-gowned doctors of the Sorbonne were collaborators. Under Bedford, the University of Paris was quit of its old rival, the royal power of France and the King's representative, the Prévôt. The Faculty ran its affairs exactly as it pleased; and in return the doctors examined Bedford's case for King Henry and found it good. Henry the Sixth was the choice of the University of Paris.

And Charles the Dauphin?

Whatever credit the Dauphin had possessed—and it had never been large—had vanished with the blow from Tanneguy du Châtel's axe that had felled John the Fearless, a favorite of the doctors, on the bridge of Montereau and avenged Valentine Visconti.

It would be difficult for anyone but an academician to regret the passing, however messy, of the Fearless. But the consequences of Tanneguy's axe were horrendous and still going on. The religious hierarchy of Paris and the Holy Office in France were dead against the Dauphin. It was this fatal combination that would destroy the body and try to destroy the soul of Jeanne d'Arc.

Master Jean Gerson, quondam Chancellor of the University of Paris, would write a defense of la Pucelle against the charge of witchcraft. But Gerson himself had been forced to flee Paris as the Butchers and their hatchetmen took over and Pierre des Essarts did Burgundy's bidding and the University elevated the twelve articles of Jean le Petit to a sanctified category; sanctifying the art of murder.*

The duc d'Alençon sat in on a few sessions at Poitiers, perhaps to guard against the possibility of Jeanne becoming confused. He need not have worried. Jeanne stalked in, wearing her tunic of black and grey; sat down by herself on a bench. The hearing was held at the Hotel de la Rose, the residence of Master Jean Rambuteau, a royal counsellor and an official of the Parlement of Paris. Jeanne was lodged in Rambuteau's house. When a squire of the Dauphin, Gobert Thibault, entered, accompanied by two clerks, Jeanne jumped up, strode over and clapped Thibault on the shoulder, saying, "I would like to see a great many men of your sort!"

She then announced with some pride that she knew not a from b.

The examination proceeded. Although under the nominal presidency of Regnault de Chartres, Archbishop of Reims, that wily cleric seems to have taken little part.** The rest of the tribunal, composed of bachelors of theology, doctors of canon and civil law, and professors of theology, questioned Jeanne as to her coming into France. She told them about her Voices and about saving the Kingdom.

* Pierre des Essarts, prévôt of Paris, that is, military governor, during the Burgundian regime following the murder of Louis duc d'Orléans. His end was curious. Suspected of complicity to betray the city to Armagnacs, Pierre des Essarts was the victim of a mob. He put on his best gown, got completely drunk, and was hauled behind a plough to his beheading, and all the while he laughed. For Jean le Petit, see Introduction.

** We cannot be absolutely sure of the Archbishop's role, because unhappily the 'Book of Poitiers' containing the minutes of this hearing vanished shortly afterward; perhaps (the thing is not unlikely) destroyed by the Archbishop himself. It was too favourable to Jeanne.

Master Guillaume Aymeri, professor of theology, made this salient comment: "You have said that the Voice told you God wished to deliver the people of France from their calamities. If He wished to deliver them, he has no need of men-at-arms."

It would never do that God could get on without Jeanne d'Arc. She said: "Name of God! The men-at-arms will fight and God will give the victory."

Seguin Seguin, a dignified man of fifty, professor of theology and Dean of the Faculty at Poitiers, took over the questioning. "What language do your Voices speak?"

Jeanne shot back: "Better than yours." Seguin had a *limousin* accent, certainly no more rustic-sounding than Jeanne's own speech. At Rouen, she would cry: "I have a great *pah-oour* (for *peur*) of the fire!"

Seguin then asked if she believed in God. She replied: "Better than you."

Disconcerted, Seguin pointed out (not unreasonably) that the tribunal could hardly recommend Jeanne to the Dauphin to take over a field army and assume responsibility for the lives of thousands of men on her simple assertion, without proof of her mission.

Jeanne flared up. "God's name! I have not come to Poitiers to make signs. Escort me to Orléans and I will show you the signs for which I have been sent." She added: "I will have all the men that I need and I will go to Orléans."

She turned to the tribunal, with her instinctive sense of the dramatic. "Four things are to come. First, the English will be defeated and the siege of Orléans raised. But beforehand, I shall summon the English. Then the Dauphin will be crowned at Reims. Third, the city of Paris will return to its obedience to the King. And the duc d'Orléans will return from England. All of that, I shall see accomplished." *

After this thunderous pronouncement, there seemed little to say. Jeanne had exhausted the subject.

Someone asked Jeanne why she called the King the Dauphin, and not the King. She replied: "I shall not call him King until he has been crowned at Reims, where I have determined to escort him."

That sounded very much as if Jeanne d'Arc of Domremy were in-

* She achieved only the first two. Charles entered Paris in November, 1437 (though the Constable de Richemont had reclaimed the capital in April, 1436), following the Treaty of Arras with Philip of Burgundy. Charles duc d'Orléans was liberated in 1440.

tending to create the next King of France. Whatever the tribunal thought about brash girls, it had been unable to turn up anything detrimental to Jeanne. She was given a clean bill of health. "She was a good Christian and lived as a Catholic." In view of the crisis in the realm, "the imminent peril in which the city of Orléans was placed, the King could well aid Jeanne and send her to Orléans."

One of the tribunal, Jean Erault, professor of theology, reminded his colleagues of Marie, 'The Gasque of Avignon,' and the prophecy of the virgin redeemer from the march of Lorraine.

The tribunal had used up almost three weeks of Jeanne's precious time. Now it might render her a service. She turned to Master Jean Erault. "Do you have pen and ink?" He had. "Then write what I say—."

It was her greatest letter; to the English task force at Orléans.

"JHESU MARIA. King of England and you, Duke of Bedford, who call yourself Regent of the realm of France; you, William de la Poule (Pole), Earl of Suffolk; John Lord Talbot; and you, Thomas Lord Scales, who call yourselves lieutenants of the said Duke of Bedford, do God's will. Render to la Pucelle, who is sent by God, the King of Heaven, the keys of all the good cities that you have seized and violated in France. She has come here by God's Will to proclaim the royal blood. She is entirely ready to make peace, if you wish to do right, provided that you give up France and pay for having kept her. And you, archers companions of war, gentlemen and others who are before the city of Orléans, go back to your own country. And if you do not, expect news of la Pucelle, who will soon be with you, to your great harm. King of England, if you do not do thus, I am war chief and wherever I shall encounter your people in France, I shall make them get out . . . and if they do not obey, I shall make them all perish. I am sent by God, the King of Heaven, body for body, to throw them out of the whole of France. And if they obey, I shall show mercy. And have no other opinion, for you will not hold the realm of France from God; but King Charles, the true heir, will hold it; for God wills it and this was revealed to him (to Charles) by la Pucelle, and he will enter Paris with a good company. If you do not believe this word, wherever we find you we shall strike you and make such a great 'hay-hay' as has not been known for a thousand years. And believe firmly that the King of Heaven will send more power to la Pucelle than you will know how to muster with all your assaults, to her and to her good men-at-arms; and by cracks on the head we shall see who has the better right. You, Duke of Bedford, la Pucelle prays and requires that you make no more destruction. If you do right, you may come in her company, when the French will do the finest deed for Christianity ever seen. And answer, if you wish to make peace at Orléans. And if you do not, a great downfall shall come to you shortly. Written Tuesday, in Holy Week."

LA PUCELLE went down to Blois.

Now a medieval army was much less an impersonal professional force than a great big quarrelsome and rapacious family. Pay was small, often non-existent; but opportunities for loot immense. The family aspect was heightened by the camp women. These women were not whores, caged like animals in a stinking brothel for the troops to relieve themselves, as in a modern army. They were free lusty beings, who gave their favors where they would; often a woman stuck to her soldier throughout a campaign. Of course, in the eyes of the Church such women were scarlet, denounceable, Babylonian; but soldiers in the field paid little heed to the Church, except to hang an occasional fat Brother or to rape a few nuns.

As might be expected, discipline varied greatly. In general, the soldiers followed a particular captain, usually a knight-banneret, went where he went, fought or retired as he did. The commander-in-chief had at best a nominal authority; in reality, the army was governed by a war council of the chief captains, an oligarchy. When for instance the 1500 Picards pulled out of the siege of Orléans, they did so at the behest of their own captains and without reference to the English. The 'God-damns' themselves operated in independent units, locked up in their various forts.

The French had an assortment of chiefs, none of them notably successful. De Clermont had been beaten at Rouvray, though this was hardly his fault. The Scots, under the rash and not overly bright Jack Stuart, Constable, had got completely out of hand, ignored de Clermont's sound dispositions, and made a stupid rush against the ingenious leaguer constructed by Fastolf. D'Alençon had been overthrown at Verneuil, along with the Earl of Douglas; while the Constable de Richemont had managed to incur the most astounding defeat of all, when Thomas Rempston and 600 Englishmen had fragmentized de Richemont's 16,000 at the 'Rout of St. James' in 1426.

At Orléans, the famous Gascon pair, Poton de Xantrailles and Etienne des Vignolles, 'La Hire,' had accomplished little and had finally quit the defense. Poton, it is true, by a brilliant diplomatic stroke had brought about the departure of the Picards; but this and the purely fortuitous cannonading of Salisbury were virtually all that the defense had been able to achieve.

At Blois, the duc d'Alençon appears to have been in command, ably seconded by the Marshals de Boussac (Jean de la Brosse) and Gilles de Rais, the latter a beautiful and sinister young man, immensely rich, who, seduced by his own uncle, had become a homosexual at the age of fourteen. Gilles de Rais had married, for money, the gentle terrified Catherine de Thouaronne; he was anything but a family man. Money he loved, and the things that money could buy; delicious boys and girls; silks and satins; marvelous tapestries, manuscript illuminations, orfevres of gold and precious stones. His own illuminations were exquisite and if the young man sometimes dipped his brush into a rich Tyrhennian colour the hue of blood, no one need suppose that it was actually blood. He had also a taste for the theatre; himself composed 'masques' set to music, with costumes of his own designing.

But especially Gilles de Rais was fascinated by the 'black art' (the blazon of de Rais was a black cross upon gold). The idea of a fellowship, not with the Holy Ghost, but with the master of the infernal regions, greatly attracted him. For just as some persons are born with a faith in the good God, so do others come on earth with a conviction of Hell. It used to be thought, not illogically, that such persons were children of darkness, conceived by the Devil.

Jeanne la Pucelle interested Gilles de Rais. Their partnership was curious; a kind of living illustration that only a hairsbreadth divides God and the Devil. He of course took to Jeanne's magical side; her Voices and visions. If one could talk with God, it must also be possible to get in touch with Hell. There was nothing Gilles de Rais desired more than a long quiet satisfying talk with Satan.

Whether Jeanne suspected the sulphur on the breath of her charming young Marshal, his dark satanic beauty, the blue glitter of his eyes, she wisely refrained from any efforts at conversion, accepting, as it were, the aid of the Devil to accomplish God's work.*

---

* It is only fair to state that from Salomon Reinach to M. Georges Bataille, Director of the Bibliothèque Municipale at Orléans, certain scholars have remained unconvinced of the horrifying guilt of the magnificent Marshal and have attributed

Besides, she had other more immediate objects of reform. Holding no rank in the army save that of a simple knight-banneret, with right to display her own banner, Jeanne la Pucelle began on arrival to give orders and to formulate policy directives for the army as a whole. First, she got rid of the camp women. Her army must be chaste. She did allow that if a soldier and his woman wanted a formal marriage, they might have it; otherwise, the woman must go.

The troops must hear Mass every day, just as did la Pucelle. Her own confessor, Jean Pacquerel, was appointed to oversee the spiritual needs of the men. Then, there must be no swearing in God's army; this astounded La Hire. He protested that he and a good many others would become inarticulate.

Well, Jeanne observed, La Hire might swear by his staff, 'par mon martin,' as she did. To a man of La Hire's vocabulary, this was like offering a chastity belt to Isabeau de Bavière. Yet, he submitted. So did the army.

Why?

The little French soldier, as fine a soldier as could be found anywhere, when properly led, brave, resourceful, imaginative, good humoured, had suffered tremendous shocks since Agincourt. He had lost faith in himself, in victory; now, when he went up against the English, the French soldier expected to be licked. And usually was. Only a few days before Jeanne's arrival, a French sortie at Orléans had been demoralized by the dread 'Hurrah!' of the English. French equipment was as good or better than English, in fact French artillery was consistently better; numerically, the French were superior; strategically, the French were fighting on their own ground with excellent supply lines.

The trouble was interior; the French spirit was sick.

Backed by an ancient druid prophecy, stainless, visionary, eloquent, Jeanne la Pucelle appeared the answer to a dream. While the captains, distrusting Jeanne's notions of strategy, excluded her from their councils, Jeanne acquired immense influence with the men. The Dauphin had

---

his downfall to a frame-up on the part of Jean de Montfort, duc de Bretagne, who was consumed with greed for the vast possessions of Gilles de Rais. It is possible they are correct; yet, unless contemporary records are to be treated as complete fabrications, bones of more than a hundred children were found in the vaults and fire-places of the Breton Bluebeard's castles. As late as September 9, 1957, *Time Magazine* reported a further discovery of bones in the oubliettes of Tiffauges, totaling the remains of forty-eight children. This item was shown to M. Bataille, who promised to investigate.

outfitted her in a suit of armour, without blazon of any kind; a Scotsman in Tours, Hamish Power, had painted Jeanne's standard, gold on white, sewn with fleur-de-lys, Our Lord holding the globe of the world and between two angels, with the legend: JHESU MARIA.

Jeanne had as well a sword. Now this sword was popularly believed to possess magical attributes, as had King Arthur's 'Excalibur.' And indeed the manner of acquiring Jeanne's sword was scarcely less marvelous than the hand appearing out of the enchanted lake with Arthur's sword.

Jeanne wrote to the priests of Saint Catherine of Fierbois that her sword was buried behind their altar, and asked them to dig it up and send it to her. They dug, found the sword, the rust and dirt flaked off as if by magic, and they, suitably impressed, made for her a fine scabbard of vermilion velvet. The people of Tours presented her with another scabbard of cloth of gold; while she herself had made a sturdy serviceable sheath of leather.

When this bright foretold Pucelle thrust into the camp at Blois, with white and gold standard, and enchanted sword, with young shining voice, with marvelous eyes—no army in the world, much less a French army, was proof against such sorcery.

She had no command; no mandate—only herself. But that was enough. When the army set out from Blois, Jeanne on a white horse bore her standard before the troops; priests and soldiers chanted the *Veni Creator Spiritus;* the ambiance was that of a solemn crusade, and a good deal more uplifting than the ambiance of many actual crusades.

The soldiers, as they went, sensed the radiant change; they longed to believe in Jeanne, because they longed to believe once more in themselves. La Pucelle was their secret strength; and before they had even fought a battle, they knew what wonder rode with them.

Soldiers of France! forty archangels look down upon you.

After months of desultory fighting, the siege of Orléans was grinding to a decision. With the Army of the Loire, Salisbury had swept down like a wolf, gutting several cathedral towns, Chartres, Janville, Jargeau, and spitting the defenders like so many trussed chickens. The English had settled first to mine and then to starve Orléans. The initial operation might well have been successful had not Salisbury himself been eliminated by a lucky shell shortly after the siege had begun.

On October 24th, the English had seized a formidable fortification of twin towers, Les Tourelles, at the south end of the bridge, and Salisbury had gone up one tower to use the top storey as an observation post. A French piece on the city wall, at the tour de Notre Dame, was loaded and laid; the master gunner went off to dinner; and during the lull an inquisitive boy, eager to see how the gun worked, put a match to the hole.

The shell struck the grated casement of the Tourelles; a fragment of iron bar tore away Salisbury's jaw. He was removed to Meung where after eight days of agony—the fee of Bellona, Goddess of War—the Earl died. The command devolved on William de la Pole, Marquess of Suffolk, debonair, handsome, a confirmed Francophile. Suffolk dug in with a minimum of fighting. On the northwest side, five forts were built: 'Saint Laurent,' 'La Croix Boisée,' 'London,' 'Rouen,' 'Paris'; then, a two-mile gap between 'Paris' and little 'Saint Loup,' on the northeast, hardly more than a lookout post. John Talbot, England's 'goode dogge' and 'the great Achilles of the field,' commanded the line of forts. Across the river, Sir William Glansdale and about 500 'God-damns' were holed up in the Tourelles, and in another smaller fort on the Isle de la Charlemagne, in the Loire. Two little forts, 'Saint Privé' on the west and 'Jean le blanc' on the east guarded the approaches to the Tourelles on the south bank.

Suffolk restrained the other captains from rash forays. An *escarmouche* or skirmish in which casualties numbered more than six was bloody. During a Christmas truce, Suffolk and the Bastard had gallantly exchanged gifts, while the tailed God-damns were transformed into joyous Yule waits, to the tootling of musical instruments loaned by the townsfolk. At midnight, all fellowship vanished; and they began banging away at each other.

Inadequate as all this seemed, when convoys got in and out of Orléans almost at will,* the siege was wearing down the French. The 'Day of the Herrings' especially had struck despair into the town. But a shrewd stroke by Poton de Xantrailles nullified, at least temporarily, all progress on the part of the besiegers. Poton conceived the idea of offering to neutralize Orléans under the protection of Philip the Good. An

---

* Not only was there this two-mile gap in the ring of forts, but Suffolk, not exactly a Black Prince, had neglected to close the river with an iron chain. Even before the Picards withdrew, on January 3rd, for example, Orléans received 154 prime hogs and 400 sheep. On April 5th, 118 hogs, six fat beasts, and two horses groaning with butter and cheese passed the siege. This does not look as if anyone in Orléans was down to cats and rats.

embassy went off to Dijon. The duke was delighted and accepted at once. Bedford was less enthusiastic; and informed his ally that he did not "intend to beat the bushes for someone else to catch the birds."

Piqued, the glorious Duke of Burgundy withdrew 1500 Picards from the forts. At one stroke, the besieging force was reduced by almost one-third. It was now impossible either to continue the line of forts and to close the ring on the north or to prevent revictualing. The 'siege' became a curious elephantine waltz about the walls of this bustling city of 30,000 souls.

The Picards departed on April 17th.

A few days later the Army of Blois marched out to the relief of Orléans. Jeanne had the notion that she was leading God's host straight into battle. The French captains knew better. First, no assault might be undertaken without the Bastard of Orléans; second, the immediate mission was to reprovision the town. The captains took Jeanne and the army along the south bank, away from the town.

When, on the evening of April 29th, she discovered the trick, she was furious. The Bastard of Orléans had just rowed across from the town. "Are you the Bastard of Orléans?" Jeanne demanded.

"I am," he replied. "And very glad to see you."

She took no notice. "Is it you who have advised that I come here, on this side of the river, and that I have not gone straight where are Talbot and the English?"

He said: "I and others wiser than I have given this advice, believing it to be the best and most certain course."

It was the moment for a burst of eloquence, of a splash of *vert*. "In God's Name, the advice of Our Lord is wiser and more certain than yours. You thought to deceive me, but it is you who are deceived, for I bring you the best help that ever came to any soldier or to any city."

She paused, dark eyes gleaming. About them fell a thin sad April rain, while across the river Orléans sprawled darkly and downstream reared the daggered shadow of the Tourelles.

"It is the help of the King of Heaven!" she cried. "It comes not for any love of me, but at God's will Who, at the beseeching of Saint Louis and Saint Charlemagne, has had pity for the city of Orléans, and He will not that enemies should have the body of the lord of Orléans and his city."

Jean, Bastard of Orléans, listened attentively. His handsome sensitive face with artist's eyes recalled that proud boy who "would rather be bastard of Orléans than heir to the noblest in the realm"; the boy that Valentine of Milan wept over, saying, "this is the one that was stolen from me, but he is fitter than any of mine to avenge his father."

Vengeance; the House of Orléans lived, breathed, dreamed retribution. *Nothing is more to me; more to me is nothing!* Shrewdly did Jeanne associate herself with the passion of Orléans; identify Orléans with the grandeur of the past, with Saint Louis and with Charlemagne. The lords of Orléans would bear much from anyone who exalted their tragic House.

Patiently, the Bastard explained that the City's first need was supplies; the army would escort the waggons upstream, out of reach of the English, to a place near Chézy where boats had been collected. The boats would sail downstream and into the city. They were waiting now for a west wind.

"The wind," said Jeanne, "will change."

With difficulty, Jeanne was persuaded into a boat. For now a fresh problem arose. La Pucelle became anxious when she learned that the army was returning to Blois. Without her, all the good work might go for nothing, the soldiers fall again into error. The men felt the same way; they were equally reluctant to part with La Pucelle.

At ten of the clock, on a rainswept night, Jeanne was rowed across the Loire to her city of Orléans. And did some prescience whisper to Sir William Glansdale, high in the Tourelles, of this mortal angel? That blunt Yorkshireman, fearing neither man nor Devil, looked out of blue ice and spat.

Oh Rouen! Rouen! You shall have great sorrow for my death . . . And all the time snakelike tongues and bracelets of flame writhed about her, glowed in the Bishop's eyes, smoked in the scorching breath of 'Our Trial.' For the red day was coming, the day of flame. The Virgin Redeemer would be washed in fire.

Or: was there a way out? Might the Redeemer redeem herself? Ceaselessly plucking, the invisible lute strings of her soul. Bargaining with the Bishop. She had long crying fits, would not eat; she began to doubt her Voices, light failed, the universe guttering out in horror and darkness.

but somewhere in time flared the image of Orléans; the banner of the angels flaunted, St. Catherine's sword flashed. . . .

"Which do you prefer, your sword or your standard?"

"I am forty times fonder of my standard."

"Who told you to have this design on your standard?"

"I have done nothing save by God's command. I bore the standard in battle to avoid killing. Never have I killed."

"What company did your king give you?"

"Ten or twelve thousand . . . I knew by my revelation that I should relieve Orléans. And I told the king that I would."

"Did you tell the men that you alone would receive the shafts and stones?"

"No; there were a hundred and more of my men wounded. Yet I told the men to have no fear. We should win. In the battle, I was wounded by an arrow in the neck. . . ."

"Knew you beforehand of this wound?"

"I well knew; and told the king. I was the first with the ladder at the fort by the bridge; and it was there that I was hit." *

All they could obtain were simple straightforward replies. Ah now! surely there was more to the case. You can trust us. We are your friends, Jeanne. Trying to help you, my dear. (Be quiet, Courcelles! can't you see the girl is doing her best?) Now your standard, my dear. Clouds of butterflies were seen following it . . . and your sword that you laid on the altar of St. Denis to be adored . . . and that mandrake you carried in your bosom. . . .

This, spiders' silken bag and newt's tongue of sorcery, the butterflies her familiars, the adoration of the magic sword, the midnight root that shrieked—they were laying their trap.

The fire crept closer. . . .

But now, the sun and shadow of Orléans, this miraculous green, the old grey stones, the cannon on the battlements, the great market where they distributed the supplies that Jeanne's army had brought (for, as she promised, the wind had changed), the barges moored at the river wharfs—but oh! that torchlit moment of her entry, the white-maned horse, the gold and white standard, the thousands of faces that melted into one great frantic face.

Jeanne! Jeanne! Jeanne!

* Fourth Session. Tuesday, February 27th. Cauchon in the Chair. Interrogation led by Master Jean Beaupère, canon of Notre Dame de Paris, canon of Rouen, acting chancellor, pro tem, of University of Paris, former rector.

For an instant even she, la Pucelle, felt cold and still and full of wonder. Could she really do what they expected of her?

And then her attention was seized by her standard catching fire from a torch. She spurred her horse, turning the standard to put out the flame. And at last they brought her to the house of Jacques Boucher, treasurer of the duc d'Orléans, near the porte Regnart, where "she was received with great joy, with her two brothers, her gentleman and their lackeys who had come with them from Bar." *

(long long afterward Catherine Boucher would remember that shy braided child of nine, herself, who slept with Jeanne la Pucelle the nights of Orléans)

And now in the infinite brown-eyed sadness of childhood, in the summer kingdom, fell the haunting cry: *France!*

The Bastard departed for Blois, leaving La Hire in charge of Jeanne and the defense—which was much like setting a stag to watch a wild mare. However, several days of calm. Jeanne rode about the city, showing herself to her adoring people, looking over the fortifications. She also composed a summons to surrender to John Talbot (Bedford had already received his). This letter was taken, under a flag, to Les Tourelles by Jeanne's two heralds, Guyenne and Ambleville. The contents so enraged the Governor, Sir William Glansdale, that he threatened to burn the heralds on the spot—an almost inconceivable breach of such customs of war as existed. Fortunately, wiser counsels prevailed; Guyenne was locked up and Ambleville sent back with an insulting message in which Jeanne was called 'cow girl' and 'whore.' After a brief crying spell over this, she returned to the charge and attempted to summon Glansdale by shouting from the Orléans end of the Loire bridge. Her appearance was the signal for a blast of insults from the bored soldiers shut up in Les Tourelles.

But their period of boredom was rapidly drawing to a close. On the morning of Wednesday, May 4th, the Bastard returned from Blois with the army and a large train of supplies. Jeanne and La Hire rode out with a company of men-at-arms to meet the supply train, proceeding along the northern bank. The English did not stir. Safely within the town, Jeanne and the Bastard dined together at eleven, at Boucher's.

* Pierre and Jean d'Arc, as well as the faithful Bernard Poulengy and Jean de Metz, were of their sister's household. To these may be added: Jean d'Aulon, her squire, Louis des Coutes, her page, and Jean Pacquerel, her confessor.

There had been rumours that Sir John Fastolf with a stout company was on his way to Orléans and Jeanne said to her dinner guest: "Bastard, if Fastolf arrives and you do not tell me, I shall have your head!" And smote the commander-in-chief on the chest.

The Bastard promised; and La Pucelle went upstairs to take a nap.

Though Fastolf did not come, that same Wednesday the French made a thrust at St. Loup; but the captains told Jeanne nothing. Aroused by a tumult in the street, Jeanne leaped from her bed and rushed down, yelling at Louis de Coutes, "Ah, you bloody boy, you would not tell me French blood is flowing!" (Only a little before she had confided to Louis that God was meditating an attack, but she wasn't sure where).

The treasurer's house was in an uproar.

Louis was all thumbs and dashed about, half in tears. Finally, Jean d'Aulon came in and armed la Pucelle (she had been stamping about, commanding Madame Boucher and little Catherine to help her with her plate armour). She kept trembling and groaning, "oh the earth is red with French blood!" They got her outside, a horse was found, and her sword and banner, which she had left behind, were handed to her out of an upper-storey window.

Hysterical, horrified, Jeanne flogged through the grey bleeding streets, a horde of town militia scraping after. At the Porte Bourgogne they were bringing in the French wounded, streaming with blood. Jeanne cried: "I can never see French blood, but my hair stands on end!"

On the plain beyond, the French were pelting from St. Loup. Now it is not clear whether the captains intended to press home the attack or whether simply to probe the English defense on the north bank. Jeanne couldn't have cared less what the captains had intended. They had not consulted her; she did not consult them. Now, as so often in the future, she took over at a critical moment—her first.

Why anyone ever considered Jeanne a master of strategy is strange. She knew only one tactic: a direct furious assault driven home. To Jeanne, war was so terrible that she could never think of it as an 'art'; a 'science'; a 'game'—or any of those fancy names by which men try to pretty up their passion for organized murder, the scorched flesh, the steel smoking in the guts. War had to be experienced at a level of terrible exaltation, her nerves strung to a shrieking sobbing tension—and her attacks had a quality of frenzy.

Riding in amongst the French, Jeanne displayed her gold and white standard. The men rallied; reinforced by the town militia, they re-

turned to the assault. Talbot, who had been leisurely getting together a
relieving force from his other forts, was caught flatfooted. Before Talbot
could move, St. Loup was overwhelmed. The soldiers of la Pucelle
plunged redbladed through the shattered fort, slaying frantic English
—as the Black Prince had sabered the French at Limoges. A few 'God-
damns' put on cassocks and ran crying to the Maid. Jeanne at once took
them under her protection. "What does it matter," she said to her protesting troops, "if there be but one priest among them? Better to save
all, than kill one innocent man."

It was hardly a point of view that ever commended itself either to
her comrades or to her foes.

St. Loup was the first field success of the French during the siege;
and it was due directly to the inspiration of la Pucelle.

But Les Tourelles was another proposition. Here the English had
devised a complicated defense scheme, based on a series of flanking
positions leading up to the massive stone bulwark of two towers which
stood squarely, British bull-like, at the south end of the Loire bridge.
A flat sandy plain stretched for miles around, on the green banks
willows and alder bushes, and in the silvery river two little islands, Saint
Aignan (patron of Orléans), and the Isle de la Charlemagne, on either
side of the broken bridge. The English had fortified these islands and
by means of them maintained liaison with Talbot and his forts. They
had also two small forts, St. Privé and St. Jean le blanc, on the south
bank, on the left and right flank of Les Tourelles.

The fortress itself was ringed on the south bank by a stockade and
earthwork, Les Augustins, built on the ruins of an Augustine Priory.
The stockade connected with the fortress by a long 'boulevard' or
barbican of wood and masonry; while from the barbican a drawbridge
and portcullis gave access to the citadel on the bridge. To the rear, the
English had broken down two of the seven arches of the Loire bridge,
to guard against a surprise from the city side. The position, as thus
outlined, was considered impregnable to direct assault. Further, between 600 and 1000 crack troops were available to defend the whole
scheme.

Before Jeanne's arrival, the French do not seem even to have concentrated an artillery barrage against Les Tourelles. Though well supplied with ordnance, most of the French pieces appear to have been
mounted on the walls of the town itself, across the river—half a mile
wide.

One French master gunner, Jean le bombardier, did indeed vastly annoy the English by shouting insults, twitting the 'God-damns' about their tails, and having drawn a few crossbolts and small shot, would suddenly collapse as if mortally hit. But as a cheer went up, the gunner would leap to his feet, rush to his piece, and blaze a shot at the English. He did this so many times that the besiegers wasted much valuable ammunition on him, to no purpose. On one occasion, Jean le bombardier even had himself carried off the field by two comrades.

While the French were plentifully supplied with powder and shot brought in from Blois and Tours, the English were facing a shortage and were expecting a convoy at the time Jeanne appeared. This may explain why no effort was made to interrupt the two large supply trains from Blois, on April 29th, and again on May 4th; and why on the second occasion Jeanne and La Hire, with 500 men-at-arms, were permitted to ride out unmolested along the north bank to meet the incoming supply train. As the siege had already lasted seven months, the English failed to realize that with la Pucelle time had enormously speeded up; that they had lost the initiative.

For whatever Jeanne's faults as a captain, she had the great gift of seizing the initiative and this compensated for many deficiencies.

But, to obtain her opportunity, she had to work against the cautious 'Fabian' strategy of the French captains. These men are not to be blamed. They had seen too many battles and armies thrown away by rash ill-considered action. They tried to restrain Jeanne; and when they could not restrain her, they tried to broaden her views as to strategy. And unlike the French chevaliers of the past, who never seemed to learn the simplest things about strategy, Jeanne was teachable in this regard.* So much so that it was due to her that the great victory of Orléans was not endangered at the moment of culmination.

On Thursday, May 5th, Ascension Day, Jeanne appeared dramatically at an army council at the house of Cousinot, Chancellor of the duchy d'Orléans. "What are your plans, messires?"

The Bastard explained: "To attack Talbot's forts."

Striding up and down, she shot him a scornful look. "Tell me what

---

* King Jean le bon, like Jeanne la Pucelle, was a great one for direct assaults and destroyed thereby several fine armies—his own. But King Jean always telegraphed his punch, his huge lumbering columns got in each other's way, and the good knight had no understanding of fire power. Jeanne la Pucelle made no such errors.

you are really planning. I should know how to keep a greater secret than that."

Well, yes they were planning a blow against Les Tourelles, in case they drew out part of the garrison. But they did have in mind first a feint against Talbot across the river.

"Why didn't you tell me?" Jeanne demanded.

Why indeed? Probably because they foresaw that she would try to take over direction of the whole operation. She warned them: "It is no use to try to deceive me. I know your plans."

And here again she displayed that secret power, her chief strength —her inner cognition of events. So thus she knew not only the captain's plans, but knew that she would lead the assault against Les Tourelles and would be wounded in the breast. Like any other young girl, she was afraid of being hurt, but this did not for a moment deter her.

"Angry as a bull, the Governor was. Marry, and I thought he'd like to burn the puzzel's heralds on the spot."

"A dour man, William Glansdale. They say he's swore to give us the cow-girl for sport."

"He'll need to catch her first."

"Take a witch to catch a witch."

"Ah, Davy, Davy, you don't think the puzzel be a witch?"

"They say the French kneel and kiss her feet. They say she's a magic sword."

"Human, Davy. Human. She'll bleed. I've a wager with Dick Hawke. He's the best eye in the company."

"We'll see, Tom. Look you! Isn't that the puzzel now? And with her friggin' French pimps. What in blazes is she up to?"

"Looks as if yon mackerel is to loose a bolt at us."

"Her damned armour, Davy. Jesus, but it must be heavy on her! How d'ye reckon she does it?"

"Does what, Tom?"

"Christ, man! Sees to herself."

"Don't you know, Davy? Our armourer was telling me. She's got a little plate, a breach plate, with a hinge there in front. She keeps a sponge inside. All you need do is to open the door and change the sponge."

"Well, fancy that! What will they think of next?"

"Did hear that, Davy? What's that she yelled?"

Read: here is news!

"Get down—the bolt!"

"Look you. It's landed yonder. There's a bit of parchment on the shaft."

"You, English, who have no right over this realm of France, the King of Heaven orders you, by me, Jeanne la Pucelle, that you give up your fortresses and return to your own country or, if not, I will make you such a hai-hai as will never be forgot. Here is what I have written you for the third and last time and will write no more. Signed: JHESU MARIA, Jeanne la Pucelle.

"PS: I, I would have sent my letters honestly; but you, you detain my messengers and you would have arrested my herald called Guyenne. Return him to me and I will send you some of your people taken in the fortress of St. Loup, for they are not all dead."

"News from the whore of the Armagnacs! What will the Governor say to that, Davy?"

The events of the following day, Friday, May 6th, are obscure. It is clear that the English were beaten, but just how and what part Jeanne played are uncertain. Jean d'Aulon, a chevalier reminiscing at fifty about the heroics of his youth twenty-five years before when he was a junior officer, relates the following tale. The French assault force against Les Tourelles crossed from the city by a bridge of boats at about nine in the morning. The Sieur de Villars, Seneschal of Beaucaire, was in command. The immediate objective was St. Jean le blanc, but the English abandoned both the fort and the Isle St. Aignan, withdrawing into Les Augustins. De Villars then, without consulting anyone, gave orders to break off the assault. During the French withdrawal, Lieutenant d'Aulon (approximately his equivalent rank today) was put in charge of the rear at the embarkation stage. The English began a sortie; d'Aulon and some hot Spaniards dashed like Bayards into the fray; Master Jean le bombardier cut down with a single shot a gigantic Englishman defending the breach in the palisade; Jeanne and La Hire arrived in the nick of time, leaped into the saddle and spurred with lances straight at the English who, quite literally, 'turned tail'—and then the body of the French came swarming back to seize Les Augustins.

This kind of basic or cautionary old soldiers' tale has been considered the 'most reliable' account. One wonders what would constitute an unreliable account.

The facts are that this was not a simple skirmish turned into heroic victory by the last-second arrival of Jeanne. The day before, the Army Council at Cousinot's had decided upon a major stroke against Les Tourelles. De Villars may have been in charge of the advance landing party, but it is incredible that the Bastard should have played no part. The captains, who had at first not even informed Jeanne of the real plan, had tried seemingly to mollify her by allowing her to participate in the feint against Talbot. But this feint never came off. Jeanne dashed toward the Porte Bourgogne (instead of the Porte Regnart, near Talbot's headquarters at Fort St. Laurent) with a crowd of town militia, well-fortified by the vintner's precious stuff. Raoul de Gaucourt, an honourable and efficient officer and the captain of the Dauphin's household, was stationed at the Porte Bourgogne to prevent just such a wild eruption, that might upset the Bastard's plan.

A violent altercation occurred. "You are a wicked man!" Jeanne flared at de Gaucourt. "With or without your leave, we shall fight and win!" Her followers added other and more explicit comments on the royal captain's ancestry and character. De Gaucourt felt his life was in danger. Jeanne got through; she and the militia rushed down to the boats and piled in.

They arrived on the far shore as some sort of withdrawing maneuver by the French task force was taking place. What it portended no one, least of all Jeanne, paused to inquire. It will, however, be recalled that the major purpose of the feint had been to draw out the English on the south bank; due to Jeanne, the feint had failed to materialize. However, soldiers can be drawn out in other ways, such as a retreat before their eyes of an apparently intimidated attacking force. It may well have been a plan improvised on the spot by the Bastard, who could not have wished tamely to withdraw, after a fine initial success without striking a blow, outnumbering the English on the south side by at least six to one, and with a wonderful opportunity to crack them up before Talbot could get into action.*

* It is possible of course that the Bastard himself, on learning that the feint had not come off, had ordered the assault broken off. But it seems unlikely. With Fastolf on the way, the French would never have a better chance at Les Tourelles. Contemporary French accounts of the action glorify Jeanne, to the exclusion of any serious discussion. And unfortunately there is no contemporary English account of the siege at all. Probably too painful.

However that may be, the intervention of Jeanne and the town militia and the launching of a premature counter-attack pushed the English back into their tough stockade. It then took the best part of a whole day to dislodge them, in repeated and costly assaults. What Jeanne really did can only be conjectured. She was not of course mounted; that would have been absurd in such an attack. We can think of her as blazing about, shouting, waving her Standard, her very presence insuring that the soldiers would not quit the field as long as she held on it. Toward the end, the steel spine of a caltrop pierced her foot and she had to be helped off the scene—but by that time Les Augustins was a blackened ruin and the remains of the garrison were withdrawing into the boulevard.

Great gentleman that he was, Jean the Bastard uttered no word of criticism, then or twenty-five years after. Significantly, he passed over la Pucelle's activities on that day.

Jeanne had gone without her lunch. She returned very weary to the treasurer's house to dine with Father Pasquerel and Louis de Coutes. Lieutenant d'Aulon, as he himself relates, stood all-night vigil with his men in the captured fort.

As pale with fatigue, Jeanne sat over her fish, a messenger from the Army Council arrived. The Council's word to la Pucelle was: "Considering that the city is well supplied with provisions, we would do well to keep (within) the city while awaiting help from the king. It does not seem advisable for the soldiers to sortie tomorrow."

It is unlikely that this message was intended to be taken seriously by anyone save Jeanne herself. The French were camping in the charred ruins of Les Augustins; they had the damned 'God-damns' on the run; every rule of war dictated that they should press the advantage. Probably the captains hoped to get off at least one attack before Jeanne arrived to take over. After all, consider how they must have felt. She had barged into two of their plans and drastically affected both. True, St. Loup had been an unexpected victory. And a useful one. On the other hand, Jeanne's intervention at Les Augustins might well have prolonged the affair by driving the English back to the protection of their stockade.

In any case, Jeanne brushed off the captains. "You have been with your Council," she told the messenger. "And I have been with mine. And the counsel of Our Lord will prevail."

She turned to Father Pasquerel, saying strictly, but not unkindly,

"You must get up earlier tomorrow and do better than you ever have. Keep near me always, for tomorrow I will have a great deal to do and more than ever I had before, and tomorrow the blood will flow from my body above my breast."

The next day, Saturday, May 7th, Jeanne was up at dawn and heard her first Mass before arming. Her host offered her a mess of little trout for breakfast. "No," she said. "Not now. Keep the fish for the evening and I'll bring you a 'God-damn' who will eat his share." She added, significantly, "And I shall come back to the city by way of the bridge."

Since the first silvery light, the French army had been marshalling on the south bank, before Les Tourelles. In these days of clanking drabness, it is often forgot how splendid a medieval army appeared. Banners and pennons, red, gold, blue, silver, green, fluttering in the radiant May; sun flashing and glinting on a thousand facets of armour; the gorgeous ostrich plumes, the great plunging horses, the shields with their heraldic devices: wolves, bears, eagles, hawks, bulls, and all manner of strange and magical signs such as roundels, chevrons, wheels, claws, and fangs.

The English, too, had a role. Far from home, in the usual beleagured and unsympathetic aspect of an army of occupation, the English upheld the greatest military tradition in Christendom. Often outnumbered, outgunned, but never outfought; soldiers of the prince who said, "I would not that we had a single man the more, for the glory shall be all the greater to those who abide here."

Agincourt; October 25th, 1415. . . .

A sense of fatality, of terrible imminence hung in the air. Everyone in the army, from the Bastard of Orléans to the youngest powder monkey, knew that this was the day; that it was to be proved here and now whether Jeanne la Pucelle was really the saviour of France, as she claimed to be, or whether she was just another crazy dreamer who talked big.

Les Tourelles thrust into the reddening sky, two grated and angry-looking towers and the ragged jaw of the boulevard. The fortress was isolated. The Isle St. Aignan and St. Jean le blanc had been lost in a useless effort to reinforce Les Augustins, the day before; while under cover of night Talbot had also evacuated St. Privé, cutting off Glansdale from the north bank. And Suffolk, that courtly gentleman, that blue and silver knight—where was Suffolk?

Presumably with Talbot. But this was not Suffolk's show. His genius was diplomatic, for negotiation, for deals behind the scenes. He and the French captains had understood one another very well. Now this mad Pucelle had crashed into the midst of Suffolk's tranquil gentlemanly siege, with bewildering effect.

"In war she was very expert . . . especially in the placement of the guns, for it was in this that she excelled."

So spoke the aging memories of the aging 'beau duc,' d'Alençon, twenty-five years after; the tribute of worsening age to the fire and glory of youth, when he was twenty-five and she was seventeen. Lovers they were of a sort; bound together in fire and blood.

Whether or not Jeanne laid the guns, the French bombardiers opened with a barrage from both the south bank and the town, pouring a concentrated fire on Les Tourelles. Twenty minutes of furious iron and from the English silence: a level-eyed damned-to-you silence. It was the moment for scaling ladders. Some ingenious mind, a little before, had come up with the idea of a 'pavois' for assault troops; the 'pavois' was a kind of clumsy wooden shield strapped on the back, so that tortoise-like the French might advance under a savage hail of fire and oil and stone.

Twice they drove across the blue scarred terrain to the walls of the boulevard; they got their ladders up and men began crawling toward the battlement—but both times the English stood to their guns, serving the pieces until the redhot barrel-loops blew to bits, and sending down a rain of crossbolts, so that the French who did reach the walls had no support. And on the second try, Jeanne herself was first at the ladders, when Dick Hawke, champion eye of the company, shot her down with a crossbolt.

They got her moaning away from the wall. The bolt had gone in six inches at the shoulder buckle, just above the breast. It was indeed a crack shot; and just missed the heart. The army chirurgeon told Jeanne it would be necessary to pull out the bolt. She told them to go ahead. These bolts had a broad flanged head, so that to pull one out was agonizing. She gave a great scream as the bolt ripped free, tearing and macerating the lovely breast.

In pity for her pain, a soldier offered her a little charm to conjure away the hurt. She shook her head; Jeanne la Pucelle wanted no sorcery. The chirurgeon applied soothing ointment and a poultice of herbs; she slept and rested awhile.

The sun stood high. Across the scorched no-man's-land, the English took off their helmets and doused their boiling heads. Anxiously, they gazed Frenchwards, for truth to tell the defenders were running short of powder and shot, as well as bolts, and if the French kept up the assault—but happily everyone had seen Dick Hawke's magnificent shot that put the puzzel out of action. Without their puzzel, these French were just the same scared monkeys the English had beaten a score of times.

The 'puzzel' had awakened, the day, her day, was burning in the west; and she sent Louis de Coutes for the Bastard. "Do not sound recall," she implored the commander. "I am going to ask God about the attack." Jeanne got on her horse and rode to a little vineyard, away from the army. She was gone about a quarter of an hour. The French rested on their arms; it was vespers, eight in the evening, and they had been fighting for more than twelve hours. The captains felt nothing further might be attempted that day.

Emerging from the vineyard, Jeanne announced that there would be another and victorious assault and that she would take part in it. The captains tried to dissuade her; but she vowed that she would go alone and that the men would follow her. Which was probably true. She had participated in two bitter onslaughts, she had been severely wounded, and she had been encased in cruel-heavy plate armour for twelve hours. No matter. Jeanne la Pucelle was going in.

(The old soldier, Jean d'Aulon, is reminiscing now: it seems to him that all the faith and wonder of the great campaign return and he is young again. And now, twenty-five years after, he tells the Trial at Paris how in the red evening he and a Basque of de Villars' company, wishing to rally the men, dash toward the scaling ladders, with Jeanne's Standard; and how Jeanne, seeing them, comes hot after, crying "My Standard! My Standard!"; and how she scuffles with the Basque; how the Basque, pricked on by d'Aulon, tears the Standard from the exhausted hysterical girl; and how the pair of heroes surge together to the rim of the deep fosse before the boulevard, flaunting Jeanne's Standard, but leaving Jeanne behind. . . .

But the Bastard is an old soldier too, and he was at that field. And how was it that the Bastard did not see d'Aulon and the Basque and that heroic dash? How was it that his most vivid memory is of great dark eyes and pale mouth, of that voice pleading amid death and terror for one more try at the barricade, vowing if need be to go alone . . .

and seeing her take the Standard and go forward. Yes, the Bastard is an old soldier, but he tells the Trial nothing of what he did. Memory like a flame sweeps over him. . . .)

This is what *he* knew:

Trumpets flared; the attack exploded. The French drove through that weary Hell, after Jeanne and the Standard of the Angels, up to the boulevard. And: the bright wild voice crying at the fosse, the old comradeship of lances, and beneath the Angels, armoured like Michael—Jeanne la Pucelle.

Desperate, the English went on shooting.

The French scrambled into the fosse already blue with dead and plunged toward the ladders. The scaling ladders swarmed with French; if they were monkeys, they were heroic monkeys. When the shot was gone and English arrows strewed the ground, the 'God-damns' flashed their steel; and as the French poured over the barbican wall they were met by sword and dagger and mace. Brains splashed, a crunch of bone and gristle, a red mist of blood—a century of iron rage was paid for.

The English were trapped. From Orléans a convoy of little boats laden with militia set out for the bridge. A fireship with flaming beautiful sails drifted toward the two bleak towers. At the broken arch the militia clapped together a flimsy plank crossing and, led by Nicholas de Geresme, chevalier of the Knights of St. John at Rhodes, one by one the soldiers crept over to take the English in the rear. The fireship reached the wooden drawbridge between the barbican and the towers.

Suddenly a voice soared above the frenzy, "Classidas! Classidas! Render yourself to the King of Heaven. You called me whore, but I have great pity for your soul."

Glansdale, waving the banner of Sir John Chandos, the paladin of the Black Prince, and about a hundred powder-blackened survivors hurled onto the blazing bridge; a ripping of timbers, shrieks, and fountains of flame. The English plunged into the river. Glansdale in his armour sank like a stone. His body was later fished out, parboiled, and the bones sent to England.

The victory was complete.

Jeanne burst into tears over the English dead. She loved victory, but she hated the cost. If only these stiff agonized forms had heeded her warnings!

She returned to an hysterical bell-ringing Orléans, the whole city mad for la Pucelle, kneeling, kissing, touching, weeping—their Virgin Redeemer, now and forever. Aching in her armour, her wound burning, Jeanne was rescued and sent to bed. She fell at once into a heavy druglike sleep. She slept ten hours. She had to call on the immense resources of her spirit, that vast communication with the deep ocean of consciousness, every time she fought. For she was not truly a warrior at all; she was an illuminée, a prophetess, and she moved and had her being in glorious light.

When Jeanne awoke, she found the army and city breathlessly awaiting her decision. For even while she slept and rested from her labours, the Lord Talbot, that 'great Achilles of the field,' who had done nothing worthy during the fight for Les Tourelles, had drawn out his army in battle array and was now challenging the French. For once, the captains did not try to interfere with Jeanne. They let her decide.

Over three thousand dogged English marshalled in the battle-tried formation of the famous past, defiant, snarling, that most dangerous of all beasts—a wounded tail-lashing Lion. La Pucelle gazed on the bristling snouts of bombards, the picked archers on the wings, the massed battalions in the centre—and over all the Standard of the Dogge.

"Let them go," Jeanne said. "We shall have them another time. God does not will that we fight this day."

It was a military decision of the highest importance and credit to Jeanne. For it is surely just as vital to know when not to fight, as it is to know when to press home the assault. The English had lost a battle; they were far from losing the war. Besides, it was not Jeanne's mission to destroy Englishmen. Her mission was to liberate the cities of the stricken realm of France.*

For Jeanne, Orléans marked the transition from the peasant visionary, tricked, shut out of councils, even lied to on occasion, to the professional

---

* This decision of Jeanne's has been much criticised by Miss Sackville-West and others, as if it were a question of overwhelming and cutting up a beaten demoralized army. This, it is said, is the way the French captains viewed the matter; and they were much disappointed. But the captains were wrong. Talbot's army was neither beaten nor demoralized; it had not been in action at all. Glansdale's force was but a fraction of the effectives at Talbot's command. True, numbers and morale were now in favour of the French; but this had been the case at Poitiers and Agincourt and other fields. On balance, Jeanne's decision cannot be faulted.

of war. The battle is the ultimate test and Jeanne had proved herself at Orléans. From now on, she was listened to; her ideas and strategy dominated; the common soldiers were worshipful.

Perhaps all this sudden success was too much; for it led Jeanne to overestimate what she alone could do. She was wonderful—as long as she had the captains and army of Blois. But her whole position teetered on the furtive will of this Charles of France, who had been waked up three times in one night to hear the glorious tidings of Orléans, who for the moment was grateful, but who was jealous and sly as a courtesan, who had no spark of the faith and gallantry that animated the men about Jeanne la Pucelle.

How long would the honeymoon last? Intelligent men asked themselves this question. Charles had abandoned one friend, one position, after another; he despised and hated his mother, the sentiment was reciprocal; he had been a party to the treacherous murder of Duke John the Fearless; he had alienated the Constable of France; he couldn't endure his scrawny son and had small joy in the company of his wife. He literally had not one true friend in the world, save two—Yolande of Aragon, his mother-in-law, and Jeanne la Pucelle.

But Jeanne could not give the knock-kneed fellow the reassurance as a man that he craved (though one might speculate that if she had really understood the problem, even this might not have been too great a labour for France), for with many men political force is linked directly with sexual power. As Charles had not conquered even one attractive woman, how could he hope to conquer the most fascinating of all: France?

Years after, he was to find the only security and happiness that he would ever know on the magnificent breasts of Agnes Sorel.

Jeanne suspected, or allowed herself to suspect, little of the Dauphin's true nature. Marguerite de la Touroulde, Jeanne's hostess at Bourges, observed that her guest was "very simple and ignorant save in matters of war." And though, especially in view of her heroic conduct of her own defense at Rouen, this be too sweeping a view, Jeanne always took a rose-coloured view of Charles.

Tributes poured in.

First, Orléans. The capital of the sombre Duchy had already canonized la Pucelle 500 years before the Church did. The Duke over the water sent a gift of a robe of *cramoisie* (vermilion) with a hood of *vert perdu* (*vert sombre sur noir*), costing thirteen crowns. Bonne Visconti, daughter of the deposed Gian Maria Visconti and niece of Valentine, wrote from Milan to ask la Pucelle's aid in recovering her 'ancestral right.' And Philippe Maria Visconti, present Duke of Milan, received a letter from Boulainvilliers that glowed with the portrait of this female Perceval. The Duke turned over the letter to Antoine of Asti, one of his poets, who produced an epic in Latin glorifying la Pucelle.*

And in Paris a greffier (clerk) of the Parlement under the entry of May 10th, Tuesday, wrote: "this day the other captains and men-at-arms keeping the siege and the bastilles about the Loire . . . set out . . . to fight foes who had in their company a single pucelle having a banner. . . ."

And Clement de Fauquembergue drew on the margin of his parchment register a curious, rather pathetic little Pucelle, with long braids and skirts, carrying a banner, sword at her side.

And again in Paris an elderly lady of sixty-seven, old pensioner of Burgundy and friend to Bedford's Duchess Anne, from her cloister strangely moved by news of this miraculous resurrection and of her that set bells ringing and hearts blazing sat down in old confessorial light to write her last poem: "I, Christine, who have wept eleven years shut in an abbey. . . ."

But to her, as to the others, the miracle had happened. She laughed once more. "Then today at *prime,* laughter took me. To laugh merrily with joy. . . ."

And she who had done this for Christine de Pisan was the one: "who has cut the cord which narrowly bound France; one cannot praise thee enough, when this land humiliated by war, has been granted peace; by a miracle, by the divine Will was sent God's Angel to the king for his benefit."

Notwithstanding the enthusiasm, Charles hesitated. He retired to Loches, unable to decide on a campaign in Normandy, a campaign in the Loire, or just sitting tight. Personally, he favoured the last course.

But Jeanne, like a troublesome conscience, was ever at his heels. She burst into his privy chamber one day, knelt and clasped those bony legs, saying, "Noble Dauphin, do not hold so many and such long councils, but come as soon as possible to Reims to receive a worthy crown."

Christopher Harcourt, a privy councillor then present, asked Jeanne

---

* Readers who would like to regard more closely the doings of the fascinating Visconti of Milan should look up a novel by Raphael Sabatini titled *Bellarion.*

if her voices had advised this course. She said they had. Harcourt then
suggested that she might describe the phenomena to the king. Jeanne
blushed and replied: "I understand what you want to know and will
tell you willingly."

However, she told them no more than they already knew, what she
had related to the commission at Poitiers, that when she could not
readily persuade anyone to God's Will, she brought the matter to God's
attention and a Voice said: "Daughter of God, go, go, go, I will come
to your aid."

As she repeated these words, a marvelous exaltation came over her
and she lifted her eyes toward Heaven. Charles, too, became radiant,
as on that first evening at Chinon.

God, it appeared, favoured a campaign in the Loire, where Talbot
and Suffolk had concentrated their forces. First on the agenda was
Jargeau, twelve miles upstream from Orléans, where Suffolk and about
1200 English lay. Just before Jeanne set out for Jargeau, the seventeen-
year-old Guy de Laval, scion of an ancient Breton family and a recent
recruit, glimpsed her for the first time at Selles-en-Berri.

"Monday, I set out with the king for Selles-en-Berri, four leagues
from Saint Aignan," Guy wrote to his mother, Jeanne de Laval, "and
the King sent for la Pucelle, who was already at Selles. Some told me
that it was a mark of favour that I should see her." La Pucelle arrived
in full armour, but unhelmeted, and bearing her lance. She was very
gracious to Guy and his brother André, and invited them to her lodgings for a cup of wine. She promised the Laval boys that she would
soon be offering them wine in Paris. Guy was quite carried away (as
what boy would not have been?). "To see her and to hear her seemed
something completely divine."

The young Breton saw his heroine off for the army. "I saw her
mount, in unblazoned armour, save her head, a little battle axe in her
hand, upon a great black warhorse which, at the door of her lodging,
resisted very strongly and would not allow her to mount. Then she
said: 'Lead him to the Cross,' which was before the church beside the
road. Then she mounted without him stirring, as if he were tied. Then
she turned toward the church door nearby and said in a womanly voice,
"You, priests and churchmen, make a procession and prayers.' Then she
turned to her road, saying, "Forward, Forward!' and a gracious page
bore her Standard displayed and she had her battle axe in her hand."

Guy then described the arrival at Selles of other captains, the new commander-in-chief, d'Alençon, whom his very junior officer had beaten at tennis (jeu de paume), the boy's brother-in-law Louis de Bourbon, Comte de Vendôme, Marshal Jean de Boussac, La Hire, and another brother-in-law Guy de Chauvigny, who told Guy that his sister had a good mien and was fatter than she ever was.

"Never went men to the field with such good will, as they go to it here," Guy wrote; and afire with this new French spirit, he begged his mother to sell or to mortgage his land or to use any convenient means to raise money for the army. "For we shall either be saved or we shall be utterly ruined and perish."

The young Comte de Laval (he received his title at the Coronation) was one of 8000 French and Bretons with a crusading flame. At Jargeau, Suffolk ringed by guns, including an enormous piece *La Bergère,* the Shepherdess, sent from Orléans in honour of la Pucelle, attempted to parley. The English commander suggested a two weeks' truce and offered to surrender if he were not relieved. Not unnaturally, d'Alençon rejected this idea; and Jeanne sent word that Suffolk and all his men might go free, on condition of departing at once and in their doublets.

Unwisely, Suffolk spurned this generous offer. Next morning, at nine, *La Bergère* began belting the city walls with solid iron shot. During the cannonade, d'Alençon and Jeanne were observing results of the careful laying on of the guns when she exclaimed: "Move from that spot, *beau duc,* or this machine will kill you." She indicated a bombard on the walls.

Accustomed to the imperatives of Jeanne's intuition, d'Alençon did as he was bade. A few moments later an unfortunate Monseigneur du Lude ventured onto the same spot and was killed *sur le coup* by a bursting shell.

Shortly after, Jeanne told the commander to blow up his trumpets and advance to the assault. A little shaky from the incident of the shell, d'Alençon wondered if an attack were not somewhat premature. But Jeanne said: "Have no doubt, the hour is at hand when it is pleasing to God." Adding that it was essential to act when God willed. "Act, and God will act."

When d'Alençon still did not budge, Jeanne taunted: "Ah! gentle duke, are you afraid? Do you not know that I have promised your wife to bring you back safe and sound?"

D'Alençon blew up his trumpets. Suffolk, on the walls, made a desperate attempt at a last-minute parley; but Jeanne was already at the ladders, gold and white Standard in hand. A stone crashed on her helmet; she fell and lay mortally still. Horrified, the French gathered around. But in a moment or two she was up, flaring the rent Standard, and that voice, bright joyous echo of the ditch at Les Tourelles, pierced the morning, "On, on, friends! God has condemned the English. At this hour, they are ours; have good heart!"

The French poured into the city. The English retreat by the bridge was cut off and Suffolk's brother Alexander slain. Suffolk, who might then have had a better death than the one he found, surrendered with his other brother, John de la Pole, and about fifty of his gentlemen.

The remaining English, eleven hundred gallant men, were massacred.

The battle of Patay began with a dinner down in Janville on Thursday, June 16th. Talbot was there and Sir John Fastolf and Lord Scales and Walter Hungerford and Tom Rempston, the pick of the English officer corps, captains of the 'fine old lineage.' Jargeau had fallen the previous Sunday; the combined forces of Talbot and Fastolf numbered some 4000 men. Against them, intelligence reported a large French array, perhaps double the size of the English muster.

Fastolf was Bedford's man and Bedford had never liked any part of the Loire campaign, less than ever after two resounding defeats. The Regent was setting about the composition of a blistering report to the King's Council in London. Fastolf therefore had been sent as much to restrain Talbot as to reinforce him. Counsels of caution were passed over the wine and walnuts. They had not enough men; they were caged on the defensive; they had temporarily lost Burgundian support.

All this inflamed Talbot. He had ridden in from Beaugency with about two score lances and some archers, leaving Matthew Gough to hold the fort.* The Lord Talbot was forty-six, as jealous of his military reputation as a lovely lady of her milkwhite body. When he rode out on his dappled destrier, men pointed: "Know who that is? That's Lord Talbot, that is. The most valiant knight in two Kingdoms!"

Lord Talbot . . .

But, now, what were they saying? "Oh—Talbot? Aye, the dog lurked in his kennel and let old Glansdale perish. Lord Talbot was had by a chit of seventeen."

---

* A 'lance' was not one man, but the smallest unit in the army. It has been variously estimated as from four to six mounted men, a man-at-arms in full armour, a swordsman, two archers, and perhaps two unarmed pages or *valet aux armes*.

By God, it was not to be endured. Suddenly it mattered not a curse to Talbot how many men he had or whether he had any men at all. He would go alone.

"God's Wounds!" Talbot burst out, for there was no Pucelle in his army. "I don't care what you do, Fastolf. I'm going to fight."

Sir John Fastolf was hurt. An English gentleman ought not to talk like that.

"English gentleman be damned!" Talbot exploded. "We're losing this war, while you old women sit on your tails in Paris."

Fastolf was shamed into coming.

The day following the dinner in Janville, Matthew Gough, warned by Suffolk's fate, had surrendered Beaugency. Meung was now threatened. There was in fact no dependable base in the Loire left to the English. Elementary prudence counseled retirement; but Talbot would not hear of it. He was in an Agincourt mood. He forgot that no longer might a single Englishman with his dread 'hurrah!' rout four or five Frenchmen.

The two armies came together two miles outside Beaugency. The French had seized a commanding position on a little knoll astride the Orléans road. Talbot, below, sent a personal challenge, offering to fight anyone in the bloody army. D'Alençon refused; the commander of the French emphasized the late hour and promised battle the next morning. But Talbot had other ideas.

Earlier that day, the French had received a surprising reinforcement. Informed that Artus Constable de Richemont was approaching with a goodly array, d'Alençon flatly refused to have anything to do with him. The Dauphin (but the cupid leer of Gorgeous Georges over the royal shoulder) had expressly forbidden it. Jeanne argued for the Constable. The debate was interrupted by news of Fastolf's oncoming army. Jeanne swung into the saddle and rode out to the Constable. Dismounting, she knelt before the gruff little Breton: "Constable," she said, "you have not come by my wish, but since you have come you are very welcome."

It was an unusually tactful speech for la Pucelle.

The Constable said to Jeanne: "Jeanne, they tell me that you wish to fight me. I do not know whether or not you come from God. If you come from God, I do not fear you, for God knows my good will. If you come from the Devil, I fear you still less."

These preliminaries over, they rode together into the French camp; and that night the Constable's men stood watch for the royal army. Jeanne's intervention had added 1200 fighting men plus the general of the armies of France to the campaign. But they still had to bait the Talbot dog.

Dawn broke on a deserted English camp. On the heights, the French rubbed their eyes and stared. Talbot had slipped away during the night. The captains debated pursuit, a lingering uneasiness about the 'Goddamns' evident.

Reports came in of English troops in the vicinity of Patay, a village eighteen miles north of Beaugency. Talbot and Fastolf were heading back to Janville. Jeanne interrupted the colloquies of the French captains. "Have you good spurs, messires?"

"What do you mean, Jeanne? Are we to turn our backs and run?"

She laughed. "No, but the English will not stand. They will be overthrown and we shall need good spurs to catch them!"

They set off in three divisions, La Hire and Poton de Xantrailles in the van, d'Alençon and the Bastard marshalling the centre, Jeanne (over her protest) and the Constable de Richemont bringing up the rear. Toward mid-day the army neared Patay.

"They cannot be far, Jeannette," d'Alençon rode up, ungloved, to the familiar white and gold Standard.

She looked at him. She had just saved him from violent death, as she had promised Jeanne d'Orléans. He would live long, too long for his own fame. Oh that one might die in the good greening time, the time of June! She herself . . .

"They are here, *mon beau duc.*"

The French captains gazed about, but all was still as the flaked gleaming sun on the green breast of the hillside, as the halted gleaming standards of the army of liberation. They were here! But no one save Jeanne in that flaring noon perceived them.

And over the captains came again the uneasiness, the memory of ruined fields and old unhappy deaths, and they looked anxious and spoke of horses. But she, she longed for the enemy as a woman in labour longs for her delivery.

"For God's sake!" she cried to those queasy captains, "it is necessary to fight! We shall have them were they hanging from the clouds. God has delivered them into our hands that we may punish them."

And she added: "Today the King shall have the finest victory that ever he knew. My Voices have told me they are ours."

And in that haunted noon, June-glistening, a cry of birds, rooks in the corn, and in the sky a kestrel volleyed. . . .

From a copse off to the right a sudden splintering snapping and a noble antlered beast bounded into view, dashed across the French line, and thrust into nearby thickets. Frozen to their saddles, the French heard a shout, "View Halloo!"—the English hunting cry. And in that instant, while the bright day whirled, la Pucelle beside the Standard flashed her sword and the voice came singing, "Your spurs, messires! Use your spurs!"

The French horse swooped on the unready English, crashing into a rank of archers, riding them down, sabering as hoofs plunged. The van with La Hire and Poton knifed through Fastolf's line and thundered up the rise toward Lord Talbot and the reserve. The routed troopers of Fastolf, skeltering in all directions, threw dismay into Talbot's men. La Hire's cavalry, the glorious two thousand, hit the English like an avalanche. It was all over in half an hour, the perfect Johannique victory: a surprise, a magnificent charge home, annihilation. Almost four thousand men were killed or taken. Fastolf himself managed to get away, with a handful of archers. But Talbot, that 'great Achilles of the field'—.

They captured him quite alone, sitting on his horse beside an elder bush amid the desolation of the dead and the beautiful clarion of the French military trumpet. He made no resistance, indeed he seemed hardly certain what was going on. Only his pale blue eyes gleamed like midnight frost.

D'Alençon could not resist a gibe when he saw whom they had brought. "You did not think this morning," he chortled, "that this would happen to you."

"It is the fortune of war," the fallen champion said.

Paris beckoned. The English had at present no field army. Bedford had panicked and shut himself in the fortress of Vincennes. The Duke of Burgundy, knowing when he was outclassed, would not lift a finger to save Paris. A city of 200,000 souls, the matchless pearl of the West— "who holds Paris holds the world"—a city like a gorgeous harlot waiting to be possessed. How could anyone compare such a prize with this

rigged and incredible ceremony of kingship? Old Regnault de Chartres
mumbling and making passes, the fishlike pink tones of the royal body,
the dried black globules of holy oil that if you could believe was
brought a thousand years before in a gold phial in a dove's beak from
Heaven direct to Clovis, you could believe anything—and the organ
thundering Zadock the Priest and shouts of 'Noel!' and the great rose
window stained with fire and gold. . . .

But Jeanne la Pucelle was of the people, and though the Kings
themselves at least from the time of that terrible man Philip the Fair
had long abandoned the mystical meaning of the rigamarole at Reims,
the people still clung to the old significance. The notion that King,
lords, and commons were really one; that the realm belonged to God
alone; and that He had delegated the King as His Deputy and the
Coronation at Reims became the outward visible symbol of this divine
investiture.

Philip the Fair did away with all this archaic nonsense. God, if He
figured at all in the schemes of the destroyer of the Templars, did so
as a huge cardboard backdrop, the kind that looms all eyes and
whiskers on some impossibly far Walpurgis. The Kingdom, then, belonged to Philip the Fair and to the issue of his loins; and far from
being one with his people, the King was not even of the same race,
but Frankish (whatever that was) and the common horde, Latin.

All very well. But when the King was stonewitted and had no male
issue, Philip's theory, strictly one-man rule, collapsed dramatically,
brought on the hundred years' war.

Jeanne's task was to restore the ancient significance of Kingship,
the King united with his subjects and God's Viceroy on earth. At their
very first talk, she had advised Charles that he must surrender the realm
to God and God would then formally appoint Charles as His Deputy,
as it had been in the time of his forebears—by which Jeanne meant
those great Kings who had honoured the divine contract, Louis the
Seventh, Philip Augustus, Saint Louis.

In this light, Jeanne's insistence on an immediate Coronation at
Reims, the traditional site for such solemnities, was a shrewd psychological stroke which, once carried through, could never be undone.
The notion that the Valois as such had any unique claim to the throne
had been heartily demolished by the Plantagenents; but a divine appointment—that was something else.

The way to Reims lay through Burgundy and Champagne, centre of the magnificent Duke Philip's influence. No better way of demonstrating the Duke's impotence before Jeanne (his first fiasco with a woman!) could have been devised than this triumphal march through the heart of his dominions. Auxerre did manage temporarily to stave off submission to Charles by greasing Gorgeous Georges with 2000 gold crowns; while Troyes, scene of the Treaty of 1420, by which Isabeau sold France and the white body of her daughter Katherine to the victor of Agincourt, slammed its gates before the royal army. Troyes was in the grip of a wild hair-frenzied preacher, Brother Richard, who had come to the city straight from a smash run at the cemetery of the Innocents in Paris. Brother Richard's speciality was Doom; Anti-Christ was on the way and the Apocalypse at hand. The charnel setting of the Innocents, the immense collection of skulls in the churchyard, the appalling mural of the *Danse Macabre* on the charnel house wall, afforded Brother Richard an admirable mise-en-scene. He packed in crowds of five and six thousand, beginning at dawn and continuing until dinner, six hours of bellowing. A single prayer of Brother Richard's had been known to fell hundreds.

When he had reduced his hearers to a satisfactory state of gibbering hysteria, Brother Richard would demand proofs of renunciation of the world. Holocausts of furniture, silks, furs, billiard cues, playing cards, dice, took place. This feature of the performance agitated the authorities; and Brother Richard was invited to carry his revelations elsewhere.

"Sow beans!" Brother Richard roared. "Sow beans, *mes bons Troyens et bonnes Troyennes!*"

They did so, in preparation for Anti-Christ; and when the ill-supplied soldiers of Jeanne arrived, they found rows of tender young bean shoots for their sustenance. Jeanne summoned the town; the burghers refused and sent letters to Châlons and Reims, announcing their resolve to fight to the last Burgundian. Brother Richard's professional nose detected a whiff of brimstone at the gates.

Jeanne blew up her trumpets; and when the white and gold Standard advanced to the fosse, her cry rang "To the assault!" Scaling ladders were already in place when the burghers displayed a desire to parley. Terms were speedily arranged: submission to the Dauphin; provisions for the army; safe passage out of the city for about 500 Burgundian troopers under the captaincy of Caboche's old friend, Villiers de l'Isle Adam.

Brother Richard came rushing out, gown flapping, arms whirling like windmills. "Approach boldly," Jeanne said. "I won't fly away!"

She gazed at him, with amused dark eyes. He had never said that she was a witch, Brother Richard protested. Jeanne entered Troyes in company with the furious friar; and Brother Richard preached a wall-tottering sermon in her praise. Afterward, she could not shake him. He went along to the Coronation, attracting to Jeanne several frayed screwloose women, would-be Pucelles, of whom the best known was Catherine de la Rochelle.

Jeanne had no trouble at Châlons or at Reims. Both submitted to Charles. The Coronation was set for Sunday, July 17th. Reims swarmed, the first Coronation in fifty years. Young René d'Anjou, Duke of Bar, came pelting into town at the head of 200 lances. He had thrown off allegiance to Burgundy and would ride for three months stirrup to stirrup with Jeanne la Pucelle, a memory that was to mark René's life and the life of his golden daughter, Marguerite d'Anjou, now one year old.

Less notable arrivals, but for Jeanne all-important, were Durand Laxart and Jacques d'Arc, who put up at the Sign of the Striped Ass. The royal treasury settled the bill and the two drank on until September, wifeless and happy.

Their girl, their Jeanne, the pride of Domremy and the pride of Greux, had no more official status at the Coronation than she had with the army. But:

"Why was your Standard carried into the Church at Reims, and not those of the other captains?"

"It had borne the peril. It was right that it should share the honour." *

So Jeanne herself. She, more than anyone there, had made this Coronation. And it was right that amid the nobles of France with their proud blazons, their military Orders, amid mitred purple prelates with jeweled gloves, should come this girl with dark intelligent eyes and page boy haircut, in a plain jacket of mail, and bearing the gold and white battle Standard, the rent mended, the grime cleaned away.

And who might say? Now beneath the spectrum flare of sun on glass, the thirty-six seated kings and queens glowing in the eighteen double lancet windows, the huge exaltation of the organ soaring to the groined heaven of the nave, an echo, always behind the echo, of valour

* Session of Saturday, March 17th.

and great dead voices, might enter into that thin crushed frame on shambling legs approaching . . . before the intricate whorls and stone saints of the rood screen, on the high altar of Our Lady of St. Remy, rose a purple-gloved hand with a golden ampulla—the holy oil of Clovis . . . and to the right of the altar, beside the Standard of the Angels, the girl with shining look. . . .

"And all things prospered for Your Highness until the time of the siege of Orléans undertaken by God knows what advice. In this time, after the misfortune happened to the person of my cousin of Salisbury, whom God pardon, there came by the hand of God, as it seems, a great evil upon your people who were assembled there in great number; this which came about in large part, as I think, by the mingling of false beliefs and crazy fears that they have had of a disciple and limb of the Devil called la Pucelle, who has made use of false enchantments and sorceries. This evil and this overthrow have not only diminished in great part the number of your people, but also have affected the courage of the rest in an extraordinary way and have encouraged your enemies to assemble in great number."

So John Duke of Bedford to the King's Council in London. His pen scratching and fading across the parchment, a feeling of doom, all his work in vain, even Anne his wife—must he lose Anne too? And in this vast decaying Vincennes, this grim final Regency, a sound of bronze far off, the evening bell of Lancaster—Bedford stared about with horror. Something whispered: in the coffined twilight, amid the dark oak paneling, the musty tapestries and ruined chairs—*Lancaster is dying* . . .

"Oh my damned soul!" . . . and Bedford, broken-bladed nose and wine-flushed face, eyes deep and blazing—if only they could lay hands on the witch! And for a moment he savoured the delight of fire and iron, she naked, moaning, she bone-cracked and shrieking on the red-hot grid of English vengeance.

Meantime the Cardinal of Beaufort, Chancellor of the King, had collected by Peter's pence an army of 3500 men to crusade against the Hussites of Bohemia; but Bedford's need was more urgent. The witch had caused to be killed upwards of 7000 of Bedford's men; but there were more, English grit, English pride—*once more into the breach, dear friends!*

For yes, they all came out of Agincourt, they had been created fifteen years ago by Harry—the sword, the Swan, the blood-dark Rose. And here in this upper room, black and scarlet westward chamber, the hero himself one suffocating August day had sweated his last, loins on fire, feet and hands ice-cold. Going out at thirty-five, all his work unfinished, his heir a ten-months' babe. Only John his brother might save Lancaster. Harry had died pronouncing faith in John.

But was it not all a dream?

Bedford perceived that Lancaster was a kind of resurrection, chivalry, the visionary past—what had perished at Poitiers—this haunting love of nostalgic men. But time slipped away, the age despised dreams. Waiting now, sometimes he had this terrifying feeling, waiting for Lancaster to die, the torn bleeding Swan, the withered Rose.

Oh my soul!

The mistakes, the load of hatred, the bitter stares and spitting, the wolves—life, life was a wolf forever slavering at the gate of one's spirit; yes, the mistakes, the blue plucked dead, the Bastard of Vaurus, his brother Denis, their tree flaring with strangled bodies, the grey skeletons moving vaguely in the Paris streets, too weak to dispute garbage with the pigs. But Bedford had plans. People of Paris! do not despair. Your Regent is thinking of you. But, the clock croached on midnight. The last candle, the empty glass—Lancaster.

If all else failed, one could still die. Always time for that. Bedford uncurled lean fingers, staring at the flung quill and black fierce scrawl.

At Poitiers, Jeanne had set forth her aims: Orléans, a Coronation at Reims, Paris, the Duke over the water. In a few short weeks, she had achieved towering success; herself 'hanging from the clouds' as with her vivid hyperbole she had depicted Talbot's army. So far, she had annihilated all available English field forces, liberated the valley of the Loire, crowned the King at Reims.

She set her sights on Paris. Prospects were good; but Jeanne ran into opposition from Charles and his advisers, who would much rather negotiate than fight. Their point of view was not necessarily discreditable; co-existence with the Duchy of Burgundy was essential. The aim was to split the Anglo-Burgundian alliance. Peace with Burgundy meant 'peace in our time' for the realm of France. It was not the principle of negotiation that was wrong; it was the way in which it was carried out by Charles that undid Jeanne's work.

Gorgeous Georges was notoriously venal; while the Archbishop himself was not above suspicion of having made off, some time before the Coronation, with the historic Crown of Saint Louis, its eight silver angels alternating with gold fleurons, and palming off on Charles a nondescript crown of inferior make. Having been elevated to a strong bargaining position thanks to Jeanne, this precious pair crawled before Philip of Burgundy; first, an immediate truce after the Coronation, neutralizing the army of liberation and allowing Bedford to rally; then, an embassy headed by Christopher Harcourt, Raoul de Gaucourt, and the Archbishop arrived at Arras in mid-August. Everything that Philip wanted was promptly agreed to: a general armistice, a peace conference in 1430 with Amadeus VIII of Savoy mediating; an 'humiliation at Canossa' for the murder of Philip's father, expiatory penance, guarantees of future good behavior, abject homage to Philip himself—all undertaken on behalf of Charles by his ambassadors. Nothing was said about the House of Burgundy expiating the murder of Louis duc d'Orléans.

This preliminary negotiation was followed by the arrival at Compiègne, French military headquarters, of a Burgundian embassy headed by Jean l'aveugle, of Luxembourg. Jeanne la Pucelle had her first glimpse of this sinister one-eyed lieutenant of Burgundy who was to play such a mortal role in her life. John of Luxembourg was the nightside of the glorious Duke; the hatchetman who screwed money out of recalcitrant vassals, who arranged 'accidents' to wealthy burghers and the forced marriage of their heiresses to favourites of Philip, who did the dirty work of intimidation, theft, and murder by which pirate Burgundy blazed forth as the golden chivalric realm.

Burgundy's lieutenant concluded a four-months' truce with Charles, affecting all territory above the right bank of the Seine. Charles also agreed to give up those towns of the Somme which had just returned to their allegiance, including Senlis, Creil, and Compiègne itself. The fate of Paris was decided during these August talks. For, not only was Bedford given time to reinforce, but it was agreed that Philip might send troops to Paris. Appeasement could go no farther.

At these conferences, Bedford had an observer, Hughes de Lannoy, a Burgundian adviser to the Regent's Council. De Lannoy submitted a confidential aide-memoire to the Council, of which the salient points were: sending an army to Guyenne to destroy Jean IV, comte d'Armagnac, an ally of Charles, hiring 2000 Burgundians to defend Paris, compensating Philip and his vassals out of French territory ("any lordships which His Grace would be happy to have"), buying off Jean V de Montfort, duc de Bretagne, with the province of Poitou, and Artus Constable de Richemont with Touraine and Saintonge, in addition appointing de Richemont the Constable of Henry the Sixth in France. This last proposal had an ironic twist, in that de Lannoy suggested digging into la Trémoïlle's lordships in Saintonge to bribe his bitter foe, the Constable!

This ambitious scheme was a long-term plan. The most pressing need was the resurrection of the English army and the defense of Paris. Recovering from his panic, Bedford had done wonders. Garrison troops were called in from Normandy, the army of Cardinal Beaufort was diverted from the Hussite Crusade, and 700 Picards were hired from Burgundy; by late July, the Regent was able to confront Charles with a force of 5000 men. Though he sent an insulting challenge to Charles, offering personal combat, Bedford was not eager to hazard his new army on a single throw. Growling about the French like a mastiff, Bedford provoked no battle but relied on the diplomacy of his ally Burgundy.

After this convention of Compiègne, Jeanne's dream of capturing Paris had little hope. She suspected the worst, but was determined not to quit. Still only seventeen, she had small understanding of statecraft. Nor were her friends, the Bastard and d'Alençon, noteworthy in that department. There was in fact no member of Jeanne's party (as it may be termed) competent to offset the influence of Christopher Harcourt, Georges de la Trémoïlle, and Regnault de Chartres.

And here is enunciated the weakness of Jeanne le Pucelle. She had no plans for the realm, other than moral uplift: regular churchgoing, no dice, no playing cards, no swearing, no sex. Her contribution was that she made it possible for those who came after her to formulate national policies.

Nowhere is there evidence in Jeanne's thinking of political and economic changes which if France was to survive in competition with a ruthless state such as Burgundy were at least as important as throwing out the English. It was not, to say the least, sufficient to get rid of a competent and devoted administrator like Bedford simply to solidify the clutch of Gorgeous Georges on the realm. God had told

Jeanne to throw out the English; she had received no information on what happened afterward.

Yet, given time, God might have come forth with plans. His legate to France was incredibly young. Jeanne had stirred the embers of national feeling to a roaring blaze; not la Trémoïlle, not Charles de Valois, not even the House of Orléans, but Jeanne la Pucelle captained the new national party. It was her tragedy that everything happened too soon; and she was not ready to seize the political chance.

Wherever she went, Jeanne was the object of veneration. Inadequately but truly, people perceived the rare and radiant being. A spate of 'Jeanne' baptisms occurred; she was *marraine* or godmother in a dozen towns. At Lagny, they brought her a baby which they said had been dead for three days. Jeanne touched the little black-faced creature and at once it began to howl, reviving sufficiently to be baptised before lapsing into another and final sleep. At Bourges, where she stayed with Marguerite de la Touroulde, the ladies of the town brought relics for Jeanne to touch. Jeanne laughed (always this pleasant grace of humour for her own adoration) and said to her hostess: "Touch them yourself. You will do as much good as me."

Marguerite also recalled that she had seen Jeanne naked, in bed and at the bath, and that la Pucelle was virgin.

In the Ile de France, at Château Thierry and other places, Jeanne broke down and wept. "Ah, what good people these are!" she cried. "I have seen no other which rejoices so much at the coming of the King. When God gives me leave to end my days, I should like to be buried in this country."

The Archbishop, listening to this cry of the heart, inquired: "Oh Jeanne, in what place do you expect to die?"

She sensed the irony. He had a vested interest in the answer. "Where it pleases God," she said. "For I know no more of the time or the place than do you. And would it please God, my Creator, that I retire now, giving up my arms, and go to serve my father and my mother in watching the flocks, and with my sister and my brother who would rejoice to see me."

But she was to be buried everywhere and nowhere, for in a sense she never died. She vanished in flame, like the phoenix, to rise forever from the ashes of her memory.

And everyone who ever spoke with her, enjoyed her friendship, suffered her sword, tormented her, collaborated in her death, received immortality for this single reason: la Pucelle. Her advice was eagerly sought, from such diverse matters as the tangled finances of the city of Toulouse to the three-way contest for the Papacy.

"My dear lady," Jean IV of Armagnac had written, "I commend myself humbly to you and beseech you for God's sake, seeing the division which now exists in the Holy Church concerning the question of the popes . . . to entreat Our Lord Jesus Christ that in his infinite mercy he declare unto us through you which of the aforesaid three is the true Pope, and which He would have us henceforth obey, him who is called Martin, him who is called Clement, him who is called Benedict. . . .

Entirely your Count of Armagnac"

Jeanne was at Compiègne, just getting on her horse to go out and harass the God-damns. There was a scuffle; some zealous partisans of Clement threatened to throw Armagnac's messenger into the river. From the saddle, Jeanne dictated a hasty reply: "Count of Armagnac, good and very dear friend . . . I am now too pressed by the business of the war; but when you hear I am in Paris, send me a messenger and I will tell you in whom you should believe; and what I shall know by the counsel of my just and Sovereign Lord, the King of all the World. . . ."

This exchange of letters has often been cited as an example of Jeanne's naïveté and ignorant presumption. Given the state of men's minds on the Papacy, the curious mingling of calculation and superstition, it probably was naïve of Jeanne to think that she could straighten out the mess. Still, there was nothing outrageous in either the Count's request or Jeanne's reply. Nor any reason why Jeanne la Pucelle might not have chosen as satisfactory a Pope as any cabal of Italians, French and Imperialists in the Sacred College.*

Despite her lack of education, the absence of any definite program other than fighting, was Jeanne intelligent? The answer must be: yes. Even if she rejected formal learning, she learnt in her own way. She had the primary foundation of a first class intelligence: an excellent memory. She conducted, entirely alone, her own defense in one of the greatest trials of all time, in the midst of savage hostility, chained, ill, constantly threatened—with no documents of her own, unable to read the documents against her, with no aid but her memory.

* This particular contest ended with Otto Colonna, called Martin V, holding the field, as Benedict XIV died and Clement VIII retired from the competition.

After this tremendous intellectual performance, an achievement greater than any feat of arms, no one can say what Jeanne might not have accomplished had not the greedy and ruthless men of her time destroyed her at nineteen. . . .

What did Charles really think of Jeanne? What did she think of him? Did she understand Charles' inferiority complex around Philip of Burgundy? Philip was everything that Charles was not, that the age vastly admired. Succeeding to the murdered John the Fearless at twenty-five, Philip presided for almost fifty years over the most glittering and orgiastic Court in Christendom. The rigid ceremonial of Burgundy, the insolence of power and riches, became a model for successful royalty. Philip's magnificent tourneys attracted knights from all over; the Order of the Golden Fleece, Toison d'Or, celebrated both Jason of Colchis and the blonde body of Duchess Isabella of Burgundy, the voluptuous Portuguese princess. Philip threw a single party, the most extravagant ever known, the Feast of the Pheasant, costing 50,000 livres d'or, with elephants and dragons, mock jousts, twenty-eight musicians in a pie, mountains of pink sugar spun into faery delights, a naked giantess with spiced wine pouring from her nipples and below the opulent breast a chained lion with the legend "do not touch my mistress." All this to proclaim a crusade that never came off!

The Duke's success with women was Casanovian. The mere glimpse of a tender young morsel was enough to fire the ducal eye and to touch off the siege guns of his gallantries. He fathered nineteen bastards before he was thirty (his knightly device was *'aultre n'auray'*—no other shall I have!); and he was much given to communal baths. Like all his House, Philip had a violent temper, which he learned to control and to mask under a gleaming hauteur; in old age this control broke in dealings with his son Charles who had an equally violent temper, never mastered.

Occasionally the great man unbent, to the delight of his subjects. His humour ran to the cruel horseplay, so dear to the age. A drunken beggar, passed out cold at the palace gate, was picked up and carted inside. Philip changed clothes with the beggar; and when the fellow came to, he was attired in velvet and cloth of gold, seated before a feast. As he was gorging, the Duke, in rags, beseeched alms. The bewildered beggar drank himself into a coma, his rags were restored to him, and he was thrown into the ditch where he had been found.

Philip, too, was the epic connoisseur, the master patron. His influence created the Flemish school, the brilliant visions, the taut true line of Jan van Eyck, Hans Memling, Roger van der Weyden, Dirk Bouts, Petrus Christus, and Hugo van der Goes. These paintings, curiously mixed, of poignant idealism, the vermilion red tempera, and the Flemish fleshpot, ultramarine blue and egg yellow—the unbearable tears of Mary, the awful Christs descending, with Arnolfini the silk merchant and Chancellor Rolin and a very nubile mademoiselle in a conical black hat. All this, the ashy taste of prosperity, the contradictions between chivalry, the ideal, and the greed and cruelty of the great Duchy, the horror of war; and at the end, the fantasies of Hieronymous Bosch—the monstrous landscape of the soul.

No more eloquent pictures have ever been painted.

By comparison with all this splendour, passion, idealism, glut of gold, the joy and corruption of worldly power, the dread secrets of the soul's underworld—Charles and his entourage seemed mean and pitiable. In addition, Charles had placed himself at a fatal disadvantage by his part in the murder of Philip's father.

If Philip condescended to negotiate, Charles could only feel deeply flattered. Philip did not, indeed, wish to dominate France, as had the two preceding dukes of his House. He was after bigger game, a new imperial state on the lines of the ancient Lotharingian Kingdom of the 10th Century. By consenting to the Treaty of Troyes, 1420, post-Agincourt, and the English Regency, Philip abandoned whatever claims he had to run France. He needed the English alliance to carry out his schemes elsewhere; and the English needed him to maintain their grip on France.

For Burgundy, Jeanne had scant respect. She had never liked the bullying gilded dukedom; and she would find incomprehensible the obsequious attitude of Charles. As a concession to the Council's views, she had three weeks before the Coronation addressed a courteous letter to Philip inviting him to participate. And on the very day of the ceremony, she had written again from Reims, begging the Duke "with clasped hands" not to make war on the French, and warning him that if he did, his men would be defeated and their blood spread wide.

Rumours of the truce agitated the cities that had submitted to Charles; and Reims sent an inquiry. Jeanne replied, saying that she "begs you and requires you that you do not doubt her in the good dispute that she undertakes for the blood royal; and I pledge you that I will never abandon you as long as I live." She goes on to say that a fifteen-day truce has been made with Burgundy and an agreement that the Duke "deliver" Paris at the end of the period, but she does not know whether she will keep the truce, as she is not happy about it. If she does, it will be for saving of the King's honour. In any case, she assures the Rémois that she will "keep the King's army together to be ready at the end of the fifteen days, if they do not make peace. For this, my very dear and perfect friends, I beg you to believe that no evil shall happen to you as long as I live; but require you to keep good watch and to guard the good city of the King. . . ." *

She wrote as chief of the national party. If the King's Council did not feel responsible for those who had risked their necks to declare for France, Jeanne did. She would go with them to the end, undeviating. The beautiful eloquence was Jeanne; her letters reflected the manner of speech that moved and astounded men.

But what was France without Paris and the Ile de France? Persuaded at last to take the field, the reluctant royal warrior moved with the impetuosity of a turtle, the army covering approximately 100 miles in thirty-six days—the distance between Reims and Paris. Even at that, Charles did not go the whole way, but set up headquarters at Compiègne; while Jeanne and d'Alençon pushed on to St. Denis. "Array your men, *beau duc!*" she cried. "And those of the other captains. For by my staff, I have a longing to see Paris!"

La Pucelle had her wish from the heights of Mont Marthe, on the evening of September 7th. Had they arrived six weeks before, they might have walked in. But Paris, nervous and giddy, that not long before had flared with the feats of Margot of Hainault, tennis champion, was now feverish with Jeanne la Pucelle d'Orléans. Rumors rioted: Jeanne would sack the city; Charles had sworn to plough and to sow with salt the site of Paris. No doubt, certain scares of this sort were set going by the Occupation to forestall any popular sympathy for Jeanne. It was true, however, that Charles had no great passion for the city, nor the city for him. The last time Charles had seen Paris a Burgundian mob, completely out of control, was howling for his blood and he was saved by the quick thinking of Tanneguy du Châtel,

---

* The Duke, of course, could not "deliver" Paris even had he wished to, for the city was in Bedford's hands. This temporary truce was superseded by the four months' armistice of Compiègne, by which Burgundy was allowed to reinforce Paris. I have made my own fresh translations of Jeanne's letters, in general relying on Regine Pernoud's text. In her eager dictating, she rushes from the third to the first person.

of the axe at Montereau. Later, the dislike of Charles would stimulate the rude Parisians to hoot his mistress, Agnes Sorel.

The French found walls bristling with guns, a determined pro-Burgundian populace ("had they been four times as numerous, they could not have taken us!" the Bourgeois boasted), stiffened by the hard core of Bedford's regulars captained by Villiers de l'Isle Adam. In the wine-gold September flourished defiant Standards, the red diagonal cross of St. Andrew, Burgundy, the red Greek cross of St. George, England.

The assault was delivered at about two o'clock, the afternoon of Friday, September 8th, the Feast of the Nativity of the Virgin. Jeanne advanced to the moat before the porte St. Honoré, on the right bank. The dry outer fosse was soon crossed; but the flooded second ditch, the water level controlled by hydraulic gates within the city, blocked the French. Jeanne tested the depth with her Standard; and called for faggots. For hours the French laboured to fill the fosse, while shot and arrows blazed. Jeanne's Standard-bearer, Richard, was killed by a crossbolt between the eyes.

Jeanne seized the white and gold Standard and plunged forward, through a torrent of arrows. "Advance! Paris is ours!"

And from the walls they yelled: "Soldiers' piece! Camp woman!" At the ditch a crossbolt crumpled her, with the muzzle velocity of a shotgun blast. She lay moaning, her thigh torn. But when they tried to carry her out of danger, she screamed and fought. "I would have taken the city," she sobbed, as they bore her away.

But the day was red and the men were exhausted. Casualties had been terrible, the worst by far of any of Jeanne's battles: 500 dead, 1500 wounded or missing. All that night the French burned their dead, to prevent dishonouring of the bodies by Burgundian ghouls. "To-morrow," d'Alençon promised Jeanne. But tomorrow never came. That evening, René d'Anjou and Charles de Bourbon, comte de Clermont, arrived with an order from Senlis, to which royal headquarters had been removed: break off the assault.

This order, the result of the convention with Jean l'aveugle, left Jeanne incredulous. She insisted on another try. The captains agreed. D'Alençon had constructed a temporary bridge across the Seine at Saint Denis; the French would strike the less heavily fortified left bank. But Charles had thought of that possibility too; and during the night he had d'Alençon's bridge broken down. If Charles was not able to stand up to his enemies, he was adept at frustrating his friends.

Jeanne made a visit to the abbaye of St. Denis, sepulchre of the Kings of France, whose stone gisants gazed from twenty tombs in the purple silence. On the high altar, where a thousand candles flickered for souls in purgatory and gold-casketed lay the heart of Bertrand du Guesclin, Jeanne la Pucelle placed her sword and armour —a final offering to France.*

(And was it now that she glimpsed the way and the flame?)

At Châlons, Jeanne had met an old acquaintance, Garardin d'Epinal, Domremy's Burgundian. He asked her how she was. "Oh, I go well," she replied. "I fear only one thing."

"And what might that be?" Gerardin inquired.

"Treachery," Jeanne replied.

And again at Compiègne, Catherine de la Rochelle was yapping about the Burgundians and how it was necessary to come to terms with them. Jeanne cut her short. "There is only one way to make peace with those people," she said. "At the point of a lance!"

And now the enemy had come, but not in the gold and scarlet of Burgundy, not in any guise that she had dreamed of, not openly, banners displayed, but on covert feet, with a mask of trust and love—her own lord. He whom by her toil and blood she had raised out of fear, out of shame and loneliness to a glorious crown. No, it could not be true.

And yet—incredibly!

They were giving up Paris. They were taking the bitter road back; the army was breaking up. *He* had delivered her to death.

"I AM NOT ALONE. . . ."

After the failure at Paris, she lingered on another eight months, smothered in protocol, dragged from one château to another, given a patent of nobility as Jeanne du Lys, with a blazon of three gold fleur-de-lys and a sword and crown upon a field of azure. She now had more formal status and less real authority than ever before. The ever-

---

* But not, it appears, her white armour or the enchanted sword. Saint Catherine's sword had come to an inglorious end; la Pucelle had broken it on the derrière of a lewd camp woman at Compiègne.

victorious Army, that had marched beneath the Standard of the Angels, was disbanded at Gien; after a brief reunion with Jeanne d'Orléans at St. Florent, d'Alençon went campaigning in Normandy with La Hire. The *beau duc's* request that Jeanne la Pucelle join him met a flat 'no' from Georges de la Trémoïlle. The Treasurer had other plans for Jeanne. He appointed a relative, the Sieur d'Albret, to the supreme command and placed la Pucelle under this watchful eye.

In October, Jeanne went forth with a little army of 2000 men, captained by d'Albret and Marèchal Jean de Boussac. First, they closed in on the fortress of St. Pierre-le-Moustier, on the upper Loire. Whatever role Jeanne now played, she was increasingly visionary, increasingly alone. In a sense, she had always been so; her legions were in Heaven.

Jean d'Aulon, lieutenant of Jeanne's Household, found her one day quite solitary, before the ramparts of St. Pierre. What was she doing there, by herself? d'Aulon wondered. She turned, with a strange look. "Oh," she said, "I am not alone. I have fifty thousand angels about me." And she pointed to the empty plain.

She had always communed with the invisible, heard Voices, seen a marvelous light; but never quite so apart from the reality of ordinary men. Worried, d'Aulon asked her if she expected to capture St. Pierre-le-Moustier. *"Oui, par mon martin,"* she replied. And, rising in her stirrups, she shouted for faggots to fill up the moat. St. Pierre fell; for the last time the old enchantments worked. But she was like a Merlin who has overstayed his leave, living on into an age of unbelief.

But she was still full of dreams.

The Constable de Richemont would lead 3000 men from Brittany; La Hire was on his way from Normandy; King Charles was raising more troops. But reconciliation with the Constable was blocked by la Trémoïlle, and it took four years and a knife thrust in that huge belly before Artus de Richemont got in to see his royal liege. As for that bandy-legged young man, far from raising troops, he was warming up to one of the most astounding and painful betrayals in history.

Following the success at St. Pierre, the royal army was sent to lay siege to La Charité, a town in Burgundian grasp a few miles down the river. The season was bitter. "Name of God," Catherine de la Rochelle said to Jeanne, "I don't see how you do it. Making war in such weather."

Poor Catherine! She was not of the stuff of prophets. Her one effort at soothsaying had been exposed as fakery. Catherine had claimed to receive nightly revelations from a 'lady in white' who gave her information as to where the wealthy had hid their treasure. Catherine told Brother Richard and Brother Richard told the King's Council —it was the type of revelation likely to interest Georges de la Trémoïlle. Putting the matter to the test, Jeanne stayed awake all night in Catherine's bed—but the white lady did not appear. After three nights of this, for which Jeanne trained in sleeping by day, to keep Catherine awake by pinchings and proddings, the would-be seeress, dead for sleep, had to cry mercy.

Send Catherine home to her husband and children, Jeanne recommended. Yet not even mortal peril cooled Catherine's craving for publicity. She turned up in Paris the following year, with a half-witted companion; at first, not averse to being taken for la Pucelle, marvelously resurrected, Catherine soon realized that this pose was a deadly game. She 'confessed,' denouncing Jeanne and her errors and heresy. Catherine got off with a few months in the grim prison fortress of Le Châtelet, but the weak-witted Pierronne la Bretonne was burned, for saying that Jeanne had been inspired by God.

The Army dallied during a month before La Charité. Supplies were running low; and Jeanne had been forced to write all over the Loire, to Riom, Clermont, Orléans, to obtain the bare necessities for the siege. The captains refused to attempt to storm the town; the Army was dispirited, the weather harsh. It was now dead December, the very lean skeleton of the year. Against Jeanne's plea, the siege was lifted; nothing further might be done anywhere until spring.

The scene shifted from the field to the Court; the action, from the military to the diplomatic level. Perceptive men, such as Hughes de Lannoy, political adviser to Philip of Burgundy, saw which way the wind was blowing. De Lannoy was useful; in addition to his memos, he did a little pimping on the side for His Grace. Now he counseled Philip that la Pucelle was finished, that Charles was as wax in the hands of the Archbishop and la Trémoïlle. There need be no rush about the peace conference; simply extend the truce. Charles had even been persuaded to write to Amadeus of Savoy, the prospective Chairman, to put off the conference from April to June.

All this delighted Philip. He was in the midst of his two most pleasurable pursuits: the body of a woman and playing at chivalry. He had just taken a third wife, blonde and sensual Isabella of Portugal;

and in her honour the doting bridegroom had founded the Order of the Golden Fleece—which some wags said celebrated not Jason of Colchis, but the blonde body of Duchess Isabella. Philip was in a giving vein; all that he asked to extend the truce was the return to Burgundian allegiance of the Somme towns, of which the chief was Compiègne.

But Compiègne would have none of Philip. The town refused to receive the Comte de Clermont, whom his troops referred to as 'Junior,' because they rightly suspected it was a prelude to being handed over to Philip. In reprisal, Burgundian hatchetmen were unleashed, raiding in the Somme; it was Philip's policy to terrorize Compiègne and other towns into submission. At Bourges, Jeanne la Pucelle began to receive frightened letters.

Could she protect the good towns of the realm of France?

She could—and she would. Her armour and sword had been plundered from St. Denis by the English; but she had new armour and a new sword, with the familiar white and gold Standard. More difficult was the matter of a company. Her friends, such as d'Alençon and the Bastard, held no present royal command; the royal forces had been thoughtfully broken up by la Trémoïlle. The King kept only a palace guard of Italian ruffians under a Piedmontese named Bartelomio Baretti, for raids and skirmishes.

Yet even this unpromising material was not immune to la Pucelle. She worked on Baretti and his Italians, evoking in those vulpine souls unsuspected valor; and when Poton de Xantrailles rode in from Brittany, and Hugues Kennedy pledged his Scots, she had a company. By March, she could no longer be restrained. Yielding, Charles for the first time gave Jeanne a field command and made her paymaster of the curiously assorted warriors. She, la Pucelle, the saint of victory, was on her own with a few hundred routiers and 10,000 gold crowns.

The campaign began well. Melun opened its gates to la Pucelle in early April; she made a triumphal entry. But it was almost the final grace in this unique and shining life. For at Melun she received the bitter news of her imminent capture. Her Voices told Jeanne she would be taken before St. John's Day, that is, June 29th. She always had a horror of confinement, she a wild free being, forest-haunted, the arching silent paths of Lorraine. She obtained no more information. She was given neither the day, nor the place.

The captain of Compiègne was Guillaume de Flavy, a cousin of

Georges de la Trémoïlle. Her own captains tried to dissuade Jeanne from putting herself in the power of this man; Soissons, nearby, had just been betrayed to the Burgundians by a Picard ecorcheur, for 4000 *salus d'or*. She shook off the well-meant advice. '*Par mon martin,* we are enough. I will go to see my good friends of Compiègne!" Jeanne exclaimed.

She rode in at the porte Pierrefonds in the early morning of May 23rd, having passed the previous day and night in the saddle and in the fields. Surrounded by cheering townsfolk, the heroine of France was pressed to make a sortie that day. Again her captains were dubious; the men were exhausted and required rest and good refreshing. For once, Jeanne hesitated. She did not know the lay of the land; neither the number nor disposition of the foe. To the innocent enthusiasm of the townsfolk, crowding about their Pucelle, Guillaume de Flavy added a more sinister note. He, too, favoured a sortie; and guaranteed to protect Jeanne's retreat. As we shall see, he had his motives.

Jeanne could seldom resist an emotional appeal. She mounted, took her Standard, and rode out with 500 men. It was between four and five in the afternoon, Vespers. As he had promised, Guillaume de Flavy manned the walls of Compiègne with a strong guard.

Now, the bridge across the Oise was protected, as at Orléans, by a boulevard and a causeway ran from the boulevard through marshy terrain to the village of Margny, held by the Luxembourgers of Jean comte de Ligny. Gold and white Standard flaring, la Pucelle swept down on Margny. Once more, and as it were, forever, Jeanne la Pucelle routed the enemies of France. Luxembourgers ran. But it happened that the one-eyed Jean himself, whether by chance or by design, had ridden out to survey the town from across the river. Margny was an advance post and Jean de Luxembourg, alerted by the clamour, despatched a summons to his base camp at Clairoix, a mile and a half away.

In a short time, Duke Philip came hot to the rescue with the crack Burgundians of his Household in their gold and scarlet. The tables had been neatly turned on the French. It would be pleasant to record that like the Immortal Swiss Guard, the Lion of Lucerne, Baretti and his routiers stood and died. *Whom God abandoned, these defended; and saved the sum of things for pay. . . .*

Nothing of the sort.

When it became apparent that the day was not only unprofitable, but was becoming downright dangerous, Baretti's men departed. Poor hired swords of a shabby prince, they had not contracted for heroism. They did what they professionally could; they covered Jeanne's retreat up to the boulevard. Now it was the turn of de Flavy, to sally and rescue Jeanne. De Flavy never stirred.

She was a few hundred yards away, surrounded by a yelling mob of Burgundians, vermilion cloth of gold cloak swinging as she made her *"attention à droit! attention à gauche!"* Her little Household, Jean d'Aulon, her brother Pierre, and a handful of others fought beside her. She was undone by her passion for fine clothes, her splendid cloak that both marked her off and offered a means of capture. An archer named Lyonnel, a Picard in the service of the Bastard of Vendôme, lieutenant of Luxembourg, caught a bit of cloth of gold in his fist; with a tremendous jerk, he pulled Jeanne from her saddle.

De Flavy never stirred.

The commandant had admitted the fleeing routiers. For Jeanne, he clanged his portcullis and raised his bridge. The silver bird of Heaven had been snared. She was escorted to an immediate interview with His Grace, Philip of Burgundy—who was overjoyed to see her.

Charged with treachery, Guillaume de Flavy would no doubt have said that he had nothing personal against Jeanne, that he was even sorry about her fate. He had his career to think of, a wife and children to provide for. In this, he was at least no worse than Judas, who also had *his* career with the Sanhedrin and who was in financial straits.

But what may be said of Charles de Valois, who owed all his career to Jeanne la Pucelle, who but for her would not be longer even King of Bourges, but who would be wearing out a hand-to-mouth existence in a Spanish garret, universally scorned? The moment she was captured, he treated her as already dead. Not a single gesture, not a word from Charles. He did indeed allow his Chancellor, Regnault de Chartres, to put out a statement on the morrow of Jeanne's capture that this misfortune was God's will, for she had been proud and wilful. He himself said nothing.

It is not impossible that Charles de Valois allowed la Trémoïlle to engineer the final Gethsemane, a deed which, if true, makes Judas Iscariot seem comparatively honest and decent. At least, Judas had the grace to hang himself; the greater horror was reserved for Charles. In the ordeal of Charles de Valois was consummated the passion of Jeanne d'Arc.*

Charles could have done much for Jeanne. He could have raised a princely ransom to outbid the English. And if the English put pressure on Burgundy, the life of John Talbot, Earl of Shrewsbury (captured by Jeanne at Patay) could have been put into the scales against Jeanne's. When they finally had her in their grip, the English treated Jeanne abominably. But after all, she had hurt them and they were afraid of her. In England, the new levies raised by the King's Council to go fight la Pucelle rioted and refused to board their ships.

What had Jeanne done to Charles, save to restore to him his name and birthright; his self-respect, his pride and royalty? Always dodging obligations, such a burden of gratitude must have terrified a man like Charles. He could never repay it, especially as Jeanne wanted none of the things most people care about: money, titles, property. When she was captured, she owned nothing but her horse and her armour. Unable to requite the obligation, unable to get out of it, Charles did nothing. If he did not actually connive at Jeanne's betrayal by the commandant of Compiègne, he gave the English notice that they might treat her with impunity; shut her in an iron cage, torture her, violate her—condemn her soul to everlasting fire and her body to pitch and sulphur—and while this was going on, Charles flitted from Bourges to Chinon, from Loches to Mehun-sur-Yèvre, arrayed in green, crimson and white, sonnets and music accompanying him, feasts, dancing, long rides in the countryside. . . .

Jeanne paid for this pleasure; paid with six months' anguish in an English hell. Charles paid too, his score being almost as terrible. But the reckoning was deferred.

And we must suppose too, on a more exalted level, that Jeanne was not merely the simple victim of an appalling injustice—though she was that. But in her life, so devoted, pure and just, she re-enacted an ancient martyrdom, the sacrifice of the Redeemer—the last essential act without which the redemption itself might fail. Rouen was implicit from the beginning.

* His end was grim. Abandoned even by d'Alençon and the Bastard, his feather-brained mistress Agnes Sorel poisoned, hated by his son and heir, Charles either voluntarily starved to death; or was murdered by order of Louis the Dauphin. This was a direct result of his frightful ingratitude to the one being in all his life who kept faith in him—Jeanne la Pucelle.

She came like music, this antiphony of the soul that inspired, that transformed . . . young she was and lonely. What did she seek, she that knew her name would ring forever? . . . She looked for nothing in the world without; the world within had given her all. Her stable of horses, her fine raiment, her armour and enchanted swords—all part of her role of angel on horseback, the image of the age. But she was greatest at Rouen, alone, beaten, manacled, starved—alone with echoes, marvelous echoes, crying and singing, the torn vision, the death and love she brought. . . .

PIERRE CAUCHON IS WITH US FOREVER!

On November 21st, 1430, Jeanne la Pucelle was sold by Jean comte de Ligny to the English. The price paid was considerably more than Judas received for Christ and even above the sum obtained by the Scots in disposing of the mortal body of King Charles the First. The price was, in fact, stiff: 10,000 gold crowns. John Duke of Bedford put the finger on the Estates of Normandy, screwed 120,000 pounds out of these canny Normans. Part of the balance was used to bear the expenses of Jeanne's trial and to sweeten the judges.

Jeanne had been comparatively well treated by de Ligny; not only was he well aware of the value of his prize, but the presence of his aunt, the Demoiselle of Luxembourg, an ancient lady of whom the one-eyed pirate stood much in awe, restrained loose behaviour. The worst indignity that befell Jeanne was an occasion when an over-friendly visitor, the Comte de Pressy, managed to feel her breasts on the pretext of measuring her for a new *pourpoint*. Jeanne boxed his ears.

The Demoiselle of Luxembourg was very wealthy and her nephew did his best to please her, even holding up the sale of la Pucelle because the old lady had become attached to the girl. But on November 13th the Demoiselle died and one week later Jeanne was turned over to the agents of Pierre Cauchon, Bishop of Beauvais, who was brokering for the English and who intended to bring the captive to trial for heresy and for trafficking with demons. . . .

Oh, it was to be a glorious Trial! Nothing like it ever seen; famous, quoted, the touch of a master. Yes, his name, this ironic provoking name, Pierre Cauchon, that sounded so much like Pierre Cochon (and he was massive!), Bishop of Beauvais, Archbishop-to-be of Rouen, would go down in the scholiarchy of time, the discoverer and scourge of the strangest heresy ever known. He would assemble a splendid bench of assessors, doctors and canons from Rouen, Beauvais, Paris— and the Grand Inquisitor of France. The Bishop would preside, conduct the proceedings, the English would have no reason to criticise him and after all the witch had been taken within the bounds of his old diocese of Beauvais.

He would astonish the learned snobs of the Faculty of Paris, who had coveted 'Our Trial' for themselves. Praise God, the English had preferred Rouen and Pierre Cauchon. Well, he would show them all the stuff that he was made of, ex-delegate to the Council of Constance, ex-secretary to Jean sans peur, privy councillor of Henry the Sixth. He was sixty, enormous, and this was his first big chance. He knew the English, Warwick, Bedford, Cardinal Beaufort; for years, he had worked with the lords from across the Manche. He believed that the English would pay well; would remember service by such prizes within their disposal as the See of Rouen.

Besides, by the Rood! he was defending Holy Church. Heresy, schism, intercourse with devils—could there be a worse case?

But from the beginning, 'Our Trial' had gone wrong. Oh, he had the assessors all right, sixty and more, and if he could not get the Grand Inquisitor himself (who was busy with another case) he had the Dominican Vicar of the Holy Office, Jean le Maistre; he had personal jurisdiction granted him by the Cathedral Chapter of Rouen. One would have thought—. But there had been that aging fool, Master Nicholas Houppeville, who had questioned the Bishop's right to hold the Trial at all and the accused's lack of counsel. Pierre Cauchon had settled with Master Nicholas. Others had interfered, why didn't the Bishop do this or do that? He had settled them, too.

But by far the most troublesome aspect was the accused herself. He had never dreamed of this. An ignorant peasant debating with the Faculty of Paris. Why, it was not to be borne. Only—it seemed that it was. And the English, with each session, becoming more and more furious, not even civil any more, Cardinal Beaufort shouting insults— oh what Pierre Cauchon had to endure for his faith!

But he was determined to see the Trial through; he couldn't quit, he had staked too much. Better that he and the accused went down together, if it came to that. Why, he had asked a question such as: "Are you, or do you believe yourself, in a state of grace?" A splendid question; however she answered, she must condemn herself.

And what had she said?

"If I am, may God keep me there. If I am not, may God put me there. For I would rather be in a state of grace than anything in this world."

And the speechless Bishop had heard an admiring murmur from the assessors and someone, he thought, had said, "responsa superba"—superb reply. It was. But it so disarrayed the Bishop that he could not think of another question, and had to give over the proceedings for that day.

But the Bishop knew a trick or two. His investigators in Domremy had been totally unable to unearth anything detrimental to Jeanne. He had shouted at them for a pack of fools; and proceeded to make his own deductions. Early in the Trial, he had seized on the wearing of men's garments by this profane girl. He had found scriptural injunction against women in tunics; * but, more importantly, he had noticed how the girl clung to her stained and filthy costume. Inadvertently, the Bishop had hit upon what he had very much lacked: an issue.

He had no idea why she made such a fuss over these unseemly rags, but it was clear the matter had assumed a tremendous significance to her. In the Sixth Session, that of Saturday, March 3rd, in the Robing Room—a sitting which began well when the accused was persuaded to take the oath upon the Gospels—the Bishop had Master Jean Beaupère, former Rector of the University of Paris, take up the question of Jeanne's attire.

"Did the examiners of the other party (at Poitiers) inquire about your dress?"

"I do not remember."

"Did you take this dress by direction of your Voices?"

"I do not remember."

"When you first visited the Queen (Marie d'Anjou), did she ask you about this dress?"

"I do not remember."

"Did the King or the Queen or others of your party require you to put off male dress and take that of a woman?"

---

* "The woman shall not wear that which pertaineth unto a man, neither may a man put on a woman's garment: for all that do so are abomination unto the Lord thy God." Deuteronomy, Chapter xxii.

"That is not in your Trial."

"Were you not so required at Beaurevoir?"

"Yes indeed. And I said I would not change it without Our Lord's leave . . . the Demoiselle of Luxembourg and the Lady of Beaurevoir offered me a woman's dress . . . and I would sooner have done it at the request of these two ladies than of any other ladies in France, except the Queen."

"When God revealed to you that you should change your dress, was it by the voice of Saint Michael, Saint Catherine, or Saint Margaret?"

"You shall have nothing more from me at present."

The Bishop was anxious to demonstrate—and she would not admit in so many words—that her Voices had specifically enjoined Jeanne to put on male attire. If the Voices had commanded anything so contrary to Scripture and decisions of Church Councils, then they must be of demonic origin. But Jeanne sidestepped the question, although, cleverly, she insisted she would not retake woman's dress until a direct revelation from God commanded her to do so.

The Bishop returned to the attack ten days later; having explored meantime other and less profitable avenues. The girl was fiendishly adept at getting out of tight spots.

"Took you this dress at the request of Robert de Baudricourt?"

"I have taken it of my own wish, and not at the request of anyone in the world."

"Did your Voices instruct you to wear man's clothing?"

"Everything good I have done, I did by command of the Voices. For the dress, I shall answer tomorrow."

"Did you think you did wrong in taking such dress?"

"No. And if now I were with my own people and wearing this man's dress, it should be for the great good of France."

The Bishop sighed. The evasive tactics of the accused complicated his problem. In every tight corner, she took a kind of heavenly Fifth Amendment, claiming God forbade her to answer, or she would promise to reply another day, say in three weeks.

Pierre Cauchon went to a question in which his English employers were specially interested.

"How did you propose to deliver the Duke of Orléans?"

"I would have taken enough English prisoners to ransom him. And if I had not enough, I would have crossed the sea and delivered him by force."

"Did Saint Margaret and Saint Catherine tell you that you should take prisoners to ransom the Duke of Orléans? Or that you should cross the sea to deliver him by force?"

"Yes. And I told the King to let me take prisoners. And if I had been permitted to last three years, I should have delivered the Duke. . . ."

The next Session, the Tenth, was wasted on a rambling and largely imaginary account of la Pucelle's "Sign" to the Dauphin at Chinon; even the most stupid assessor might perceive that Jeanne was making sport of the Bishop in this tale of angel bearing a crown of gold. Bourbon saw the angel, she said. D'Alençon saw it. La Trémoïlle saw it. And if Georges saw an angel, anyone could.

The Eleventh Session considered the question of Beaurevoir and whether Jeanne were not in a state of mortal sin as a result of her suicide leap.* She denied an intent of suicide; and went on to warn the Bishop concerning his own state, the risk that he was running. What risk? Pierre Cauchon wanted to know.

Why, she said, if he judged her wrongfully, God would punish him. She had regular information on the subject of the Bishop from her Voices. She commented further that Saint Catherine had promised aid in the present crisis. Either she would be delivered from her cell or a disturbance would arise during the Trial, to free her. She would be released by a "great victory." And, her Voices advised: "Take it all cheerfully. Do not despair on account of your martyrdom, for in the end you will come to the Kingdom of Heaven. . . ."

This rather took the doctors' breath away.

This peasant girl bestowing salvation on herself. What became of Holy Church? Of a thousand chantry chapels? Of a million Masses for the dead? Of the power to bind and the power to loose? . . . *thou art Peter . . . upon this rock shall I build my Church.* . . .

And the Bull *Ecclesia Unam Sanctam,* which set forth for all Eternity the authority of the Church.** What would become of all of them, if

---

* In August, Jeanne had leaped from the sixty-foot tower of Beaurevoir. She had been wildly excited over a report that the English intended to storm Compiègne and put every living thing to the sword. Incredibly, Jeanne suffered no broken bones or serious injuries, though she was unconscious three days.

** Pope Boniface VIII, in 1302. Persecuted by Philip the Fair, Boniface tried to defend himself by immense spiritual claims. He has been described thus: "Boniface any Jacques Bonhomme might claim a private revelation from God Almighty concerning salvation? This girl—and her military triumphs had persuaded millions that she spoke truth—proclaimed that God talked regularly with her, regarded her in a special light as His Daughter. This was powerful medicine, worse than witchcraft. Witches were often spoilt nuns or saints in skirts of flame, the necessary obverse of the Church Militant.

But she—she—oh wondrous she!

Needed nothing; asked nothing; was not even interested. *Would you not like us to arrange a fine and notable procession for you, to bring you to God?* . . . but all she desired were the prayers of good Catholics everywhere.

Oh surely, surely, Pierre Cauchon knew heresy, schism, when he smelled it. There he sat, huge and purple, wheezing;—and his Promoter and his Vicar of the Holy Office, and the sixty assessors . . . Soldiers of God! fourteen centuries of Catholicism look down.

For this was another war, a war for the immortal soul. And what happened here—at Rouen—rippled out to the edges of Christendom and the vast night of the dead.

In the Fourteenth Session, held on Thursday, March 15th, the Bishop had sprung his trap. He knew how Jeanne hungered for the Holy Sacrament, hovering about the Chapel Royal of the Castle, asking innocently, "Is this where they keep the Blessed Lord?"—and how the Promoter, Jean d'Estivet, had rushed up one day just in time to seize the girl as she was entering the Chapel.

D'Estivet was an irritating fool. Something might have been made of so passionate a need. The Promoter was just one more of the crosses that Pierre Cauchon had to carry in the labours of 'Our Trial.'

"Should you hear Mass, would it not be more fitting to do so in a woman's dress? Which, then, do you prefer: to wear a woman's dress and to hear Mass; or to continue in man's attire and not hear Mass?"

"Promise me that I may hear Mass if I wear a woman's dress and then I will answer you."

"I promise you that you shall hear Mass, if you put on woman's dress."

(She was caught. She had not expected so prompt an agreement.

---

was prepared to style himself *Imperator,* and in the general sublimity of his pretensions he is thought to have outdone all his predecessors." *Cambridge Medieval History,* Vol. VI, pp. 628, 644–645.

Now she must either reject the Sacrament or put off her unseemly costume. She took refuge in evasion.)

"I will think this over and then answer you."

"You must take a woman's dress, unconditionally and absolutely."

"Bring me a dress like that of a citizen's daughter; a long *houppe-lande,* and I will wear it, and also a woman's hood, to go and hear Mass." *

It had been a good day's work. Jeanne had been backed into a corner, as a result of her odd insistence on wearing man's attire. The following Saturday, March 17th, the Bishop pressed his advantage:

"What say you as to the woman's dress?"

"As to the dress, I will not take it yet, not till it please Our Lord. But if I am found guilty, I beg you to grant me a woman's dress and a hood. . . ."

"If by God's command, you wear a man's dress, why do you ask for woman's attire for your last hours?"

"It suffices that it be long."

"Now, as to your godmother, Jeanne Aubrey, the one who saw the fairies. Is she considered a wise woman?"

"She is an upright woman of good sense. She is not a witch."

"You say that if we let you go, you will take a woman's dress. Is this pleasing to God?"

"If you let me go in woman's dress, I will put on man's attire and do as God commands me. And never shall I swear not to take up arms or wear male dress."

(To be sure everyone grasped the point, the Bishop grouped questions on the subject of Jeanne's dress with those concerning submission to the Church Militant.)

"Do you submit to the decision of the Church?"

---

* The choice of garment is significant; for a *houppelande* style was common to both men and women in the 15th Century. The idea that Jeanne wore her tunic to protect herself from her keepers is nowhere borne out in the trial records; but two witnesses, Martin Ladvenu and Pierre Cusquel, stated that she confided this explanation to them, when they testified at the Trial of Rehabilitation. But this is surely specious on Jeanne's part, if she did employ such an explanation. Chained and helpless as she was, it can have made little difference what she wore if the keepers were determined to have her. There were three of them at all times in her cell, two to hold her and one to outrage her. It may be noted also that she was equally adamant on the point at Beaurevoir, when she was in no danger of abuse. Some other cause must be sought for her insistence on wearing her tunic and hose.

"I refer in this to Our Lord Who sent me, to Our Lady, and to all the blessed Saints in Heaven!"

"There is the Church Triumphant, where are God, the Saints, and the souls that are saved; and there is the Church Militant, that is, our Holy Father the Pope, God's Vicar upon earth, the cardinals, the prelates of the Church, and the clergy, and all good Catholic Christians; and this Church, when assembled, cannot err, and is governed by the Holy Spirit."

"But I come from God, from the Virgin Mary, and from all the blessed Saints in Heaven, and from the Church Triumphant on high, and by their commands, to Charles of France. And to this Church I submit all my deeds."

"Will you submit to the Church Militant?"

"You shall have no other answer."

After dinner that same day, the Bishop, gorged on capon and claret, had swirled back for a turn at the Voices. The Catholic line on such phenomena was explicit: it emanated from either God or the Devil and only the Church might decide. Jeanne, as the Bishop had been at pains to point out, had never submitted her Voices, or any aspect of her mission, to final judgement of the Church, at Domremy, Vaucouleurs, or Poitiers. At Poitiers, she had been formally examined, but her own mind was already made up and she did not in any sense seek the advice or aid of the tribunal.

The more precise the descriptions of the phenomena, the more likely that the Fiend had assumed a guise to trap the unwary. Corporeal limbs, clothes, odours were significant evidence. Earlier, the Bishop had asked Jeanne if Saint Michael were naked when he appeared to her. She had shot back: "Do you think God has not the means wherewith to clothe him?"

Now the Bishop tried again:

"Have you ever kissed or embraced Saint Catherine or Saint Margaret?"

"Yes, both."

"Do they smell pleasant?"

"Assuredly (*il est bon a savoir,* lit. it is good to know)."

"When you embrace them, do you feel warmth—or anything else?"

"I could not embrace them without feeling and touching them."

"What part did you embrace, above or below?"

"It is more fitting to embrace them above."

"Have you not given garlands?"

"Yes, often. But only to the saints' pictures or statues in the church. Not to the Voices."

"Those garlands you hung on the tree of fairies, did you put them there to honour your Voices?"

"No. . . ."

"What do you know of those who consort with fairies?"

"I never did that or know anything of it. But I heard it said they went on Thursdays. I put no trust in it. It is only sorcery. . . ."

(*I heard it said they went on Thursdays!* . . . the echo of Jeanne of Lorraine, this country girl, twenty summers come Epiphany, whose body and soul were in the dock in the greatest trial of all time . . .)

The point of submission was hammered. On April 18th, a Wednesday, several examiners crowded into the evil hole where Jeanne lay manacled, pale and weak, too ill to attend public sessions. She had suffered a nervous breakdown from abuse by Warwick's 'strawnecks.' *

"If you do not accept counsel and follow the Church's advice, your body is in mortal peril."

"Seeing the illness that I suffer from, I am in great danger of death. And if so be God's Will, I ask you to hear my confession and to give me my Saviour, and that I be buried in consecrated ground."

"If you wish to have the privileges and sacraments of the Church, you must do as good Catholics should. *You must submit!*"

"I cannot tell you anything more now."

And again on May 2nd, when by order of the Earl of Warwick, captain of Rouen, the guards had been changed and the abuse of Jeanne halted, so that she began to mend and was able to appear at a public hearing of admonition. Satisfied, the Bishop had intended only to nail down what she had said in her cell; he had no thought of jeopardizing all the labour of the past few months. The Session had begun in quite

---

* It is apparently only since about 1870 that persons are allowed nervous ailments by academic historians. For those living before that time, such writers accept all sorts of fantastic diagnoses dreamed up by medieval quacks, *le médecin malgré lui,* and overlook the plain evidence of the real trouble. Henry VI, for instance, is always called an 'imbecile'—as if some Mongolian tendency were involved; the truth being that Henry, a neurotic from childhood, suffered a complete nervous crack-up, which took the form of schizophrenia. Jeanne is said to have had an attack of ptomaine in prison; it is quite possible she did, but the more important fact is a nervous breakdown.

a routine way with Master Jean Chatillon, doctor of theology of the University of Paris, leading for the tribunal.

"Do you submit to the Church Militant?"

"I believe in the Church; but for my deeds and words, as I said before, I refer the matter to God, Who has caused me to do what I have done."

"Do you mean that you have no judge on earth? The Holy Father?"

"I will tell you nothing else. . . ."

"Would you submit to a General Council of the Church?"

"You will drag nothing else from me."

"Would you submit to our Holy Father the Pope?"

"Bring me to him and I shall answer him. . . ."

At this point, there was an unlooked-for and startling interpolation. The accused who, as usual, was sitting by herself on a little stool before the tribunal, giving her replies in a sullen monotone, suddenly got to her feet and made the following declaration: "I will submit to the Council of the Church at Bâle."

It was exactly as if a bomb had exploded under the Bishop. In theory, any person charged with heresy had the right to appeal to a General Council of the Church or to the Pope; in practise, the local 'Ordinaries' of the Church conducted proceedings. But so jealous was the Bishop for his jurisdiction that his creature, Nicholas Loiseleur, canon of Rouen, secretly introduced into Jeanne's cell as a fellow prisoner, had encouraged her never to submit to the Higher Authority of the Church Militant.

Now, in an instant, all the careful planning and strategy of months was imperiled. God knew what would happen if the Bishop lost jurisdiction to Bâle.* At the least the splendid See of Rouen would vanish forever; and the Bishop would be fortunate if he kept out of jail. The English were not likely to sympathize with problems of canon law. Indeed, it was in the highest degree improbable that they would ever let Jeanne out of their grip, to go to Bâle or anywhere else. She would disappear into an English dungeon.

If this appeal were allowed to stand, no one would really gain anything: not the accused; not the Bishop; not the Church (whose authority would almost certainly be flouted by the English).

---

* The Council of Bâle had not yet convened, but was scheduled for the autumn. Pierre Champion makes out a strong case against either the Council or the Pope, Eugene IV, withdrawing jurisdiction from the Bishop. Still, it is important that Jeanne made the appeal.

The Bishop arose. He fixed a terrible glance on Brother Isambart de la Pierre, who had begun to speak in favour of the motion and whom the Bishop rightly suspected of having egged on the accused in this threatening course. "You—idiot!" he said to Brother Pierre. "Hold your tongue!" He turned magisterially to Guillaume Manchon, recorder.

"Shall I write these words?" the scribe asked.

"No!" the Bishop thundered.

At this, the accused leaped up. "Ah, you write what is against me, but not what is for me!"

"Pass to the next question," the Bishop said.

It had been a near thing. The Bishop decided to take no more chances, but to proceed to judgement. The sixty-one Articles of Accusation drawn up by Master d'Estivet and containing all kinds of wild charges such as prostitution, murder, and mandrakes, had been redrawn and reduced to twelve by Thomas Courcelles, for the opinion of the University of Paris.

On Saturday, May 19th, the tribunal assembled in the chapel of the archepiscopal manor of Rouen, the Bishop trying out, as it were, his anticipated chapel. With Master Pierre Maurice of the Faculty leading, the censures of the University were brought out, point by point.

The first, second, third, fourth and eleventh articles dealt with Jeanne's supraliminal experience, second sight, precognition, apparitions, voices from the unseen; all these works were stigmatized as superstitious, pernicious, idolatrous and proof of demonic intercourse. The fifth article concerned the wearing of the tunic and hose and the haircut en ronde, in page boy style. This was judged blasphemous, idolatrous, and very possibly heretical. The sixth article denounced Jeanne's bold letters to the English, in which she summoned the enemy to surrender before she launched the attack. She was considered cruel and a murderer, one who revelled in blood. The ninth article concerned the claim to direct information on salvation and freedom from mortal sin; this was judged false and presumptuous. The twelfth and last article referred to the duty of every good Catholic to submit to the Church; and Jeanne was judged schismatic in her refusal.

Master Pierre, the youngest doctor there, just trying his dialectical wings, preached the admonition of his life. "Jeanne, very dear friend. . . ."

He pointed out the long struggle of the Church against error, the insidious wiles of Satan able to counterfeit at will the shape of men or of angels; and how only those skilled in detecting such lies and tricks might distinguish God and the Devil. It followed that if the untrained person saw an apparition or heard a voice, it was his duty to submit any such experience to the judgment of the Church—which Jeanne had consistently refused to do.

The soldiers of the Church were Christ's warders at the gate of truth, the defenders of the Castle of Salvation, as the gendarmes of the King protected the outposts of the royal domain. "If your King in the exercise of his power had given you charge of a certain place, forbidding you to allow anyone to enter; and someone appeared, saying he came by the King's authority, you would not allow him to enter unless he brought you letters or some other certain sign that he came with the King's authority; likewise, Our Lord Jesus Christ, when He ascended into Heaven, leaving the government of the Church to Saint Peter and his successors, forbade them to receive any coming in His Name, if they were not sufficiently assured, other than by their own words, that they came from God. . . .

"Wherefore, Jeanne, you must understand that, if in your King's realm, when you were there, a knight or some other subject had arisen and said, I will not obey the King, nor will I submit to any of his officers, would you not have said that he should be condemned? What would you say therefore of yourself, brought up in the Faith of Jesus Christ by the sacrament of baptism and made the spouse of Jesus Christ, if you do not obey His officers, the prelates of the Church?"

Master Pierre went on to warn of fire, both satanical and English. He laboured with Jeanne to submit. "For He has said to His prelates, He that heareth you heareth Me; and he that despiseth you despiseth Me . . ."

It was a brilliant effort. Eschewing the turgid violence of a d'Estivet and the subtle web of a Courcelles, young Master Pierre had preached a most eloquent exhortation; briefly, the Trial, despite its presiding genius, took on a mighty dimension, Aquinian in scope.

But Jeanne la Pucelle was equal to the occasion. "Oh Master Pierre, beau sire! . . . I will maintain what I said at my Trial. And if I were to be condemned and saw the fire lit and the wood prepared and the executioner who was to burn me ready to cast me into the fire, still in the fire would I not say anything other than what I have said. And I will maintain what I have said until death!"

If the Bishop did not encourage Jeanne to submit to Bâle, he greatly desired her to submit to him and to confess herself in error. This would accomplish what was for the English the main purpose of the Trial: to obtain proof that la Pucelle was inspired by the Fiend.

But for the Bishop such submission would crown his efforts; he would go down as one of the great Inquisitors of all time. And he was still young, barely sixty, for office in the Church. He might look beyond the See of Rouen, to the Rota in Rome, even to the white and gold triple tiara and the See of Peter. Yet all his labours might have gone in vain had it not been for Warwick.

Between the public admonition on May 2nd and the abjuration of Jeanne, a selected bench of assessors had debated the use of torture. They had even taken Jeanne down to the torture chamber of Castle Rouen, where she might behold the fire, the pincers, and the iron wheel. But she, unblenching, had only said to them that what by torment they extracted from her one day, she would deny the day after.

The Bishop had believed her; and only two out of the thirteen assessors, Courcelles and Loiseleur, the fox and the jackal, had voted for the brake. Yet there were other, more effective methods. Jeanne had already suffered one nervous collapse from abuse; now Warwick loosed his 'strawnecks' on her again. Worn down by months of horror, Jeanne was ready to sign anything to get away from the English.

Pierre Cauchon would have been happier had Jeanne yielded to his persuasion. But the English would brook no more delay; they wanted to get the business over, the witch staked. Superstitious, the English captains were even holding up the siege of Louviers, until their scourge should be a handful of grey ash.

The formal abjuration of Jeanne la Pucelle took place at the cemetery of Saint Ouen, on Thursday, May 24th.

The accused scarcely displayed humility. When Master Guillaume Erard, bachelor of theology, former Rector of the University of Paris, was preaching to Jeanne, she interrupted several times, and when he referred to Charles de Valois as "heretic and schismatic," the impenitent girl shouted: "I swear that my King is the most noble Christian of all Christians!" And on the conclusion of the sermon, she had once again tried to by-pass the Bishop, by appeal to Rome. "I have already told you that for what I have done I appeal, after God, to our Holy Father the Pope. . . ."

The appeal was not of course allowed; and the Bishop explained to

Jeanne that the 'Ordinaries' of the Church had full power to judge her case. The Bishop then proceeded to a reading of the sentence: Jeanne, as heretic and schismatic, was cast out of the Church and turned over to the secular power. This meant: the stake. While the Bishop was reading, those on the platform with Jeanne urged her to abjure, Brother Pierre and Brother Martin Ladvenu anxious to save her from the flames, Nicholas Loiseleur doing the Bishop's bidding.

From the crowd, shouts arose: "abjure! abjure!" From the English came roars and threats. Jeanne stood there, amid the gaping graves, a pile of bones yellow and smooth as ivory, skulls squirming with maggots—the ancient horror of the dead. The girl swayed; gasping and sobbing. The Bishop paused. Brother Martin produced a written abjuration. In the confusion, it was not read to Jeanne. She was given a pen; laughing hysterically, she traced her name.*

Nicholas Loiseleur congratulated her and said she had done a good day's work for the welfare of her soul.

A good day's work for the Bishop, as well. He had an alternative sentence ready: "Wherefore, that you may make salutary penance, We have condemned you to perpetual imprisonment, with the bread of sorrow and the water of affliction, that you may weep for your sins, and nevermore commit them. . . ."

She listened, in dread. Perpetual imprisonment was almost as great a terror to her as the fire. But at least she would be quit of the English, lodged in a ward of the Church. The Bishop's next words destroyed all hope. "Take her back," he said to Brother Jean Massieu, "to that place where you found her."

She cried out, struggled . . . inexorably, Pierre Cauchon moved down from the platform.

The Bishop had done his best; but the English were not pleased. In their muddled English way, they expected both abjuration and the stake —all in the same day's work. How this was to be accomplished within the laws of Holy Church, they neither knew nor cared. They had paid for a certain result, and now it looked as if that result eluded them, thanks to the Bishop and his obsession with canonical rules.

Cardinal Henry Beaufort was pointed. Encountering the Bishop just

---

* Carl Dreyer in his glorious film, "The Passion of Jeanne d'Arc," has been the first person to perceive the shrewd psychological use of the setting of St. Ouen in working Jeanne up to an hysterical state.

after the scene of abjuration, he said: "What do you do here, Bishop?"

And the Cardinal's Secretary yelped: "Are you a traitor, Bishop?"

Pierre Cauchon recognized in the Cardinal certain kindred traits, remorseless ambition, a mastery of men and the ways of the world; but he also perceived in him a kind of utter grossening of mind and spirit which fitted him little better than Master Jean D'Estivet for the management of so complex an enterprise as 'Our Trial.'

He replied, with cold dignity, "I am not a traitor." Gathering his purple skirts, he went on his way. He knew what he was doing.

The next move was up to the English. Warwick cut off all access to the captive; the strawnecks went to work. When the Bishop next saw Jeanne, on the Monday following, she was wearing her old ragged tunic and babbling of her Voices. He had no choice but to declare her a relapsed heretic. He did not inquire how the relapse had come about; it was enough that it had occurred. He guarded the citadel of faith; representative of the Church Militant, he had through skill, patience, will, and power of mind brought this dangerous heretic to abjuration, where the English would have burned her at once—and made a martyr of her.

Imperfections existed; but in the main it had been a notable and splendid Trial. Ah, the Church and all that vast crowded future, shadowing out to an infinite succession of unknown days, would have cause to remember Pierre Cauchon!

He must nudge the Cardinal about that See of Rouen. . . .

❖ ❖ ❖ ❖ ❖ ❖

JE MAINTENDRAI. . . .

When Brother Jean Massieu, *huissier* or bailiff of 'Our Trial,' stooped into the small greylit tower room, he saw Jeanne sitting upright on her pallet with the great iron chain tripled about the frail body and clamped to a huge log. Her dark eyes were shining with tears, her face distorted with shame and death; and Brother Jean knew that the swine had been at her again. Not even on her last night could they leave her in peace. For a moment, Jeanne seemed not to know him. Despite her shame, she appeared to be in quite another place. He spoke to her as gently as he might.

"Oh, Brother Jean," she said, weeping, "shall I make my confession?"

He told her that she should, that Brother Martin Ladvenu would soon be with them. Her face lightened. Brother Jean did not tell her that Bishop Pierre Cauchon had granted this extraordinary permission

[Manuscript register of the Parlement of Paris, in Old French cursive script, with a marginal pen drawing of Jeanne la Pucelle]

y authentic drawing of Jeanne la Pucelle made during her lifetime, presumably by Clement de Fauquem-
es, clerk of the Parlement of Paris. De Fauquembergues, however, had never seen Jeanne. Dated Tuesday,
0th, two days after the liberation of Orléans. Register of the Parlement of Paris; ARCHIVES NATIONALE.

II. Miniature of Jeanne, from an illuminat[ed] manuscript of the Fifteenth Century. T[he] Standard has been painted with exactitude, co[n]forming to Jeanne's description. The Lo[rd] stands between two angels, blessing the wor[ld] while on the streamer are the words: IHS MAR[IA]

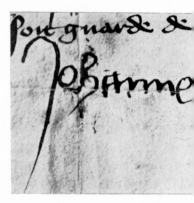

III. Signature of Jeanne from her letter t[o] the people of Reims, March 14, 1430.

IV. Jeanne driving the daughters of joy out of the French camp. *Les Vigiles de Charles VII* by Martial d'Auvergne.

because this was the day the English would burn Jeanne as a heretic. She, a lapsed heretic, had no right to absolution. Brother Jean did not understand the Bishop's permission, unless it be that even in his gross and merciless spirit lurked some tiny spark of regret for Jeanne la Pucelle and the secret knowledge that she had not lapsed. For now she wore the filthy black tunic, the man's garment, by means of which the English had tricked her to their fire.

She had told Brother Jean how, having abused her, the guards had taken away her woman's dress; how she had lain naked all morning, weeping and pleading; how the guards brought her the tunic forbidden by the Bishop; how at last, for a need of nature, she had put on the tunic and had been taken out—and how the soldiers, who always accompanied her to the *petit cabinet,* and held the door open while she was within, had called everyone to witness that she had broke her vow of submission.

This treachery was the most shameful of all the cruelties inflicted on Jeanne la Pucelle.

Brother Martin Ladvenu, canon of Rouen Cathedral, of the Order of Preaching Friars, entered the cell; he was accompanied by another friar whom Brother Jean had never seen before. Brother Martin, a small brisk Norman, halted at the sight of the girl's face.

"Jeanne," Brother Martin said, "I am come to tell you—."

"I must die!" she cried. He nodded; and all the Brothers were silent, regarding her.

"And how shall it be, Brother Martin?" ·

"It shall be by fire, Jeanne."

An almost insane terror crouched in the girl's eyes. She beat with her palm upon her shaven head. Rocking, she moaned: "Alas, how can they use me so—cruelly, horribly? Oh that my body never yet corrupted should be burned to ashes! Oh I would that my head were cut from my body seven times than to suffer death by fire!"

Brother Jean felt tears stinging; he dared not look at the others. He knew that what she said about her body could not be literally true. The English had violated her, held her down shrieking, until word of this had come to the Earl of Warwick, captain of Rouen, that Jeanne was going mad, that she vomited everything she ate, and Warwick had changed the guards, threatening to hang anyone who assaulted her again. Brother Jean understood her to speak figuratively, that never had she consented, and she was therefore inviolate in spirit.

Jeanne shuddered, long hysterical gasps, crying, "Oh if they had put me in a prison of the Church, with Church people about me, I should not have been so used!"

And, abruptly, she staggered up in her chains, eyes mad and shining. And that voice, oh that eloquent thrilling voice that once had charmed men to tears and glory, now echoed amid the old ruined light, stark, terrible . . . "Before God, Who is the great Judge of us all, I call to witness what they have done to me—."

And words, dreadful words, scenes that Brother Jean could not have believed possible save in Hell—the captivity of Jeanne la Pucelle amongst the English. She had forgot nothing, not an instant. She told them how three English soldiers slept in the cell with her, how they continually cursed and spoke foully to her, how they would describe to her, hour after hour, the various ways they intended to abuse her, how they had beaten and starved her, given her rotten food, kept her chained like a beast.

And the nights! the nights of Jeanne la Pucelle amongst the English. She told them . . . each act, how she lay naked for hours in chained darkness, how much of the time she was senseless, how at dawn they would relate what they had done to her—accusing her of participating.

She told them . . . and Brother Jean felt sick with horror; and the other Brothers stood pale and mute.

Bishop Pierre Cauchon strode in. His bulk filled the cell, obscuring what weak tormented light there was. Jeanne looked as if Satan himself had just entered. "Bishop, I die because of you!" she burst out.

Oh to be a Bishop, to be Pierre Cauchon, righteous, true and pious! For Pierre Cauchon is with us forever; and if, miraculously, he did not exist, he would have to be invented. But he exists; he very much exists, filling the room in his episcopal scarlet.

He gazed at Jeanne, eyes small shrewd and winking, at this girl whom he had done his best to destroy. "Ah, Jeanne—patience! You die because you have not kept your promise. You have returned to your wickedness."

Jeanne said quietly, "If you had put me in a Church prison, in the keeping of *religieux,* good and proper people, this would not have happened. Bishop, I charge you before God."

The Bishop shook his head, in a discouraged way. "Always impenitent," he said.

Brother Jean feared that at the last moment the Bishop might revoke the permission for confession. But the Bishop said nothing more; the Bishop's work was done and he went out, robes swirling, a vast impersonal horror where he had stood.

Brother Martin glanced about in exasperation, finding neither candle, napkin, nor stole. "This was ill-done," he said. He sent Brother Jean to fetch the articles.

While they waited, Jeanne said: "Oh Brother Martin, where shall I be tonight?"

"Have you no faith in Our Lord?" he asked.

"Oh yes. Yes!" And her eyes cried her longing.

Brother Jean returned and now it was necessary to call in one of those foul creatures who reeked at the door, the ordure and shame of the English Army. The guard, filthy, unshaven, stinking of wine, shambled in. He bent over Jeanne, gaunt face and leering hands. Unchaining her, he touched her breasts and privy part.

Was it because Jeanne had beaten them in battle, shamed their greatest captains—and this was the only way they could dominate her? Was it because her purity, her innocence, outraged these *hauspaillers?* * Ah, but they would not have dared lay a finger on her, a captive bought for 10,000 gold crowns and worth many times that amount to the English High Command, without permission.

Was there a more sinister explanation?

The English believed Jeanne a witch, a mistress of the forbidden. And it was well known that sexual congress with a witch was the best way to the secrets of the black art.

Jeanne crept from her pallet of verminous straw. Brother Jean was shocked at the wasted body, that body once so young, fresh, and round-bosomed. In only one part of the cell was it possible to stand upright beneath the slanting eaves; and whatever time of day it was outside, here, in this terrible little room, it was always iron twilight. The English had boarded up the casements.

Brother Jean shivered. He turned away, not bearing to look at la Pucelle. What had happened to this girl was the worst horror that he had ever heard of—dwarfing in cruelty the martyrdoms of old.

He tried to think—but his mind refused the anguish—of those unutterable nights, lying here in her chains, and those swine . . . oh God, about her the bright swords of angels flashing, the terror and

* literally, 'strawnecks'; i.e. soldiers of such mean status that the protective gorget and breastpiece were made of straw, instead of steel.

madness—why, why? And here it was always dusk or the grey dead hour, the hour before the dawn; here the only sound was drunken horrible breathing, curses and moaning—Saint Catherine and Saint Margaret! Here, hour after hour, day after day, the ritual—drinking, urinating, beating, abusing, snoring.

By order of Richard Beauchamp, Earl of Warwick and captain of Rouen, this *chevalier sans peur et sans reproche,* this perfect gentle knight, the guardian of Henry the Sixth and a very Perceval for prayer, three of the foulest beings that could be found dwelt constantly with Jeanne.

But it was over now, the ordeal finished. Not even the English could think of anything worse than what they had already done. And Jeanne was on the other side of the room, murmuring in confession to Brother Martin Ladvenu.

In the Vieux Marché, or Old Market Place, of Rouen, near the soaring Cathedral, the sound of hammering rang upon the May. Workmen swarmed, putting the last touches on a scaffold; and already groups of townsfolk were milling and gossiping. For it was the thirtieth of May, a Wednesday, and this was the day they were burning Jeanne la Pucelle.

The Rouennais were a thrifty cautious lot, collaborating happily. The last conceivable possibility was a popular uprising in favour of the angel of France. Still, Warwick took no chances. Soldiers began to stream into the market place, wearing the white surcoat with the red George cross, their iron salades or helmets like inverted soup tureens. They carried glaives, an eight-foot thrusting weapon with a flanged blade.

On the way to the Vieux Marché, riding with Jeanne in the open two-wheeled cart, Brother Martin told Brother Jean that never had he heard such a confession. It was, he said, the confession of a saint. And Jeanne had also described publicly and outside the seal of confession her torments. Brother Jean asked about the night before.

Brother Martin's face became grim. The guards had abused her; and then—.

"An English lord," he said. "A great captain."

"Warwick?"

Brother Martin shook his head. "She did not know. It was dark and the soldiers held her, while the lord had his will of her."

Brother Jean was silent. They were rattling through the old grey streets of Rouen, Jeanne la Pucelle standing upright in the cart, the tall mitre cap coming down over her eyes. And on the cap was writ: HERETIC APOSTATE IDOLATRESS.

Oh there had been a moment, one of those tense horrible moments when everything might have failed over a word. Brother Martin had heard this beautiful unbearable confession; and had realized that he had not specific power to bestow absolution and the Blessed Sacrament. It was necessary to send to the Bishop. Brother Jean had been cold and sweating. The Bishop could so easily refuse, logically ought to refuse. But Pierre Cauchon had granted absolution to Jeanne la Pucelle!

Presently, in the Vieux Marché, a group was seen approaching, a curtained litter and robed men, men in velvet chaperons walking. They proceeded right across the Square, past the mailed ranks, the red George crosses row on row, the heaped unlit faggots, and over all the spired dove-haunted Cathedral. The curtains of the litter parted and a huge bearlike form, wrapped in purple, was helped out. Henry Beaufort, Cardinal-Bishop of Winchester, Chancellor of the King of England, walked slowly toward the temporary stand on the north side. Wheezing, choleric, already stricken with the stone that was to kill him, Cardinal Beaufort took his place along a railed *banque* fronting Jeanne's scaffold, flanked by Warwick, Humphrey Lord Stafford, Thomas Lord Scales, Jean de Rinel, canon of Beauvais and Secretary to the King of England, a nephew of the Bishop's, then Colart de Mailly, political adviser to the Duke of Burgundy, and finally John Grey, Bedford's observer and the captain of Jeanne's guard.*

This was the secular arm.

And on the other side of the Place stood the platform where was massively enshrined the Bishop, surrounded by the glinting faces of his helpers. Immortal as the Bishop, hovering forever in the greygold light of Rouen, the yellow lichened glow on old stones and pavements of the soul . . . Master Jean Le Maître, bachelor of theology, Dominican Vicar of the Holy Office, in his pocket twenty *salus* of English gold for his "labours"; Jean d'Estivet, canon of Beauvais and of Bayeux, Promoter (Prosecutor) of 'Our Trial,' who like his English masters treated Jeanne la Pucelle as a whore (he would one day be found in a sewer, strangled); Nicholas Midi, newminted canon of Rouen for his

---

* John Grey was a gentleman in Bedford's Household, later knighted. Whether he was also the Sir John Grey of Groby, cavalry commander for Queen Margaret, this Grey was hardly of the lowest orders of the army. While Grey was the officer in charge, the brutal and depraved 'strawnecks' under him were chosen to break Jeanne's spirit.

"services," shuffling his sermon (he would one day become a reeking horror of leprosy); Master Pierre Maurice, canon of Rouen by grace of Henry the Sixth; Master Jean Beaupère, canon of Our Lady of Paris, canon of Beauvais, canon of Rouen by grace of Henry, in his pocket thirty pieces of silver in token of England's gratitude. . . .

And Thomas de Courcelles, young Master Courcelles of the University of Paris, Instructor in theology, this "solemn and excellent Thomas" who wished to break Jeanne's bones with the Question (his memory would fail utterly when twenty-five years later he was asked about this and other acts of enthusiasm for the Bishop).

But now they are all here, assembled forever, in the old stonelight of Rouen. All save one, Nicholas Loiseleur, bachelor of theology, canon of Rouen, so steadfast for the Bishop that he stole secrets of the confessional and carried them to Pierre Cauchon—how could Nicholas Loiseleur miss this moment?

Nicholas Midi began his sermon, taking as his text, "Where one member suffer, all the members suffer. . . ." First Epistle to the Corinthians, twelfth chapter.

It was nine o'clock, *nones,* the third hour of prayer. Jeanne la Pucelle stood rigidly on the scaffold, the faggots heaped below. The mitre cap hid part of the girl's face. Beside her a placard had been nailed, proclaiming: "Blasphemer, liar, dissolute, trafficker with demons, apostate, schismatic. . . ."

And this monstrous emanation of evil, now so mute, so still, before all those eager staring thousands, this girl of the oakwood and the flashing fountain, remembering as in a dream the sun that lay in golden pools upon the forest path. . . .

Master Nicholas droned on. The English showed signs of restlessness. This moralizing was not what they had come for. But the Bishop, as always, knew what he was doing. If he could wring a final recantation from Jeanne, it was worth a little time. After all, they had all Eternity.

And Brother Jean Massieu, on the scaffold with Jeanne, felt as if they were getting ready to burn him. And he recalled how at the end of the Trial, after Master Pierre Maurice had laboured mightily with Jeanne to submit her words and deeds to the Church Militant, she had replied: "I will maintain what I have always said at my Trial. And if I were to be condemned and saw the fire lit and the wood prepared and the executioner who was to burn me ready to cast me into the fire, still in the fire would I not say anything other than what I have said. And I will maintain what I have said until death."

Well, the wood was prepared, the executioner ready, the fire about to be lit, and did she recall her words, did she waver, as once she had wavered, to sign the Abjuration? Brother Jean perceived that the girl was still as death, unmoving in the greygold lancing light. And again he had that odd feeling that she was not with them, that she had got to another place where they might never come.

(It was noon, golden summer noon, and she was in her father's garden, and on the right hand a strange light, an utter falling away of sound—and the gleam of Voices. . . .)

Cardinal Beaufort was glowering at the preacher. From the English side came whistling and shouts of "Get on with it!"

Master Nicholas Midi wandered to a climax. The Bishop waited hopefully. But there would be no second Abjuration.

For now she was alone, solitary with her vision, her dream of redemption that once had illumined the forest ways of Lorraine. And of those gaping thousands, tiptoed to see a witch burned, not one might intervene between her and her light. She thought of Jacques d'Arc and Isabelle Romée; of her brothers Pierre and Jean; of Hauviette; of Charles the King; of d'Alençon and the Bastard; of those who had believed in her and fought beneath her Angels. But even they were now far off and like shadows about this high terrible altar on which she stood.

Suddenly, off to the right, a black-gowned man broke through the steel rank. He came running. It was Nicholas Loiseleur, canon of Rouen, canon of Chartres, spy, stool pigeon, the most despicable creature that crawled—it was Nicholas Loiseleur who had rigged a pretended confessional in Jeanne's cell, to trap the sick tormented girl, and who had a concealed confederate take notes for the Bishop.

He scrambled up the scaffold, gasping "Jeanne! Jeanne!" Collapsing at her feet, he tried to kiss her hand. *"Pitié pour moi, Jeanne. Pitié pour moi."*

Jeanne glanced down, her lips moved. Soldiers dragged Loiseleur away, screaming and sobbing. The English were very ill-content with the delays and interruptions. The English dinner hour was promptly at noon and nothing was allowed to interfere with the sacred ritual of beef and wine. Pierre Cauchon rose majestically.

"I want a Cross," Jeanne implored Brother Martin. "Please get me a Cross." Brother Martin Ladvenu sent Brother Jean to the parish church of Saint Sauveur.

The Bishop was booming on, pronouncing the formula of excommunication, excommunicating the spirit that he had just allowed to receive absolution and the Blessed Sacrament . . . "therefore we, Pierre, by divine mercy Bishop of Beauvais and Master Jean La Maître, Vicar of the renowned doctor Jean Graverent, the Inquisitor of Heretical Error, both competent judges in this Trial, declare that you, Jeanne, commonly called la Pucelle, have fallen into divers errors and crimes of schism, idolatry, invocation of demons. . . ."

Brother Jean clambered up the scaffold with a Cross. The English glowered; but did not interfere. Jeanne's face became radiant; she kissed the Cross.

". . . after this Abjuration of your errors the author of schism and heresy has arisen in your heart which he has seduced and since you are fallen again—O sorrow!—into these errors and crimes, as the dog returns to his vomit. . . ."

The executioner brought more faggots. The scaffold was built very high, the highest that Brother Jean had ever seen. He feared the executioner would not risk the cord.

". . . we denounce you as a rotten member, which, so that you shall not infect the other members of Christ, must be cast out of the Church, cut off from her Body, and given over to the secular power; we cast you off, separate and abandon you. . . ."*

Noon gleamed. Above the spire of Saint Sauveur, doves wheeled. Behind the English glaives a kind of quiver ran through the crowd.

"By the Body of Christ Our Master, by Our Lady, and by all the Saints in Paradise, by Saint Catherine and Saint Margaret, by Blessed Michael!" Jeanne's voice rang. In the frightened day, out of the world's rejection the haunting cry of love—"I pardon the wrong done me here. Oh, good people, I beg you, pray for me. And you, priests and clerks, pray for Jeanne. Let each of you say a Mass for me. And you English, do you pray too for Jeanne!"

Brother Jean was weeping. Brother Martin and Brother Ysambart de la Pierre were kneeling beside Jeanne. She gazed about, the steel and the sun, the huge crowd face suddenly torn by horror and grief . . .

* From Pierre Champion's edition of the Latin transcription of the Trial, rendered into English.

"Oh Rouen, Rouen, you shall have great sorrow for my death!" she exclaimed.

Among the English, some were pale and silent; others shouted, "Burn the witch! Into the fire with her!"

And to Brother Jean Massieu, praying with Jeanne la Pucelle, came an angry yell, "Well, priest, do you mean to make us dine here?"

The bailly of Rouen, a big burly Englishman, approached. "Do your office," he ordered the Executioner. No sentence was read. Jeanne was to be put immediately into the fire. The Executioner clambered up to chain her to the stake.

"Give me your grace, Jeanne," he said.

She regarded him; tears fell slowly, a bright stain upon the May. "Yes," she whispered.

"I can't help you," the Executioner said. "They've built the scaffold too high."

It was as Brother Jean had feared. Under cover of the first smoke, a humane executioner might strangle the victim with a knotted cord before the flames roared up. But this man dared not remain with Jeanne. There was to be no mercy of any kind for her.

The faggots were crackling as Brother Jean thrust blindly away. He heard a great "ah—ah!" from the crowd; and an English soldier leaped onto the scaffold. He gave Jeanne a little wooden Cross made from the broken baton. She kissed the rude Cross and put in into her bosom, next her flesh.

And now: in red dancing light, horror-staring, alone . . . she would be delivered by a great victory—a victory over death . . . Forever would she rise, young and shining, from the ashes . . . out of flame and smoke soared the cry, "Jesu! Jesu! Jesu!"

The fire blazed, red licking tongues and curling smoke and a whish! as the Executioner threw on sulphur. As smoke, oily and black, stifled her, and the scorching breath of Hell seared her—a mighty organ-gasp of agony dissolving into fire and air—came the last wild "Jesu!" Her head slumped; flames curtained her.

Messire Warwick stood up; gave a sign. The Executioner and his assistants began to scatter the fire, knocking aside the blazing faggots. Jeanne reappeared; or rather the crowd in the Vieux Marché glimpsed a blackened cindered mass hanging in chains.

Warwick sat down. The Executioner kicked back the faggots. The black thing vanished in a torrent of flame.

He came in the citadel of dusk, just past Vespers, with a furious jangling of the convent bell and a voice bawling for Brother Martin Ladvenu. Admitted to the Convent of the Preaching Brothers, he stood wavering at the wicket, muttering to himself.

When Brother Martin appeared, his arm was seized in an iron clasp. "Listen to me," said a hoarse drunken voice. "Want to tell you something."

Brother Martin recognized the Executioner. "I used oil and charcoal," he said, swaying. "I used brimstone. The heart wouldn't burn. The innards neither. Couldn't get them to burn. Orders were, straight from the Guv'nor, Messire Warwick, make ashes of the Puzzel. Ashes, he says. Don't want anything left. No friggin' relics. Want ashes!"

He belched and swayed. Oh in some damned and forgotten sepulchre, some corner of the ruined night! "Threw the heart in the river," he said. "Innards, too. Want no friggin' relics, the Guv'nor says." He burst into tears. "Orter threw myself. It's damned I'll be—damned and burnt in Hell. She were a saint."

"A saint?" Brother Martin repeated.

"Aye, a saint," the Executioner said, weeping. "She's with the saints and I—I'm straight for Hell. God's Blood, man, a dove flew out of the fire. Didn't I see it? Flew up to Heaven! And you're telling me she's not a saint?"

"No," Brother Martin said. "You may be right."

"I know bloody well I'm right," the Executioner said. "Don't you ever say she's not a saint. If I ever hear you—." He knotted a huge fist.

"Peace, fellow," Brother Martin said. The Executioner gazed at him out of red drunken eyes. He began again, as in a litany. "I used oil and charcoal," he said, staggering away. "I used brimstone."

He stumbled down the Night.

✢ II ✢

RENE AND MARGUERITE D'ANJOU:

the tragic geste

"Peace, O my stricken lute!
  Thy strings are sleeping.
Would that my heart could still
  Its bitter weeping!"

RENE AND MARGUERITE D'ANJOU

HE WAS a storybook prince, legendary in his fame and misfortune, maintaining in his lifetime and after an aura of romantic splendour, of high-hearted noblesse that is the very vision, the crenellated dream of those moonwhite magical towers on the gilded page. Other princes admired these visions; it did not occur to them that life could, as it were, step from the lovely folios chained in their libraries.

Very early, he was confirmed in the conviction that life was far stranger than a dream, that near at hand was the bright door and young secret voices, that everything he had castled in his mind was true. At twenty, he had encountered at the unsavoury Court of his rapscallion father-in-law, Charles Duke of Lorraine, a peasant girl in a red kirtle. The girl was called Jeanne; she was seventeen and came from a village cross-roads in Lorraine, a place known as Domremy. She had been sent to Nancy, to the Duke, by Robert de Baudricourt, Sire de Vaucouleurs.

A victim of the 'mal des ardents,' sliding into a disreputable grave, the old Duke had heard that the red-kirtled visitor claimed miraculous inspiration. Perhaps she could prescribe for him.

Curt, as always, with noble acquaintances, Jeanne said to the ailing Duke, "I know nothing about your sickness. But you would do well to give up this vegetable-seller's daughter you are living with, and return to your good wife."

The Duke choked; and René of Anjou, his son-in-law, noted that

115

the girl, far from being impressed by a great lord, seemed barely to tolerate the sick old man. The Duke asked her what she wanted. Jeanne replied promptly, "A horse, your son, and some good men to escort me into France."

The knightly young Duke of Bar had not escaped the notice of the sharp-eyed peasant girl. Besides, René was her immediate feudal over-lord, as Domremy lay in a valley of Bar. What more appropriate for so traditional-minded a girl as Jeanne as to ride to Chinon, to the Dauphin, in the company of her feudal lord?

The Duke of Bar was willing; it was just the sort of madcap adventure that he fancied. But Charles of Lorraine dared not offend Burgundy, the ally of the English; he could not get mixed up officially in this girl's wild schemes.

Couldn't she do anything at all for him, the old man pleaded. Cannily, the girl's eyes narrowed. She had a warm brown face and black braided hair. Well, she would think about it. If the Duke would help her, she would pray for him.

Charles offered four francs and a black horse, as far as he dared go. The girl accepted; it was a beginning, *the beginning*—of the marvelous adventure, the miraculous life and most piteous death of Jeanne, that young René of Bar had seen pass red-kirtled and glowing, like a tinted legend.

After Jeanne had taken leave, Alison Dumay, the vegetable-seller's daughter, came out from behind the arras and they had a good laugh, Alison imitating the girl's coarse rustic accent. But in the midst of a hearty bellow, the old Duke suddenly broke off and gripped his side. Pain shot through his groin. Perhaps, he thought, as if her intervention were a final hope, the peasant girl might pray for him!

This occurred on February 10th, 1429. Less than six months later, Orléans had been relieved, an English army had been overwhelmed at Patay, and Charles the Dauphin had staged a triumphal progress from Bourges to Reims—all the work of this red-kirtled Jeanne with the rude accent, who had cropped her hair, put on armour, and was leading men to battle under a white gonfalon sewen with gold *fleur de lys* and two angels kneeling before a blue and gold Virgin.

It was an irresistible vision. The Duke of Bar forgot practical politics, counsels of friendship with mighty Burgundy; he seized a quill and despatched a defiance to John Duke of Bedford, Regent of Henry the

Sixth, for whom the very mention of Jeanne was enough to stir a dangerous choking fit.

". . . I, Regnier, King of Jerusalem and of Sicily, Duke of Bar, Marquis de Pont, Comte de Guise, warn you that as my very dear uncle, the Cardinal of Bar, has a little time previous come before you in pursuit of various matters and among other things has on my behalf and in my name, by virtue of my letters of authorization to him on these lordships, put his hands in yours, as you the so-called Regent of the Kingdom of France, in token of faith and homage for lands and domains that I hold in fief of the Kingdom of France and has promised you obedience, I, for certain causes which do move me, renounce all homage, faith, oath and promises whatever. . . ."

Having hurled this gage, René galloped off to the Coronation at Reims of Charles the Seventh, on July 10th. The blazing light of redemption—the light of *la Pucelle*—as Jeanne now styled herself, aroused the chivalric spirit of men like René of Anjou, and Jean Count Dunois, and the young d'Alençon; fired with devotion the rough captains such as La Hire and Poton de Xaintrailles; made heroes of thousands who had been convinced they could never beat the English 'godons' (God-damns) or redeem anything, including their own souls. But this miraculous light did not transform the mean contemptible soul of Charles, King of France by courtesy of la Pucelle. The seventeen-year-old girl could shame the paladins of Harry of Agincourt and break the spell of English invincibility; she could not change Charles. He was her great failure. The real leader of the French was a bastard of the House of Orléans, Jean Count Dunois, who at least was indisputably a Valois, natural son of that gay swaggering Louis Duke of Orléans. Isabeau, mother of Charles, had publicly branded the knockneed stuttering prince a bastard; and until the advent of Jeanne many Frenchmen had taken Isabeau's word on the matter.

When René of Anjou, with other captains of la Pucelle, Dunois, d'Alençon, the glittering homosexual Gilles de Rais, over whom Satan already brooded, laid siege to Paris in September, their King hovered at Compiègne, betraying his army with Burgundy. The assault failed, Jeanne was wounded by an arrow in the thigh and had to be dragged from the ditch, sobbing. Charles seized an excuse to break off the siege. He chose René to inform Jeanne, indicating the favour the

Duke of Bar had with the inspired *illuminée* who had bannered French arms to victory—for the mission must have been anything but pleasant.

Charles and his Council broke up the army (not wishing to do anything to irritate Burgundy!); and René never saw Jeanne again. She went her flamelit way, to the terrible glory at Rouen, while henceforth René interpolated his own vision with the golden life, wine and peacocks, sundrenched gardens, delectable girls.

Yet Jeanne never vanished from his world.

Orange groves, the singing, and the sun . . . boating parties on the Loire, the *baillée* or fishing net contest of the girls of Angers, tournaments and masques, those great caravans that yearly set forth by water from Angers to Tarascon, laden with pipes of Anjou wine, sweet and demi-sec, kegs of butter (for the lord of Provence did not fancy oil in his cooking), furniture, chests of linen, silk, velvet, strongboxes of gold and silver plate—all this magnificence, as under striped awnings a plaint of lutes floated over the water and stupified crowds gathered on the shore.

Good King René made his annual progress from his northern to his southern domain.

He had the soul of an impresario, not that of the necromantic Gilles de Rais, who had gone from lavish productions such as the *Mystery of the Siege of Orléans* (produced, directed, designed, and played by Gilles de Rais!) to secret horrors in his blood-drenched castles, but a tender glory in which smoke-gold and caressing the light lingered on the Loire; and René bestowed a kiss on the dimpling winner of the yearly seine contest (and perhaps, observing with connoisseur's eye plump thighs and ripe breasts, took her night). Or, Italian players strolling from the Campagna, performed a masque, a 'farce' of antlered husband, lover, and popingay wife with breasts bursting from a foam of lace. Or, in serious vein, the canons and acolytes of the Cathedral chapter of St. Maurice put on a mystery, *Wedding Day at Cana,* which never failed to stir enthusiasm at the dramatic pitch when the curtains of the silver reliquary were rolled back and gleaming in red porphry splendour was the very vase that had held the water changed into wine by the Lord Jesus—acquired by King René for two hundred crowns, gold, in Marseilles.

Or, winter had come, snow prowling on white cat's feet in the Angevin night, the castle flaring and magical. . . .

And the inspired hand was at winter work, moorish or round dances in the Great Hall, Twelfth Night revels, a Lord of Misrewle; singing and the haunt of lutes, old Provençal airs, improvisations in the troubadour style; or the Seigneur's own composition set to music. And everyone wore vermilion and the Hall was hung in sable; or everyone wore white and the Hall was hung in green. And in the dancing, the masks, the dimples, the gaudy costumes (designed by René) would hover an aura of sexual passion; the girls, the young men transformed by the torchlit sorcery of the artist-King; and love, the dancers locked together in ecstasy, in the dreaming halls of Tarascon.

None of this was real. Or, rather, it glowed in another realm. Did Louis the Eleventh spend hours over costumes for a revel or in painting miniatures on glass? Did one surprise Charles the Rash labouring a sonnet or judging a girls' fishing contest? Or Francis of Brittany designing a garden and painting a mural of it on his privy chamber wall? Gilles de Rais had done some of these things, but everyone knew how he had turned out.* These others were men of affairs, craving power. And power is manifested variously, the power to bestow death in which Charles excelled; the power to manipulate lives, a specialty of Louis; the power to betray and sow suspicion, than whom none surpassed Francis.

When René ventured beyond the dream, he suffered. He was only a cadet of Anjou, but when his brother Louis the Third died suddenly in 1434, René became heir to Anjou and Provence. His mother, Yolande of Aragon, had already arranged that he be adopted by the Cardinal of Bar as heir to the Duchy of Bar; the marriage with Isabelle of Lorraine, daughter of Alison Dumay's ailing elderly lover, ensured René's succession as Duke of Lorraine. In addition, if he could ever persuade the English to get out, he had a claim to Maine, adjoining Anjou.

So, René had as fine a set of appanages as any Prince could wish. It was not enough; or, rather, the trouble was that all these shining

---

* All homosexuality is tinged by a sense of fatality and death; but in the case of Gilles de Rais this aspect overwhelmed everything, like a black poisonous growth in the soul. Only Gilles, and perhaps Charles d'Orléans, could be said to rival René as a noble amateur of art during the period.

lands, these demi-Edens, had been handed to René. He had done nothing to earn them. A 'quest' in Arthurian tradition was essential. An object was available in the Kingdom of Sicily and its Queen, Giovanna the Second. The lady fair was hardly up to Guinivere standards; she was aging, she was fat and coarse, her morals aroused comment even in Naples. No matter. She was a Quest.

Queen Giovanna, 'Giovanna the Good,' as quaintly she came to be known to unborn generations of humble Neapolitans, had willed her throne to Louis d'Anjou; when Louis died, she had switched to Alphonse of Aragon, but Alphonse proving not very satisfactory in bed, Giovanna bethought herself of the dashing young René d'Anjou. Giovanna's heirs were expected to give proof of their capacities during the Queen's lifetime.

Alphonse attacked Naples; Giovanna, in distress, called on René. The knight errant was delayed, due to an unfortunate fray with a Burgundian company of routiers, in which he had been captured. Duke Philip had not forgot René's letter to Bedford. He shut René in the fortress of Dijon, one of the two ducal capitals, the other being Bruges. Here, René languished; while Philip meditated the ransom.

The unhorsed knight—who had come to grief through emulation of John the Good and leading a frontal charge on horseback—occupied his hours in painting miniatures on glass, of the noble House of Burgundy. It was an acceptable tribute, but Philip, the 3rd Duke, was not so carried away that he failed to fix a stiff ransom: 400,000 crowns.

By the time René reached Naples, Giovanna the Good had passed to her eternal reward; and Alphonse of Aragon was fighting with Francisco Sforza over the Kingdom. Five years were wasted in an utterly pointless campaign—worse than the campaigns of John the Good—which is painful even to read about. René, a master at staging tournaments, had no idea of conducting an actual war. Time and again he was deceived by his allies, foxed by Alphonse, betrayed by the Neapolitans. Huge sums were raised; Isabella pledged everything, personal jewels, household silver, works of art—all disappeared into the maw of Italian mercenaries who had two infallible professional rules: 1. never injure one another 2. shake down the employer for every denier.

On his return to Angers, René was broke and had not a single result of five years of ruinous campaigning. He still owed Philip of

Burgundy more than half his ransom. He was very willing to listen to envoys from the Duke of Suffolk, Chancellor of Henry the Sixth, when they appeared at Angers, early in 1444, seeking a bride for the King of England. Another embassy, under Bishop Thomas Beckington, was at work on the problem in Armagnac. René's first daughter, Yolande, was pledged to Ferry of Vaudemont; but Marguerite, the second, was available. Born at Pont-a-Mousson, in Lorraine, March 23rd, 1429, Marguerite was now almost fifteen. René was delighted at the prospect of Marguerite becoming Queen of England. To be sure, glancing about, he glimpsed nothing visible that might make a dowry, but the English were evidently so sold on the marriage that the girl herself should be enough.

Besides, Marguerite was a wonderful match for any king.

René dilated. Oh, she was belle, sunlike and flashing. She was devoted (he himself had chosen her motto, *humble et loiall*); she sparkled with wit, spoke Italian, Spanish, read old Tully and Aristotle in their own tongues. As for music and dancing—

The envoys of England looked doubtful. Was the girl pious? did she know her catechism? King Henry was a veritable Edward the Confessor. René reassured them. Marguerite had been brought up in the strictest faith: one grandmother was Yolande of Aragon, the other Marguerite of Bavaria, for whom the girl had been named. Both women were famous for their piety.

And now, if the envoys would please—

The hearthflames made a dancing glow in the room, for it was winter, and the birds painted on the walls, the white peacocks, the red pheasants, the golden bird of paradise came alive on their boughs and the envoys were gazing into a lovely garden that seemed to hover, blazing with flowers, just beyond the wall.

She glided into the room; and the envoys turned dumb with wonder. For René had not deceived them. Marguerite d'Anjou was a dancing gleam of sun, bright flowing hair, marvelous fair skin, a gold-flecked luminous gaze. She curtsied, spoke a few words in English, which greatly pleased the envoys. They wanted her likeness at once for the Lord King; how delighted he would be! How happy Milord of Suffolk and Milord Cardinal of Beaufort and the English Nation with this radiant child!

And in the dancing light, the bloodred flames a coronal of reflected light upon the brighthaired girl, her round face and full sensual mouth, while the envoys of England smiled on their Queen and beyond the casements, white towers leaned into dusk and there came the mad far off keening of the mistral—whoo-oo-whoo-oo—and the grey river that lapped the walls . . . and did René think—draw back for an instant from the Night—that this would be an adventure far more terrible than any he had ever read of, a destiny beyond imagining cruel and dark? . . . then might he have clasped Marguerite in his arms and sent empty-handed the envoys.

But to René, as to almost everyone, God's only mercy was ignorance. He could perceive nothing, not the madness and the terror (the mistral of the soul), not the fields of snow and blood . . . and this lovely dancing child in the crimson light, this flashing gold of innocence, the loveliest Angevin in three centuries, and what dread vision shrieked and grew upon the happy walls? In a tender garden, in a King's gold-haunted revery, the bird of paradise, the peacocks and the sun —and the crazed withered shadow that crept amid these shining memories.

They spoke of money; of lands and titles. René wanted to clear his title to Anjou, formerly occupied by the English. Then, he insisted the English quit Maine, an appanage of Anjou. The first demand was readily granted; the second was crucial and had to be referred back to Suffolk. After, came the embarrassing question of dowry.

René fumbled around the topic, hinted at a valuable claim to the isle of Majorca, which he was willing to turn over to Marguerite! The House of Anjou had claims galore; it was possession that was the problem. The envoys listened, but heard no mention of cash. If Suffolk wanted Marguerite, not only would she bring no dowry, but the English would have to pay all her expenses—trousseau, wedding, voyage. This extraordinary, if not unique, marriage proposal would also have to be referred to London.

Meantime, Master Hans might get on with the portrait.

For once, René had all the best of a bargain. Suffolk agreed to everything, and himself promised to come over as Henry's proxy.* Now followed weeks of glittering preparation—on credit—and the

* Suffolk led an English delegation to Tours, to negotiate peace with France. The Anjou marriage was an integral part of the peace settlement, but the commissioners could not agree on the other terms, especially the future of Normandy and Guyenne. Three days after the proxy marriage, Suffolk signed a two-year truce with Charles.

delighted interest of Charles of France, who himself could not have thought of terms more advantageous to his Kingdom. Maine was the strategic key to Normandy; once clear Maine of God-damns and Normandy would drop like a ripe fruit into the lap of France. Charles had only one doubt. Would the English deliver?

René pooh-poohed this doubt. Of course the English would deliver. He had Suffolk's word. Charles had a speculative look; the marriage terms had not yet been made public, he reminded his brother-in-law.

Wednesday, the 25th of May, was a white and blue day, Lancastrian colours for a Lancastrian bride. At Tours, in the Abbaye of St.-Julien, Marguerite d'Anjou and William de la Pole, Marquess of Suffolk, stood before the legate of the Holy Father, Pierre de Mont-dieu, to make their vows. The proxy-groom was fifty, a blue and silver knight, a gallant image; the bride had turned fifteen; she gazed with loving eyes on her cavalier, come like a Prince of dreams, bearing fortune and a crown.

Trumpets flared.

In the old grey streets of Tours, through crystal morning, passed the cavalcade amid bells, flowers, and shouts. Everywhere, on bridle and martingale, on the green, white and red livery of Charles of France, on the blue and silver of Suffolk, on the black and tawny of Pierre de Breze, Seneschal of Normandy, on the mailed blaze of English and Angevin cavaliers appeared the enamelled white marguerite with ruby heart.

Cavaliers of the Queen!

Gleaming, sunroyal amid the armour, she rode a white hoby . . . she was fifteen and a Queen and would never die!

"A Queen not worth ten marks"

Marguerite embarked at Cherbourg early in April on the *Cokke John,* a fore-stage vessel with master mariner and a crew of 100 men. The voyage was rough; the young bride was violently ill, and Suffolk had to carry her ashore in his arms. At Southampton, where Marguerite temporarily lodged, a wild storm burst, augury of the monarchy to come. Henry, who had been occupied in various financial expedients, including a loan of 2000 silver marks from Cardinal Beaufort, to defray Marguerite's expenses, had rushed down from London. But the bridegroom found the door shut. Marguerite had the pox. For a fortnight she suffered, ministered to by Master Francis, a royal physician, while Henry languished. (Was not this affliction also an augury of the terrible end, when her whole body, so satin-white, lovely and tempting, would be ravaged by a mysterious skin ailment, originating in the malaise of her soul?)

Happily, the case was light; and Marguerite emerged with no ill effect, save that she was marked for life by the tiny pitted scars of erupted pustules. They were married in Titchfield Abbey, Thursday, April 22nd, the sixteen-year old bride receiving a gold ring with shining blood-drop of a great ruby—this too the gift of Cardinal Beaufort. She stole sidelong glances at her lord, the twenty-two year old Henry of Windsor. He was, she perceived, slightly built with brown silky hair and a pale pointed face. Most remarkable were the young King's eyes: velvet brown, limpid, pleading—a look glimpsed in the eyes of a fawn. Marguerite remembered Katherine of Valois, mother of Henry; and the terror that had swept over Katherine's life, the madness, lechery, murder, war—every foul thing had haunted her before she was twenty. And beside Marguerite, now, from under long feminine lashes the fawnlike gaze of Katherine of Valois—pleading and vulnerable.

Afterward, the bridal couple came to London.

At once the shape and substance of her Monarchy was revealed. In the sly ironic smile of Duke Humphrey of Gloucester, the King's uncle and Heir Presumptive; in the massive bustle and bland loan-shark look of Cardinal Henry Beaufort; in stiff pontifical Richard Plantagenet, Duke of York; in gay glib Edmund Beaufort, 2nd Duke of Somerset, and nephew of the Cardinal.*

Uncle and nephew, a Beaufort bloc, took possession of the bride. They were Suffolk's political allies; and had backed the Angevin match against Humphrey and his hotblooded Gasconne girls, daughters of Count Jean of Armagnac. Humphrey's notion had been generous; he had intended to have painted portraits of all three sisters and to allow Henry to choose his fancy. However the King chose, Guyenne would be sealed to England by the match. Like most of the Good Duke's projects, the idea was well-conceived, but ill advanced. Humphrey

---

* He was at this time Marquess of Dorset and Earl of Mortaigne, not raised to Duke of Somerset before March, 1448, on the surrender of Le Mans. However, to avoid confusion of too many titles, he is referred to throughout as Somerset—by which he is known to history.

lacked staying power. Not one of the portraits was completed; and meantime his rivals rushed in with a splendid likeness of the daughter of René of Anjou. Henry made his selection. The Good Duke did not hide his chagrin. When, on his return from matchmaking, Suffolk demanded in Parliament a fifteenth for his charges, Humphrey commented, "Parliament hath bought a Queen not worth ten marks."

Yet Humphrey did not know the worst. René had spent vastly; on wars and entertainments; on the upkeep of his lands. Marguerite was one of the few liquid assets that he had. The English Nation, not unreasonably, expected that a Queen from abroad would bring with her some tangible token of her love and devotion to her new people. René, on the other hand, expected to be compensated for Marguerite. Backed by the Beauforts, Suffolk agreed to turn over to René the Duchy of Anjou and the County of Maine. Humphrey did not know about this transaction; nor did anyone else. When it came out, the reaction would mean Suffolk's head.

No doubt if he had been *au courant,* Humphrey would not have been quite so gracious, quite so much the good loser, when he met the Queen with an escort of 500 men wearing the ostrich feather; and had Marguerite as his guest of honour at a feast in the peach-brick palace of Greenwich.

Suffolk counted on the charm, grace and wit of Marguerite to smooth his own path. He had her sumptuously crowned on Sunday, May 30th, 1445, at Westminster Abbey—a day chosen by Marguerite for her consecration. Some in the joseph-coated crowd upon the parvis, before Henry the Third's great Abbey, may have recalled that this golden day for a golden princess was the same day of fire and death for that strange girl out of Lorraine, exactly fourteen years ago.

And remembered too when the bells began thronging for this princess, herself born in Lorraine, and the glow and glory of her royalty, as if come now to redeem and consecrate the vision of the peasant girl of that country, how on this same parvis, thirty years before, they had heard the triumphant thronging of Westminster bells for King Harry, the great organ note of Nationhood, the soaring hymn, "Our King went forth to Normandie."

Remembered and wept; for Harry, for the dead, and for the days that would never come back, for pride and valour and all that great lost time, like banners in the dust.

On tiptoe, craning, apprentice London; and Nell and Doll and Bess.

Queen Marguerite came in a horse-litter, trapped in white gold-powdered damask; her gown was white and gold, and her bright hair flowed to her shoulders, while she wore a diadem set with pearls and rubies. And with her came a masque of angels, singing praises; and the Mayor and Corporation in violet; and all the fountains plashing wine, both white and red.

(And once in Rouen that dream of peace and the little Lord Henry, the Voices calling *Jeanne! Jeanne!* . . . on a pallet of rotten straw, in the old chained Norman dark, hands clenched, weeping and listening, *England, England*—a dream, a passion, a torment . . .)

Scarcely had Coronation bells hushed and the fountains of wine run dry than the young Queen was thrust into a tense battle: Humphrey against the Beauforts. The Good Duke had been stripped of his Protectorate; he had been driven out of the Privy Council; his Duchess, Eleanor Cobham, had been convicted of sorcery and banished.* Humphrey's friend, Richard Duke of York, would be recalled from his post in Normandy, where he had gone far to retrieve the ruin created by the campaigns of John Beaufort, 1st Duke of Somerset, and sent to Ireland. The Beauforts were warming to a mortal climax: Humphrey had to be got out of the way before the deal with René was made public.

Part of this strife was sheer lust for power; rival aldermanic gangs. But part was a bitter row over the most crucial issue of the day: should England get out of France? A policy of disengagement offended national pride; while not a few persons had made a very good thing out of the invasion and occupation of France. But to hang on meant ever-increasing occupation costs, which could no longer as in Bedford's time be squeezed out of the French. It meant, essentially, the absurd spectacle of a nation of three million trying to sit on a nation of fourteen million, with the richest patrimony in Europe.

The policy of Gloucester was ossified, completely out of date. It was based on the political and military realities of the year 1415. It had only one merit: it was immensely popular. It solaced and fed soothing promises to the national image. The Cardinal and his friends

---

* She was arrested at the King's Head in Cheapside, a kind of open air pavilion, whence she had come to dine and view the Marching Watch, on St. John's Wort, June 25, 1441. She and her familiars, Roger Bolingbroke and Margery Jourdaine, were tried for sorcery, especially melting waxen images of the King. Bolingbroke cracked under torture and admitted everything; he and Margery Jourdaine were burned, while the Duchess was banished to the Isle of Man.

well knew the peril of pricking an humiliated lion. When a French Embassy made its appearance to demand a settlement for Marguerite, the Cardinal had to do something—fast.

As he had secured the flank of his peace policy from Scottish assault by marrying his niece Joan Beaufort to James the First, so the lynx of Winchester tried to safeguard the main position, the front with France, by marrying the niece of King Charles to Henry. He miscalculated one vital aspect; the slender youth with brown pleading eyes was incapable of possessing a woman. Just escaping female sexuality, he had not attained manhood. His marriage was, in fact, a white marriage.

The Cardinal, usually so observant, might have noticed hints concerning his royal nephew had he not been so bent on his own schemes. There had been the occasion when "a certain great lord"—perhaps well-meaning—had suddenly introduced several girls gauzily clad and with naked breasts into the King's presence. After the initial stupifying shock, Henry, who had just been discussing the canonization of Alfred, rushed from the room, shouting, "Fie! Fie! Ye be much to blame!" *

Or there had been Henry's trip to Bath, then as later a centre of thermal immersions. "Riding by Bath, where are warm baths in which the men of that country customarily refresh themselves, the King, looking into the baths, saw men wholly naked. At which he was displeased and went away quickly, abhorring such nudity."

He had been as shocked as any Abbess of 'Ancren Rewle.' But: why had Henry been peering into the baths? The answer may be found in another practise of his, that of peeping at the amours of his servants. He was in fact a *voyeur,* a classic mark of inability. "He took great precautions to secure not only his own chastity, but that of his servants. For before he was married, he would keep careful watch through hidden windows of his chamber, lest any foolish impertinence of women coming into the house should grow to a head and cause the fall of any of his household."

Before his marriage . . . Marguerite at least put a stop to the peeping, though she must have been aware very early on (and allowing for the customary humiliations of the bridal night) that her lord would never make a woman of her. In addition, Henry's mortifications and hair

---

* This and the following excerpts and description of Henry's curious habits are taken from Blacman's *Henry the Sixth,* as translated by Montague Rhodes James.

shirts, his practise at table of having beside his plate a large confection in the form of Christ's five Wounds as it were red with blood, made him a curious companion for a passionate young girl, nurtured in the love-mystique of Old Provence. After every course, Henry would rise from his chair and offer a short prayer.

What did they talk about, these two, since the exquisite charms of his bride were not compelling to Henry?

Besides the canonization of Alfred, Henry took an interest in the education of boys. He had recently founded Eton, a grammar school for 'pore scolers' at Windsor; and King's College, Cambridge. Henry's chief concern was the religious side; and he used to say, "I would rather have them weak in music than defective in knowledge of the Scriptures." He also warned the Eton boys against the corruption of the Court at Windsor. Despite this warning, the boys did visit the Castle, where they encountered their Founder in one of his characteristic get-ups of friar's rough gown, wooden beads, and thonged sandals. "Be ye good boys," he would say to them. "Teachable and true."

Marguerite was inspired to found a college.

She endowed Queens College, Cambridge, with a grant of 200 pounds from her privy purse, intending to supplement it, but the disasters of Henry's reign prevented her. Andrew Duckett, a Carmelite friar, was the first Provost, serving for almost forty years, through the wars and the Sunne of York. Ultimately, Queen Elizabeth Woodeville provided additional funds. Although Henry himself, with the aid of his master masons, Robert Westerly and Reginald Ely, is said to have designed the plans for his Colleges, it is unlikely that Marguerite played such a role—but she might have got advice from her husband!

Their dinners together, at Eltham or at Windsor, with the gold service enamelled with little white marguerites, the bride's daisy flower, that Henry had given to her (but that Cardinal Beaufort had paid for), conversations by candlelight, she winging from topic to topic, colleges, silk women, Alice Chaucer, tournaments; he, grave, long-lashed, given to nervous birdlike cries *St. John! Forsooth and Forsooth!* No one, glimpsing them together, could have imagined these two in bed.

Cardinal Beaufort, a vigorous fork, was a frequent guest. His eager hostess had cook prepare roast swan, one of the Cardinal's favourite dishes.* Between mouthfuls, the Cardinal talked of the coming Parlia-

* Recipe: "Kutte a swan in the roof of the mouth toward the brain enlonge (and lung), and let him blede, and kepe the blode for chawdewyn (hot wine); or else

ment. The chief business (everyone had thought) would be the marriage deal; the French were becoming unpleasant. But the Cardinal dropped a blazing match into the touch-hole of speculations. The principal item on the agenda, he announced, would be the treason of the King's uncle, Humphrey Duke of Gloucester! Marguerite paused, startled, in the midst of a description of one of René's tourneys. Henry's glance fluttered. Certain evidence had come to hand, Cardinal Beaufort went on—oh he could tell them! He lowered his voice. They waited in the candleglow, the light glinting on the gold dinner service with enamelled marguerites, the bright-haired girl with shining breasts, the thin sad youth in vermilion robe.

Gloucester was scheming to kill the King and to seize the throne. He had been discovered just in time. Beaufort remembered Duchess Eleanor, her waxen images, her familiars. . . .

Henry picked at his lentils, beside his plate a large obscene-looking Wounds of Christ with red juice oozing. He was pale and incredulous. Humphrey, he insisted, must have a fair trial.

The Cardinal reassured him. The noble Duke of Gloucester would be summoned to Parliament, arrested, and tried before his peers. Cardinal Beaufort might suggest but one precaution: a change of venue. Humphrey had too many friends in London. Let Parliament be convoked at Bury St. Edmunds, on February next. Henry had a vague look, said nothing. Amid the reddish gleam of gold the Cardinal's thrusting glance met Marguerite's eyes.

The Good Duke came to Bury with eighty followers. It was Sunday, February 18th, and very cold. He was intercepted by Sir Thomas Stanley, an officer of the royal Household, with the solicitous word that in view of the weather Humphrey should proceed at once to his lodging, where a fire was laid and dinner on the way. Humphrey did proceed; and at eleven he sat down to a hearty dinner. At just after the stroke of twelve, John Viscount Beaumount, Constable of England, with Edmund Beaufort and various officers, appeared; Humphrey was under arrest.

The Good Duke was never seen again alive. Preparations for his trial got under way, but on the Thursday following his captors an-

---

knytte a knot on his nek and so let his nekke breke; then skald him. Draw him and rost him even as thou doest gose in all poyntes, and serve him forth with chawdewyn." *Two Fifteenth Century Cookery Books.*

nounced that Humphrey had succumbed to a stroke. The body was exposed to view the next day; no one of the Duke's friends could detect anything amiss or any reason to halt the burial. On the Saturday, the body was taken to St. Albans for interment. Parliament broke up in confusion; and Cardinal Beaufort escorted the King to Eltham, where Marguerite was waiting. At table that evening the Cardinal was eloquent: on the sins and temptations of this world and the abrupt way Heaven strikes down the proud.

It was an appropriate text. Cardinal Beaufort himself was to afford, just six weeks later, an equally vivid illustration. When he heard the terms of the Cardinal's Will, Henry wept. The good man had bestowed on his indigent nephew the sum of 2000 pounds. It was too much, Henry protested. He would not touch a penny. "He was a very dear uncle to me and most liberal in his lifetime. The Lord reward him. Do with his goods as ye are bound; we will receive none of them."

The astounded executors suggested the money go to the endowment of Eton and Cambridge. Henry assented; adding that the gift should be made for the "relief" of the Cardinal's soul. Was Henry beginning to have second thoughts about Bury St. Edmunds?

The dead Cardinal may have had racketeering instincts; but it was racketeering on a grand scale. No doubt he wanted peace partly because he expected to make money out of trade expansion and deals with the French. Still, his critics wanted war partly because *they* expected to profit. At least the Cardinal was in tune with reality. Not all the loud empty voices prating of honour and glory, of Poitiers and the Prince, of Limoges and the wasted hero carried in his litter along the line to rally the men for a final massacre, of Harry at Agincourt thanking God they were so few for victory must be the more splendid, not all this might obscure the fact that English policy in France was a fraud and a failure.

But the Cardinal's political heirs, his nephew Edmund Beaufort, 2nd Duke of Somerset, and William de la Pole, Duke and Marquess of Suffolk, were not men of the same mettle. The leader of the war party, Humphrey, had been 'taken care of'; for the moment, the horizon was clear. Yet in three years Somerset and Suffolk had fumbled away their advantage; their party was completely discredited, one leader murdered and the other openly assaulted in the streets.

What had they done?

They had, chiefly, delayed the delivery of Maine and Anjou until relations with the French had become electric. Somerset had then taken over in Normandy, and a trigger-happy mercenary had precipitated war by a frontier raid into Brittany. Three armoured columns, with great parks of artillery, drove into Normandy under Charles the Victorious. Like his brother John, who had vowed to burn his shirt if that shirt knew the secret of his strategy, Edmund Beaufort by a plausible exterior concealed the emptiness within. He had no policy and no strategy. He shut himself in Caen, while the excellent French artillery, under Jean and Gaspard Bureau, flattened one English stronghold after another. Suffolk scraped together a relieving army under Sir Thomas Kyriel, one of Talbot's captains. At Portsmouth, in January, 1450, the soldiers mutinied over arrears of pay. Adam Moleyns, Bishop of Chichester and Lord Privy Seal, was sent down as paymaster; the scoundrels promptly murdered him. Marguerite never forgave Kyriel this outrage. After this inglorious beginning, Kyriel and his men departed for Normandy. The little force of 4500 was caught in a trap at Formigny, assailed front and flank by the French under de Clermont and Arthur Constable de Richemont. The cavalry with Matthew Gough escaped; but the remaining 3000 were wiped out. It was England's last stand.

With Formigny, the Beaufort Coalition that had governed the realm for almost ten years was done for. The Cardinal's death had removed the heart and soul of the Ministry, the one man who might have averted ruin and made the peace policy work. Somerset struggled on in Caen for another six months, but his position was hopeless. The Parliament of January, 1450, was solidly Yorkist; the Speaker, William Tresham, was an avowed partisan of the brusk Duke of York, while in the Lords, John Mowbray, Duke of Norfolk and Earl Marshal, thundered against Suffolk.

The grand design of 1447 had wreaked a hollow victory. A childless aging bachelor Prince of Lancaster had been eliminated to make way for the prolific warrior House of York. By 1450, the Duke of York had sired nine children, six boys and three girls, of whom six survived. Forty years of age, the Duke had a formidable reputation as soldier and administrator, in trouble-shooting posts in Normandy and Ireland. Further, the Duke had a strong dynastic claim through Anne Mortimer, his mother, descendant of Lionel, second son of Edward the Third, whereas the House of Lancaster was descended only from the fourth son, John of Gaunt. Up to now, York had refrained from asserting his claim, remembering that his father, Richard Earl of Cambridge, had been shortened by a head in the conspiracy of 1415 against Lancaster.

If York was formidable, his wife Cecily was equally so. Youngest daughter of Rafe Neville, Earl of Westmoreland, Cecily or 'Proud Cis' as the neighbors called her, was arrogant and ambitious, as well as intensely pious—a familiar combination. Cecily was tall, commanding, hawknosed; she dominated the five foot six Duke, both physically and psychologically. The pair were utterly in contrast to a radiant quick-silver being such as Marguerite d'Anjou. Humphrey of Gloucester, the dead Opposition leader, had been a connoisseur, a cultivated inquiring mind, a lover of books. It is doubtful if the 3rd Duke of York ever read through a folio in his life, unless it were some dry treatise on siege warfare; he had no use for music or for poetry. Two thousand years of philosophy had passed him by. He had one of the least original minds of his generation, a little surprising in view of the fact that Anne Mortimer had been a learned woman and that the Duke's uncle Edward, 2nd Duke of York, had written a fascinating study of venery, *The Book of Game*.

Cecily, on the other hand, read a great deal; but mostly works of a godly uplift . . . Music, she allowed if it were devotional. "The Lives of the Saints" was preferred to Aristotle. At Fotheringay and Baynard, those citadels of the House of York, the green and gold tapestries depicted Old Testament themes, "Susannah and the Elders" and "Potiphar's Dream."

Cecily was austere. Her children were a little afraid of her. Like the deacon's daughter, they tended to go to extremes when out from under parental control.*

Not yet asserting his dynastic claim explicitly, the Duke of York struck hard at the Lancastrian ministers of Henry the Sixth. In Commons, Speaker Tresham hymned York's praises, while he prepared the indictment of Suffolk. The Chancellor was accused of stealing sixty thousand pounds of public funds, of plotting with the King of France to destroy England's domain overseas, and of conspiring to seize the

---

* George drank; Anne and Margaret were notorious for their affairs, and Anne had two broken marriages; Edward played Sardanapalus, whenever he had the money. Only Richard was his mother's boy; pious, moralizing, sermons in his Proclamations.

throne by marrying his son John to the infant Margaret, heiress of John Beaufort.* These charges were ridiculous; Suffolk readily defended himself in the Lords. But in the atmosphere of emotional frenzy created by the failure in France an appeal to reason made no headway.

Behind the attack on Somerset lay hatred of Marguerite, of the foreigner, the 'Frensschewoman,' the very symbol of the power that had humiliated England. The words of William Gasciogne, Chancellor of Oxford and intimate of Humphrey, were freely quoted: "Lately, in a certain Kingdom, a woman was married to a certain King, and the person who contracted this marriage, by a secret and false compact, alienated a great Duchy from this Kingdom."

Marguerite was compelled to keep silent, while her great friend and protector was savaged. Suffolk threw in the sponge; his conviction and at the very least his attainder were inevitable if he stood trial. He offered to resign and get out of the country, until tempers cooled. Norfolk and Tresham accepted, on behalf of Richard Duke of York, who sat in Dublin Castle, pulling strings. No doubt, they intended to keep the bargain with Suffolk, but they reckoned without the mood of murderous rage that they themselves had helped arouse.

Suffolk's little convoy was halted off Dover by a tall fore-stager, a royal ship, the *Nicholas of the Tower,* Walter Whitmore, Master. Suffolk's knees broke when he beheld the ship's name. John Stacy, the astrologer, had warned Suffolk to beware the Tower; but the Duke had bethought him only of London's Tower.

Insulted ("Welcome, traitor!"), buffeted, stripped of Garter and fine doublet of mailed blue velvet, Suffolk was thrust into a little 'cock bote' with a brace of ruffians. Seizing a cutlass, one filthy losel, a galley wight, 'the lewdest of the ship's company,' hacked off the Duke's head. They laid the body naked on Dover sands, the bleeding head beside, and rowed away.

This atrocity occurred on Saturday, May 2nd. In a kind of curious medieval wake, the Sheriff of Kent (who himself was shortly to come to a terrible end) and Suffolk's own men watched the headless body

---

* The Beauforts were barred from the throne by two Acts of Parliament; that prevented no one from speculating on their chances. Margaret was the first in line, being the only child of the first Duke of Somerset. Her claim descended to her son, Henry Tudor, who became, by virtue of this outlawed Beaufort claim, Henry VII.

on the sands—"and his men sit on the land by great circumstance and pray"—while news of the murder came crying to London.

Marguerite became hysterical. She rushed to Wallingford, to Alice Chaucer, the dead man's wife. They wept together. Then, the proud cruel spirit of Yolande of Aragon possessing her, she turned Spanish and quiet; considered what she must do. Her chevalier must be avenged. Tresham would die in September, cut down by the dagger of Lord Grey de Ruthyn, a partisan of Marguerite. Norfolk would be shamed in battle. But York himself would pay at Wakefield the most fearful price of all. Now Marguerite knew the face of her enemy; and that face was fanged and savage, wolf-like, utterly merciless. She, the Queen, might be torn in pieces—at any corner of a sunny afternoon.

The Duke of York, in the heady glow of success, overplayed his hand. A fierce insurrection burst upon the Lancastrian monarchy; and in their desperate plight Henry and Marguerite evoked the sympathy forfeited by the surrender in France.

"WHO THEN WAS THE GENTLEMAN?"

Their lives were mean and cruel. They were old at thirty, used up at forty. If skilled, they earned 4d a day; if unskilled, 2d a day— rates fixed by law. If lucky enough to have a few acres of land, they paid manorial rackrent, either in labour or in money. Poll taxes of a shilling a head, as much as ermine-gowned burgesses paid, were squeezed out of them. They wore the same rags day in, day out; their 'shoon' were wooden clogs or ankle boots of stiff oxhide. Their houses were clay hovels, rat-infested; they slept on verminous straw. Their hours of labour were from sunup to sunset; afterward, their time was their own. They were free to get drunk, which they did frequently, on dark bitter ale. Or they could fornicate, which they also did frequently. Beds were few and icy; the only way to keep warm was to crawl in with a hot posset and a wench. They might also read, but most of them were unlettered; and if by some odd chance they could spell out a few words, no one had any books. It was dangerous to be caught reading. Only Lollards read; and Lollardy was punished by the stake.

On Sundays and Feast Days, they were expected to put on their least filthy tunic and to appear in Church. They were also expected

Marguerite d'Anjou kneeling in prayer. ... m the stained glass portrait in the window ... he Chapel of the Cordeliers at Angers, prob- ... late Fifteenth Century and taken from

IOTHÈQUE NATIONALE

w: VI. René d'Anjou in his study. From an ... minated manuscript produced by King ... é's artists at Tarascon.

IOTHÈQUE NATIONALE

VII. René d'Anjou. An anonymous drawing of the Fifteenth Century.
PHOTO GIRAUDON

Below: VIII. Henry VI, King of England
After a contemporary portrait.
NATIONAL PORTRAIT GALLERY

to tithe. Of course, if they did not have the cash—and generally they saw very little cash—they might work off their tithes in the fields or gardens of the local monastery. Or they might bring a sheep or a goat to the parish priest. Additional fees were collected by the Church for baptisms, confirmations, marriages, and funerals.

They were never alone. They lived in herds, disease passing like a train of Greek-fire through each in turn. They dwelt continually with death; and when their souls passed to the unimaginable ice-palace of Heaven, of which the priests spoke, their uncoffined bodies manured the earth; and as the Nation grew and was sustained by their living toil, so the very earth of England was nourished by their decay.

They were the labouring commons; the apprentices and journeymen, the peasant tenantry. . . .

In 1450, Kent in southeast England was a forge and working-house of discontent. Roving the highways were old soldiers from the wars, "those who sit broken-legged in the soft warm Sundays, to beg silver"; the wrecks of Lollardy, gaunt inspired men, shambling along, muttering alone . . . *John Ball hath rungen your bell; and greeteth you well. Now right and might, will and skill. Now God haste you in everything* . . . a horde of wayfarers, pack pedlars, grinders, tinkers, fortune tellers, workers in glass, pottery, wood and leather . . . and a whole ragged rainbow with nothing to sell but sweat and muscle.

Into this fermenting bowl, Richard Plantagenet in Dublin (Duke of York and Lieutenant in Ireland), supping with the Devil, reached a very long spoon.

A stranger appeared one day in Kent. He had a knowing air, was approachable and friendly. Jack Cade, he called himself. The word 'cade' means a small barrel or cask. No one seemed to know where the newcomer hailed from, but folk noted that Jack spoke with an Irish lilt. With Jack, the talk usually got around to the evil state of the realm and the King's bad counselors, William de la Pole, Marquess of Suffolk, and Edmund Beaufort, Duke of Somerset. Nothing surprising in that, for conversation in Kent often touched on these matters. Kentish folk remembered Wat Tyler and the 'hurling tyme' of 1381.

But, unlike the usual rambling inconclusive memories, talks with Jack Cade seemed to have purpose; he was getting at something. Kent found out what when Suffolk, former Chancellor and head of the peace faction, was murdered at Dover by hirelings of those favoring war with France, of whom Richard Duke of York was certainly one. It was a grassfire signal. Jack, it turned out, had organized committees of sturdy rogues all over the shire. In case of an emergency, he explained.

Well, the emergency had arrived. It was Wat Tyler come again. Horsemen dashed over the shire, carrying the word. *When Adam delved and Eve span, who then was the gentleman?* . . . the old cry of John Ball on Blackheath.

And they heard; and they answered.

They downed tools, left plough and workbench, crept out of their evil cavelike dwellings into the shining day. They stood like men, laughing and weeping, shaking hands; life was good and the 'great Captain of Kent'—Jack Cade—would make it better. Soon, they collected a mighty company at Canterbury, sanctified by the memory of Tyler, where old Wat and Jack Straw and John Ball had assembled a wild and faggot-throwing array of the commons of Kent, in the time of Richard the Second.

It was a company of rags and patches, men without banners. But Jack, it seemed, had thought of everything. Those who knew the use of arms (and they were not a few!) were issued swords and billhooks, collected by Jack's committees. There were even yew bows and cloth-yard arrows of ash wood. In the Market Cross of Canterbury, Jack appeared on a scaffolding and made a talk. They were come together, he announced, to restore the ancient rights of freeborn Englishmen —*a field full of folk!* as long ago Piers Ploughman had proclaimed. They would go to London, to see King Henry. And Queen Margaret! a tinker shouted. Jack laughed; and put a hand to his hip, with a haughty air. The crowd roared.

They would get rid of the traitorous knaves who had sold England's right in France and pocketed the money, Jack promised. He named no names, but everyone knew he meant the Duke of Somerset and other friends of the murdered Suffolk, men whom Queen Margaret still kept in power. The Duke of York, that fine gentleman far away in Dublin, whose heart bled for the suffering peasants, would be recalled to the King's side. Taxes would be abolished; and the cruel Ordinance of Labourers that forbade a man to sell his skill where he would, at a living wage. Elections to Parliament would be made honest.* Finally, Jack shouted, the commons of Kent would give short shrift to clerks and lawyers. Wat Tyler of glorious memory had hated lawyers, tools of the rich and of the Church.

And now, as a reminder to the lords in London that the Kentish folk meant business—.

Jack rapped out an order. Men appeared, dragging a black scarecrow trussed like a sheep carcass on a pole. They hoisted the scarecrow onto the scaffold; and it was seen that this was a real scaffold after all, with rope and crossbar. Jack himself pulled the trap; the black thing leaped and danced, about the scrawny neck dangling a pen and inkhorn—symbols of the clerk.

The crowd roared.

Presently, they hit the road to London, no longer an aimless horde, but a marshalled array, with the Constables of the Hundreds marching at the head of their musters. And at the fore, on his silver horse, rode Kent's great Captain, Jack Cade—'John Amende-alle,' as his ecstatic followers termed him. Beside Jack rode his principal officers: the Banner-bearer with the stiff square Standard of the White Wolf, the strange device that Jack had chosen for the Company; the Sword-bearer, Robert Poynings; the Herald of Exeter, in blue and silver tabard, whom Jack had persuaded to throw in with the Company; and Harry Lovelace, Jack's second-in-command.

Still they came, Wat and Will and Dickon, the word flashing through the wold that Amende-alle was a-marching; came running, some from shires distant as Wilts and Somerset, and some travelled all night to join the Company. The great days had come again. This was the shining moment; laughing, singing, shouting—*when Adam delved and Eve span, who then was the gentleman?*

Oh yes! the Kingdom of God was at hand, and they wept to think what Tyler would have said. They had slain Wat Tyler at Smithfield, William Walworth, London's Mayor, and others of the King's escort had struck down Wat, and him trying to parley with the young Richard; but Wat's spirit had returned to lead the people. Already

---

* As Professor C. W. Oman points out, this was hardly a revolutionary program; more like a program drafted by Richard of York than by a firebrand such as Wat Tyler. The peasants, however, continued to identify Cade with Tyler, until the glaring inconsistency of his conduct destroyed him.

the men of Kent saw the heavens opening and the wonderful things
that Jack had promised. No more taxes, no more tithes, no more
sweating like a slave for lord or bishop (down in Wiltshire, the
Company of Kent heard, the commons had just hanged a bishop, "a
wonderful covetous man"). To sleep, gentle Jesus! in a fine bed.
White bread and brown ale for the asking. New woollen hoods and
shoes of supple Spanish leather. And wenches, wenches with fiery
tongues and succulent thighs. For Amende-alle was come!

Along the road, forty miles to Blackheath, a vast flaring column,
ten thousand strong, with the Standards of the Hundreds going on
before and the White Wolf fang-gleaming in the sun. Ankle-deep in
marigold, amid murmurous fly-drowsing June, the ragged cheering
boys, the old men who wept, the beggars with huge festering sores
and crazy gait, hopping on crutches, hair matted with burrs—all, all
trailing after the Company of Kent.*

God thundering from pillars of fire, Canaan ahead, and on his silver
horse a marvelous Moses, in glinting helmet, carrying a sword. The
very last day of Creation . . . God's children in the mighty fellowship of Kent, and London again, London with golden spires and
flashing red tiles, the great gates, the gleaming river, the nineteen-arch
Bridge.

Oh London, we are coming!

While England shook to the march of the Dispossessed, Parliament
like a set of queasy debtors was shunted from Blackfriars to Westminster, and finally to Leicester. Queen Marguerite had never liked London; the feeling was reciprocal. Marguerite was just twenty-one. A princess of Anjou, she was proud, defiant, and beautiful. Wedded to a
crowned anchorite, Henry the Sixth, Marguerite now had, with Suffolk's
murder, the chief burden of the House of Lancaster. Leicester, the
young Queen felt, might provide a less controversial setting. But no
change of scenery might alter the bitter review of 'Lancastrian misrule.'
After Suffolk's beheading in an open boat, off Dover sands, in June
1450, the war party was gunning for Edmund Beaufort, Duke of
Somerset and Lieutenant in Normandy. Again, John Mowbray, Duke

---

* It is obvious that Richard Duke of York, by no means a Richard Egalité, could not
countenance the abolition of tithes or the hanging of bishops. Equally clear that
the peasants were taking direct action on the lines of their own conception of social
reform, as in Wat Tyler's time.

of Norfolk, and William Tresham, Yorkist Speaker of the Commons, prepared the attack.

Marguerite marked Speaker Tresham; short, peppery, wattled—the turkey cock effect of so many of York's partisans and of the strutting Duke himself. But Marguerite had friends in Parliament, among them Lord Grey de Ruthyn. She discussed with a sympathetic Lord Grey the Speaker's abuse of her, his responsibility for Suffolk's tragic end, his present clamor against Somerset. Lord Grey promised to 'take care' of Tresham; and would do so with a dagger, ere the year was out.

It appeared certain that with Somerset out of the way, Marguerite herself would be the next target of the irreconcilables. Victory of the English in Normandy!—the vision blazed, Lancaster's failing final hope. Somerset was shut up in Caen with a mutinous garrison; three French columns under Charles the Victorious, with great parks of artillery, were driving at will through Normandy, cleaning out nests of English. Had Somerset been the Black Prince, he could not have averted ruin. Yet, was not this English doom what Queen Marguerite had secretly longed for? Her enemies said as much. Brought to England by Suffolk and the peace faction, Marguerite had always symbolized an end to the strife between the two Kingdoms—even if that meant the English getting out of France for good. René of Anjou was writing to his daughter Marguerite that it was as if Jeanne la Pucelle had come again; soon all France would be rid of the damned 'God-damns.'

In the midst of this Parliamentary fray burst the news of Cade. Marguerite perceived the deadly meaning; Kent's great Captain was the climax of the threats, murders, and hurlings inspired by Richard Duke of York. The King's Council, headed by John Kemp, Primate of England, Cardinal-Archbishop of Canterbury and King Henry's nominee as Chancellor, called on the Staffords, Humphrey and William, cousins of His Grace of Buckingham, to put down the rising. Equipped with but a modest force, more in the nature of constabulary duty than to fight a pitched battle with a strong army, neither the Council nor the Staffords seemed to have any notion of Cade's power.

At Blackheath, outside Southwark, where Tyler had gloried and drunk deep, the gorse was fenced off into a huge camp, by night the twinkling cat's-yellow of hundreds of cook-fires, by day a flashing savannah of steel, a torrent of colour. Cade himself, as befitting the leader and thinker of so mighty an enterprise, had established his headquarters apart from his humble following, at the White Hart Inn, Southwark. Here, the great Captain held court, couriers coming and going, while negotiations went on with Mayor Thomas Charlton for the surrender of London. Possessed of seemingly irresistible power, Cade had already begun that policy of fencing himself off for the sources of his strength that would in the end destroy him.

Wat Tyler never made this error. Tyler was undone by the very enormity of his popular success. Wat's fatal conference with the boy-King Richard the Second at Smithfield was a miscalculation, profound in result, of the mystique of English kingship that yet remained after overwhelming humiliation of the temporal power.

For the moment, however, Cade was supreme. A servant of Sir John Fastolf's, one Payn, was caught by the rebels prowling about their camp and brought before Cade. Fastolf was military adviser to the King's Council; the mention of his name inflamed Cade. The Captain of Kent rated Payn as a horse-stealer and ordered the Herald of Exeter to make "four Oyez (public cry) at four parts of the field; proclaiming openly by the said Herald, that I was sent thither for to espy their puissance, and their habilements of war, from the greatest traitor that was in England or in France, as the said Captain made proclamation at that time, from one Sir John Fastolf, knight, the which diminished all the garrisons of Normandy and Maine, the which was the cause of the losing of all the King's title and right of inheritance, that he had beyond the sea." *

The two horses, blooded mares, belonged to Fastolf; and Payn had attempted to take these horses plus some valuables of Sir John to safe-keeping at Caister Castle, Norfolk. Cade appropriated the mares; he then delivered a blast against Fastolf, raking up the old canard of Fastolf's cowardice, his running away at the battle of Patay—the familiar line, now taken over by Richard of York, to explain the English defeat in France, the beginning of a 'stab-in-the-back' legend.

Significantly, Cade said nothing about Fastolf as a landlord; nor did he dredge up any social grievances.

On June 18th, the Staffords, with King Henry close behind, reached Blackheath. Cade had evacuated his camp, ringed about with a stockade, and retreated into Kent. The Staffords pressed after, not realizing that this retreat was a maneuver to avoid being pinned down in the stockade and perhaps starved out. At Sevenoaks, the Company

* J. Payn to John Paston, *Paston Letters*, XXX; ed. by James Gairdner.

of Kent suddenly turned and fell upon the Staffords. The royal army was wiped out; and both commanders slain. Cade rigged himself in Sir Humphrey's gold-studded brigandine, embossed with the Stafford Knot.

Henry himself had taken the field, urged on by Queen Marguerite; but the wrecks of Stafford's command streaming into Blackheath demoralized the King's array. His men refused to fight, compelled the surrender of Lord Say, High Treasurer, to the rebels, and melted away. Henry and Marguerite fled to the fortress of Kenilworth in Warwickshire. Henry's first effort to play the Leopard in the teeth of mutiny had ended disastrously, while the Queen was but young in terror.

A change took place in Jack Cade. Heretofore, the Captain of Kent had been a man of the people, risen up to avenge their wrongs and to teach the lords a lesson. But now Jack became a lord himself. He took up his old quarters at the White Hart; and proclaimed that he was no longer Jack Cade but John Mortimer, noble cousin (though on the sinister side) to the last Earl of March, a claimant to the throne.*

No plain man might get in to see Jack; in fact it was worth a man's whole skin to be heard talking of Jack Cade, that was. Poor wights had their heads broke just for speaking the name. He that had been the most easy of fellows was now withdrawn behind a governance more rigid than that of a prince. He issued commands through Lovelace and Poynings; proclamations were cried at Blackheath by the Herald of Exeter.

To the White Hart Inn came Humphrey Duke of Buckingham, commander of the King's army, and Archbishop Kemp, the Chancellor; they were received by a seated and covered 'Sir John Mortimer' (he had recently added knighthood to his honours), consuming a pork pastry with a continually replenished mug of foaming ale at his elbow. The delegation asked 'Mortimer' what his intentions were. Wiping the suds from his mouth and shouting for the drawer to rush another growler, as Tyler had once rinsed and spat before young Richard,

---

* Anne Mortimer was heiress to the Claimant and mother of Richard Duke of York. His own claim, such as it was, derived from Anne Mortimer rather than the Dukes of York. Richard II had appointed Roger Mortimer his heir; and York recognized Richard as the last rightful King. By taking the name of Mortimer, Cade verged dangerously near a claim to the throne. This, no doubt, was his intention once he had liquidated Henry. As for Richard of York, he was fairly hoist with his own petard.

'Mortimer' demanded a personal interview with King Henry, to discuss the state of the realm. There was no more talk of the Duke of York, that fine gentleman whose heart bled for the people. 'Mortimer,' it now appeared, had resolved to take the government on himself.

Appalled, the Chancellor and the Army chief returned to Kenilworth. 'Mortimer' prepared his state entry into London. The citizens had long since given up any idea of armed resistance and the rebels had behaved with such discipline in Southwark that Mayor Charlton himself had arranged a welcome at the Guildhall.

In goldstudded brigandine, Stafford-embossed, flashing and glittering, the Captain of Kent rode into London across the nineteen-arch Bridge on Friday, July 3rd. Rode into glory, amid frantic cheers, with agate eyes and cruel smile. Before him pranced the Sword-bearer with a gilded sword of state borne upright; and after, the Banner-bearer with the huge snarling Wolf—"old Whitey," the cowed peasants whispered—the badge of the noble House of Mortimer; and drums flaring, trumpets skirling, this was the hour of Amende-alle!

(but he wasn't John Amende-alle any more, some magic had gone out of him, and presently the frightened folk who trooped after would discover this)

By Old St. Swithin's on Candleswick Street, the Captain of Kent struck his sword on London Stone and cried: "Now is Mortimer lord of this City!"

At the Guildhall next morning, 'Lord Mortimer' (he was continually improving in rank) thrust aside speeches of welcome; the men of Kent had work. 'Mortimer' had dragged along in his triumphal procession Sir James Fiennes, Lord Say, the High Treasurer; he now gave Lord Say a drumhead court martial on charges of having sold out to the French, with Suffolk. Say, the third royal officer to be publicly and atrociously murdered in six months, was beheaded at the Standard in Cheap. Meantime, at Mile End where Wat Tyler and King Richard had held their first conference in 'the hurling tyme,' the Kentish men had caught Sir James Cromer, the Sheriff of Kent and a relative of the slain Treasurer. Cromer was beheaded forthwith. The two heads were placed on poles and paraded through the streets, at every corner a halt, bestial howls, and a gruesome kiss between the heads.

Mayor Charlton and his fellow officials began to have doubts. Fun was fun; but Charlton was feeling queasy about those heads. Who could say that the Kentish lads might not become fond of this sport?

At this moment, 'Mortimer' in his mad arrogance—for he had passed to a visionary world of paranoiac splendour—broke the discipline imposed by himself on the Company. A self-invited and doubtless rather trying dinner guest at Gristes House in Tower Street, 'Mortimer' requited the hospitality by plundering his host of everything movable. "And Jacke Cade, captaine of the rebels in Kent, being by him in this his house feasted, and when he had dined, like an unkinde guest, robbed him of all that was to be found worth the carriage." *

Later, either that day or the next, "the unkinde guest" went on to Cornhill, where he broke in "a fayre house of olde tyme called the Grene Gate. Since the which tyme Philip Malpas, sometime Alderman and one of the Sheriffs, dwelling therein, and was there robbed and spoyled of his goods to a great value by Jacke Cade." **

After this suicidal knavery, Mortimer withdrew across the massive London Bridge, crammed with lean-to redroofed houses, to his headquarters in Southwark. Lord Scales, Constable of the Tower and a Lancastrian, whose offers of military aid had been hitherto rebuffed by the Yorkist-inclined city, now saw his opportunity and pressed upon Mayor Charlton the services of Matthew Gough, recently returned from Normandy, with several hundred archers and men-at-arms from the Tower of London, to keep out the wild bands of Kent.

That afternoon, July 6th, 'Mortimer' found the drawbridge at the south end raised, while armed patrols swarmed the London side. Exeter's Herald sounded the alarm; the Standard of the Wolf was unfurled in the silvery river sky.

The battle began about evensong. It went on all night, by torches and flares, lighting the green-ghastly faces of the dead and the steel flashing up and down the great Bridge. The shrieks of the wounded, trampled underfoot or pitched into the river, were lost in the roar of Tower bombards, the tongues of orange flame leaping from the battlement. Poor Payn, Fastolf's man, dragged about in 'Mortimer's' retinue, was forced into the fray. "And then at night the Captain put me out into the battle at the Bridge, and there I was wounded, and hurt near-hand to death; and there I was six hours in the battle and might never come out thereof." ***

Nobody knew the number of the dead. They perished obscurely, plunging into a river like a mirror of glittering flame; and were

* Stow's *Survey of London,* ed. C. K. Kingsford, 2 vols. Oxford, 1906.
** Ibid.   *** Paston Letters, *opus cit.*

washed with the tide to Gravesend. Matthew Gough himself fell, covered with wounds; and in the red exhausted dawn, the London captains proposed a twenty-four hour truce. The Kentish men retired to Blackheath. But while Kent's Captain drank and meditated blood, word spread that King Henry had promised pardon to all who would lay down their arms and go home.

The Great Company listened to the bishops, Kemp of Canterbury and Wainflete of Winchester, Lord Privy Seal, now guiding the King. The flame was gone; the redemption. This Moses was clayfooted, a covetous cruel braggart. The Company began to break up. 'Mortimer' perceived that the game was done; by the wall between 'Lord Mortimer' and the obscure devoted thousands, he had destroyed himself. John Amende-alle, the Captain of Kent, was a cry of resurrection; of banners out of dust. 'Lord Mortimer' was naught but the pseudo-bastard of an extinct Norman line.

The discredited deliverer, no longer even a glint in the eye of the Duke of York, asked for and received a pardon—made out in the name of 'John Mortimer.' His most pressing anxiety was for his pilfered goods; he loaded them into a wherry, to convey them to Rochester. But straightway came to him the mortal news that Jack Cade had no pardon, but only a mythical 'John Mortimer.' This irony on the part of the Bishops, who now dominated the Council and who by jesuitical skill had quelled the rising when the men of war had utterly failed, stirred a panic in that cold and terrible heart.

He abandoned his baubles, his boats, his men—those few who still kept a ruined faith in him—and fled an outlaw into Kent.

It was almost the last act.

Even a hunted wretch must eat. For a week this apparition, doomed to bear the name of Cade through eternity, wandered southeast England, a mangy beggar raiding gardens, living on roots and berries. What mighty wind of God failed here; this pitiful scrabbling creature, on all fours, digging and chewing.

On the night of July 13th, he was scrounging a garden in Kent when the owner, Alexander Iden, appeared. Cade put up a fight; but Iden was the better man. Only later did the Kentish squire learn that these swordstrokes were the most profitable he had ever bestowed, for a price of 1000 silver marks had been put on Jack Cade—alive or dead.

The remains came up to London, where short days ago the great Captain had swaggered and promised laws. They quartered the body and impaled the four quarters on four gates of London, while the leering crow-plucked head adorned the tallest spire of London Bridge.

❖ ❖ ❖ ❖ ❖

> MILADY OF PLEASAUNCE: *the world without is fair of view, green and white and red; the world within is black of hue and bitter as the dead!*

SHE did not invent faction. Years before she appeared, the Monarchy had been split by hate: Humphrey of Gloucester, Protector, against Cardinal Henry Beaufort. Brawling in the streets, secret devisings—they struck at Humphrey through his Duchess, Eleanor of the White Hand. Eleanor's disgrace and banishment to the Isle of Man was a prelude to murder.

Some said Humphrey had been slain by a white-hot spit thrust into his fundament, as Edward the Second had been served at Berkeley Castle. The Earl of Warwick, however, favoured a simple explanation of throttling. Whatever the method, word went out among Humphrey's friends—and he had not a few—'Beaufort.' Cardinal Beaufort was the Boss in the back room, endless games of solitaire, a string of whorehouses, an immensely profitable loan shark business. Beaufort gave the orders and a host of obscene creatures translated into action.

Two months after Humphrey's end, Beaufort, choleric, massive, had been suddenly stricken in his episcopate palace of Waltham. "Apoplexy," remarked Humphrey's friends, with a wink. "Apoplexy" had been the diagnosis given out by Beaufort and Suffolk at Bury.

So accustomed was the Boss to the power of gold that on his sordid and instructive deathbed, he shrieked: "Will not Death be hired nor money do nothing?" It seemed not.

The dead man, whose evil legacy still wracked the land, had cultivated the forlorn young Angevin bride. Shrewder than his enemy, who could think of nothing better to do than to make speeches in Parliament denouncing the financial condition of the bride's father, Cardinal Beaufort had welcomed the girl, petted her, given lavish dinners, loaned money; he was always available for avuncular counsel. He foresaw Marguerite's importance in the Monarchy; she was also the key to his peace policy. The first English politician to come out for peace, Beaufort had a touch of Papacy fever; he had his eye on the triple tiara and wanted a European reputation as mediator between the two greatest realms of Christendom.

Richard of York, next in blood, succeeded Humphrey as heir; he also took on Humphrey's role as head of His Majesty's not-so-loyal Opposition. For there were plenty of Beauforts to step into the Cardinal's buskins; Edmund, 2nd Duke of Somerset, had three bold sons, Henry, Edmund, John, to match York's eaglets.

For the young Queen, the real danger was that a childless Henry might be by-passed by both prolific branches of the Royal House. Only a miracle, it seemed, might restore the rightful position of the Monarchy.

The miracle happened.

In February, 1453, Richard Tunstall, Chamberlain and Reader to the King, announced to an astounded Henry that his wife was with child. It was like the Immaculate Conception. Henry suspected the "Holy Ghost"; others, especially the Duke of York, settled for a less celestial intervention.*

The rumblings from Fotheringay grew more and more ominous. The Duke himself had recently sired a twelfth child, a puny sickly boy with the mighty name of Richard; but the pride of York's heart were his stalwart sons Edward and Edmund, now eleven and ten years, who, the Duke had fondly expected until this most disconcerting event, would carry on the line of England.

As usual, when mischief was afoot, Somerset was suspected. York's program for the weal of the Realm and the bill of articles he had presented to the King "how be it that it was thought they were full necessary, were laid apart, and to be of no effect, through the envy, malice, and untruth of the said Duke of Somerset." ** And when the Duke had at length 'persuaded' Henry (the persuasion taking the form of 5000 armed men) to remove Somerset from office and clap him in the Tower, Marguerite had immediately intervened, to have her favourite released. On the strength of Henry's tenuous promise, York had disbanded his company, only to have Somerset—who was hid behind the arras—suddenly interrupt the conference with the King and demand York's own incarceration.

The Duke of York was convinced that Somerset had sired Marguerite's

---

* Henry's remark is quoted by the gossipy envoy from Francesco Sforza. Calendar State Papers, Duchy of Milan, Vol. I, p. 58.
** York's petition to King Henry, in Fenn's *Paston Letters*, Vol. I, p. 65. The Duke's letter to citizens of Shrewsbury, in Ellis, *Original Letters*.

child. Somerset was in his fiftieth year, having been born in 1404; Marguerite was twenty-three and an intimate friend to Somerset's Duchess Eleanor. As with the case of rumours linking Suffolk and Marguerite, when the Queen's devotion to Alice Chaucer had dispelled suspicion, her affection for her "right dere and entirely welbeloved cousin" Eleanor Beauchamp, should have cleared the air. Warwick himself, who was more objective about these matters than his friend the Duke, felt that Jamie Butler, Earl of Wiltshire, an Irishman lately come to Court, had been sharing Marguerite's bed.* Butler was thirty-three, "the best-favoured knight in the land; and the most feared of losing his beauty." Elizabeth Butler, Wiltshire's Countess, was one of Marguerite's ladies; but stood hardly in the same intimacy with her royal mistress as Alice Chaucer or Eleanor Beauchamp. Even so, for the Queen to desecrate her Court and her own faith and honour with adulterous lust for the husband of one of her ladies seemed inconceivable. Marguerite herself had been among those casting the heaviest stones at Agnes Sorel, 'Madame de Beauté,' the lovely playmate of the King of France. Agnes had been maid-in-waiting to Marguerite's mother, Isabella of Lorraine, and the d'Anjou family had never forgiven the girl, especially as another d'Anjou, René's skinny flatchested sister Marie, played the role of betrayed and neglected wife.

But even 'la belle Agnes,' however much her lush charms might tempt to sin the reigning monarch, had never dreamed of bastardizing and degrading the Succession itself. Yet, unless Henry's version was to be accepted, some earthly agent had to be the father of Marguerite's child. Henry himself, as we have seen, was a most unlikely candidate; while Somerset at least had the merit of being of the blood royal, though on the sinister side. But the claims of Henry Beaufort, Somerset's eldest boy, barely twenty, appear to have been entirely overlooked—even by the Duke of York. If the matter is considered from Marguerite's view, there is much to be said for Henry Beaufort. He was young; he was handsome; he had wonderful personal charm. He was of the blood royal, from Old Gaunt and the ardent Fleming, Katherine Roët. Above all, Henry Beaufort possessed the great virtue of being unmarried. Marguerite rightly considered her own wedlock a white marriage and adultery in such circumstances might have an extenuating aspect

---

* He was heir to Ormonde, in Ireland; and succeeded to that earldom in 1454 or early in 1455.

in the eyes of the Church; but there could be no extenuation, no forgive-ness, for tempting another to break his solemn vows. For Marguerite, the degree of the sin was of immense import.

For a romantic youth of twenty, Marguerite was a marvelous piece of luck. Henry Beaufort adored passionate women and, if possible, he liked them royal. Later, he was to have a torrid affair with Mary of Geuldres, the amorous widow of James the Second of Scotland. Henry may not have known he was the father of Marguerite's child; she might have considered it dangerous to let him think so. For all young Beau-fort knew, he need not have been the only one in this delightful bed. Nor, as a blood and bone Lancastrian, was it up to him to question the official explanation that King Henry had suddenly become po-tent.

What Beaufort could be sure of was that he loved Marguerite a great deal more than she loved him. A passion that never failed, even in the black night of Lancaster, after Towton, when Henry riding his splendid luck was pardoned by the victor; became the confidant of the King, the Captain of the Guard, the dashing companion of the first 'Merry Monarch.' And his beloved, she that had been a dazzling Queen, wan-dered in rags through the jeering towns of Burgundy. She called to him, to her lover; called to him when she was nothing and he stood in the blazing light of the Sunne of York.

He heard this cry, broken-winged through the desolation of memory; and for that memory, that lost night—he threw away all, fortune, honor, life.

Now, romantic and jealous, he could not fail to perceive how his idol invited attentions of other men, Butler, the good-looking Irishman with his blarney, Sir John Grey of Groby, a cavalry officer, and Henry's own sire, Edmund Duke of Somerset. Even old John Talbot, eighty, with a body as lean and dry as hickory, entered the lists. Better than the others—or perhaps because by reason of age he was removed from hopes of other triumphs—Talbot knew what pleased his lady. He had made for her an illuminated manuscript, as fine as the Horaire of René himself, in his workshop at Tarascon.

So Talbot—just before, a true knight, he went out to die for his lady at Castillon, has illuminated for all time this golden being who tore men's hearts with beauty and that fatal charm of Provence. She sits on a low divan in her peach-coloured palace of Pleasaunce, and on her head is a diadem of gold set with pearls and rubies; her bright hair, a fountain

of sun, flows to her shoulders, while the heliotrope mantle with a gold
band falls away from magnificent breasts. And around her and above
her is an azure canopy with golden fleur de lys; and her ladies, all
aflame in silk and velvet, with heart-shaped head-dresses; and her cavaliers in brilliant coats edged with miniver. Old Talbot himself is in
the scene, kneeling before his lady and offering his book—and she ex-
tends a slim hand blazing with rings.

It was all very well for Old Talbot to cavort around an amorous
French piece. Everyone knew the old boy was getting childish; he was
not the man he was at Agincourt. So ran the sulphurous comment about
Fotheringay.

Was the Duke of York to be found in a lady's presence-chamber,
capering to the lascivious pleasing of a lute? He was not. Richard of
York was to be found in the saddle, defending England's honour, which
the King's Ministers had betrayed or bartered away. Did Duchess Cecily
load her strong capable Westmoreland hands with jewels she could
not pay for? Did she walk about half-naked, exposing her breasts, like
some tart at the Cardinal's Hat?* She did not. She dressed soberly, wore
the plain gold band given her by the Duke almost twenty years before;
prayers were heard at Fotheringay thrice daily.

Only one course remained. Duchess Cecily was adamant. York—she
always called her husband 'York'—must speak privily to the King, get
these knaves dismissed and in the Tower. He had tried that already,
York reminded his Duchess. The King's promise was worth nothing.
Ah, but had York not acted hastily—disbanding his array? This time
he should keep his company about him.

York cogitated.

Meantime an event occurred which threw all plans into confusion.
The King was down at Clarendon, having dinner with his friend the
Bishop of Chichester. They were discussing Henry's foundation at
Eton, a favorite royal topic, when suddenly the King's face changed and
he went dumb. The Bishop could get no further word out of him. It
was like a visitation of God. Perhaps, the Bishop thought, the weather
played a part; it had been a sultry August. They bundled the sick man,

---

* One of eighteen whorehouses in Southwark. By city ordinance, they were forbidden
to hang out signs, but allowed to paint emblems on the rear walls fronting the
river. Hence: the Cardinal's Hat; the Flowers of Lucy; the Cross Keys; the Gunne;
the Crane.

still speechless, up to London and Marguerite, whose body was beginning
to swell with England's heir. Marguerite and Somerset took over; gave
Henry the best of care, while they prepared a formal regency.

The news burst on Fotheringay with the impact of a train of bombards. That wicked French minx had devised the whole thing, Cecily
asserted. She had probably drugged Henry. Not even the Duke of York
was willing to go that far. Cautioned by Warwick, he braked his reaction and waited to see what would happen. Men carrying the Duke's
Falcon credence went quietly about the eastern shires.

On St. Edward's Day, October 13th, Marguerite was delivered of a
bonny boy. He was christened Edward, a lyon name in English legend.
The bells tolled and the culverins crashed; only the sick man continued
sick and unable to recognize his heir. From time to time he was visited
by delegations of peers who tried out such remedies as "they moved
him; they shook him; but he heeded them not. They had him taken
out of one room and into another, and strove by pulling him about
to rouse him from his lethargy."

These hound-and-saddle healers were dealing with an advanced case
of schizophrenia, one of the toughest and most baffling of all mental
illnesses.* No one will marvel that the patient did not respond to their
notions of treatment. Little better were the official medicine men in
their green Court dress with harrowing prescriptions of: "electuaries,
potions, waters, syrups, confections, laxatives, clysters, gargles, head
purses, bathings, fomentations, embrocations, shaving of head, unctions,
plaisters, cerates, blisters, scarifications."

These green-coated magicians were men born too soon; electric shock
gadgets and the frontal lobe would have fitted extremely well into the
program.

It was said that King Henry had inherited the 'Valois madness.'
Blame the French for everything, even schizophrenia. It is doubtful
that there was any such thing as the 'Valois madness.' Assuming, as
legend has it, that Jeanne de Bourbon, wife of Charles the Wise, was the
guilty carrier, there were two hundred years of Valois in direct and
collateral descent from Jeanne de Bourbon, and hundreds of individuals,
and only one, Charles the Sixth, is known to have been mad.

* This portrait is the only attempt in English to deal rationally with the problems of
Henry's madness and impotence. Marguerite has not been happy in her biographers.
Mary Anne Hookham is unreadable; Bagley, equally so. Agnes Strickland is read-
able, but out-dated. Miss Strickland, whose collected works were dedicated to the
late Queen Victoria, was not well equipped to tackle the Freudian side of life.

Where then is this 'Valois madness' so glibly proclaimed by academic historians gulled by the old wives' fables in the chronicles of retired grocers and susceptible monks? *

The 'Valois madness' existed only in the overheated imaginations of chroniclers. Schizophrenia is not, like dementia praecox, inheritable. It has nothing in common with such blood-linked mass idiocy as generations of Jukes and Kallikaks. Its true cause is as obscure as that of multiple personality; and there may well be a common factor in the causes of schizophrenia and multiple personality.

Schizophrenia is a massive retreat from reality. In Henry's case, it was a renunciation of a world which had become unbearable. The King was not an imbecile; nor was he lunatic in the Bedlamite sense. He was a person who had come to view with horror his surroundings: the greed, the violence, the lust. Nor does the fact that up to now he had appeared to accept his lot with sweetness and good temper argue anything save the total repression of his true reaction, which must ultimately result in a personality explosion.

It is most likely that Marguerite's pregnancy was the precipitating cause. Henry's love and admiration for his dashing wife were unbounded; whatever his sexual deformation, he knew the quality of Marguerite d'Anjou. And in an instant, in the twinkling of an eye, his whole fragile world, all his precarious pitiful defenses, had come crashing down. Her body, forever unattainable, had been given to another; and the King of England—what was he? A poor weak husk of a creature, crying stunned and alone. . . .

Marguerite understood. Henry was good; good as she might never be, as few on this earth might hope to be. Set apart from the brawling cruel and stupid nature of man. But before all, she was a daughter of her House, of Anjou pride in war, the sweet false glory of the kingdoms of the world—the world without: "green and white and red."

Henry was the dark world within, the monsters and the horror, that Brother Hieronymous Bosch would celebrate. . . .

* Professional historians, by which is usually meant teachers of history on the faculty of a college or university, are all too often woefully ignorant of the uses of modern psychiatry, bristling at the very name of Freud or of Jung; much as fifty years ago political and military historians, obsessed with politics and war, were ignorant of the applications of Marx to history.

Candles at twelfth night. . . .

In this same year, 1453, that saw the birth of Edward, Prince of Lancaster, and Henry's madness, Isabella of Lorraine died at the early age of forty-three. Never robust, Isabella's health had broken down traipsing about Calabria in the wake of mercenary captains who badgered her incessantly for money, plundered her of everything not nailed down, and when she had been milked dry, deserted to Alphonse. She had also waged a strenuous campaign with her cousin Antoine de Vaudemont over the inheritance of Lorraine. When the old Duke died, Alison Dumay had been hooted through the streets of Nancy, pelted with dung, and beaten to death, while Antoine had moved in on the duchy. In this crisis, René had been little help. He was either sitting in a Burgundian jail or wandering the wilds of Calabria, questing for Giovanna the Good. After a lengthy tussle, Isabella and Antoine had compromised: Yolande of Anjou was betrothed to Ferry of Vaudemont, and Lorraine would pass to their descendants.

At Isabella's death, René was inconsolable—for six months. The very mention of his wife's name set off fresh spells of weeping. The sable-shrouded prince displayed to his friends a picture he had painted: a bow with a broken cord and the haunting device, *Arco per lentare, plaga non sana.* Love was a broken bow, the string snapped by the launching of the arrow which had stricken René with an irreparable wound.

But: consolation was at hand.

There were girls in Old Provence as fair and tempting, with strawberry-tipped breasts, as any who ever walked the earth; their kingdoms of joy would restore to life this grieving prince. A man could not remain in the old stone darkness, a pleurant crying at the bolt—*and here sits Memory, down whose cheeks the tears are pouring.* . . .

Re-entered, by the gate of passion; the orange groves, the singing, and the sun.

Two bastards were born, Jean and Madeleine. Both were to disappear in the mysterious and tragic doom which, at the end of René's life, would strike down the House of Anjou. In this year also, he met Jeanne de Laval, daughter of Guy XIV, Count of Laval, a Breton seigneur.

Jeanne was no beauty. In the masterly evocation of Nicholas Froment, the tryptych of *The Burning Bush,* she has a long sallow face, sharp nose, and pinched mouth. Intensely pious, Jeanne was seldom heard to laugh. Twenty-one yet unmarried, she was chilly and 'good.'

But René was smitten. After all, he was close to forty-five, triple-chinned and unwieldy; and a virgin of twenty-one was a tender morsel. He was inspired to a pastoral ode on the subject of this vintage romance, *Regnault et Jeanneton,* depicting in a mere ten thousand verses a debate on love between a shepherd and a shepherdess, with a pilgrim wayfarer as arbiter. A composition which caused that rascal François Villon to guffaw; and to remark that in his experience the shepherd girls of Anjou got to the point much more quickly!

But then, the author of *The Hanged Men* and of *Fat Margot,* the friend of Guy Tabarie and of Huguette Duhamel, *larron, scelérat,* and the greatest French poet of the age, had the usual professional's irony for efforts of noble amateurs. Visiting Angers in 1456, where he had hoped to shake down a rich uncle, Villon was not received by the prince of patrons in his castle with fourteen towers; a little too unwashed and ironical, with the smell of the Châtelet, the poet was not quite suitable. Villon was received by René's elegant friend, Charles d'Orléans, at Blois. He managed to hang on for several weeks of ortolans and roast swan, paying for his dinners by a few painful staves on the nativity of the Duke's daughter Marie.

'Regnault' and 'Jeanneton' were married in the Abbey of St. Nicholas at Angers, September 10th, 1454. The groom settled princely tokens of love on his young bride: the city and castle of Saumur; one-third of the revenues of Anjou; one-half the revenues of Bar; the product of the *gabelle* or salt tax in Provence. The newly-weds honey-mooned at Saumur, that castle of cloud-hung visionary towers on the Loire. In the passion of white nights, a renewal of the idyll of a storybook prince, René composed his finest geste, an allegory of the *Chevalier Coeur d'Amour*—the quest of the Knight Coeur for the Lady Doulx-Merci, held captive in the dungeon of Castle Rebellion. Borrowing from *Le Roman de la Rose,* from *Tristam,* and from a galaxy of quests, René created his own version. With his companion Desir, Coeur wanders forests and seas in search of Doulx-Merci; he sails to the Isle of Love, where are found whole pavilions of hospitalized knights groaning with love, Charles d'Orléans, Charles de Maine, Pierre de Brézé, René himself. This touch allowed René, who was by no means devoid of humour, to work in a gentle satire at the expense of the pretensions of courtly love, as celebrated by his noble friends. The presence at the Isle of Charles of France is indicated by the royal badge of a stag above a closed door, though in this case the anguish was real enough, for

Charles had been recently bereft of the one passion of his life, Agnes Sorel. At length, reaching Castle Rebellion, Coeur d'Amour is grievously wounded in a fight outside the dungeon door of Doulx-Merci. Transported in turn to the Isle of Love, Coeur d'Amour seems on the point of expiring as the allegory ends.

Overlong, a pastiche of 'quests,' the *Chevalier Coeur d'Amour* has nonetheless moments of enchantment; and has passed supremely well the final test—survival.*

While René was celebrating in allegory the Arthurian gloss on chivalry, his daughter Marguerite was involved in the realities that underlay the prophetic vision. These English knights who on April 23rd observed the Feast of their patron Saint, George of Cappadocia, and who wore the blue belted Garter of the paladins of Edward the Third, partook of quests as well, but they were pilgrims for power, for lands and money. And though Queen Marguerite might have been in some sense a Doulx-Merci, the quarreling barons were concerned not with her distress but with their own schemes. Neither Somerset nor York had any desire to compromise; each wholly disbelieved in the integrity of the other and the only reason fighting had not broken out was lack of preparation.**

But on both sides activity was now feverish. Somerset was mustering in London, with headquarters in the Strand, without Temple Bar. He had also developed a far-flung intelligence service, his agents disguised as friars and seafaring men with tarry pigtails, to report on the doings of the Duke of York. That old front fighter was marshalling in the shires, and calling in wild kerns and galloglasses from Ireland. The Crown itself had no army, nothing resembling a police force. Lack of funds had prevented raising even a palace guard to defend the Royal Family—in striking contrast to the Kingdom of France, where Charles the Victorious had for some years maintained a royal guard of 900

---

* Beautiful reproductions of text and illuminations have been made; critiques have discussed the significance for French art of this pioneering work; a film has been made with the hypnotic voice of Maria de Casares rendering René's lines. The paintings are glorious, but critics dispute whether René had anything to do with them.

** York had been taken aback by the excesses of the Jack Cade Rising, which he had sponsored, and by the way in which public opinion had rallied to the Government. More preparation was essential to swing the Nation to acceptance of an armed challenge. One aspect of this was to pretend that Henry was illegal anyhow, and York with his captains constituted a kind of rightful Government-in-exile.

cavalrymen, plus the Scottish Guard of 300, and the royal ordnance under the brothers Bureau.* These permanent units formed the nucleus of the French Army and greatly contributed to English defeat in Normandy and Guyenne.

Henry's madness was a godsend to York. Hitherto, Marguerite and the Lancastrian ministry had sheltered behind the nominal authority of the King; now, York might challenge the Queen directly. For a few weeks, York played a waiting game. Marguerite was twenty-three; she had little conception of the formidable threat. She assumed that she would become Regent and take upon herself the management of the Realm, as Isabella of Lorraine had done in the absence of René. But England was not Anjou, nor were the English devoted vassals. In fact, this same year had brought Talbot's catastrophe at Castillon and Marguerite's subjects were bitterly anti-French.

The Queen sent a bill of five articles to the Parliament of January, 1454. "Item . . . whereof the first is that she desireth to have the whole rewle of this land; the second, that she appoint the Chancellor, Treasurer, Privy Seal, and all other officers of this land; the third, that she may give all the bishoprics of this land, and all other benefices belonging to the King's gift; the fourth is, that she may have sufficient livelihood assigned for the King, the Prince, and for herself; but as for the fifth article, I know not what it be." **

Such a bill had not the wildest chance. It tipped York's hand; and very soon after, "the Duke of York will be at London justly on Friday next, coming at night. And the Earl of March rideth with him. The Earl of Salisbury will be at London on Monday or Tuesday next, coming with seven score knights and esquires, besides other menies. The Earls of Warwick, Richmond, and Pembroke come with the Duke of York, each with a goodly fellowship. Every man that is of the opinion of the Duke of Somerset maketh him ready to be as strong as he can make him." ***

Everything was for the best in the best of all possible York worlds, when an unexpected snag occurred. John Kemp, seventy-four, Chancellor and Cardinal-Archbishop of Canterbury, refused to quit. This was infuriating. The Chancellor could not simply be shoved aside, like Marguerite and Somerset. The first prelate of England, Kemp had a long

---

* Colonel Burne, in his *The Agincourt War,* somehow arrives at a figure of 9000 cavalrymen in the royal guard. This is manifestly incorrect.
** *Paston Letters;* News-letter of John Stodeley, January 19th, 1454.   *** Idem.

and honourable record of public service; he could not be accused of treachery in France or anywhere else.

York resorted to intimidation. The choleric bullying John Mowbray, Duke of Norfolk, who had already delivered a scathing blast in the Lords against Somerset, invaded the Chancellor's office with a threatening harangue; * other lords were pressed into like service; and even delegations of tradesmen, such as the dealers of the wool staple, who crowded in to clamor against Lord Bonville's piracies on their mercantile associates, the Flemings. The old man had not a moment's peace and was "so threatened by some lords, especially by the Duke of Norfolk, that he chose rather to die than to live in fear."

And, in fact, the courageous Archbishop and loyal servant had a heart attack on March 22nd, dying the same day. As England was not the domain of the Grand Turk, and "an Amurath succeeds not an Amurath," no one suggested that Kemp was helped into eternity. Still, his death was mightily fortuitous.

At the last moment, Marguerite and Somerset drew back from blood. In the last days, Somerset House was the scene of taut midnight conferences, with frantic messages to and from Westminster Palace. Confused by Kemp's sudden death (and perhaps warned!), the Queen and her minister hesitated; York chose the hour, rallied his great hooded troop, closed the gates—and struck. Somerset was arrested in the midst of a conference with the Queen; "in the bedchamber," York gave out, allowing his auditors to infer the nature of the conference which the husband of 'Proud Cis' had righteously interrupted. Somerset's men were rounded up and disarmed; a complaisant and rather frightened House of Lords rushed through a bill granting full powers of Protector to Richard, Duke of York.

York and Warwick must have toyed with the notion of settling with Marguerite for good, now that they had her at their mercy; of shutting her in some clammy fortress, like Isabella the She-wolf at Hertford, from which she would never emerge alive. It is astonishing that they did not do this. They were certainly not deterred by any consideration of pity; nor by public opinion, which in any case was not at the moment sympathetic to French women. Somerset was in the Tower; the other

---

* It is easy to see what sort of man this Norfolk was, in the recital of ugly bickering, and occasional violence, between him and his tenants that occurs in the *Paston Letters*. He survived to appear dramatically on the right flank of Lancaster at a crucial point in the battle of Towton, swinging the victory to York.

foes of York cowed. The lords of the White Rose could have rigged a case against Marguerite, "dealing with the enemy," as later they tried to do in the Sandwich raid. What probably restrained them was the fear of provoking Marguerite's kinsman, Charles of France, to reprisals, especially attacking Calais, which the party of York required as a strategic overseas base for future operations in England. And, as usual under-valuing her, they felt that the young Queen could be bought off. York offered Marguerite £1000 yearly, plus an additional 2000 silver marks and the Earldom of Chester for the prince. It was like a divorce settlement; only, the aggrieved party had not the least intention of allowing the Duke to get away with any such terms. She took the money, and kept quiet—for the present. Henry, he must get well; he must come to himself. She would make him!

Astonishingly, she did. . . .

It was at Windsor on the Monday past Christmas, with candles at the casements, the risen day already descending into dusk, and she a mother (like the Mother), in her arms the child of England, and without the snow on white cat's feet, prowling . . . the glow of Twelfth Night, English voices in the white falling dark . . . *the last day of Christmas, my true love sent to me.* . . .

And in the chambered light, the old sad flicker of the candles, sat the King wrapped in a blue furred robe, fingers plucking shadows. "Who is this child, lady?"

"It is your child, Lord Henry."

He cried out for joy; tears glistened. His! His! It was *she* who said it (and had he forgot, the old bright terror, the listening and the stillness?)

And in the chambered dusk, the lords saw with wonder that their King had come back to them, from his terrible sleep.

"What is the child's name, Lady Margaret?"

"His name is Edward; for he was born on Edward's Day, at three of the clock."

"Then God be thanked!" He lifted pale starved hands. Suddenly weeping, he turned to the others, "Oh my lords, I wist not where I was nor what was said to me until this moment." He looked at her, oh wondrous her! so proud, so golden in the candleflare. "But tell me, Lady Margaret, who are the boy's godfathers?"

"His Grace of Buckingham, Milord Edmund of Somerset, and the good grey Cardinal that was."

"Saint John! Saint John! It was well done, gentle lady. But said you not, the Cardinal that was?"

"The Cardinal is dead, Lord Henry."

He gazed about, in the Christmas glow, the candles burning, burning for Twelfth Night—and without, the snow. . . . "I never knew," he whispered. Then, eyes deep-wondering, staring, "The wisest lord in this land is dead."

OF SHIPS AND MEN AND GUNS. . . .

Richard of York grumbled about the shires, no longer Protector, his enemy Somerset in the saddle and Queen Marguerite flaunting. Proud Cis buzzed at her lord to act. Delay might prove mortal; remember Humphrey, the Good Duke. By May, 1455, York had arrayed a field force of 5000 men, with Warwick and Salisbury his adjutants. It was proposed to march on London and to 'deliver' the King from his wife and friends.

The move was not unexpected. With Buckingham and Somerset, Marguerite prepared to meet the challenge. The royal army was smaller than York's, 3000 men, but it was well-equipped and counted most of the old baronage of England among its captains. For them, several times on the brink of blood, York's overt defiance came as almost a relief from the long tension of threats, hatred, and calumny endured by all those who loved Marguerite.

Henry himself was nerved to an astonishing belligerence by his wife. When the two forces collided outside St. Albans, on the morning of May 21, and York demanded that Somerset be yielded up, Henry issued a blast worthy of his sire, famous Agincourt. "Now I shall know what traitors are so bold as to raise a host against me in mine own land. And by the faith that I owe to Saint Edward and the Crown of England, I will destroy them, every mother's son, to have example to all traitors who make rising of people against their King. And for a conclusion, say that rather than they shall have any lord here with me at this time, I will this day for his sake and in this quarrel stand myself to live or die."

Through this royal reply shines the voice, the very style of Queen Marguerite d'Anjou.

Henry's army barricaded in the town, while the Yorkists tried to crack the wooden barriers erected on the causeway across the town ditch. The defenders held firm through a sleet of arrows until the Earl of Warwick, just turned twenty-five and experiencing his baptism of fire, resourcefully hacked through the back walls of houses fronting on St. Peter's High Street. Warwick's men erupted in the town at Holywell Lane, blowing up their trumpets and shouting "à Warwick! à Warwick!"

It was the coup de grâce. Jamie Butler, heir to Ormonde and blarney-kissing High Treasurer, suspected of sharing Marguerite's bed, was the first to make a quick exit, closely pursued by the Standard-Bearer, Sir Philip Wentworth. The Earl of Northumberland and Lord Thomas Clifford were killed in a desperate charge at Warwick's line. Somerset was mortally hit and crawled up on the steps of the Castle Inn to die (long before, a Welsh woman had said to him, " 'ware the Castle!"). His son Henry Beaufort, Marguerite's only real love, was left for dead in the street. Buckingham, royal commander, went down with an arrow in the face; while King Henry himself, standing limply beside his fallen Leopards, was wounded in the neck. He was led into a tanner's nearby, where Richard of York found him, to sink on his treacherous knees and wrench out hypocritical croaks of loyalty.

And the King? Bleeding, the blood seeping down his neck, staining the mailed doublet, trembling and horrified, the dread darkness coming on once more, crying alone while his cousin of York—he listened through a thickening terror—rumbled on, saying it had been all Somerset's fault, wicked Somerset now lying dead on the steps of the Castle Inn, and the King was restored to his own again, to his good friends of York, oh they were round him like bucklers, and why was His Highness crying, he need never cry again, for York was here and would never leave him!

Somerset was dead. Adam Moleyns, Lord Say, Suffolk, John Kemp, good grey Cardinal, now Somerset—all dead, struck down by York. Her friendship was become a way-station to doom. Walking up and down in the roselight of Greenwich Palace, the Queen brooded. She could not protect her friends, she could not protect herself. And always at her back, in the gilded rooms of Greenwich, she heard soft pursuing footsteps, the voice of Humphrey, mocking—oh she thought, did she, that by getting rid of him all troubles would be at an end? Well, she could see now. Half England hated her, 'the Frenssche scold'; and one by one her friends were 'holped' to God. The dead mocking voice went on and on, ringing and echoing in her ears, until she could not bear it, she longed to run shrieking through the roselight.

For the voice spoke truth. She was misunderstood and hated. She had come to England with naught but love in her heart; but the English did not want her love, they did not want her at all. Even her Chamberlain, Sir John Wenlock, had turned against her, acting as Yorkist Speaker in the White Rose victory Parliament following St. Albans. Yet she clung to the hope of changing these stubborn English. She would go amongst the shires, dwell with her subjects; oh she was simple, good and kind, she was a wife and mother, like the good wives of Chester and Norwich—they would see!

And her ladies, beside tall lancet windows, the three Elizabeths, Elizabeth Butler, Elizabeth Grey, Elizabeth Lady Dacres, and Lady Margaret Ross, did they not love the Queen? Her ladies, who saw her daily, who knew her? She would rouse such a flame of devotion as had never been seen in England!

And she would have for support her Henry Beaufort, 3rd Duke of Somerset and now Chancellor, and good William Wainflete, Bishop of Winchester and Keeper of the Seals. For, after St. Albans and York's brief flurry of triumph, she had once more restored the King out of darkness; forced out a bitterly protesting York.

But all her resolves and benign hopes split on the rock of ambition. York would be a king, Salisbury his first minister, Warwick his captain and admiral. Henry pleaded for a 'loveday,' a feast of reconciliation, mortal foes hand-in-hand. Marguerite agreed; and they had a loveday at St. Paul's, a rare sweet sight, Marguerite walking hand-in-hand with the Duke of York, Salisbury with Somerset, Warwick with Henry Holland, Duke of Exeter, and King Henry in vermilion robe leading the tender procession.

Their hands might be gently locked, but death was in their hearts. This loveday perished like a July flower. Warwick was the first to break the compact. As Captain of Calais, Warwick was a blackbrowed Hawkins in armour, breezing up and down the Channel, ignoring the Government's treaties with friendly nations, his cannonades smashing the decks of Spain, the Hanse, and Burgundy. In the style made famous on the Spanish Main, Warwick's buccaneers would descend with dirk and cutlass on peaceful trading vessels, wreaking terror and death and seizing the ships as prizes. Complaints poured in to the Council at Westminster. The final straw was the violation of England's treaty with the Hanse, a running fight with the salt fleet of Lubeck, and five great ships seized and taken into Calais.*

Marguerite had Warwick summoned to Westminster, the more readily as he recently and without the least proof had publicly accused her of betraying England with the French raid on Sandwich by Pierre de Brézé, cavalier of bridal blue and white—so long ago. Well, here *he* was, red-handed, destroying England's commercial accord for his own profit.**

He came reluctantly, not trusting her, yet not sufficiently distrusting her to avow he dared not face a woman. Debarking at Westminster on a sullen day in November, 1458, Warwick strode with only a score of his red-jackets through the grey vast planes and granite sky of the esplanade, past the stone Clock Tower, and into the vaulted Duchy of Lancaster. The Council, presided over by young Somerset, blood-feud foe of all Nevilles, received the brigand in frigid silence. Warwick had only begun to make his defense when the base court rang with "Warwick! Warwick! Name of God!"

Warwick plunged down a crumbling stair and out into a frenzy of killing, his red-jackets against kitchen black-guards armed with cleavers, spits, and fire forks. Warwick's men cut a way to the boat-stage; died, hacked and split, that the Ragged Staff might live. Blood-spattered, Warwick leaped into his wherry, rowed furiously toward Lambeth, on the Surrey side. From mid-river, he glimpsed Marguerite's scullions on the landing-stairs, cleavers and forks dripping blood. Warwick never forgot.***

And now, between Marguerite and the party of York was nothing but death. She in the roselight, scheming, the dream within her dying, no more talk of her colleges, of books, of the poor girls, her 'silk women' that she had taken off the streets and taught a trade . . . now she

---

* Warwick's latest biographer has referred to these forays as "knightly exploits" (Kendall, *Warwick the Kingmaker*). Warwick's raiding was as knightly as lovable old Henry Morgan's bloody swathe along the Spanish Main.

** Warwick had superseded Exeter during York's second Protectorate; and it had proved impossible to oust him from Calais. Exeter had a dirty deal from York all around. He was thrown out of his naval command; his wife Anne, second daughter of the Duke of York, divorced him; Anne's brother Edward attainted him; and finally had the wretched fellow murdered. Exeter's only discoverable fault was loyalty to his Sovereign, Henry the Sixth.

*** He believed that Marguerite intended to have him murdered. There is no proof of this, but Warwick had managed to achieve a kind of sublimity of loathing in the Queen's eyes, most particularly for the scurrilous stories that he spread about her.

spoke of ships and men and guns; those lovely lips, made for kissing, proclaimed death; and she would imagine heads clotted with blood. Or she would pace up and down, a harsh manlike stride, spitting commands.

Henry would watch beneath long quivering lashes, the pain and wonder grew, he was afraid of her, afraid of the being that she had become.

In that lost and orient light of childhood, that happy island of the soul, she had dreamed of love—of a kingdom. Secretly, secretly, this is the voice of Yolande of Aragon, proud steelblue consonants, the sound of royalty cutting like a blade: she shall be a queen, hard stainless diadem-glittering . . . then to remember, yes at midnight, René's step upon the tower stair, the room floating in moonlight, the lap and murmur of the river a hundred feet below, and in the shining dark the whisper of her name, *Marguerite d'Anjou . . . Marguerite d'Anjou . . . Marguerite d'Anjou. . . .*

But then, then, she had not learned to kill. Her eyes blazing with tears, the music of childhood, the bells of Provence, and she remembering, remembering.

And her mother, was not Isabella beautiful and gay, a princess of mirth, loving? But the years, the years that the locust hath eaten. The rain, the coughing, the dark cruel faces of the mercenaries—and a woman alone, dying, weeping, hardly a decent gown. Blessed Virgin! what was it all for?

And she too, had not this passion of hers been Isabella's ruin, this mad levy of death, this frenzy of kingdoms, when she had not means wherewith to buy a gown?

It availed not, for she was embarked on that quest of hers, a quest more lonely and terrible than any visioned by her poet-father.

She went from the dreaming and scheming of rose-red Greenwich to Cheshire (the most beautiful Lady of the West Countrie!), where she arrayed. Five thousand men with the Swan badge, Edward's badge, they went forth under Lord Audeley. But this fine array, the work of months of travel and crusading for the Rose, had been shattered by Salisbury at Blore Heath, in Staffordshire. Oh if ever she might lay hands on Salisbury!

But then, what happened did not bear thinking of. She had levied yet another army, a splendid army, high-hearted, sworn, a gleaming

terror. At first, all had gone wondrously. Her men had caught Richard
of York, Warwick, Salisbury—the whole nest of traitors—at Ludlow.
Desperate, York had spread a report of Henry's sudden death; ordered
a mass for the King's soul. But Henry displayed his Leopards; the
Calais regiment, 800 men in crimson coats under Andrew Trollope,
came over to Lancaster. York's spirit broke.

Then: Northampton. In ten months, York made a blustering recovery;
was on the march to London. The captains of the Rose entrenched;
deep dykes, palisades, rows of bombards snout to snout. *Impregnable,*
old Buckingham vowed. And John, Viscount Beaumount agreed.

How brilliantly it had begun, had she not seen it from a rise near
Northampton? Young Edward of March, gigantic and grinding to
the attack, the red leaping roar, the crash of chainshot, the shrieks
like music of York dying . . . eagerly she reckoned, making the score
for Blore Heath.

The broken attack streamed away; the rain began, thin black needle-
points in thunderous July.

And again, trumpets. Again, the huge crunching of boots on boggy
earth, banners torn and limp—she remembered banners in Calabria,
long ago—and the doomed silent faces as they crunched by the dead.
And March, young gigantic March, with his Standard of the Sunne,
clanking to the dyke like some fabulous monster, his great sword, his
axe—she prayed. . . .

The thing happened in a flash. She gazed upon a long steel rank
milling in the sodden ditch; her gunners to their touch-holes with
glowing matches, her archers with bent bows, noble Grey de Ruthyn,
her devoted avenger, beside his Standard. She heard a wild shout,
madness seemed to flare out of the dark thunderous morning—archers
threw down bows, gunners doused matches; her men rushed to the
ditch with outstretched hands to pull up their new comrades of York.

The rest was ruin: a savage fray in the camp, old Buckingham cut
down before his tent. So perished her second army, destroyed by Grey
de Ruthyn.

SHE WAS THE SWAN AND THE ROSE. . . .
Plundered by Stanley's thugs, the Queen of England fled through
dripping woods to the safety of Harlech Castle. It was the first of many

attempts to terrorize her and to drive her out. And there was always the hope that in these sordid scuffles Marguerite herself might get in the way of a swordstroke.

The swaggering brotherhood of the Falcon did not reflect that outrage and humiliation would array this proud woman in a Nessus-robe of vengeance; and that the House of York would pay a fearful price for insults to the Queen. Never very intelligent about Marguerite, her enemies appeared to think she could be frightened out of her crown.

But Marguerite had learned much since the days when, young and alien, she had tried to impose her monarchy through the tortured nerves of Henry the Sixth. Henry had proved a failure in every department of statecraft. While it is not true, as his detractors claim, that the King on alternate days had appointed lords of the Red and White Rose to the Chancellorship, he was capable of follies almost as extreme, such as making simultaneous promises to Somerset and to York, pledging each that his opponent would be put in ward. Henry was always, as he put it, "in charity with all the world"; and he was probably the one person present who considered the 'loveday' at St. Paul's, in January, 1458, to have been aught but a solemn farce.

Indeed, by the deal with Warwick whereby he disinherited his own line, Henry would take himself out of consideration as even the formal leader of Lancaster. Henceforth, the Swan and the Rose was Marguerite d'Anjou.

She, the former dinner guest of Cardinal Henry Beaufort, "the best-hated man in England," had set out years before to court popularity. As hardly any 'Frenssche' Queen had bothered to do so before, the English were immensely flattered. With the King's two uterine brothers, Jasper and Edmund Tudor (later the father of Henry the Seventh), Marguerite had toured the Midlands in the spring of 1452. She spent a few days in April at Norwich, where she held open house and was visited by, amongst others, Margaret Paston and Elizabeth Clere. The two girls, cousins, borrowed each other's finery for these exciting calls on the loveliest Queen in English memory and talked over their matrimonial problems with Marguerite. "When she (Elizabeth Clere) came in the Queen's presence, the Queen made right much of her, and desired her to have a husband, the which ye shall know of hereafter; but as for that he is never nearer than he was before; the Queen was right well pleased with her answer, and reporteth of her in the best wise, and saieth, by her truth, she saw no gentlewoman since she came into Norfolk that she liked better than she doth her." *

In neighbouring Oxfordshire, Marguerite was a frequent guest at Wallingford, the country estate of Alice Chaucer; while the Queen's daisy emblem, a red stone in white enamel, was familiar at Beaufort manors in Somerset and Exeter. Her personal capital and favourite of towns was Coventry, where on occasion she held royal estate with the King and Prince Edward. But of all shires, Cheshire was the most devoted. Marguerite had inspired the creation of Edward as Earl of Chester in 1454. The Queen and her son had gone in royal progress through Cheshire, distributing the White Swan badge and mustering the first Lancastrian army, the ill-fated five thousand that under Audley fought Blore Heath. At these Lancastrian fêtes, Marguerite appeared in an azure mantle with the great jewel of the Garter blazing on her left forearm; while her gentlemen wore the red and black livery of the six-year-old Earl of Chester.

These years of party preparation, of evoking a Lancastrian spirit in opposition to the busy remorseless Falcon of York, gave a mighty reward. Marguerite had been Queen of England for fifteen years; for ten of those years she had been the chief adornment and most active partisan of Lancaster. No doubt, she would have preferred to reign unchallenged, above the flames of faction. But she had no choice— other than an intolerable surrender. As she said herself, "when on the day of my betrothal, I took the Rose of England, did I not know that I must bear it entire with all its thorns?"

At Harlech, Marguerite seems to have hesitated over the next move. The rout of Northampton had scattered and demoralized the forces of the Rose. Up to this time, Marguerite had always operated through Henry and the Council; now Henry was in the custody of York, while the ministers were either dead or in flight. Lancaster appeared done.

But the victorious little Duke, astute in adversity, now demonstrated the perils of prosperity. His London entry had been triumphal; no returning Caesar laureled with the slaughter of druidic tribes might have displayed more tootling and drumbright pomp than Richard of York. That these laurels had been gained at the expense of his own

---

* Margaret Paston was in love with Richard Calle, the bailiff of her family estates. For this heinous affront to class feeling, Margaret was beaten several times a week by Agnes, her mother, and had her head "broke in two or three places." She eventually got her man, however. *Vide:* Letters LI and LXV, Fenn's Edition.

countrymen bothered York not a whit. He had been long abroad; and he had come to think of his foes as he did hot-handed French or rebellious Irish. He might have used his victory wisely; offered amnesty; refrained from agitating the Succession. He had the reality of power; all he needed to do was consolidate. Instead, he made it clear that those who had served their King were to be attainted and outlawed; while the House of Lancaster that had ruled England for sixty years and had produced one shrewd governor, one legendary St. George, and one saint, was to be utterly degraded.

York's first act was to turn King Henry out of his apartments at Westminster, breaking down the door. His next: to summon a packed Parliament to incarcerate Henry in a monastery and to acclaim Richard the Third. York did have a strong dynastic claim, through the Mortimers and Lionel of Clarence, but he ignored what for instance his sons kept ever in mind, that since the turn of the century England had been moving toward a monarchy based more on popular consent than on strict blood-descent. His arrogance was too much even for this carefully weeded assembly and when he laid his hand on the chair of state in Westminster Hall and made as if to sit down, he was greeted by a granite silence.

The Earl of Warwick was appalled. He rushed about behind the scenes, talking to key lords and gentry, trying to patch up a compromise. Henry, alone, badgered, bewildered, was persuaded to accept Warwick's formula: to retain the kingship, nominal of course, for the rest of his days, and to settle the Succession on Richard of York and his blood.

But for once the Kingmaker erred. In view of what happened, he would have done better either to have avoided the question at all or to have rammed York's claim down the throats of gentlemen of the White Rose. Warwick wanted to avoid civil war; he succeeded in precipitating it with the Duke's title in a cloudy state.

For news of these proceedings provoked fury at Harlech. Isolated, penniless, dependent for her very bread on Welsh chiefs, Marguerite was at once roused to action. Destitute in a material sense, she had enormous resources of spirit—of will, intelligence, courage—which might match anything her foes could produce in that line. She fired off letters in all directions: to the King of France, to the Regent of Scotland, and to the lords of Lancaster. The letters had the same motif: that her son Edward was the rightful heir to the crown of England, that she meant to fight for his heritage, and that she requested aid in her battle. An Angevin, she was not so naïve as to expect help without some *quid pro quo*. To France and Scotland, forever plagued by suzerainty claims of the King of England, she could offer renunciation of those claims and treaties of friendship and alliance; to her Lancastrian lords, Marguerite could offer power and privilege.

But France and Scotland, though such terms would have delighted both twenty years before, now expected more. England was a defeated divided nation, powerless to threaten. Charles the Very Victorious, who about this time was having his ugly mask immortalized on canvas by Jean Fouquet, wanted Calais and an indemnity; above all, he wanted a vigorous ally against Burgundy. Margaret could promise none of this without wrecking her son's chance in England.* Scotland, under the Regent Mary of Gueldres, wanted Berwick and other border fortresses; while Mary herself had a Burgundian bias, being daughter to Arnold of Gueldres and niece to Duke Philip the Good. Determined to try a personal approach, Marguerite set out by ship for Scotland in October.

Mary greeted her desperate visitor at Dumfries, on the west coast near Carlisle. The Scottish Court was in mourning for James the Second, killed the preceding August by a bursting bombard at the siege of Roxburgh, but Mary bundled Marguerite on a festive tour of the kingdom. The food was good; and there was plenty of French white wine to lubricate conversation. Mary paid for everything. If Marguerite had been in a house-party mood, the occasion could not have been bettered. But the Queen of England could think of nothing but her foes, who had dishonoured her. How many times must Marguerite have tried to introduce the dreary subject of English politics, between the roast swan and the subtletie of pink spun sugar, and been put off by a gay laugh from her hostess and the remark that there would be time for all that sad business. Only there never was.

There must, too, have been some jealousy and submerged feminine tension going on beneath the kisses and the compliments. They were too much alike, in certain respects. Both were proud and passionate, the mainstay of dynastic causes in a turbulent political situation. Both led troops in the field; both hated and loved with equal intensity and disregard of all but their inward burning vision. Both aroused fierce

* By his anti-Burgundian policy, Warwick ruined the very promising Lancastrian restoration of 1470–1471.

loyalty and scorching enmity; and scandal like an evil moon glimmered on them. But while Marguerite maintained a fiery dignity amid the worst humiliations, Mary's name deteriorated and former lovers commented freely on the Queen in her shift. Yet Mary never allowed jealousy of the younger woman to erupt; she was kind, she was generous, Marguerite would always have a welcome. But in the end she was forced to realize that Mary either would not or could not give her substantial aid to recover England. James, son of the lovely Lancastrian Joan Beaufort and the poet-King, might have swung Scotland for Marguerite; but James was dead and his heir was a child, while the Estates kept tight rein on their purse-strings.

But if Marguerite drew a blank at Perth, far different was the case with the lords of Lancaster. Results exceeded all expectations. It was as if the ruined captains of the Rose had been waiting a lead, to strike. Marguerite had appointed a rendezvous at Kingston-on-Hull, in Yorkshire. The choice seems curious, as the Queen was not nearly so well known in the North as in the Midlands and West. But Northampton had for a time broken Lancaster in these parts; while many of the chief captains of the Rose were Northern men: Clifford, Dacres, Welles, Roos, Northumberland. With the onset of winter, the North began to rally.

FIRE AND ICE: *these be three silent things, the falling snow, the hour before the dawn, the mouth of one just dead. . . .*

Descended in beauty, in royalty, blazing from the wild—the secret flame, an army out of a woman's terrible heart. They came from five Northern counties: Yorkshire, Durham, Northumberland, Westmoreland, Cumberland; and York City alone sent four hundred men. They came from the march of Scotland; they rushed from the south in old ragged coats, toting rusty blades and yew bows that had done service at Agincourt. In the winter sky, standards flared: the Shacklebolt of Percy, the fiery Cresset of Exeter, the Portcullis of Beaufort, the Redwinged Wyvern of Clifford, the Dolphin of Devon, the Swan and Rose of Lancaster. Old horses, rotten leather, heroes of rags and patches —they swarmed to Margaret.

It was as if she had stamped that small foot and twenty thousand men had leaped to arms. All the bitterness of defeat in France, all the ageless anger of the Dispossessed, had found a cause and a Leader.

What was Cade, what was Tyler himself, beside this glorious Margaret? The Lancastrian camp blazed with hope and singing. This time they were going to win, this time there was no turning back!

In London, beneath a December sky, they saddled in the court of Baynard Castle, breath like steam swirling from stallion nostrils. The Duke of York was riding; beside the short grim lord in the tawny cloak stood his son Edmund, seventeen, Earl of Rutland, "the best disposed lord that was in this land"; York's brother-in-law, Salisbury; his Mortimer uncles, Sir John and Sir Hugh; his nephew, Sir Thomas Neville; his Chamberlain, Davy Hall; and Harrow, the captain of the London Volunteers. They were riding north, with a company of men-at-arms, and five hundred silver marks granted by London's Council to hire additional forces. Strange rumours filtered from the North, of roads choked with armed men, of helmeted riders against a low ashgrey sky.

They would be back for Twelfth Night, York assured his Duchess. He swung into the saddle; the iron gate rattled up; with a trumpet flare, a stiff square Standard, the Maltese Falcon in gold fetterlock, with six White Roses, the company jingled over the bridge.

"I'll bring him safely home, Milady!" Harrow cried, waving his cap.

Safely home! Suddenly empty, alone in the immense sky, Duchess Cecily stared. A cold wind passed over her.

They broke camp on the morning of December 27th; and the mighty company began to roll south, Clifford's mounted Dragons in the van. Past greenrobed conifers, bleak dales, frozen brooks, into sleek Norman England, England of the conqueror's pirate hoard. She was Captain Margaret now and she rode beside the White Swan (the Standard of Agincourt) with Andrew Trollope and two hundred men-at-arms with the Swan on breast and sleeve. She led her bright avengers into the land that had cast her out.

Trollope, lean-jawed sleepless turncoat, loving glory as he did Margaret, strategist of old unhappy wars—Master Andrew had a plan. But it was Margaret who made the Army Council accept Trollope's plan. Only Clifford, haunted by his father's voice, had backed this baseborn genius of aristocratic war. Northumberland, Somerset, Devonshire, and Exeter all favored a waiting game; let York make the first move. Who ever heard of campaigning in the terrible Northern winter? While the others argued and temporized, Clifford talked war. Did he not perceive the secret of their quest: vengeance and death?

Margaret was thirty; she had cast off the dream of a complete woman in the Provençal legend—a golden kingdom where like Eleanor of old she inspired poets and painters, gleamed amid Courts of Love and Beauty. That woman was dead, or had never been. Out of madness and grief, out of the pageant of her reign, had come the woman who had learned to hate. As in earlier days, when she had exchanged sonnets with Suffolk, inspired Talbot to magical creations of art, discussed with Alice Chaucer foundations to faith and learning, now in the iron December of her monarchy she discovered others to her purpose—deathmakers, men of blood.

On December 30th, the Army of Lancaster reached Pontefract. Sendal Castle, crag-perching lair of the Falcon, was a few miles away. Clifford's Dragons went into action. Through the iron glades, under the black and dripping branches of the Forest of Galtres, rode horsemen of the Redwinged Wyvern, at their head a young lord with smouldering eyes.

Sendal brooded two hundred feet above Calder plain, the horn-shaped river and market village of Wakefield. Defying direct assault, rock-lonely in a screaming wind, Sendal displayed sheer granite at every point save the south, where a postern gate opened on a natural ramp of declining ground.* Within the gates, storehouses were sufficient only for the normal garrison of a few hundred archers and men-at-arms. To provision the Duke's four thousand, constant foraging was necessary.

Clifford's mission was to intercept a foraging party and draw out the Duke.

Richard of York was in the midst of dinner. He had kept an old-time Christmas, a northern Christmas, with yule logs, mugs of steaming brandy, a gallery of joyous waits, 'God rest ye merry, Gentlemen; let nothing you dismay!' Abruptly, as in a masque or disguising of doom, Death upthrust an ashy face at the board. York heard the

---

* Demolished by Cromwell, the Castle is reduced to a jagged projection of what appears to be the wall of a strange massive cloister; while a little way off, like a ruined tooth, is the broken base of a tower. Sir Clement Markham claimed in his *Richard III* to have discovered a plan of the Castle, which he reproduced, and from this plan I have taken the southern postern, that in any case conforms to the lay-out of the present terrain.

harbinger's shriek—and purpled. That the French bitch dared! He
roared commands.

Davy Hall, who had been with the Duke in Normandy, advised
caution. They did not know Lancaster's strength. An army under
Edward of March, the Duke's eldest son, was on the way from Wales;
Sendal could hold out on short rations a fortnight, ample time for
relief. Caution was the last word that Richard of York desired to hear.
"Oh, Davy! Hast thou loved me so long and now would see me dishonoured? Thou never saw me keep fortress when I was Regent in
Normandy and the Dolphin with all his power came to siege me, but
like a man and not like a bird in a cage, I issued and fought with mine
enemies, to their loss ever and to mine honour. Would thou that for
dread of a scolding woman I should shut my gates?" *

Andrew Trollope had correctly gauged Richard of York.

By two o'clock, York had marshalled. The Falcon Company, four
thousand strong, marched out the south gate. On Calder plain, Clifford
had slaughtered the foragers and set ablaze their waggons; now he
formed his troop across the moor, backs to the river and the Bridge
of Nine Arches. On York came, clanking over the iron ground, the
afternoon lowering into dusk, snow falling. In that pale winter light,
he glimpsed the shaggy rank of northern ponies, grey glint of steel
and snowmantled horsemen of the Dragon; and here and there,
clumps of bootless dead.

York's archers notched their shafts.

With the hissing greygoose feather, the clothyard arrow of English
yeomen, this strange white battle joined; and the Falcon swooped.
Outnumbered, Clifford's troop fell back, toward the black river; dying
and listening, Rolands at the bridge, for Margaret's trumpets. Lancaster was coming, through tree-hung frozen lanes, soldiers of the
wind, lean, ragged, fed on pease and black bread—they were shouting
and singing (aye, long long they would remember and tell of Wakefield, that iron glory beside the Bridge).

And with them rode their Lady of Snows, their Queen of fire and
ice, on a silver jennet given her by the Queen of Scotland, and wearing a long black habit and black bonnet with a silver plume. She

* As Edward Hall, a descendant of Davy, tells the story in his *Chronicle,* ed. 1809.
Hall has been much blamed for misstating Rutland's age, but this is almost certainly a copyist's error, as he refers to Rutland as "a fair gentleman and maiden-
like person"—which would mean a youth, and not a child.

longed for armour and a sword, a Maid of Lancaster redeeming her bloodred Rose. Jealous, wary, her lords wanted no Jeanne. But she was their Captain, their mortal Margaret. The Lancastrians swirled from the wood, onto the snowy plain and the masses locked in bloody rage before the Bridge.

Four o'clock.

In twenty minutes, the Falcon Company—overpowered five to one —was surrounded, cut off, beaten to earth. They who had flared from Ireland to the North now bled beneath the Hawk. No quarter—there would never be quarter again!—only the slow red dying in the trampled snow.

Here cracked a noble Neville heart; here gasped the last of the great accursed House of Mortimer; here, before a mound of dead, stretched Salisbury and Harrow, the London mercer. And nearhand, Duke Richard—rash sunsoaring Falcon crowned in blood—and devoted Davy Hall, who had foreseen this dread twilight.

At the Bridge of Nine Arches, Clifford's Dragons had caught young Edmund crying snowhooded and with a broken sword toward Market Wakefield. "Spare him!" a squire begged. "For he is a Prince's son, and may do you good hereafter."

But Clifford knew; and nothing under the frozen sky might do John Clifford so much good as the blood of a lioncel of York. He leaped at Edmund, shouting, "Thy father slew mine; and so will I do to thee and to all thy kin!"

Darkness on the ruined field, the icy dead, the snow, the soft the secret snow. Darkness and manes of bloody torchlight, the haut pale lovely face beneath the black bonnet, the little party of lords now approaching. . . .

A gift for our Lady, for our Queen of fire and ice—the head of Richard of York upon a pole. She stared at those glazed wide eyes, the wreath of frozen blood about the brows, the crown of paper— stared and drank deep of vengeance. She shuddered; shrieks of laughter stained the night.

"Hail, King Richard! Hail, Lord without rule!"

Darkness, snow falling on three thousand huddled bodies; in the west, iron hills hurled into a massive sky and down the icy edges of the night—far off, mad and broken—echoed the howling of wolves. And: another gift for our Lady. Longlocked goldenred hair, sweet murdered face—Edmund. In the crimson light, flickering and glowing on that head, the woman in black gazed and shrank; she turned, shivering . . . Above the silver jennet the pale face and rigid eyes, the magnificent column of the throat . . . oh gentle sirs! had there been another day, another Monarchy, another woman, tender, visionary, to whom someone had presented, not a gory head on a pole, but a beautiful book? And that someone now dead, that lady dead, too —and the book all covered with blood.

LANCASTRIAN military headquarters was established at York. The old temporary headquarters at gloomy ghostridden Pontefract, haunted by the shrieks of Richard the Second, were now insufficient for the mighty rally of the Rose.

Ancient many-spired York! Roman capital Ebor, then Northumbrian citadel, now a bustling thriving mart of 20,000 with huge lime-white walls of Tadcaster stone pierced by four giant barbicans: Monk, Bootham, Walmgate, Mickle. And of these, the highest and southernmost, Mickle Bar, "the Great Gate," bore a row of rotting heads, Richard Duke of York, Edmund of Rutland, Old Salisbury, Sir Thomas Neville, Sir John Harington, and five other Yorkist knights. "Let York look down on York!"

Vengeance of Margaret.

Wakefield had been her battle; hers, the vision and the victory; hers, the snowmantled terror. Wakefield had forged the soul of Lancaster. At the improvised chancellery in St. Mary's Abbey, presided over by Sir John Fortescue, Justiciar and author of the erudite work *The Governance of England,* and Dr. John Morton, a rising ecclesiast whose career was at last beginning to move after twenty years of Chancery nibs (and who, twenty-five years after, would preside in oddly similar circumstances over another Lancastrian chancellery in Paris), the business of organizing and maintaining the immense forces now massing demanded constant attention. Wakefield had illumined the northern sky like a comet of blue and white flame. Scores of volunteers were coming in every day, in old leather jackets and broken shoes, carrying rusty billhooks. A riotous contingent arrived from Scotland. On the march of Wales, a company of Welsh with Irish kerns and a few Bretons picked up God knows where, devoured the countryside under Owen and Jasper Tudor and the bonny Earl of Wiltshire, Jamie Butler. They were expected to rendezvous with the northern

Lancastrians. The losses of the Dragon troop—the only serious casualties of Margaret's army—were more than made good by two full-strength cavalry Standards from Devon and Lancashire, under Sir Baldwin Fulford and his son Thomas, and Sir John Grey of Groby, the husband of the Queen's lady, Elizabeth Woodeville.

The city of York doubled its contribution: "and to ther grete charges and costs not oonely sent unto the battell of Wakefield cccc armed and wel-arrayed men to doo hyme service, conveing afterward *the Quene grace there being,* and the famous prince Edward ther sonne, unto the battell of Saint Albones, with othr cccc of like men to th' assistance of ther soverain lord, but as wel after the same feld kepid his grace and the said Quene and prince and other lords and true ligemen at all tymes during ther pleasour within your said citie, releving them with vittals and other goods to the uttermost of ther powers. . . ." *

Eight hundred men out of a population of 20,000 was a very handsome offering; exactly ten times what the city gave its 'Crumplin' Dick'— His Sovereign Majesty King Richard the Third—for the fiasco at Bosworth.

As she had played a leading role in the war councils of November at York, setting the stage for Wakefield, Margaret now became the ruling spirit of the January debates. The Queen longed to create a triple entente with France and Scotland, rightly judging that permanent occupancy of the throne depended on strong alliances abroad. Though she could not at present meet either Scottish or French terms (Berwick and Calais), Margaret kept the negotiations simmering, a marriage project between Prince Edward and the infant daughter of Margaret's high-living Flemish friend at Perth. In England, Margaret's political objective was to march on London and deliver King Henry; this was a simple program that everyone could agree on, but beyond this the political horizon was vague. The House of York had become facile in propaganda appeals to the Nation, proclamations and speeches setting forth a platform of detailed reforms; Lancaster had no platform and issued no proclamations. The Lancastrian coalition of English gentlemen, moss troopers of the March, Scots, Irish, Welsh, and Bretons might well have broken up over a specific program; broad indisputable objectives insured unity for the working day. The real

---

* Davies, *York Records,* Appendix, p. 129. Italics are mine; the passage affords evidence of Margaret's presence at the battle of Wakefield.

problem would be what to do when London had been retaken and Henry had been restored.

However, the immediate question before Margaret and the Council was how to feed their huge array, more than 30,000 in a sprawling squatter's camp on the Knavesmire, outside the walls of York. Many of these ragged recruits had never worn shoes, but a kind of wooden sandal with a leather thong; many of them wore fleecy coats of ill-cured sheepskin and the camp stank for miles around; many had strange fur bonnets and caps of foxtails. They hardly ever washed; their garbage disposal notions were simply to throw everything into a malodorous pile beside their tents. The irritating and offensive task of policing the camp, to prevent a serious outbreak of plague, had begun seriously to worry Mayor John Thrisk and the members of the York Corporation.*

Hints became broader that York would like to see their locust-plague of Lancastrians move on; not less, one may suppose, because many of these fur-bearing yokels had taken to raiding henhouses and smoke-rooms with their huge delicious hams and sides of beef round about the Riding. But Margaret as usual had no money. She had, how-ever, a terrifying army at her back; she was very much a going concern and she could have borrowed in the money marts of Belgium or Italy at the usual twelve per cent. But this would take time; valuable weeks of travel and negotiation. And meanwhile the soldiers of the Queen were increasingly turbulent and talking of forays on their own in the southern shires. The York Corporation shelled out Margaret's expenses at York; gave 800 men 'defensably arrayed' to her army; and begged the Queen to remove the menace to health and to property outside their walls.

Margaret knew very well the quality of her army. The Duke of York and Jack Cade had taught her the frightening power of the dispossessed. From her lodgings at the Abbot's House near Bootham Bar, it was but a small distance to the wild and almost continually drunken camp of her army. Her periodic appearances in her black riding habit and her black chaperon with the silver plume, her Herald *Lorraine* and a trumpeter beside her, set off torrential demonstrations. They called her 'Captain Margaret'; and vowed to die for her. And, poor lads—most of them did.

---

* This was no idle fear. In the great plague of 1351, York lost almost 3000 citi-zens in less than two years.

Margaret came to a crucial decision. Her army would "live off the country." Morton and Fortescue protested, pointing out the political consequences. The rest of the Council was split, the Northern lords, the Earl of Northumberland, senior field commander, Welles, Dacres and Clifford going along with Margaret; while the Duke of Somerset and the Earl of Devonshire, both of whom had extensive properties in the south, were opposed to a Mongol raid. But the Queen's proposal prevailed, because no one could think of an alternative.

On January 20th, the huge fire-breathing dragon got on the move. The lords proposed to drive straight down the Great North Road, from York to London. Master Andrew Trollope had a somewhat different idea, but it was not possible to develop Trollope's scheme until the Council knew what Warwick would do. Captains and soldiers looked forward to a golden piracy in the south.

Not often did English folk behold a Queen leading men to battle; the last had been Isabel the She-wolf of France, almost 150 years ago. The novelty of the occasion, the sudden limpid stroke of January sun in the midst of the worst winter of the century, jammed the casements and rooftops along the line of march. Queen Margaret and her escort rode from the Guildhall, a magnificent new building dedicated in 1460, with tiled floors, great windows of painted glass, and a fanwork ceiling of oak. Mayor John Thrisk, Recorder Guy Fairfax, and the members of the Corporation bade Godspeed to the Queen of England.

The cavalcade passed down Coney Street, through cheering and wonder; into Spurriergate (the haunt of spur-makers) to the intersection of High Ousegate, turning right at St. Michael's Church and proceeding down Low Ousegate to the bridge, six arches and eighteen feet wide, with a two-story common gaol, an upper prison and a lower prison level with the river in whose dank greenish air the inmates perished in three days. On the roof of the upper prison projected the blackened heads and parboiled quarters of offenders against royal justice.

The January sun gleamed on Margaret's bright hair. In black and silver she came, riding her silver jennet with white-enameled marguerites on bridle and martingale—proud, gleaming, incredibly regal. And beside her rode Prince Edward in black and crimson with the Swan on his breast, sitting his pony like a soldier. And then, Margaret's trumpet-banner in an azure mantle; her Standard, a stiff square of goldsilk tissue bearing the White Swan and six Red Roses; and *Lorraine,* the Queen's Herald, decked in the arms of England and of Anjou, the

Leopards and the Lilies, and for Anjou an azure field sewn with gold fleur-de-lys and bordered in gules. And after, rank on flashing rank, the iron guard of the Swan, the sworn two hundred, jingling through ancient York. The air glistened with valour, gold and steel and the lovely bright-haired Queen, the royal boy, the Herald on his coal-black horse, cara-coling with silver rosettes at the black ears, the blaze of trumpets.

Down broad Micklegate to the great Bar and twelve-daggerd port-cullis, where the city watch in buff coats with the badge of York on breast and back presented arms. The Prince of Lancaster glanced up-ward.

"What are those black things upon the Bar, Madame Marguerite?"

"They are the heads of wicked men, my son."

(*Marry, sirs, now looks he like a king!*)

"What did they do, Madame Marguerite?"

"They betrayed you, my son."

Blackbrowed Warwick and the boyish giant Edward of York grap-pled with disaster. Rumour had made exultant devils of the victors, with Margaret playing a kind of Salome role. Richard of York had been captive on the field—so ran the brut—and put for mockery on a molehill, his brows dishonoured by a paper crown. Edmund's bloody head had been paraded on a pole; and when old York began to sob, Margaret with a fiendish laugh had dipped a napkin in Edmund's blood and handed it to the father wherewith to dry his tears. She had then danced about the molehill.* None of this was remotely true; but Margaret as an image of terror had acquired such currency with the men of the south that they believed every word.

At Baynard, torchlit conclaves with Duchess Cecily resulted in an appeal to the manhood of the whole south, a levy *en masse*. Margaret was proclaimed a usurper, her son an adultered bastard, and the north-ern lords mere pirates. The House of York was of true ancient stock, defending English right.

* Precisely the way Shakespeare depicts Margaret in *Henry the Sixth, Part Three*. A German scholar has traced the evolution of the severed head as an Elizabethan stage prop from the John the Baptist head on a silver charger of medieval mystery plays. Thus, the stage direction of *Henry the Sixth, Part Two*, IV: Enter Margaret, fondling and kissing Suffolk's head—"Here may his head lie, upon my throbbing breast." Or the wildly apocryphal scene after First St. Albans in which Richard bursts in with Somerset's head, rolling it across the stage like a basketball and shouting "Speak thou for me, and tell them what I did!" Vide: Schucking's *Character Problems in Shakespeare's Plays*.

No one bothered to consider that York had as much admixture of
alien blood as Lancaster; * that if Edward of Lancaster was a bastard,
he was at least of royal Beaufort descent; that the dead Duke had raised
up a menace to old right as alarming as Margaret's in the Jack Cade
rebellion. Recruits poured in. Warwick and Edward were able to organize two armies—one to resist the northern Lancastrians and to deal with
the western army, in Wales. The commanders of the White Rose had
the advantage of interior lines; they could bring the lesser foe, Butler
and the Tudors, to battle first. Edward, who was already at Gloucester,
threw an army of eleven thousand across the Lancastrian line of march.
On February 2nd, the Vigil of the Purification of the Virgin, at nine
o'clock in the morning, the orphaned heir of York fought the battle
of Mortimer's Cross, in Hereford. Like Constantine at the Milvian
Bridge, Edward attacked under a heavenly sign: the parhelion, an
atmospheric trick seeming to display three suns—at once interpreted
as a sign of the three brothers of the Sunne.**

Lancaster's army of eight thousand was wiped out. In the rout, Jasper
Tudor managed a getaway, while the bonny Earl of Wiltshire, like the
Duke of Plazzatora, was first of all his corps-a—from the field! Poor
old Owen, either through negligence or some hitherto well-concealed
martial ardor, got himself captured. He was not, however, greatly
worried. The man who had charmed his way into a royal Valois bed
believed he could charm the heir of York into a pardon. He little knew
the ruthless nature of the redgold godlike being who held summary
court on him at Hereford. Edward had a father and a brother to avenge;
besides, he had never liked this pushing Welshman. Even when he
stood in his doublet at Hereford Market Cross, before a crowd on
tiptoe, the curly-haired Owen "trusted on pardon and grace till the
collar of his red velvet doublet was ripped off. Then he said: 'That
head shall lie on the stock that was wont to lie on Queen Katherine's
lap.' " Oh, he was always himself, incorrigibly vain in the throat of
eternity.

But the conceited charmer was not forgot. The handsome head was
set "upon the highest grice of the market cross, and a mad woman

* The House of York was of direct descent from Peter the Cruel, by Isabella, second
daughter to the Cruel and wife to Edmund of Langley, first Duke of York. Richard III was great great grandson of Peter the Cruel.
** As noted elsewhere in this work, "Richard the Third," the two younger brothers,
George and Richard, had been sent to Utrecht for their safety, by Duchess Cecily.

combed his hair and washed away the blood from his face, and she got candles and set about him, burning, more than a hundred." *

While Edward at one blow destroyed Lancaster in the west, Warwick around London had a far more corrosive task. He had to defend against victorious Lancaster of the North, a mighty company flooding a paralysed countryside, sacking and burning. Below the river Trent was enemy territory for the Queen's men, a naked garden of spoils. As the red glow of Margaret's passing flared like Judgement on the horizon, the shires sent desperate appeals to Warwick. But the Earl could not unguard London; at most, he agreed to incorporate the ancient Abbey and town of St. Albans in his defense. Abbot Whethamstede and Henry himself—appalled by reports of his wife's following—had begged Warwick to save St. Albans, the shrine of Alban, the first martyr of Britain.

Warwick was an excellent soldier, but he was not at all the same type of commander as Edward. His sea victories in the Channel were models of dash and valour, brilliant improvisations against a superior but unwary foe. However, when it came to fighting on land, Warwick, with the single exception of his fiery sortie at first St. Albans, favoured a strategy of massive defense. Warwick hated casualties, whereas Edward was quite prepared to leave half his army on the field if only he might gain the victory. Warwick had a vital and quite modern understanding of logistics, looking after the food and drink of his men, transporting his artillery, keeping open his supply lines. Neither Edward nor his father paid any attention to this aspect of military strategy; and in fact it had been Duke Richard's improvidence in this regard that had forced him to fight the battle of Wakefield against vastly superior odds and all but destroyed the cause of York.

At second St. Albans, Warwick's over-all strategy was simple: to bar the way to London. He rightly judged that if he could administer a decisive check to this discordant horde, it would begin to break up from frustration and lack of discipline. The remnants could then be mopped up by Warwick and Edward, in conjunction. It was a strategy eminently sound and in accord with political and military realities. There were, however, two drawbacks. The tactical alignment forced on Warwick at St. Albans was ill-advised; more significantly, the other side possessed two tacticians with military ideas approaching genius,

* Gregory's *Chronicle*.

Andrew Trollope and Margaret herself, who refused to play the game of war as kings and knights had for centuries played it.

The cathedral town of St. Albans perched on the nether spur of a steep rise, the Hadley-Barnet plateau which at its highest elevation, Barnet itself, three miles south, reached an eminence of four hundred feet above sea level—the greatest elevation for miles around. Beyond the town, the ground was a patchwork of uncultivated fields and wood, broken by dykes and hedges. Beech Bottom, an ancient ditch, very deep, interposed a barrier for about a quarter mile between the town and an army approaching from the north. The Benedictine monastery of St. Albans was well down the rise, southwest of the town, near the river Ver and the ruins of the old Roman Verulamium.

On Monday, February 16th, the day before Shrove Tuesday, Warwick marshalled on this dispersed and ragged terrain. His total front extended almost five miles, from the town ditch on the west through Barnard's Heath and a wild tract called no-man's-land on the northeast. The Earl had upwards of twenty-five thousand men, hastily assembled and by no means perfectly integrated. They ranged from Warwick's own Household array in trim white and crimson, to men of Suffolk and Norfolk bearing badges of the Ape-clog and White Lyon, to Kentish volunteers in any old outfit, and to Londoners in the city livery of blue. London, indeed, had been generous: and after the rout of Wakefield had given the cause of York an additional 2000 marks. The army was distributed thus: a strong company of Warwick archers in the town, anchoring the left flank; heavy detachments lining Beech Bottom and forming a massive centre; a very elongated right wing, sprawling over the countryside and split into small units, defending isolated hedges, hillocks, and patches of scrub.

This was a very modern conception of troop dispersal, depending on excellent staff work and efficient communications. In neither was Warwick fortunate. His principal assistants were his brother John Neville, the Marquess of Montague, a brave man but one who had a fatal inability to make up his mind; the aging ailing querulous Duke of Norfolk; the young untried Duke of Suffolk; and Harry Lovelace, a captain of Warwick's own Household, who had been put in charge of Kentish companies on the right wing.* Warwick's intelligence reports

---

* It is stated in Flenley's *Chronicle* that when York went north in December, he took "one Lovelace, a gentleman of Kent, with great ordnance of guns and other stuffs of war." Lovelace may have been at Wakefield; but the tale, as

served him poorly. Of the scouts or 'prickers' that the Earl sent out to advise him of the Queen's movements on this crucial day, "the prickers came not home to bring no tyding howe nigh that the Quene was, save one came and sayd she was IX myle off . . ."

But this one that returned, though his information as to distance was approximate enough, failed to advise the Earl of the vital news that the Northern army had turned off the Great North Road and was now at Dunstable and poised on the Watling Street, or alternative Roman road to London. Lieutenant Poynings and his two hundred men of the White Rose, whom Warwick had stationed as an advance guard in Dunstable, could have informed the Earl; but Poynings was dead and his whole band either slain or in irons. So well did the Lancastrians keep the secret of their strategy.

At sundown on February 16th, Warwick's field intelligence added up thus: the huge disorderly array of the Queen was about a day's march off on the Great North Road; Margaret would certainly halt for the night, to rest and refresh her men; Warwick could expect a direct frontal assault sometime in the late afternoon of Shrove Tuesday. When he went to bed at Yorkist headquarters at Sandridge, three miles outside St. Albans, Warwick could feel additional assurance in the ingenious surprises he had prepared for his foes, inventions which demonstrated how well-equipped the Earl was to refight Poitiers or Agincourt—assuming the oncoming army was willing to wage that kind of battle. Always strong on artillery, Warwick had brought along every bombard, culverin and falconet he could lay his hands on; he had hired hand-gonne men from Burgundy; his front was mined with caltrops and nets of cord with upright nails.* Movable lattices with steel barbs protected the gaps on the right wing; the bombardiers, besides their guns, were provided with short-range devices that fired flaming arrows with great heads of iron, while they—for greater protection—stood behind large shields loop-holed for firing and bristling with spikes. In case of retreat, the bombardiers might cast down these shields before them, spikes upright.

One cannot but admire the ingenuity that improvised this formidable

retailed by Waurin, that he was captured and then sent to Warwick to betray the Earl sounds like moonshine.

* Vide Gregory's *Chronicle*. A caltrop was a steel ball with five or six razor-sharp projections, so positioned that however the ball fell (and one may assume that on occasion the caltrop was employed as a grenade and thrown before an oncoming assault) at least one dagger was upright.

defense in a matter of weeks. But Warwick's Maginot Line, like the more elaborate constructions of later times, suffered from one fundamental deficiency: the enemy would not behave as he was presumed to do. One could bar the Great North Road, assuming the foe was on that road and preparing to deliver a frontal assault. But: what if Margaret and her men took another route? What if all strategic bets were off, because the opposing commander was a woman and had original ideas of her own?

❖ ❖ ❖ ❖ ❖

FIRE AND ICE. . . .

Margaret had known men would be killed; she had understood blood would be her portion. She was God's angry woman whom life had denied. Her love must ever be furtive, half-realized, furiously disavowed. She had found another, fierce satisfaction: blood-hate. But Wakefield had made Margaret pause. Was she this terrible being, who had murdered the blood royal of England and had gloried in the deed? Was she this woman, without pity and without love—as her enemies charged? Ashes of Vengeance—and a dead Falcon. What was there about death that made the dead so much more vital than the living? For she saw now, always with her, blooded, gazing and real, the slain. It was no use—at least it was no use to her—to protest that they had been rebels in arms, traitors; that they had stabbed her friends, dishonoured her name, driven her half-mad. She was the nervous knife-edged kind of woman who was torn to bits by her own cruelty; she was eloquent in cruelty, but she could not endure the punishment to her nerves.

Sacred Virgin! If by a word of hers, she might restore to life young Edmund of York, she would cry that word. She had never desired his death (but why then did she allow his head to be displayed on Mickle Bar?). She had not wanted this terror, this frightfulness (why then had she taken up arms?). She had not wished that her name be a knell of dread over half England (why then turn loose a horde of brigands on her subjects?).

These questions that tantalized her and made her frantic were unanswerable. The only recourse was action; but action increased her dilemma, provoked new, more appalling questions. She took to glossing over Wakefield, even implying that she had not been there at all and that John Clifford was responsible. In a sense he *was* responsible, for his hatred and his nerves were even worse than hers. Presumably, a

man can exist for death as well as for life; from the first, Clifford had
probed the essential meaning of the war. He cared nothing for political
programs, even the future of Lancaster. The whole aim—for Clifford—
was vengeance and death.

Margaret was deeply disturbed; yet sympathetic. She perceived the
madness that infected Clifford, the need to kill; but she knew, too, that
Clifford was disinterested, as no one else about her was. He was not
seeking titles or manors; the war itself was his opportunity. To kill the
persons who had struck down his father. While others schemed and
maneuvered for power, here was Clifford, stainless, incorruptible—
shining with death.

And Margaret would need such ironshod fury for the work ahead.
Warwick, she hated with all her heart. Warwick had publicly branded
her an adulteress and sealed the sign of bastardy on Edward, her son.
Warwick had contrived the insulting bargain with King Henry. And
Warwick was the most dangerous of her foes; the shrewdest and most
loved by the commons. Warwick must be destroyed.

With 'Grand Captain' Andrew Trollope, whose strategy at Wakefield
had been so brilliantly right, Margaret devised a new attack. Trollope,
she had never altogether understood. What did he want? He had been
a Warwick man, adjutant of the Calais garrison. At Ludlow rout,
Trollope had crept across the lines by night, with eight hundred men,
to join Lancaster. York's army had dissolved without striking a blow.
How Warwick had cursed! If ever he laid hands on Master Trollope
or any of the eight hundred who broke their oaths to the Bear—it would
mean impalement.

What might she bestow on him who daily risked a horrible end for
Margaret's sake? She had one reward in her keeping, the only one that
he cared about: herself. Yes, like so many, Trollope had fallen hopelessly in love with the commander-in-chief. But loving her was loving
a flame that shriveled. She knew, better than they; oh far better! what
it meant to love Margaret of Anjou. . . . She came back to the war,
to the army and Warwick skulking behind his barbed tricks at St.
Albans.

At sundown, this Shrove Tuesday eve, this iron Lancastrian Lent,
the trumpets blew. Long northern files surged after the Standards,
sergeants shouting, ordering the march; cavalry swung by, in sallets
and steel jacks, horses' hoofs muffled with straw. Through blinding
tears, Margaret, Captain Margaret, Prince Edward beside her, beheld

the passion of the Rose. Within her breast was a great blazing light, a crescendo of flame.

. . . in Dunstable Cross the dead men lay, row on sabered row, with blue silent mouths. . . .

"The road was a ribbon of moonlight!"

(they came in loneliness and in silver, down the river road and haunted meadows of the moon, a column of glinting armour, horses sculptural in the frozen light: Clifford's Dragons, then Grey's Lancashire horse. Two approaches curled up the rise from the river: George Street and Catharine Lane, both leading into St. Peter's High Street, the main passage of St. Albans. These riders of the moon intended to strike the elaborate defense on the left flank.)

Behind, in the vast granite dark marched the Army of Lancaster, a swinging northern stride, foxtailed caps and curving billhooks making patterns of sorcery in the moonlight. An army of hunters, an army of lean hickory-hard warriors with murder on their minds. They stalked the Earl of Warwick. And with them rode Queen Margaret, shadowy, elusive, hooded, with strands of bright hair escaping in the wind.

At this hour, this strange blood-tryst, Margaret saw before her all the strangeness and terror of her life: the irreparable wound of the bridal night; the white monarchy of love, young Beaufort, the old pleading wonder of Provence, for a moment, a breath of time, an instant only! and then madness and the candles burning for Michaelmas; the men already dead for her, and the great death to come; blood and snow . . . Margaret trembled, biting her lips. About her, in the naked wood, the light made pools and raindrops of silver, sprinkling sallet and breastplate. . . .

At the town barrier, a yell broke the night. Archers of the watch had only time to close the high wooden gate, where the road intersected the town ditch. Shrove dawn glimmered on a furious skirmish, arrows and a confused shriek of steel. Clifford's suddenly assailed Dragons fell back; to counsel by St. Michael's Church, at the curve of the river. Grey's company, a hundred yards down the road, had better luck. At Catharine Lane, the barrier was down, the ditch unguarded. As Grey's men prowled upward in the pale Shrove light, they heard trumpets flaring.

The army of York had been alerted.

But the dismayed Earl of Warwick understood little of what was happening. Up Catharine Lane and into Folly Lane went the Lanca-shire troopers, erupting like ghosts into winding St. Peter's, opposite the Castle Inn on the steps of which, five years before, Edmund Beaufort had bled to death, crying out and calling on Margaret.

"The lords of King Harry's party pycched a fylde and fortefyd it full strong, and lyke unwyse men brake their array and fylde and took another, and before they were all sette a buskyd to batayle (ready for battle), the Quene's party was at hand whythe them in toun of Synt Albones, and then all thynge was to seke and owte of ordyr. . . ." *

Warwick had, in fact, fallen into panic. Roused at Sandridge head-quarters by a dawn alert, Warwick concluded that Lancaster had sud-denly appeared in overwhelming force on his flank; and that he was about to suffer the fate of his father and the Duke of York at Wake-field. He did not know that as yet only Grey's dismounted company was "at hands" with the archers in St. Albans; and that the shock of the surprise might be retrieved by quick support of the archers.

Warwick decided to write off the archers and to abandon the formid-able defense along Beech Bottom, lest the position be turned. He at-tempted what would in any circumstance have been a hazardous ma-neuver, but which in Warwick's plight was a passport to ruin; to with-draw his divisions of the left and center and swing about on an axis diagonal to the previous line, creating a new front.

While Warwick was occupied in demoralizing his hitherto unen-gaged divisions, the archers who might have been the Earl's salvation were allowed to die. Though Grey himself went down, mortally hit, his company triumphed with aid from fresh Standards. By mid-morn-ing, St. Albans was firmly Lancastrian; the Swan and the Rose flaunted from the Clock Tower, in St. Peter's Way. Abbot John Whethamstede, whose horrified gaze had looked down on the first battle of St. Albans from this same Tower, was cloistered in emergency prayers. For days, he had dreaded some such disaster. That Margaret was intensely devout did not allay fear. She had come to punish.

The Queen appeared in St. Albans, with Herald and trumpeter. She had beaten the best; her strategy had destroyed the greatest army York had ever assembled. Already flames were licking Frenchman's Row

---

* Gregory's *Chronicle.* "King Harry's party" was Warwick; the hapless King had been taken to the field, for what purpose is obscure, and had been left in the care of Sir Thomas Kyriel and Lord Bonville.

(where John the Good had been briefly quartered) as Margaret's Herald proclaimed the inviolability of the monastery and Cathedral Chapter. Lancaster's victory must not be sullied. Foxtailed, black with grime, cleaning their sword grooves of blood, the terrible hunters listened and laughed. . . .

Afternoon at St. Albans. . . .

The ragged welt of Warwick's new line thrust one thousand yards diagonally across Barnard's Heath, tilted precariously in the air on the left and intersecting the Great North Road on the right. By herculean efforts, groaning and tugging, guns were dragged up the slope and re-trained; lattices, caltrops, netts were hauled into place. But before the sweating nervous soldiers had done (God's Wounds! had *she* not left three thousand dead at Wakefield?), the cruel wind blew on them; and out of St. Albans poured regiments of long-striding furcapped northern men. And for the first time echoed that strident northern battle yell.

The southerners froze. Men of Sussex, men of Kent, Burgundians in gold and scarlet with the white St. Andrew's Cross, Londoners in City blue, they had not bargained for this. Their captain was a mere boy with no field experience, eighteen-year-old John de la Pole, Duke of Suffolk. But where was Warwick? He could not be everywhere; he had gone to rally and close up the scattered right wing in no-man's-land. All thumbs, terrified into statues by the hoarse murderous screeches, the gaping mouths, the feeling that the very air dripped madness, the Burgundians could not get their guns lighted; and of those that did, the firing pans, ignited too hastily, blew up in their faces. The bombardiers jammed their muzzles, cursed over damp powder and sputtering lights.

The netts and caltrops had a brief success, breaking up the first wild rush, the 'Grand Captain' himself, fighting under the gaze of his Margaret, going down, instep pierced by a barb. But the northern fury was only momentarily halted. The oncoming horde berserked through the mine field, York field pieces going off in all directions. "And ere the gunners could levylle their gonnes, they were busily fighting, and many a gonne of war was ordayned that stode in lytylle avayle or nought . . ." *

They died beside their useless guns; behind their netts, their great

* Gregory's *Chronicle*.

cauls of iron, their bristling spikes. Died; listening for Warwick with tears of rage and longing—why had Warwick left them to perish? "The southern men, who were fiercer at the beginning, were broken very quickly afterwards, and the more quickly because looking back, they saw no one coming up from the main body of the King's army, or preparing to bring them help, whereupon they turned their backs on the northern men and fled. . . ." *

These were the divisions of Northumberland; the wild and drunken Scots; the desperate shirtless of the March—thrown into this afternoon exploit, to triumph with a brilliant flame, in the madness of their on-slaught.

And afterward, Clifford's Dragons. Riding down the fugitives, with lance and belt axe. Wakefield, again. . . .

Warwick rode across the heath, scurryers and banner-guard about him, and straggling after a long column that he had gathered to the support of his new line, digging them out of pockets of resistance all over Barnard's Heath. For, as his position had been turned, his grand pattern of defense no longer had meaning. Warwick had to shore up what hasty barrier he could. The men came reluctantly, their officers arguing with Warwick's pursuivants; ** and some refused to come at all. They felt safer where they were.

It was mid-afternoon, a grey desperate Evensong, with snow sifting down, when Warwick reached the last ridge and bracken of his hasty front; heard the fierce yells, the brazen echoes; saw, as in a far and chilling dream, the scarlet Burgundians lying under the beechwood, the huddled Londoners in blue; and scattered wide the backs of fleeing men. Black brows above black armour, Warwick saw all in a single glare of ruin, instantly and forever.

Haunted and bedeviled by a woman, by a she-wolf who had wrecked his elaborate scheme—how might such things be? For a moment para-lysed, he sat his roan gelding; and even as he gazed there blew upon him the northern battle cry, banners burst amid the bracken, and his own company began to dissolve. Warwick had just time to get away; he could imagine himself on a molehill and Margaret dancing. Break-

---

* Whethamstede's *Register* (trans. from the Latin).

** A military officer with assimilated rank of Herald-at-Arms and a usual function of performing liaison between staff headquarters and various sections of the front. On formal occasions, the pursuivant wore his stiff gold-tissue tabard athwart; that is, with sleeves back and front and principal parts at the sides. It is, I be-lieve, the way the Heralds appeared in *Alice in Wonderland*.

neck he rode, to that last redoubt in no-man's-land, captained by his own Household officer, Harry Lovelace of Kent. For here was a fortress-heart of Warwick valour, six thousand lads of the old devotion, sworn as Trollope had sworn, to die for Warwick; and now in this soul's gaunt February flared that resolve to die here, upon this ruined field, among his men; that was to flare again at Towton and last, in tragic splendour, at Barnet.

For he was to be denied even valour. The redoubt, a bald hillock spearing from the desolate land, had been abandoned, guns spiked, netts hurled aside, and grey descending twilight—the dusk of dishonour. Once more, a trusted officer had hideously betrayed Warwick on the field. Harry Lovelace had deserted to Margaret.

Even now, past all hope, the savage running fight continued; across the wild dusk, five miles and more of terror, the Dragon troop (oh this was war! this was sport!) in a wild sabering chase, swinging belt axes, lancing down with steel shard and long ashwood haft—and the crunch of bone and gristle, the agonized frosthaunted scream as some poor wight was jolted between the shoulder blades by eight inches of barbed steel, as a hunter might spear a beast. The troopers called it 'boar-sticking' and considered it rare sport.

For Warwick, the shame and loneliness, the cruel north blowing on him as he galloped, hunted through the bloodripped twilight, the Lenten terror, in that proud damned spirit an anvil that echoed to the hammer of Roan William's rocking pace, beating out a cry—*Edward! Edward!—the last, the last, the King!*

They brought her, in dignity and in terrible beauty, that pale pock-marked royalty now radiant, to the Abbot's House of St. Albans, while on the heath the killing raged—blood calling to blood across the twi-light—and Clifford crying on the sacred work. Margaret for an instant was the old old Angevin promise fulfilled, the warrior Redeemer, the iron angel . . . She turned out Abbot John Whethamstede and his black monks; and even as she greeted the Lord Henry, laughing and exclaiming in his fond foolish way, *St. John! St. John!* the tall lancet windows of the Abbot's guest house glowed redly.

St. Albans was burning.

While she stood there, embracing the mad laughing being in his "blew gowne, none too clenely kept," the radiant Lancastrian joy burst-ing over her, the name *Margaret* pulsing within her like fierce hot blood, the flames swept over the town, a coronal of blazing light that

peasants saw for miles around and knew Captain Margaret once more
had gained the victory.*

FIRE AND ICE: *and all the season it snowed.* . . .

Margaret was delighted when they brought Lord Bonville and Sir
Thomas Kyriel, guardians of King Henry at St. Albans (he had been
found during the battle under an oak tree, alone, laughing). She knew
them of old; and unfavourably. Bonville was a turncoat; Kyriel, the
captain whose men had stabbed Bishop Adam Moleyns at Portsmouth.

She thought of Edward, administering justice. The boy was eight
years old, exactly one year older than the youngest prince of York,
small wizened Richard. But this heir of England glowed with health;
he had chestnut curls, a strong well-knit frame. He had been cradled
in royalty, in his nursery echoes of pride and doom. Margaret had
taken him about the country, exhibiting him to gaping crowds, teach-
ing him to lisp little speeches as he handed out his badges of the Swan
and Ostrich Feathers. Edward was a favourite even if, as many suspected, he was bastard-born. Whenever Margaret had presented her son
in his livery of black and red, the White Swan of Agincourt on his
breast, recruiting had flourished.

Moved by some demon of Anjou, Margaret had destroyed that innocent image, worth regiments to her cause.

As if to reveal her unsurpassed mastery of symbols of doom—those
heads rotting on Mickle Bar!—she had seated Edward on a tall scrolled
chair, like the Coronation Chair, with Bonville and Kyriel before him.
Manacled and silent they stood, while the harsh light of February
slanted across hawk-nosed faces, the Cavaliers of the Rose. Queen
Margaret like a gorgeous wasp wore black and gold, on her white swell-
ing bosom exposed almost to the nipples a silver crucifix. Edward appeared in purple velvet overlaid with gold mail. The Abbot's Hall was
hung with blue and white, Margaret's bridal colours (on her finger the
blood-drop of her marriage ruby, *when I took the Rose of England*—.)
and the colours of Lancaster as well.

"Fair son, what manner of punishment shall these men before you
suffer?"

* Second St. Albans has been reconstructed from the Chronicles, the writer's own
explorations of the terrain, and the shrewd analysis afforded by Colonel Burne,
in *The Battlefields of England*. Neither biographer of Warwick, C. W. Oman or
P. M. Kendall, give anything but vague general accounts, such as may be found
in any history textbook.

"What have they done, Madame?"

"They have broke their oaths. They have levied war against the King."

"Are they traitors, Madame?"

"They are, my son."

"Then let them have their heads taken off!"

Old Kyriel stared, unbelieving. Twenty years in foreign parts had Tom Kyriel fought for England and his King. He had been one of Bedford's captains. And now: death from the mouth of a child. Kyriel's gaze shifted; to the black and gold Queen, the lovely wasp. Her lips curled; eyes flared.

Kyriel understood. "May God punish them, who taught thee this manner of speech!" he cried to the boy.

They took the two men away.

These executions caused shivers. Patterns, English folk said. First, Wakefield and the Christmas heads; then, the swathe of terror where she passed; now, murder of two honest knights. Death from the mouth of a child. *This boy,* they whispered, *already speaks of naught but vengeance and of cutting off heads.*

Mayor Richard Lee, grocer, took to his bed, pale as a corpse. The Council sent three women, dove-bearing emissaries, to work on Margaret's gentler side, the dowagers of Bedford and of Buckingham, and Lady Scales.

She could not make up her mind. For days she brooded, one moment about to order regiments to the assault, the next to withdraw altogether. Where was the voice of doom, Our Lady of the Snows? Now victory, shining and imminent, victory bright as blood in the sun—and she could not, her magic failed, blood swirled about her. Blood on her lips, on her hands, on her silken gown, flowing in dreams a crimson freshet, as at St. Albans she had heard men speak in horrified tones of Womere, the Woe Water that ran blood for nine days and nine nights, while across the East blazed a great hairy Star, with a flaming tail, and in the frozen air voices cried "Woes! Woes!"

She asked for bread; and London threw her a stone. The supplies and money sent by the Council were stolen at Cripplegate, among the thieves Sir John Wenlock's cook and scullions. Still she held back the thunder; repressed the word that would have hurled 30,000 men against the undermanned defenses.

"She had one poynt of a very woman, for, often tyme, when she was

vehement and fully bent in a matter, she was sodainly, lyke a wether-
cocke, mutable and turnyng." Instead of an all-out effort to crack
London's shield, to punish the insolent City, she sent Sir Baldwin Fulford with 400 Devon light horse to demonstrate about the walls.

She had no 'gonnes,' no siege machinery of any kind. Her famous
foot-cavalry were equipped with only what they might carry or wear on
their backs. She was the goddess of lightning; of the deft mortal thrust.
But now, badgered by Henry and the three women, frightened at her
own terrible fame, she rejected destiny. She promised not to sack the
City (a prospect which had for months beguiled her men); she wrote
in Edward's name a reassuring letter to the Council; * but with all
this useless parley, she lost time—Lancastrian time that would never
come back.

On February 23rd, the seventh day before London and the high tide
of Lancaster, the Council broke off negotiations. Margaret had hesitated overlong. Warwick, whom she had imagined as a Lear upon the
heath, wandering the wold with a few mad companions, had made a
remarkable recovery. He had acquired fresh levies and had joined
victorious Edward of March at Chipping Camden. They entered London, with 12,000 veterans of the White Rose, on February 27th.

Margaret's game was up. Quartered on a countryside smoking with
hate; in London, the Army of York; about her, franc-tireurs killing
and raiding. She had but one course: retreat. To the North, out of
which this host had burst. That long march into legend, that visionary
Kingdom of whiteness and silence—and at the last the Great Death. . . .

Marching! Marching!

Columns of the Rose, winged with terror, ever North, into the grey
polar light, the brief sullen days, the infinite nights. Weeping and
singing, victorious, lost . . . and where they passed, short days ago,
the crackle and hiss of flaming shires. These were Margaret's men,
scoundrels in rags and patches, bits of rotten leather, horses with sores.
Furcapped, shouldering billhooks and claymores. Swarming—suddenly
into frozen light, the winter Kingdom, the light that fell forever on
this striding horde.

In their midst rode Captain Margaret, silver-plumed upon a silver

---

* "God defend that we, rightly and lineally born by descent of the blood royal
to inherit the pre-eminence of this realm, should intend the destruction of that
City that is my lord's greatest treasure and yours . . . And we promise you that
none of you shall be robbed or wronged by any person coming with us." Harleian
MS 543 (Stow's transcription).

horse. She was silent, proud, pale; like Cade of old she had lost her magic. Her men no longer cheered; they gazed at her like baffled dogs, out of hurt reproachful eyes. Why had she failed them? They had loved her so much. Not even Wat Tyler had been loved as Margaret. They had won two fierce battles. They had marched hundreds of miles in their broken boots, to the very gates of London. And she had failed them. At the last instant, she had turned back.

She herself did not know why. But the magic had fled. She was not Jehanne or Yolande, she was just a woman with a sick useless husband, a little boy, and no money. As she rode into the North, the green and silver heart-gleaming North, she remembered the great march across England and the moonlit sorcery of St. Albans. She was haunted by a dead happiness, the red knife of February . . . *oh now you look like Margaret; all this while you were disguised!*

The coronation of blood at Wakefield was now followed by a coronation of popular joy, Warwick's kinging of the dead Duke's son Edward, this redgold giant of York who won battles as he bedded women, carelessly, exuberantly. At Smithfield on March fourth red banners flaunted in the sun, a Neville day for a Neville king, and a London crowd looking for a meal and drink, and crying, "Let us walk in a new vineyard, and let us make a gay garden in the month of March with this fair white rose and herb, the Earl of March." *

Recruiting began immediately, the new-made monarchy gilded by four thousand pounds from London. Ten days after the ceremony at Smithfield, the Army of York, already doubled, marched out Bishopsgate in pursuit of Margaret. Picking up levies on the way, Edward and Warwick surged north. They drew near the host of Lancaster on Friday, March 27th, at the river Aire in Yorkshire.

Margaret's men bivouacked that night on the banks of the Aire, near Pontefract. Clifford had galloped on, to seize the ford at Ferrybridge. He caught Lord Fitzwalter and a small company of York lances at

* This impromptu royalizing of Edward had not the least foundation, in law or practise. Even assuming—a very questionable assumption—that the House of Lancaster had been illegally on the throne for sixty years, it would require acts of Parliament to depose Henry, declare the throne vacant, render null and void the statutes of the Lancastrian kingship. And in theory, at any rate, Parliament had no right to depose a king who refused to abdicate. Warwick's act was strictly extra-legal, a necessity of war, and he knew it.

their evening mess; Clifford sabered them to the last man, it was Wakefield and Dunstable again. But this was the Dragon's last swoop.

Riding back to camp through the moonfrosted dark, silvery gleams
on naked trees, Clifford ran into Falconbridge's cavalry at Castleford.
The horsemen clashed amid the trees and cloisters of the moon, Yorkists wearing white scarfs on the left arm; a wild melee, with shrill
panic of horses, blaze of curses, and the gristle-crunch of steel. By some
hand unknown, Clifford was hit by an arrow in the throat, went over
reeling and gasping.

The Dragon troop, the eyes of Lancaster, was wiped out.*

But this did not greatly affect the lords of the Rose, who had left
Clifford to perish, less than two miles from camp. Their plans were
made. Brushing aside Margaret (a woman's war, forsooth!) and her
stealthy backfence strategy, the lords resolved on a massive frontal
wedge in the good old English style. What was good enough for their
sires and grandsires to smother in was—eftsoons!—good enough for
them. Not all Margaret's pleading and royalty might stir these lords
from their ruinous obsession with masses of armour. They advised
the Queen, indeed, that far from ordering troops and plotting strategy,
she would do well to take her sick husband and her little boy to York
and there abide the victory.

She went; burning. She had won two royal triumphs for the Rose,
and now was put aside. Even Henry Beaufort, commander of forty
thousand men at age twenty-five, even *he* took a tone of masculine
privilege with his mistress and asked her please God to stay in York
and not to make difficulties.

Ah, she knew them, these lords! Their ferocious pride, their cock-
thrusting manhood, their war lust. With jealous hearts, they laid siege
to glory; they would rather die in glory than share a woman's scheme
for victory by unmanly sneak attacks. Sometimes she suspected they
were secretly ashamed of the triumphs that she and her grand captain,
Andrew Trollope, had wrought.

But why did she dread the morrow? Was it Henry? His presence had

* Varying estimates of time are given for Ferrybridge, from Friday eve to Sunday
morning. The action might conceivably have occurred early Saturday morning,
as Colonel Burne has it, but it could not have been later, for the whole tactical
purpose was to secure the crossing of the Aire and prevent York from marshalling
on the further side. The element of surprise and the statement that Fitzwalter's
men were at their meal makes Friday eve most likely.

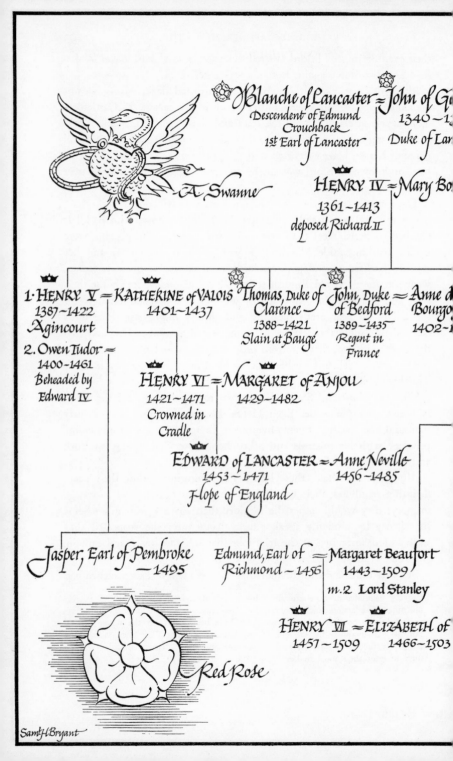

Blanche of Lancaster = John of G[aunt]
Descendent of Edmund
Crouchback
1ˢᵗ Earl of Lancaster
1340~1[...]
Duke of Lan[...]

A Swanne

HENRY IV = Mary Bo[...]
1361~1413
deposed Richard II

1· HENRY V = KATHERINE of VALOIS
1387~1422   1401~1437
Agincourt

Thomas, Duke of
Clarence
1388~1421
Slain at Baugé

John, Duke = Anne d[...]
of Bedford   Bourgo[...]
1389~1435   1402~[...]
Regent in
France

2. Owen Tudor =
1400~1461
Beheaded by
Edward IV

HENRY VI = MARGARET of ANJOU
1421~1471   1429~1482
Crowned in
Cradle

EDWARD of LANCASTER = Anne Neville
1453~1471   1456~1485
Hope of England

Jasper, Earl of Pembroke
—1495

Edmund, Earl of = Margaret Beaufort
Richmond ~1456   1443~1509

m.2 Lord Stanley

HENRY VII = ELIZABETH of [...]
1457~1509   1466~1503

Red Rose

Sam H Bryant

Payn Roët of Hainault

Katherine Roët
m. to Hugh Swynford

~~~~ WRONG SIDE OF BLANKET

⚜ John Beaufort
~1410
legitimatised by Richard II

⚜ Henry Cardinal Beaufort
1380~1447
Evil genius of
Lancaster

...phrey, Good Duke of Gloucester
1391~1447
...rdered at Bury St Edmunds

John, 1st Duke of Somerset
1404~1444

⚜ Edmund 2nd Duke of Somerset
1405~1455

⚜ Henry 3rd Duke of
Somerset
1434~1464
Beheaded at Hexham

⚜ Edmund 4th Duke of
Somerset
1444~1471
Beheaded at Tewkesbury

⚜ John, Earl of Dorset
1450~1471
Slain at
Tewkesbury

...argaret = Humphrey,
Lord Stafford

...nry 2nd Duke of Buckingham
54~1483 · Beheaded by Richard III

👑 = KINGS & QUEENS, PRINCES OF WALES

👑 = Princes of Lancaster

⚜ = Beaufort Line

CHART A
House of Lancaster

always brought defeat. Or was it the memory of that glittering horse-man, now armoured in death, whose sword had flared the way to Lan-caster?

Clifford's death had removed her chief support in the Army Council. Trollope, even with the knighthood that she had persuaded out of Henry for him, could not tell these haughty barons what to do. Only she, the Queen, might do that and she had lost her sway over them by the failure at London. Still she trembled for them, mistaken valiant knights of the Rose. Devon—Dacres—Exeter—Ormonde—Northum-berland—and her Henry Beaufort, 3rd Duke of Somerset; the proud names rang in her heart. How many would she behold again?

Musing on by candlelight, amid the walnut shadows of King's Manor, the glow of leather and brass and the rich glint of silver plate, worthy of the dead Cardinal her friend—and in the shadows, in the old hoarded light, Henry watching, eyes full of dark pain (was he going mad again?), and Edward, restless, bored, pounding up and down on a wooden horse (not nearly so much fun, though, as cutting off heads) —until she thought she would go out of her mind, and knowing all the time that ten miles away her army fought the most terrible battle ever seen in England, and she was not there.

Ferrybridge occurred on Friday eve, March 27th. All next day the masses lumbered into position for the awful shambles; forty thousand Lancastrians wedged onto a narrow plateau between the villages of Saxton and Towton, the right wing tilting on a steep bluff above the river Cock. Across a gulley the horde of York assembled, thirty thou-sand on a stripped ridge opposite Lancaster. But not all the White Rose was up; they listened for Norfolk's trumpets, the tramp of his five thousand Essex men. But Norfolk did not come.

The terrain was perfectly adapted to the kind of battle that both sides intended to fight, the kind for which Warwick had prepared at St. Albans. There was hardly any room at all to maneuver on the high broken ground and both armies could build up a massive frontage, thirty deep, along the narrow ridges. It would be a battle such as might be fought in a butcher shop, between teams of huge panting butchers, armed with maul and cleaver.

Although Henry had forbidden any fighting on Sunday (his sole contribution to Lancastrian strategy), the lords went ahead. They might have done better to heed Henry.

Palm Sunday, March 29th, dawned icily, a stiff southeast wind blowing and overhead a sky that seemed to hurl darkly toward the shivering soldiers. In the gloom, snow fell; at first, tiny flakes whirling in the wind; then, thicker and thicker, a torrent of whiteness.

William Lord Falconbridge, commanding York's advance division, sent his bowmen to harry Lancaster. They moved out to the rim of the dip and fired a single volley at the packed mass on the opposite height. Blinded by the snow that the wind now drove directly into their faces, the Lancastrian archers retaliated with volley after volley. But sly Falconbridge, the little Dragon-slayer, had at once withdrawn his men and Lancaster's shafts fell short. When the fire slackened, Falconbridge ordered another volley; York's archers, shooting with the wind, raked the enemy line. Along the Lancastrian front a few billmen, infuriated by the shooting, death striking from phantasmal bowmen, plunged into the gulley and clawed up toward the invisible enemy. Their numbers grew, without command or trumpet, until suddenly, like a rotten wall, the whole center gave way, rolling in a mad gallop down the ravine.

The line of York loomed a gigantic shadow on the ridge. Neville captains stood beside their Standards, the brothers Richard of Warwick and John Lord Montague, beside the Bear and Ragged Staff and the Dun Bull, their uncle, Falconbridge, beside the Fish Hook. Three-quarters of this host were Neville men, including London's blue-liveried company and the levy of Kent under Robert Horne. The others followed provincial lords rising with the Sunne: Wenlock, Scrope, Stanley, Hastings, Blount—and the traitor Grey de Ruthyn with his ominous Standard of the Black Ragged Staff. And still Norfolk had not come.

At his command post with York's reserve, remembering Mickle Bar, hovered the Nevilles' king, Edward the Fourth. He bestrode a white horse, Warwick bestrode a red. But this battle was no cavalry action. As Lancaster's banners—the Shacklebolt of Percy, the Cresset of Exeter, the Dolphin of Devon—flared from the gulley, trumpets shrilled and masses of York armour floundered toward the foe. They shocked together at the edge of the dip; the monstrous wedges dissolved into small savage clashes, erupting and disappearing in the storm. Nobody knew the colour of the day, who failed, who fled, who triumphed. For each man, the battle became a patch of sloshed and bloody snow. Soldiers slipped in blood.

Because nobody knew, the nightmare had no end. Four times the Lancastrians drove into that white whirling hell, four times iron shrieked as the lines crashed and they locked in mortal wrestle. Inter-

ludes occurred, strange dreamlike pauses while fresh supplies of blood
were hurried to the front. During a lull, Lord Dacres took off his
helmet to drink a cup of water and to confer with Somerset and at
that moment was slain by a crossbolt. Other lords went down. Percy
of Northumberland was dragged off the field bathed in blood; Lord
Welles had his head smashed by a mace; Courtenay of Devon was captured, to be killed after the fight; Jamie Butler of Ormonde made off
at the first onset.

The Army of the Rose fought on. Heroes of the lost, the defeated
and the damned—this bloodsloshed ridge and gulley their final kingdom. In wind and snow, the great death that blew upon them, they
fought on. And in the frenzy grew a wall of bodies, dead or smothering.
The living crawled over the slain, to get at one another.

As Clifford had foreseen, the Rose had become a mystery and a
passion of blood: a terrible altar such as these altars of the dead and
living-dead, a voice continually moaning for blood.

Toward Vespers, on the day of Christ's entry, the Yorkist ridge
was a blaze of steel, shrieks rent the dusk, blood channeled long fur-
rows across the snow. The morning blood had frozen in a crimson
necklace on the white; but the field was laved by fresh outpourings.
Lancaster's weight, that succession of ferocious onslaughts, began to
tell. In a last flare of Captain Margaret, Trollope surged out of a dawn
ambush in Castle Hill wood with his Calais veterans, to assail York's
rear and create a panic amongst the horseholders. The Red Rose was
about to wrest control of the field. Hurled back, dying into fragments of
bone and agony, broken shards of steel, York staggered toward the
chasm.

Warwick galloped up to Edward's command post, where the huge
King stood with his last reserve. He dismounted and drew his sword.
"Fall back! Fall edge! Let him who will void the field. I shall here
resolve our quarrel or perish." Warwick made a dramatic pass at Roan
William, as if to slay the horse. Edward calmed the Earl. The day was
not yet fought, he cried; debonair amid the blood.

And, incredibly, the ruthless young giant was right.

Out of a darkening sky screamed trumpets, in the twilight loomed
banners like phantasms of the dead. Norfolk! Coming hard from
Dintingdale, five thousand Essex men to strike the Lancastrian left
flank. The divisions on the left reeled; fell back on the turmoil of the
center and right. Their captains were dead or useless; but the soldiers

did not break. Fighting front and flank, retreating to a black wind down the vast horror of the evening and naked silence of the dead; once more into the ravine, toward Somerset's Standard, the Portcullis, on the ridge.

Death shone on the soldiers of Lancaster, with a cold and brilliant gleam.

They had nowhere but the river. Doom blazed through that ruined host. They began to pant down the steep slope, to the swirling stream. A flimsy plank crossing was torn to pieces and the maddened horde plunged into the icy water; exhausted, thrashing about in their iron, sinking and piling up a bridge of drowned. Thousands fell on the heights; other thousands weltered on the slope and in the shallow reddening river.

"The Heralds counted 28,000 dead on the field." *

But this did not reckon those who crawled away to die of their hurts in some merciful cottage; nor those pursued and sabered by Lord Falconbridge, as Clifford had been wont to do. More than half the muster of Lancaster perished.

In York, Queen Margaret heard the news, the messenger sweating out the tale on his knees. It had all come true, as her daemon had whispered: the mighty Army out of rags and failure, the blood-passion of the Rose, the redemption and winter glory—and the huge death.

She had only time to saddle; to gallop for Scotland, while York patrols hunted her. With her rode Henry, her son Edward, and five others of whom one was Richard Tunstall, the King's Chamberlain. But where was the forty thousand, the Army of the Rose? The vision that she had conjured from the North, the long-striding terrible heroes of Captain Margaret? Where, in sooth, was Captain Margaret? Where. . . .

these be three silent things: the falling snow, the hour before the dawn, the mouth of one just dead. . . .

---

* Edward's own estimate, in a letter to Proud Cis directly following the battle. *The Hearne Fragment* gives 33,000. Edward's breakdown of his figure is: 8000 Yorkists; 20,000 Lancastrians. Who should know better than one of the commanders on the spot and the man who had the appalling task of shoveling immense grave pits for the bodies left on the field.

✣ III ✣

RICHARD III

Give me my battel axe in myne hand,
Sett the crowne of England upon my head soe high,
For by Him that made both sunne and moone
Kynge of England this day will I dye!

—*Song of the Lady Bessy*

RICHARD III

STOP 299

HE WAS a man full of age and grief before his time. Look upon his portrait, that portrait painted in his thirty-second year of age and first year of kingship. The principal impressions of the lean sunken face are pain and intelligence. Both impressions remarkable for his blood and circumstance.

This sickly undersized boy, the twelfth of thirteen children, was born of a royal line—the Leopard line that during four centuries had been enthroned in the Confessor's Chair at Westminster. The Plantagenets, descending directly from Norman and Angevin, were a haughty race. Warriors, conquerors, rulers, men of iron and battle—the Black Prince, Edward, eldest son of Edward the Third, was the beau ideal, the crystalized perfect Plantagenet. The Black Prince consumed his whole life in war, from his christening of steel at Cressy in 1346, until the desolate end, almost thirty years later, when, shivering and mortally ill, the Heir of England was borne on a litter about the ochre wastes of Andalusia.

This latest Plantagenet was the great great-grandson of Edward the Third, tawny lord of battles; a monarch so proving in his own career the vanity of men and the mortal regality of even Plantagenets that upon his deathbed the raddled body was stripped by the servants, while rings on the stiff arthritic fingers were torn off by pretty Alice Perrers, the old lion's mistress and vicious Lady Meed in the contemporary

203

Vision of Piers Plowman. An experience in all its ashy horror that fell likewise to the Norman sire of all Plantagenets—William, surnamed "the Conqueror," who made a hideous death in Rouen.

But so far was this pale boy from the sobering lessons of earthly monarchy that at his birth—October 2nd, 1452—no fewer than five lives barred him from a throne: his father and three elder brothers of York, and the reigning Lancastrian Henry the Sixth. A sixth bar was soon to be added with the birth of a Prince of the Red Rose, Edward. Further, while the blood of York was of true undoubted right to the Crown, the descendants of Edmund Langley, first Duke of York, had long been supplanted in the succession by the usurping House of Lancaster.* The boy's grandsire, Richard Earl of Cambridge, had been beheaded by Henry the Fifth for aspiring to royalty; and the boy's father had but recently crept from under the disgrace of his sire's attainder to assume his hereditary role as Duke of York and first peer of the Realm.

The newborn prince was christened at Fotheringay Castle, the White Rose citadel in Northampton. The Duke and Duchess of York bestowed upon their youngest the proud old name of "Richard"—the name of two gleaming kings, memorable and tragic.

This: unadorned fact. But there are other accounts of the boy's birth, sinister and dramatic. And so involved was this Richard's career, from the onset, with dark legend that these tales bear hearing.

The portents of October second were ominous. "Scorpio stood in the House of Mars"—denoting a turbulent warlike character. The same chronicler, John Rous, chantry priest of Guy's Cliffe, Warwick, informs us that the boy came into the world "feet foremost." He was "born with teeth"; and with "hair hanging down to his shoulders."

Equipped with this information, that ex-horseholder, ex-propboy, turned genius-poet, has set the stage in his fabulous manner. At the dread birth, "the owl shrieked; the night-crow cried . . . dogs howled and hideous tempest shook down trees . . ." Richard's nephew, the

---

* Of the seven sons of Edward the Third, two—William of Hatfield and William of Windsor, the second and seventh—died young. The House of Lancaster traced its descent from the fourth son, John of Gaunt. York descended on the uterine side from the third son, Lionel, and on the paternal side from the fifth son, Edmund. Further, Richard the Second, deposed and murdered by Henry of Lancaster, had named as his heir Roger Mortimer, son of Philippa, daughter of Lionel; Mortimer was grandsire of Anne Mortimer, the mother of Duke Richard of York.

young Duke of York, proclaimed that his savage uncle could "gnaw a crust at two hours old."

So William Shakespeare, minion of Edward de Vere, Lord Oxford. . . .

But the Prince of York's earliest biographer, Saint Thomas More, aged five at Richard's death, has furnished the most inspired touches. ". . . (he was) little of stature, ill-favoured of limbs, crookbacked, his left shoulder much higher than his right, hard-favoured of visage, and such as in states called 'warlie,' in other men, otherwise; he was malicious, wrathful, envious, and from afore his birth ever forward. It is for truth reported, that the Duchess his mother had so much ado in her travail that she could not be delivered of him uncut; and that he came into the world with the feet forward, as men be born outward, and (as the fame runneth also) not untoothed. . . ."

The saintly authority of More has given the weight of historical fact to pamphleteering; and has, apparently for all time, established the little Prince as a kind of newborn troll. What did Richard really look like? We have three portraits: one in the National Portrait Gallery, one at Hatfield, one in the Royal Collection at Windsor. There are superficial variations, but all three are presumably faithful copies of an original painted during Richard's lifetime.*

The eyes are light brown, flecked with gold; they have a strange piercing quality. Nor is this a stylized effect of the artist. For we have other royal portraits of the time: the three Lancastrian Henrys and Edward the Fourth, whose images convey totally different impressions. Richard's hair is reddish brown, worn long to the shoulders and curling at the ends. The face narrows from a broad thoughtful brow to a sharp chin. The mouth is thinlipped and tight, with a hint of cruelty. The impression is royal; but royalty infused by taut perception, by pain and bitter nights.

In that haunted face is none of the delicate and piteous glance of the sixth Henry, the cold priggishness of the Hero-King of Agincourt, the bold mockery of Edward the Fourth. The last Plantagenet is a being apart, "a dazzling sojourner" in a world of terror and splendour.

---

* My good friend Alexander Clarke, President of the Friends of Richard III, has recently unearthed another in a New York antique shop! I am indebted to Mr. Clarke for the shrewd suggestion that the Lancastrian tradition of the de Vere family, patron of the Bard, played a strong part in Shakespeare's determination to make of Richard the most monstrous villain in all English history.

For the myth of deformity, we have illuminated drawings of Richard that reveal no hint of a twisted body, save for a slight lifting of one shoulder. "Richard liveth yet," had written William of Wyrcestre, as if the bone disease that had seized York's son in its iron clamp were like to take the boy the way of his dead brothers, Henry and William. But Richard survived, with only the physical legacy of the raised shoulder and a slight limp. The ancient Countess of Desmond who lived to the incredible age of one hundred and forty could remember Richard as "the handsomest man in the room" at a dancing party in Edward the Fourth's time. And sturdy Nicholas von Poppelau, a wandering German *ritter* and Richard's house guest in 1484, spoke of his host as "lean, with delicate arms and legs, also a great heart."

But incontrovertible is the evidence of battle. Whatever the bone disease—polio, rickets, a form of meningitis—he had not only come through the ordeal, but had steeled his slender body in arduous exercises of war. At nineteen, Richard became High Constable of England, the chief military officer of the Kingdom. He had to wear eighty-pound plate armour, flourish a heavy sword or battle axe in his right hand and manage a plunging horse with his left hand. No withered hunchback, however malignant, could have performed the blazing exploits of Barnet and Tewkesbury; the expedition against the Bastard of Falconbridge; the final heroism at Bosworth.

But if the physical monster is a legend of Tudor devising, what of the twists in the mind, the hump upon the soul? To discover in what manner truth has been raped and despoiled by Tudors and Italians, it is essential to know something of Richard's time.

Richard, Prince of York, was born three years before the first battle of St. Albans and the outbreak of the merciless conflict of the Roses. Before the boy's eighth year, his father Duke Richard and his elder brother Edmund had been savagely slain at Wakefield and their blood-glazed heads set atop the Mickle Bar of York City, upon the Duke's brow a paper crown. "Let York look down on York!"

It seemed as if the House of York might be wiped out by Marguerite d'Anjou and the victorious Lancastrians. Duchess Cecily sent Richard and George, born at Dublin in 1449, to Utrecht, to the friendly care of Duke Philip the Good of Burgundy. It is likely that the Household tutor of York, Richard Croft, accompanied the boys to ensure that they did not pick up ill habits at the golden pleasure dome of the Duke's Court. Croft, a Herefordshire man, chosen by Duchess Cecily for stern governance, had already laid his harsh discipline on the two elder princes, Edward and Edmund. Relations between these two and Croft had become so strained at Easter, 1454, that the princes had written from Ludlow Castle to their father, complaining of "the odious rule and demeaning of Richard Croft."

A letter that no doubt made Duke Richard's square mustached face crease into a grim smile. . . .

Richard gave Croft little trouble, but George—ah, George! He would slip away, the Courtiers of the Golden Fleece would give him wine and very soon George would be drunk. To make a drunkard of a twelve-year-old boy gave small concern to a Court where the Great Duke himself was nightly carried to his mistress. The ruin of George began with this trip; he became a slave to drink, especially malvoisie wine, the sweet white wine from the Canaries.

Towton! Bloody Towton! This crushing victory of York on Palm Sunday, March 29, 1461, brought home the young exiles. The scourge of Lancaster, nineteen-year-old Edward Duke of York, six feet four inches of gorgeous manhood, was crowned Edward the Fourth in a ceremony at Clerkenwell, outside London, staged by the Earl of Warwick and his Neville relatives. After an orgy of bloodletting, England enjoyed brief uneasy peace. One of the first acts of the new monarch was to create Richard, the Duke of Gloucester, and George, the Duke of Clarence. Previous lords of Gloucester had borne the title to their peril and ruin.* But for the present, glory shone on York and the young Duke. Richard was soon to go as a page in the household of the Earl of Warwick, nephew of Duchess Cecily. Warwick was the mightiest baron in England and the pillar of the new Monarchy.

Few men rise above their age. Henry the Sixth did; but Henry hardly lived in the world at all. Richard had been infused with falcon pride and ambition by his mother, "Proud Cis"—as northern relatives called her. From earliest years, he had heard about life's jewel: a crown. The crown that had belonged of old right to his House of York. The heirs of Richard the Second had waited sixty years to assert their claim. Duke Richard had temporized—fatally. How many times after Wake-

---

* Gilbert de Clare, the "Red Earl" of Gloucester, had fallen at Bannockburn; Thomas Despenser, Earl of Gloucester, had been torn to pieces by the Bristol mob; Thomas of Woodstock, sixth son of Edward the Third and Duke of Gloucester, had been murdered at Calais by order of his nephew Richard the Second; Humphrey, Duke of Gloucester, had been murdered at Bury St. Edmunds by the party of Marguerite d'Anjou.

field had ancestral Fotheringay and Baynard Castle echoed to the bitter lamenting of Proud Cis, who might have been a queen. The painful lesson of opportunity missed, of waiting too long, of being cheated by the scruples of others.

Duke Richard had actually prepared his coronation. He had broken into the royal apartments at Westminster, turning out poor fuddled Henry. He had assumed regal state among the lords of the Yorkist Parliament of October, 1460. The Duke, remarked Whethamstede, "staid not till he came to the chamber where the King and lords used to sit in the parliament time . . . and being there entered, stept up to the throne roiall, laieng his hand upon the cloth of state, seemed as if to take possession of that which was right."

As a special insult to Queen Marguerite, Duke Richard had ordained that October thirteenth, Saint Edward's Day, should be his Coronation Day. October thirteenth was the birthdate of Marguerite's son, Edward.

Warwick intervened. Warwick!

For the first time the tall blackbrowed Earl set his will against the House of York. The eldest of ten children, the grandson of a man who had twenty-two children, this fortune-hunter strangling in a sea of relatives—who was the upstart who ordered England's monarchy after his own desire?

The immense luck of Neville began with the siege of Orléans, that fatal trap which incarcerated so many English hopes save the ambitions of the House of Neville. Before Jeanne the saviour appeared on the scene, the English siegers were commanded by the Montague Earl of Salisbury, who was accustomed to view the beleagured city from a grating of the tower of Tournelles. During one noon lull in operations —and while the captain of the French artillery was off having his lunch—an apprentice bombardier applied match to touch-hole and his shot pierced the grating and tore away the half of Salisbury's face.

This brilliant bit of luck not only disorganized the siege, softening up the English for the later triumphs of the Maid, it made a landless younger son Earl of Salisbury—for the only heir of the slain Earl was a daughter married to a man named Richard Neville. And though this Richard Neville was an Earl's son—Ralph of Westmoreland—he had twenty-one brothers and sisters and his worldly possessions were not large. Suddenly master of the extensive fiefs of his father-in-law, Richard Neville Earl of Salisbury laid the foundation for a spectacular fifteen-

year rise to magnificence on the part of his son, the younger Richard
Neville and the man known to us as "the King-maker."

For the younger Richard was even more blessed than his father. He
had taken to wife Anne Beauchamp, daughter of that knightly Earl of
Warwick, whose English fires had burnt all of Jeanne save her heart.
Earl Richard's son and heir was Henry Beauchamp, a most promising
youth. But—Neville luck held. Henry Beauchamp died suddenly, in
his maying time, aged twenty-three; and throughout England crimson-
jacketed liverymen of Warwick crooked the knee to Richard Neville.

To the new Earl went huge holdings in South Wales and Herefordshire (the old Despenser lands); another block of estates in Gloucester-
shire; the town and castle of Warwick; numerous manors in Worcester-
shire; and scattered manors in sixteen other shires.* And in the fullness
of time, when Salisbury was slain at Wakefield, his son, the Earl of
Warwick, inherited the Montague lands in Wessex and the Castle of
Middleham in Yorkshire.

A man could hardly be blamed for seeing the hand of God in such
bounty.

The psychological heritage was of equal import. The lords of Warwick were fierce and beautiful; even their cruelties were on an exalted
scale. Guy, the "Black Dog of Arden" and murderer of the Gascon
mignon and royal favorite, Piers Gaveston . . . Thomas, the paladin of
Poitiers . . . Richard, courtly warrior and executioner of Jeanne . . .
Henry, sweet perfection of his race, dead at life's golden door, when
summer burned and rooks cried in the corn. . . .

The spirit of these men entered into Richard Neville and he into
them. He became the strong shoulder of England in a ruinous time,
loved by the commons and "those of meaner sort." The lavish hospitality of London's Warwick Inn at Warwick Lane: six whole oxen consumed at the Earl's breakfasts; servings of six hundred at dinner;—"all
the taverns were full of his meat and a man might carry away as much
beef as he could bear on the point of a long dagger."

Red-jackets with the badge of the White Bear and Ragged Staff;
Warwick red-jackets from every shire in England. Glancing about the
feasting, the loyal shouts, the epic fires, the inexhaustible beef, why a
man—any man—might mistake this cheer for royalty, bear himself

* C. W. Oman: *Warwick*. In English Men of Action series.

as a king. He—the architect of glory—he the crownbearer had to save York not only from Queen Marguerite; the magnificent Earl must save York from York.

So did Warwick confront at Westminster this scowling Duke, who had laid brusque hands upon the throne. . . .

The Duke is "leaning against a sideboard. And there were hard words between them, for the Earl told him that neither the lords nor the people would suffer him to strip the King of his crown."

The two lords hover in a suffused oriel light, the oaken light of medieval England, about them hunting tapestries, curtains of gold and blue, cressets of wrought iron upon the wall, highbacked chairs rising in three scrolled fleur de lys. And then: between the Duke in crimson doublet goldbraided with the Falcon and the black-mantled Earl comes this youth, this Edmund of Rutland, who passes briefly, tragically. "The best-disposed lord in this land," men say of Rutland . . . but soon, the winter of Wakefield, the Christmas death. . . .

"Fair sir"—it is Rutland speaking to Warwick—"be not angry, for you know that we have true right to the crown, and that my Lord and Father here must have it."

The royal tone of the youth who, beside the Chapel of Our Lady at the Bridge of Nine Arches, is to fall by Clifford's murderous falchion. Now the other son of York, the bland and jovial Edward Earl of March, seeing their great friend stare and darken, advises Edmund: "Brother, vex no man, for all shall be well."

But—argument has flared. And "the Earl of Warwick would stay no longer when he understood his uncle's intent and went off hastily to his barge, greeting no one as he went save his cousin of March."

Tempers cool. The Duke hesitates—and is lost. He pledges to Warwick's bond with Henry the Sixth: the piteous weakwitted king shall reign during his life; and Richard of York and the heirs of Richard's body shall come after. A covenant that flames with war, that cries publicly the scurrilous York brut of the bastardy of Edward, son of Queen Marguerite. A covenant that leads to the mortal North; to Wakefield. And the only crown the Duke is ever to wear will be a paper crown placed upon the grey severed head by Lord John Clifford—Marguerite's cavalry captain.

❖   ❖   ❖   ❖   ❖

Loyaultie binds me!

Winter, 1460–1461 . . . what images of iron and death blazoned the boy's mind? We do not know. But we may be certain that the Duchess spared her son no more than she spared herself. He knew his father and his brother Edmund had been slain in battle. He knew their heads rotted on Mickle Bar, the highest gate of York City—a gate that he himself had seen when on occasion he had been taken by Master Croft about the splendid town of York.

The boy knew, too, that this cruelty had been wrought by a French-woman—an evil stranger in this England—and that wicked men about the King, whose names he could tell over by heart so oft had he heard them, names like Suffolk, Somerset, Ormonde, had brought this woman from France and married her to the Lord King. And until this woman was dead or sent back to France, there would never be peace or a door secure. The woman had given birth—"whelped" they said at Baynard—to a son after nine barren years with her lord. Reminders of this son —born in October and but a year younger than Richard—made Duchess Cecily crimson; made her cry out "French strumpet!"

He loved his mother, but he was uncomfortable with her; she was so holy, so unrelenting. At Baynard, they had matins every morning at seven; later, Duchess Cecily heard a low Mass in her privy chamber; then they had breakfast and after they went to divine service in the chapel of the Castle. During dinner, the Duchess usually read aloud to the family from some pious work such as the "Lives of the Saints" or "Hilton on Contemplation." At Evensong, they heard low mass in the chapel. At supper, the Duchess discoursed concerning the intent and meaning of the passages read aloud at dinner.

From earliest years, he had been surrounded by God, by prayers and sacred readings. He knew the English saints by heart and his favorite exclamation—the only one his mother allowed him—was "By Holy Paul!" Perhaps if Richard had not been so chained by sickness in his boyhood he would have done as his adored brother Edward, that now kept royal state at Westminster, and would have weaned from family devotions. Edward had escaped early from prayers, but Richard and his older sisters Elizabeth and Margaret, never missed a sermon.

Edward! how Richard longed to be like that kingly brother! Edward's beauty, Edward's courage, Edward's wit—there seemed nothing that Edward did not have. Ah, to be twenty, handsome, victorious—and a king!

The undersized boy—for he grew little after his sickness and even at age twelve stood just under five feet—warmed in Edward's sun. He was not jealous, for how might one be jealous of a god? His own sallow image pleased him little and he gazed not often in the looking-glass. For him, it was enough to be the brother of such a being as Edward; to know that Edward took notice of him; even—it seemed—loved him. In October's bannering scarlet, before Wakefield, the boy had lodged with Mistress Elizabeth Paston in London and his brother Edward, though no man was busier, came every day to see him and give him news.

Loyaltie, that was the boy's banner. Loyalty to York; to Edward; to his mother. He desired nothing so much as to serve. He dreamed of knighthood and a sword—to mold his frail body into the iron likeness of a soldier.

First, page; then, Esquire. Rising with the first light, the boy prepared to serve his lord's voide, or breakfast cup. He took station in the Great Hall of Warwick or Middleham, between credenza and trestle table, bringing ewers, napkins, cups, trenchers, crocks of cheese. He must keep silent, advance and retire quickly, bear the lord's cup on high, held in both hands above the page's head, so that the wine might not be touched by his breath. . . .

Breakfast over, the noble lads of the Household trooped to the tilt-yard. Richard's friends were Robert Percy (distant cousin of the lords of Northumberland) and Francis Lovell. A favorite exercise was that of quintains. From a standing position two squires tilted with long wooden lances, endeavoring by skilfull play of the round leather buffs on the lance heads to upset one another. Or with the same lances they ran at each other on horseback, thrusting across a wooden tilting barrier. It was rugged sport, with constant danger of broken bones or cracked pates.

Next, the toughening of the body to armour. Buckling on back and breast plate; gorget about the throat; pauldons for the shoulders; thigh tassets; loin guards; leg greaves; pointed sollerets for the feet. And though this armour was tempered and sized for a youthful frame, it was no easy trick to wrestle into this cage of iron and to manage a horse and lance.*

* No trace of any armour belonging to Richard has survived. In fact, any complete suits of Fifteenth Century armour are extremely rare. But a few years later, at

Richard worked and sweated, jolting about the tilt-yard. Tears burned in his eyes. What might have been for mighty Edward the merest play was for him an exhausting labour. Only pride, only ambition kept the young Duke of Gloucester on his chosen way of a military career. *stop*

The Warwick dinner, a red-jacketed revel, came at one hour past noon. If the Earl were in residence, squires and pages were constantly busy. And even if he were not, his steward kept open house for red jackets from every shire. Dinner at Middleham, Sheriff Hutton, or Warwick was an object lesson in statecraft.

Little escaped the eye of the sallow limping squire. As his mother "Proud Cis," had imparted to him the gift of eloquence, the moralizing and exalted religious note, so did his mentor Warwick reveal the practical ways by which men's hearts might be won. This lavish public manner, this welding of friendships through gifts and honours, was to mark the kingship of Richard the Third, twenty years later. And as Warwick greatness seeped into his soul during this apprentice time, so arose in that falcon fledgling a strange tenderness for Anne of Warwick.

Born in 1456, Anne Neville could have been no more than ten at this period. She is one of the saddest shyest beings in the gallery of time. It was her fate to be heiress of this vaulting Earl, who had no son. To her and to her elder sister Isabel would pass all these castles and manors, these gorgeous lairs of the Bear. And the meaning of the Bear in the kingship and baronial might of England. Upon this frail brown-eyed Anne would fall the terrifying weight of history.

She stirred the affections of both Richard and Francis Lovell. Her own preference—can it be doubted? For handsome courtly Lovell. The little lame Prince was never one to inflame a girl—save perhaps once. And then love, romantic, dark and ruinous, love of the blood, was mixed inextricably with ambition. Except for this occasion, Richard belonged to his mother; to Proud Cis. He early took on the qualities of the confirmed bachelor: strong and subtle; disdaining and lonely; masterfully self-concentrated. He should love but where ambition lay.

How shocked and bewildered the boy must have been when his idol, when dearest Edward married for love. And married a penniless widow with two half-grown sons and a horde of greedy relatives. Dear God,

---

nineteen, Richard possessed a suit of "white" polished steel which he wore at Barnet and Tewkesbury. It is possible that this handsome armour came from the forges of Flanders, the gift of Philip of Ravenstein, who rode with the White Rose at Barnet.

might a man do worse! Edward's union with Lady Elizabeth Grey, born Woodeville, was the beginning of that fatal rift in the House of York which ultimately would ruin all. This marriage, secretly performed in a New Forest hunting lodge on May 1st, 1464, antagonized Warwick; infuriated Duchess Cecily and Edward's brother George of Clarence.

". . . (Gloucester) She may, Lord Rivers! why, who knows not so? She may do more, sir, than denying that: she may help you to many fair preferments; and then deny her aiding hand therein, and lay those honours on your high desert. What may she not? She may, aye, marry, may she . . . (Rivers) What, marry, may she? . . . (Gloucester) What, marry, may she! marry with a king, a bachelor, a handsome stripling too: I wish your grandam had a worser match. . . ." *

Echoes of indignation reverberating through Baynard Castle and the noble Hall of Middleham. Nor did King Edward's own reaction to the fury improve matters. "Why, by God's Blessed Lady," the young bridegroom quoth in his hearty way, "I that am a bachelor have some children too; and so, for our better comfort, there is proof that neither of us is likely to be barren."

Richard shared the general indignation. He early acquired a contempt for the Widow Grey and all her blood; and never after saw reason to alter his view. Tales stole about on rat's feet that the widow's mother, Jacquetta of Luxembourg, had bewitched the infatuated king. But the real witchery? The blonde treasures of the Widow Grey, treasures temptingly offered—but only with a ring. She said to Edward, with just the effective touch of bland calculation and matronly virtue, "Sire, I am not good enough to be your wife, but too good, I trow, to be your mistress."

An irresistible line with a man who took what he wished from women of all degree.

Richard could never be snared like that. When in the sun and grandeur of Middleham he gazed longingly at Anne Neville, he beheld the richest heiress in England—a glorious prize.

Anne had a price. She was hostage to her father's schemes. Just as Warwick himself had married into greatness, so did he think of Isabel and Anne as negotiable possessions—pearls of great price—in the maneuverings of statecraft. In this, Warwick was most like his age. For anyone with property—or who ever hoped to acquire any—mar-

---

* *Richard the Third;* Act I, Scene 3. This wonderfully expresses the mood of York.

riage had a hard practical core. Love was a golden bird crying in a moondrenched garden, the lost Night of the South . . . Aquitaine! . . . Aquitaine! Marriage was money and politics and land; marriage was an heir. The price of Lady Anne was service to the House of Neville.

It was a price that Richard was not prepared to pay. . . .

❖   ❖   ❖   ❖   ❖

RICHARD, DUKE OF GLOUCESTER was fourteen. In this year of Grace, 1466, he departed forever the Household of Warwick. Already Admiral of England and royal duke, further honours were heaped by a generous brother—the patent of loyalty, York loyalty, at a time when relations with his House were sorely tried. Richard himself had been tempted by Warwick—in what manner remains uncertain—but he had withstood the crafty Earl and cleaved to Edward.*

Richard: created Earl of Richmond; Constable of Corfe. To this burgeoning boy were granted forty-six manors accruing to the Crown through the attainder of John de Vere, Earl of Oxford (who was the victim of the denunciation of his own son Aubrey; and both father and son perished on Edward's scaffold). In addition, young Gloucester received all the castles, manors, and wardships formerly in the holding of the attainted Henry Beaufort, Duke of Somerset. Edward crowned his fraternal benefices by creating his brother a Knight of the Garter in February, 1466. This "Order of the Blue Garter" had been founded by Edward the Third in 1344; some said to commemorate the chaste thighs of the Countess of Salisbury, that the King mightily desired but never achieved. However this may have been, the Blue Garter was part of Edward's revival of the Arthurian Round Table at Windsor; and to attract promising knights to his projected campaigns in France. The Order consisted of forty knights from all Christendom, bound by an oath of personal fealty to Edward the Third, who was also Sovereign of the Garter. Richard was the youngest knight ever to be received into the Blue fellowship; and the solemn ceremony with its oaths, vigils,

---

* George and Richard were "enticed" to Cambridge by Warwick in 1464, the former being then fifteen and the latter twelve. Warwick attempted to make a deal; promising Isabel to George and Anne to Richard. Clarence agreed; but Richard did not commit himself. When news of this came to Edward, he "rated them soundly" for meeting with Warwick. Richard was shut up for a time; and never after gave cause for mistrust. See: *The Usurpation of Richard the Third* by Dominic Mancini; ed. Armstrong.

bestowal of sword and spurs, must have made an immense impression
on the boy.

The young knight took as his device: *Loyaultie lie me!*

Fast sliding into disaster, the monarchy of the Sunne had need of all
the loyalty it could muster. The new Kingdom must needs call back
yesterday, bid time return—the mighty honour of the dead. And what
better captain to head the solemn pageant than the pale proud unsmil-
ing Richard, the child of glory and blood. Richard would re-inter the
bones of his father Richard Duke of York and of his murdered brother
Edmund, Earl of Rutland. The fourteen-year-old knight, his blue ribbon of the Garter buckled on his left knee, his pendant George about
his neck, captained the escort of the hearse from Pontefract of Fotheringay. The sombre ride would set crying in his mind the wonder and
Trojan royalty of York: the black-draped funeral char drawn by seven
sable horses trapped to the ground in black sarcenet sewn with the
Duke's arms, and on that mournful bier an angel robed in white bearing a crown of gold.

At Fotheringay Castle, on July 30, 1466, requiem masses were chanted
for the souls of the Princes of York. The Heralds of Britain offered at
the altar the arms of the dead Richard: Norroy King of Arms offered
the coat of arms; March King of Arms, the shield; Ireland King of
Arms, the sword; Windsor Herald of England and Ravendon Herald
of Scotland, the helmet.

And now: York valour!

In June of the following year a magnificent tournament was staged
at Smithfield. The principals were Anthony Lord Scales, brother of the
Widow Grey and England's Queen, and Anthony the Great Bastard
of Burgundy, bar-sinister son of Philip the Good. The two were well-
matched. Lord Scales, twenty-four, knight and poet, famed for courtoisie
and skill in arms. The Great Bastard, crusader, champion of the Golden
Fleece, the very glass and mold of Burgundian chivalry.

What visions the scene must have conjured! And not least for the
eager youth beside his regal brother. The pavilions of coloured silk,
the Arab horses trapped in gorgeous velvet, the ermine and purple
Court beneath the Standards of York: the Flowering Sunne, the Whyte
Lyon, the Falcon Unfettered, the Gold-horned Black Bull. This was
all the wonder and joy of York, as the young Richard had ever
dreamed. . . .

Beneath goldmisted English skies the champions battered each other for two days. On the first day, the Bastard was unhorsed when his steed was blinded by the protruding horn from the chanfron of his opponent's horse.* The second day they fought on foot, with axes and swords. Scales had the better of it when the spur of his axe hooked into the Bastard's visor (Scales was fighting with an open helm); and King Edward threw down his warder.

Richard bore no active part; but Clarence was in the Bastard's corner, acting as the bearer of the bascinet. No doubt Clarence was greatly disappointed at the result, for he must have longed to see a Woodeville unhorsed.

In keeping with the spirit of the age, that preferred its cash transactions in romantic garb, the visit of the Bastard had a serious political purpose: the marriage of Margaret of York, Edward's sister, to Charles, Count of Charolais, the turbulent heir to Burgundy. Third daughter of Proud Cis, over-shadowed by Anne and Elizabeth, who had made substantial English marriages,** Margaret was to prove in some respects the most remarkable of her House. But at this time no one dared predict splendour for the shy long-nosed girl with the immense searching eyes. She was "Meg" to Richard; and he was "Dickon" to her. Neither could have dreamed that blue-arching day in June, 1468, when Margaret set forth to wed Charles the Rash of a time when brother and sister of York would become bitter rivals for headship of the House. They kissed farewell; and Margaret was gone across the Narrow Sea to Bruges, to wed at five o'clock in the morning at the village church of Damme the violent heir to Burgundy with his pinched forehead and stringy black bangs.

With Margaret of York's marriage the deceptive hour of Malorian monarchy concludes. A new and harder time is on the way for this merriest of kings. Queen Elizabeth Woodeville and her blood are at dagger point with Warwick and the House of York. The King, poor man, is in the middle—torn between his mother and his wife.

Edward had got himself into a situation almost hopeless for any man, but wonderfully disastrous for a wealthy (and amorous) monarch. He had espoused a woman emotionally chilly but intensely sexed, who

* On this occasion, too, the Bastard is said to have cracked: "Today, I fought a horse. Tomorrow, I shall take on the man." The warhorse's head armour, with a long steel horn protruding from the forehead, was called the "chanfron."

** Elizabeth to John de la Pole, 2nd Duke and Marquess of Suffolk. Anne to Henry Holland, Duke of Exeter; and subsequently to Sir Thomas St. Leger. Both marriages tinged by the carmine hue of Lancaster's Rose.

possessed five brothers looking for a soft touch, seven sisters burning for union with the noblest heirs of England—plus a pushing and insatiable father. The Woodevilles were solid Northampton gentry, descended from William de Wydeville and the Saxon Emma. No Woodeville for three hundred years seems to have made a significant marriage. The family seat was at Grafton; and the office of Sheriff appeared to represent the maximum Woodeville attainment during this long seeding-time of ambition.

In 1436, Richard Woodeville (who had not even become a Sheriff) married the noble Jacquetta, daughter of Jean of Luxembourg, Count of St. Pol, and widow of Prince John of Lancaster, Duke of Bedford. Elizabeth who by her marriage to King Edward made the family fortune was born in 1437.

At first, the Woodeville bent was Lancastrian. Elizabeth married a Lancastrian knight, Sir John Grey of Groby, who fell in Margaret's battle at St. Albans. But with the lucky daughter's second marital venture, at twenty-seven, to King Edward, the Woodeville clan rushed to embrace the White Rose. Edward proved the ideal son and brother-in-law. The Woodevilles had the pick of the marriage mart; and right shrewdly did they pick. To Anthony Woodeville, went the heiress of Lord Scales; to twenty-year-old John Woodeville went eighty-year-old Catherine, Dowager Duchess of Norfolk; * to Thomas Grey, the Queen's elder son, went the heiress of Lord Bonville; to Anne Woodeville fell the heir of Bourchier Earl of Essex; to Mary Woodeville, the heir of Lord Herbert; to Eleanor Woodeville, the heir of the Earl of Kent; to Katherine Woodeville went one of the greatest prizes, the royally descended Henry Stafford, Duke of Buckingham (a helpless ward in the hands of King Edward, this exploitation of the young duke was to redound with awful consequence upon the House of York).

Nor did the uxorious Sunne of York show himself mean when it came to other honours and appanages for the Queen's male relatives. Richard Woodeville, the father, became Earl Rivers, a tremendous boost in the social scale for the Northamptonshire squire. Anthony Woodeville was created Lord Scales, in right of his wife Elizabeth. Lionel Woodeville became Bishop of Salisbury. Edward Woodeville

---

* This Union, though strictly in accord with marital principles of the Age, shocked even the calculating Fifteenth Century. William of Wyrcestre remarked: "Catherine, Duchess of Norfolk, a Skittish damsel of some eighty summers, was wedded to John Wydeville, brother of the Queen, a man of twenty, a devilish marriage."

became an admiral; and Thomas Grey received the patent of Marquess of Dorset.

King Edward had always been lucky. He had won when the chips were down, when he had to win: Mortimer's Cross and savage Towton. Would not this splendid luck continue, Warwick, still his nominal Prime Minister, make peace with his Queen and her blood? And Clarence, too? Meantime: there was the marvelous fortune of being twenty-nine and the handsomest King of England in history. There was the gluttonous delight of a twelve-course feast, the joy of velvet wine, the weekly baths in a closet strewn with fragrant herbs, crisp inviting sheets and a pair of succulent thighs . . . oh there was everything to make a man happy, if only other persons would be reasonable. . . .

He grew careless and fat. . . .

"I have three harlots," Edward said (he meant three 'regular' harlots): "the wittiest, the merriest, the holiest harlot in England." The merriest was Jane Shore, she of cherry lip and melon breast, the wanton wife of William Shore, goldsmith, in Lombard Street. The wittiest was Elizabeth Lucy. The holiest?

But others were offended by all this ease of life, this Lucullan pleasure. Persons in some manner, however indirect, affected by the Woodeville honours and marriages. Persons who had taken seriously the King's promise to take the field to recover ancestral lands in France; the old dream of a Yorkist Agincourt. Persons who themselves had no talent for physical joys; and who deemed conditions at Edward's Court a kind of outrage.

And, remembering the public shame inflicted on Jane Shore by King Richard, it is certain that the youthful Gloucester must have viewed the proceedings at Westminster with revulsion: the righteous anger of the strict and gloomy youth against licentious elders.

Dorset's marriage was a direct affront to Warwick, for it had been intended that George Neville, Warwick's nephew, should marry the heiress of Exeter. But Queen Elizabeth gave the Duchess of Exeter four thousand marks to break off the match. Worse followed. Lord Mountjoy, one of Warwick's closest friends, was abruptly dismissed from his post as Lord Treasurer and Earl Rivers appointed in his stead. A further shake-up occurred in the Chancellorship, held by Warwick's brother, another George Neville, and a churchman of infinite ambition. To crown all, Warwick himself was sent on a humiliating and useless mission to France—to get the Earl out of England—while King Edward did his real business with the enemy of France, the Great Bastard of Burgundy.

At first, Warwick did not show his hand. He stayed away from Court, which in any case could not have been for him a pleasant atmosphere. Mysterious risings were fomented in the North, the seat of Neville power; proclamations hissed forth like rockets, evoking the familiar style of the reign of Henry the Sixth: the rebels mingled protestations of loyalty with a determination to rid the King of evil advisers. But Edward knew—nay England knew—that behind Robin of Redesdale and his blasts lurked the dark-browed Warwick and the tormented Clarence. It was not enough to catch Robin of Redesdale (probably a pseudonym for Sir John Conyers) and behead him. Other Robins arose with fresh proclamations to purge the realm.

Poor Edward!

He thought that he had all England with him; as if the smiles of a pretty lass could rally troops or as if the triumphs of the bedchamber might atone for the ominous silences of the Council Board. When it came to a fight, Edward was abandoned. Warwick and Clarence went over to Lancaster. Invading England on behalf of Henry the Sixth, they had an easy victory. Edward's troops deserted wholesale; his gentlemen fled; Montague, commander of the Royal Guard, betrayed his master; and the King himself was forced to leap out of bed at dawn (no doubt, not uncompanioned) and flee from his realm in a little fishing smack.

THE MIRACLE OF SEVENTY-ONE.

The King-maker allied to Margaret of Anjou! The enormity of such a union can only be comprehended when it is remembered that for fifteen years they had held each other in perfect hatred. Warwick was Captain-General of the White Rose; as Margaret was Captain-General of the Red Rose. Without the ambitions and mortal enmity of these two the dynastic conflict in the House of England would long since have been compromised. It was Margaret who beheaded Warwick's father, Salisbury, after Wakefield; Margaret who laid a plot to massacre Warwick at Westminster, in 1459. And it was Warwick who spread around the word that the Queen of England was a French whore and her son an adultered bastard got secretly by person or persons unknown.

Now came the extraordinary spectacle of Warwick proposing to marry his daughter Anne to Margaret's Edward; and promising to establish this youth upon the throne of England. Margaret agreed to accept Warwick as her chief minister and the de facto ruler of England.* For this result, Louis the Spider had laboured vastly; and blessed the queasy embrace of his two friends with a grant of ships and money.

It was not, however, French gold that enabled Warwick to capture England. Edward's subjects abandoned Edward; and flocked to Warwick. He was one of those fortunate politicians who seem to have a psychological impact on "those of meaner sort" quite apart from particular merits or abilities. Warwick was a very able man; but he was not the only able man in England. However: Warwick clearly projected a father-image to the people of Fifteenth-Century England. The campaign of September, 1470, was not so much a military foray—there was no fighting to speak of—as a kind of general election; an election won hands down by Warwick.

True, the Woodevilles had greatly annoyed the ancient nobility; but the commons could hardly have been affected by these rivalries. The government of Edward, despite the drinking and the strumpets about the Court, was neither oppressive nor disorderly; ** and it was certainly far more efficient than the regime of Henry the Sixth which Warwick proposed nominally to restore. But the people had this deep emotional attachment to the Earl of Warwick, their father and protector; he had no son, but the people of England were all his sons and heirs. They scarcely felt this way toward the callow redgold youth, who laughed constantly and took their wives to bed.

Warwick himself felt that he was a symbol of reconciliation; above faction. London opened its gates; and poor dazed Henry, more fuddled than ever, was brought from the Tower, "in a blew gown none too clenely kept" and displayed to the people. He sat on the woolsack in Westminster, limp as the sack itself, and spoke the phrases of peace and forgiveness set down for him by Warwick. The only one of Edward's officers to suffer was John Tiptoft, Earl of Worcester and High Constable. By his cruelties, Worcester had put himself beyond the pale.

---

* Warwick favoured a Mayor of the Palace set-up; with himself as the Mayor and a younger Plantagenet playing Dagobert. It is obvious that this would not have satisfied for long Margaret of Anjou. England was tranquil for six months because neither Edward nor Margaret was there.

** A pleasing glimpse of the young King is given by Stowe's "Annales" for the year 1462: "In Michaelmas Terme, King Edward sate in the king's bench three daies together, in open Court, to understand how his lawes were executed."

Found hiding in a tree in Weybridge Forest, he was summarily tried before the Earl of Oxford, his Lancastrian successor as Constable, and beheaded.

Queen Elizabeth Woodeville, who had rushed into Sanctuary at the overthrow of Edward, was kindly treated; and allowed every attention for the birth of a Yorkist prince, Edward, in November 1470. The Lancastrian Parliament of 1470 undid the attainders against old Lancastrians; approved a policy of trade and alliance with France; recognized Warwick as the Lieutenant of the Realm and Clarence as his Deputy and the Lieutenant of Ireland. The Parliament also passed a Royal Succession Act, settling the crown on Henry the Sixth and the heirs of his body; and, if Henry's line should fail, on the Duke of Clarence and his heirs.

England, that had known so much woe and blood, settled into the most tranquil six months of the century, under the strong hand of the father-protector, Warwick. Contrast, for an instant, this policy with the hangings, the murders open and covert, the guilt-by-association victims, the wholesale attainders in the times of those Welsh tribal axemen, the early Tudors!

The tranquillity and promise of this brief Restoration has been too often minimized because it did not in fact last. But the Restoration of Lancaster failed to survive through no conceivable fault of Warwick and his handling of the domestic situation. It failed because the nation of England which in the past had intervened so ruinously and at such dreadful cost in the affairs of other nations across the Narrow Sea had now become the prime object of the fierce rivalry between the Duchy of Burgundy and the Kingdom of France.

Charles the Turbulent who, on the death of Duke Philip the Good in 1467, had become master of the richest realm in Christendom had but one stable aspect in his policy: to get himself crowned Emperor of the West. The conception itself was by no means foolish; it was quixotic for Duke Charles to think he had the skill and intelligence to bring it off. Of Lancastrian descent through his mother Isabella of Portugal, Charles had been at one time a fervent Lancastrian. But that was in the days when his father Duke Philip had favored York; and whatever his father favored, Charles was against. Now his father was dead and hatred of Duke Philip had been replaced by hatred of a former friend and ally, King Louis the Eleventh of France. Louis was a strong partisan of Margaret of Anjou and of Lancaster; hence Charles now inclined toward York. He had marked his reversal of policy by his marriage in 1468 with Margaret of York.

The rulers of Burgundy busied themselves to upset Warwick's regime. Nothing was too good for the penniless exiles of York. They were welcomed at Bruges by the Seigneur de la Gruuthuus—the Lord of the Great House *—Louis of Flanders; given clothes, horses, money, entertainments. Christmas was passed in Bruges; Twelfth Night; and they were well into February, still subsisting on the bounty of Charles' vassal, Louis.

Edward spent a great deal of time in hawking; and in other pastimes, for the girls of Bruges were then, as now, large, blonde and comfortable. Richard kept close touch with their sister the Duchess; and through her, with the Turbulent. The Turbulent did not wish to become openly involved; it is typical of his policy that he thought to help his brother-in-law and at the same time to fool the King of France. But the Universal Spider was not fooled for a moment. He knew all about the ships being readied at Zeeland; the companies of halberds and archers, the "hand-gonne" men. He knew about the handsome loans to these princes of York. What he did not know about, however, was to prove the most effective preparation of all: Clarence. . . .

In 1470, George Duke of Clarence was twenty-one. The sole noteworthy action of his career had been to betray his brother Edward and to help substantially in the collapse of York's monarchy. He was handsome and eloquent, especially in defense of what he conceived to be his "rights." Yet, with the years, his personality grew more difficult. Where Edward was bland and jovial, Richard grave and subtle, George of Clarence was all rough edges and anger. He was the senior brother of the King; yet he saw his rightful position usurped, first by the Woodevilles, and ultimately by Richard. He had a grievance, certainly; no one took him seriously, paid attention to him. No one, that is, save Warwick. And here again we must admire that masterly man, who took the most unlikely material and molded it to his own use.

The young man was immensely flattered. Here was the wonder-work-

* This noble mansion is still standing; and is now being restored as the show-piece of Bruges. What remains of the 15th Century lodgings where resided Edward, Richard, Hastings, and others, is now thoroughly confused with alterations of succeeding centuries. The lay-out of the Courtyard, however, is still intact; and there is a splendid collection of Burgundian armour in what must have been the huge medieval kitchen.

ing champion of York, the great Warwick, listening to him, sympathiz-
ing, nodding gravely as the bitter young duke, with an ever-handy
glass, ticked off the catalogue of complaints against his royal brother.
Warwick went further.* He did not confine himself to sympathy, but
made constructive suggestions as to the future. He himself had been
sorely wounded by the King's indifference, not to say downright ingratitude. Edward had changed since that widow had appeared; he
was not the same Edward any more. To take action against this man
would not be to betray a friend and brother; nay, it would be simple
justice on a catspaw of the upstart Woodevilles. Now if Clarence would
but harken—.

Clarence harkened; and presently he found himself married to Warwick's daughter Isabel, a part of Warwick's entourage, going from one
Warwick Castle to another, and then across to Calais—and irreparably
involved in proclamations and uprisings against his brother—and finally
ending up at Angers, taking a solemn oath to a woman whom even he
must have realized hated his guts and who had murdered his elder
brother Edmund at Wakefield. Perhaps he thought there would be
some opportunity to negotiate, to recall Edward to the claims of blood.
But everything happened too quickly; York's monarchy collapsed and
Warwick and Margaret were the rulers of England. And Clarence?
Well; he was the Lieutenant of Ireland, a post to which his brother had
appointed him, in the days before he had fallen in with Warwick. He
also had a very hypothetical right to the succession, in case Henry's
line should fail. But he must have perceived that by no stretch of the
imagination would he or a son of his get on the throne as long as
Margaret of Anjou was around to prevent it.

All this had been equally perceived and the young man's measure
accurately taken by two others, his brother Richard and his elder sister
Duchess Margaret. At this point, Richard Duke of Gloucester, heretofore in the regal shadow of his brother Edward, emerges to play the
dominant role that henceforth he will never relinquish. He had gone

---

* The shrewd judicious Earl; the jealous Duke, frantic with alcohol and spite—
what colloquies they must have had! "Why, my lord, think you to have him kind to
you, that is unkind to me, yea, and unnatural to me, being his own brother?
Think you that friendship will make him keep promise where neither nature nor
kindred can provoke or move him to favour his own blood? . . . I swear if my
brother Gloucester would join with me, we would make him know that we were
all three one man's sons, of one mother and lineage descended, which should be
more preferred and promoted than strangers of his wife's blood."

willingly into exile with Edward; he had shared the poverty and anxiety
of the early days; and, when prospects began to improve, he—at eighteen—had assumed management of the shattered affairs of York's
Monarchy. Edward must have been bewildered. His fall had been as
speedy and as total as Lucifer's; and worst of all—he could really blame
no one but himself. He was only too willing to listen to the counsel of
Richard; Richard who, it seemed, had been preparing his whole brief
life for this hour.

Richard had studied Warwick's political position; and had correctly
gauged the Earl's vulnerable salient—Clarence. If Clarence could be
brought to renounce his allegiance to Warwick, a vital tactical victory
would be won.* Duchess Margaret eagerly cooperated; and sent emissaries, unsuspicious persons like priests and women, to England. Con-
tacts were established through Duchess Cecily and her daughters Anne,
Duchess of Exeter, and Elizabeth, Duchess of Suffolk. Clarence was
receptive; the Earl, it seems, was not quite so sympathetic any more.
He was too busy to listen to Clarence. And saying what a splendid lad
was young Edward, Queen Margaret's son!

He drank and brooded. . . .

They played him, Richard and Margaret, as an angler plays a large
fish; until they felt confident that even with this fish the barb was
fast. The stage was set for an amazing campaign.

Charles the Turbulent—anything but lavish save for war—disgorged
fifty thousand florins; he hired archers and "hand-gonne men"; in addition to the Burgundian ships nesting in the desolate marshes of
Walcheren, he engaged for Edward fourteen tall ships of the Easterlings,
or Germans of the Hanse. In all, Edward had some 2000 men; of whom
a few hundred were old front fighters of the Rose, come to join their
chief in exile.

They sailed on March 11th, anticipating by more than a crucial
month the passage of Queen Margaret, who fretted for a wind at
Harfleur from March 24th to April 13th. The East Anglian coast was
strongly held by Oxford, the Constable; Edward thereupon turned his

---

* Commines claims that negotiations were opened by Edward in England, *before*
he lost the throne. Commines retailed a great deal of gossip in his history; and I
find this version most difficult to accept. Everything points to the fact that Edward
considered himself in a virtually unassailable position. Why should he make offers
to the wandering rebel, his brother? Further, even if he did put out tentative
feelers, the much more elaborate and precise conspiracy was later developed by
Richard and Margaret.

prows due north and ran under a sleeting gale for the Humber. He leaped ashore at Ravenspur, in the grey torrent of a Yorkshire dawn; on the very spot where, seventy years before, Henry Bolingbroke had come home to wrest golden laughing Richard's diadem.

Omens. . . .

The adventurers were surrounded by a cloud of country people, out of Holderness, led by Martin of the Sea and a priest John Westerdale. Far from rousing the hearts of Yorkshiremen, the throneless giant created numb silence. He wandered toward York, a lewd and unwanted prophet "compassed about by a great cloud of witnesses."

York must open its gates. If York remained shut, the gamesters lost on the opening throw; no one would join them. Again, Richard's genius intervened. Edward, he advised, like Bolingbroke of old, should proclaim that he arrived to claim his duchy of York; as of ancient natural right and had no design upon the throne. So, ostrich feathers in their chaperons, they paraded before the walls of York, hallooing for Henry and the Prince.

Loyalty? Aye; no man more loyal to Lancaster than his cousin of York. An oath? Certes . . . and they all knelt down in the pig wallow before Bootham Bar, swearing to bear true faith to Henry the Sixth. The Bootham portcullis glinted upward—for one night. . . .

It was the eighteenth of March. All over England, men took weapons from the wall. The adventurers went on to Sendal, that windswept eagle's lair of York, brooding above the Calder Plain. A few old retainers of York, cap-twisting, weeping and laughing, joined the young Duke. He found horses for his retinue, country cobs that made up in endurance what they lacked in points.

Warwick remained confident. Henry of Northumberland and Warwick's own brother John Neville, Marquess of Montague, were lieutenants of the North; Oxford, lieutenant of the Midlands. Their combined forces totaled not many less than ten thousand warriors, more than ample to deal with Edward and Richard and their hired Flemings. But Northumberland, son of that Percy who died for Lancaster at Towton, and who would one day abandon Richard on the field, now deserted Warwick. Oxford and Montague turned wary; they hung back, refusing to attack. Was there not some bright magic in this Edward, this beloved of the gods? Some happy gift of sorcery that saved him at night's edge?

He continued his march: Newark, Nottingham, Leicester. And as it became clear that Edward roved unhindered, he received men in harness to his Banner: 600 under Sir John Harrington; 3000 retainers of Lord Hastings in the Midlands. Now Edward threw off the mask of loyalty to Henry; unfurled the Standard of Edward the Fourth. "Now are these our Princes all come home again. . . ."

Warwick shut himself in Coventry with 6000 men; awaiting the forces of Oxford, Montague, and Clarence. Mustering in the southwest, Clarence had written his father-in-law, begging him to avoid battle until the Duke should arrive—a small masterstroke in which the hand of Richard may be discerned.

Clarence, with 7000 men of the Red Rose, now drew near Edward. At Banbury, this Judas of York perpetrated his final and most deadly betrayal. He arrayed his men for battle; rode out from the lines to meet Richard. The brothers embraced; and Clarence knelt, begging forgiveness. His men tore off the Swan badge, revealing the White Rose cockade underneath. A welkin-splitting cheer went up for Edward; and the armies rushed to embrace.

It was a fearful disaster for Warwick. He had been completely outplayed by Richard. Clarence in their power, the lords of the Rose now used him as a propaganda mouthpiece. He was encouraged to send messages to Coventry, urging Warwick to abandon Lancaster and promising to intercede with Edward for the Earl. But Earl Warwick was not this manner of man. Hideously betrayed by the youth he had befriended; ruined by his own heir, he might consider such appeals as the most devilish mockery—.

"When the erle had heard paciently the dukes message, lorde, how he detested and accursed him! crienge out on him that he, contrary to his othe, promise, and fidelity, had shamefully turned hys face from his confederates and allies. But to the dukes messenger he gave no other answer but thys: that he thanked Almighty God to be always lyke himself and not lyke a false and traitorous duke; and that he was fully determined never to leave war tyll either he had lost hys own naturall lyfe or utterly extinguished and put under hys foes and enemies."

Clarence's treachery broke open the defenses of London. Edward and Richard drove at forced marches along the Watling Street, while Warwick sent frantic pleas from Coventry to his brother, the Chancellor, in London. But George Neville was not the type to die on the barricades.

He was strictly a career politician; and he perceived his brother's star rapidly dimming in the rising splendour of this Sunne of York. Besides, he had not the men to hold London. He did, as a gesture, lead King Henry about the streets; but the sight of the broken sick old man, on his way to martyrdom and unofficial sainthood, was hardly a trumpet call to arms.

Warwick sent desperate messages about the shires. "Henry, I pray you, ffayle me not now, as ever I may do for you." But Henry Vernon of Haddon Hall, already tampered with by Clarence, failed Warwick; as did many another. By relentless effort, Warwick collected about 17,000 men. Departing Coventry on April 8th, he surged in pursuit of Edward and Richard—but the brothers of York managed to keep a day's march ahead. They came down to London and Chancellor, the Archbishop Neville, on Ash Wednesday. They penetrated the Tower by the postern that same day; and Edward made his state entry on Maundy Thursday. The suave smiling Chancellor was on hand to greet the Rose of Rouen on the steps of St. Paul's, Henry in tow. Warwick's cup was full.

The value of French money was cried in London, a scut: four sous —the men of York were still being paid out of the Burgundian loan. There was cried also a levy of horse and foot. Edward marched out of London on Saturday, Easter Eve; an army of 15,000 in bannered array. Richard commanded the van. Nineteen: his first battle! As he swung ahead of the long glinting column, what sense of splendour, what joy of York blazoned his heart.

Green April gleaming on their lances and Banners, the Falcon Un-fettered, the Flowering Sunne, the Goldhorned Black Bull—the proud horses, the scarlet saddle cloths, the trumpeters and archers, the Sunne patch of gold sarcenet on the blue and murrey jackets. The Army of York; the great company of the Sunne . . . blazing and singing toward Earl Warwick.

Barnet is not far from London, perhaps ten miles, near St. Albans. Yet York's army did not come up with Warwick, camped on the heights above Barnet, until long after nightfall. The Yorkists pitched down much nearer the Lancastrian lines than was usual; Edward was determined to force a battle before Warwick could unite with his allies, Falconbridge and Queen Margaret. In the dark the alignment of the armies was askew. Hastings, commanding York's left wing, was out-flanked by Oxford with Lancaster's right; but Richard, commanding

York's right, fronting Market Hadley, outflanked Exeter and the Lancastrian left.*

Earl Warwick had taken up a shrewd position on Hadley Ridge, highest point between London and York. The battlefront of England's champion extended 2000 yards right across the ridge and athwart the Great North Road; below, the ridge sloped away to Gladsmore Heath and York. Should Edward and Richard attack, they would be in for a warm reception. Not only did Oxford's seasoned division, with its badges of the Blue Boar and Radiant Star of de Vere, straddle Hastings' ward, but Oxford's front was protected by a thick brambled hedge. Additionally, Warwick's centre, under the Earl's personal command, was mounted on the highest point of the ridge and protected by the guns of Montague, in position to enfilade an enemy assault.

Warwick did not intend to stand on the defensive. This was not merely a military foray to him; it was a bitterly personal trial of arms. His whole life as leader of the English nation was in the balance. Warwick determined to attack. He wanted to destroy York; destroy the House that he had made great and that had rejected and cast him out. These arrogant and treacherous brothers!

Long before dawn, Montague's guns roared and tongues of orange flame stabbed the night. The darkness awoke in terror; shivering and cursing, Edward's men scraped shallow foxholes as the murderous chainshot screamed over them. A young lieutenant of guns, sweating, sent a runner to headquarters at Barnet, begging for permission to open fire on Montague. Edward refused, with an oath. He was damned if he would give away his own position to Earl Warwick; let the losels sweat!

But all this rage of secrecy and Plantagenet guile was wasted on the great Earl. He had prepared a "subtletie" of his own for the brothers of York; and Hastings' lads, crouching in the roaring dark, were to bear the brunt of Warwick's surprise. Just at the first silver in the East, Oxford's crack division went forward, through previously sheared

---

* Colonel Burne and C. W. Oman, who have both written excellent accounts of Barnet, give the Red Rose centre to Beaufort duke of Somerset. But by the best contemporary authority, *The Arrivall of King Edward,* Somerset, duke and Captain-General of the Rose, was not at Barnet. Here are the words of the chronicler: "Edmund, calling himself duke of Somerset, John of Somerset, his brother, called Marquess Dorset, Thomas Courtenay, calling himself Earl of Devonshire, had knowledge that Queen Margaret and her son . . . were purposing to arrive in the West Country; wherefore they departed out of London, and went into the west parts, and there bestirred themselves right greatly to make an assembly. . . ."

breaks in the hedge, as barbed wire is cut for a surprise attack from entrenchments in the present age. Men of the Midlands and of the South, archers in blue and silver, a terrible moving wood of pikes and bills, they went silently into the ghostly halls of dawn, their boots trampling the wet grass.*

Had King Edward, that incomparable strategist, arrayed his men in a normal position of defense, instead of immediately under the shelf of the ridge, they might have had a chance to organize a stand. But Oxford's division hit them with awful impact. Surprise and shock were complete. Hastings himself was one of the first to void the field. His men were thrown into a panic swarm, abandoning guns, weapons, armour, yelping down the slope toward Barnet village, a mile away. And many cried on into London, wailing York ruin through the green and silver light of Easter morning. . . .

Yet, all was not lost. The great problem of medieval armies was field communications; and in the dawn mist Oxford's men pursuing into the single ragged street of Barnet had become hopelessly separated from the remainder of Warwick's army. Clearly, the Earl's battle plan was to coordinate Oxford's shattering thrust with a blow from his own magnificent troops of the centre: old Calais front fighters, red-jacketed soldiers of the Bear, wild sailors of the Channel Fleet. York, assailed flank and front, must be driven off the slope and torn to shreds.

But it did not happen. It did not happen through any fault of York, the great Sunne banner tottering, the flame going out forever . . . saved —by a wizard's mist; by a last fantastic stroke of fortune. Lost in the mist, a blue and silver company of Oxford wandered in a broad circle, ending in the rear of their own lines, instead of assaulting Edward's flank. Perhaps this lost company bore the Banner of de Vere, a Radiant Star, silver Molet on a blue field, and in the confusion Warwick's men mistook this quartering for the Standard of the Sunne-in-Splendour.

Shots were exchanged; and all along the labouring lines of Warwick exploded a cry of "Treachery!"—a powder fuse igniting disaster. Old Lancastrians and red-jackets fell to slaughtering one another; while the Earl and Montague looked on, filled with rage and horror, unable to believe that fortune, the fickle jade, had turned so cruel a face.

On York's right flank, Richard was heavily engaged with Exeter,

* For a dramatic and poetic evocation of this battle, which attained high levels of drama and poetry, the interested reader is referred to the author's novel, *The Swan and the Rose,* published in November, 1953, by A. A. Wyn; New York.

John Talbot, Earl of ...ewsbury, presenting an il...inated manuscript to ...ary VI and Queen Mar-...rite d'Anjou. This work ... specially commanded by ...ot for Marguerite, to-...d 1450.

...ISH MUSEUM; MSS. ROY-...5 E. VI, FOLIO 2B.

...Court of Edward IV. Ed-...d receiving *The Book of* ...*onicles,* executed toward ...5, from the Burgundian ...er, Jean de Waurin. In ...er left hand, Richard ...ke of Gloucester wearing ...e hose and murrey jour-...e with an ostrich plume ...is hat. This is a rare con-...porary full-length like-...s of Richard. He appears ...ll but well-formed.

...ISH MUSEUM; MSS. ROY-...5 E. IV, FOLIO 14.

XI. Richard III, Kir
England. The very fine
Hatfield portrait after
contemporary original
probably by John Serle
Court painter.

Courtesy MARQUES
SALISBURY K. G. and
lish Life Publication

XII. Edward IV, Kir
England. An early por
seldom reproduced. *A*
unknown.

SOCIETY OF ANTIQU

duke and Admiral and husband of Richard's own sister Anne. And he, outflanked on his front, as the ruined Hastings had been on his, not much of a soldier and even less of an Admiral, fought manfully this day and was left for dead on the field. He held up Richard some precious time; but gradually the young falcon of York drove his steel talons deeper and Exeter reeled back into the wild shouting mass of the broken centre.

Warwick's position was now terrible. His right wing had vanished into a Glendower's cursed mist; his centre was furiously entangled with bits of Oxford's division; his left was bleeding from Richard's slashing strokes. The Earl was urged to flee. Any lesser commander would have done so, but he, mindful of his oath and that he fought in the blazing stare of the whole English nation, stayed on the field.

Edward's trumpets shrilled, a brazen shriek of victory; the huge shining Captain of the Sunne came forward, mass on glinting mass crushing up the slope, blue and murrey bowmen, dismounted men-at-arms in flaring armour, a murderous thicket of curved partizans and glaives . . . and on the right Richard's exultant company thrusting toward Warwick. The last red lines broke; Warwick and Montague fought on with an honour guard of Calais men, nine hundred of the old immortal legend sworn to die for the Bear and Ragged Staff. Edward had issued his customary order of "no-quarter"; and the iron battalions of York gorged on English blood. Now, it was done: the legend, the dream, the vision of a united realm and the last best hope of the Rose. In Dead Man's Bottom the Calais men lay, beneath the swarming flies. Earl Warwick fell near the edge of Wrotham Wood, cut down by Richard's swordsmen of the Sunne. Richard, that he had made a warrior in the lost summer-land of Warwick, long deaths ago. . . .

It was just on ten of the clock. The battle had endured almost three hours. The hiding sorcered Sun, the Herald and splendour of York, had ruined Warwick and given the victory to Edward. But now the Sun glowed from a burnished blue; Resurrection morning, and York that was dead had risen again!

Edward gazed on the mighty black-armoured dead. His great enemy; and his brother and friend. The man who, more than any other, had made him. And oh! now even in that gross and greedy spirit might stir some tiny glow of regret, a little flare of grandeur at such a death.

And he, now truly Edward the Fourth, *consecratus invictus,* plucked an iron gauntlet from his hand and gave it to a squire. The youth was to ride hell-for-leather to London town, with the King's gauntlet as token of victory. . . .

Earl Warwick and Montague, his brother, lay naked on the pavement of St. Paul's for three days; let the people know their Earl was dead! But for the victor, scant time to savour the delights of kingship: the arab war horses, the gold sarcenet and purple velvet, the ropes of pearls, the luscious bodies of harlots, the stupifying feasts—all the fairy-tale magnificence of this gorgeous make-believe monarch. No time for galliards . . . for Captain Margaret landed at Weymouth on Barnet day. Great York mustered; and the morrow of St. George's Day, April 24th, the Sunne-in-Splendour flared forth from Windsor toward the Cotswolds and Margaret.

But: was this the Margaret that had broke York's heart with the brilliant stratagem of Wakefield? That had plumed the night attack of Second St. Albans? Or was this an aging embittered woman, the past festering in that sick heart, the future a frightening blank? And most of all: constant terror for Edward, for her son . . . Her lords and captains, Somerset, Devon, Langstrother, Audeley, Gervase Clifton, the Sire of the Rose, rallied in the southwest: country billmen, lads with old rusty ploughshares; a few young squires on country cobs (the Swan Guard of the Prince); guns from Bristol and Exeter; the Recorder and a city company from Bristol (oh the shining scarlet-booted legend of the Queen, to compel this middle-aged lawyer from fat wife and dusty office!).

She brought with her out of Touraine a company of Lancastrian exiles, 2000 or more; but she had not this time that Norman Cyrano, Piers de Bracy, and his gallant band who had so oft cried Margaret!—and let loose the hounds of war. De Bracy and his Normans missed that last blue door of glory, sweeping the silver halls of Heaven with their blades. . . .

Instead: she had Wenlock. Sir John Wenlock, Lord Wenlock, deputy of Calais, freebooter of war's anguish, old Lancastrian, old Yorkist, old sword of Warwick, with skull-grey face and cowled gaze. Margaret made him commander of the Swan Guard and her military adviser—as had been brave dead Trollope in the mad trumpet time of her youth. Might not Wenlock devise another St. Albans?

But swinging through the Cotswolds, on the ancient Roman Fosse Way, the brothers Plantagenet on their dappled arab destriers had little fear of Wenlock devising another St. Albans; or anything of a menacing character. For Sir John was their man, bought and sold. Again: the hand of Richard. As he gleamed in his white armour down the green lanes of Gloucester, the young duke had reason to be pleased. His stratagems had been successful at every turn. He had even got up a religious miracle for the benefit of Edward: the miracle of Daventry. At Daventry, on the road to London, the boards about the image of the Blessed Anne had cracked; and the saint had gazed upon Edward. He had sworn to name his next girl, "Anne." * And now; Richard had bridged a way to Wenlock, as he had done with Clarence.

A grateful Edward had made the nineteen-year-old youth, High Constable and Admiral of England. Very likely, other rewards were touched on in private conversation between the brothers. For the heritage of Warwick was vast. And though Clarence had understood he was to have it all, as part of the deal by which he destroyed his father-in-law, that might hold good only so long as Anne Neville had no claim. Anne was now the bride of the Prince of Lancaster, in accord with the agreement of Angers. Prince Edward enjoyed excellent health; but, after all, he had ventured on perilous ways, and if anything should happen to him—.

Despite the discomforts of the march, for the brothers drove their men in an effort to cut off Captain Margaret from Wales and Jaspar Tudor, Earl of Pembroke, Edward and Richard were in fine spirits. Coln Rogers, Cirencester, Tetbury, the neat grey slatestone towns dreamed in the white blaze of May. The echoing endless tramp of foot-soldiers slogging in the red dust, the wheels of the provision carts and the gun-waggons grinding the broken road, the delicate high-stepping arab mounts . . . the surging hammering rhythms of an army on the march. . . .

Provisions ran out, for Edward, always saving on the men, had brought insufficient rations. He had some vague notion of living off the countryside; his countryside. But not only did the country folk refrain from rushing out laden with hams and pasties to cheer their "liberators"; they ran in the opposite direction. Edward found it expedient to collect a herd of them as hostages, to avert guerilla attacks. The troubles of the men were increased when the horses of the captains

---

* Which, in fact, he did do. Anne Plantagenet was born in 1476; she married Thomas Howard, Earl of Surrey, and had two sons, both of whom died young. Anne died in 1513. Let it also be recalled that Anne Mortimer was the Heiress General of Mortimer and of Clarence, from whom York claimed the throne.

and the men-at-arms so churned up and riled the little streams that the foot soldiers who with burning throats slogged behind could get no cooling drink.

At Sudbury, at noon on Thursday, May 2nd, Richard's scurryers clashed with a detachment of Lancastrian horse. Galloping up with a mailed company, the young Constable routed and cut up the Lancastrians. Edward arrived; and, convinced that the main Lancastrian force was close at hand, decided to halt at Sudbury for the night.

The master strategist was completely fooled. The Queen had merely made a feint in the direction of the Cotswolds and while Edward hurriedly dug in at Sudbury, Captain Margaret was straining to reach Gloucester, the "Shining City" of the Celts; and the Severn Bridge. After a brief halt at Berkeley on Thursday night, the gallant little army of seven thousand hit the Gloucester road in the early hours of Friday.

At Sudbury, Edward's snores were interrupted by an espial's urgent report: Queen Margaret had given them the slip. Edward tumbled out his army; and despatched a pursuivant with orders to kill his horse if need be but to reach Gloucester before Margaret and command the Governor, Sir Dickon Beauchamp, to hold the city at all costs. The pursuivant won the race; and Beauchamp warned off Margaret's Herald, *Lorraine,* with a crossbolt from the battlements. The soldiers of the Rose toiled on to Tewkesbury and the Severn crossing at the Lower Lode. They arrived just at dusk; and a half-mile from the town, Somerset, Captain-General of the Rose, threw up a hasty defense behind hedges, streams, dykes, and ditches—"a right evyll place to come to as anie man might well devise. . . ."

The Army of York bivouacked at Tredington, on the old Cheltenham Road, three miles from Tewkesbury; reconnoitering Somerset, the scurryers brought back word Lancaster would be tough. Edward gave the honour to Richard.

Who were the young Constable's men? He had not yet those frost-haunted northern castles, that blue-eyed fresh-cheeked devotion. He had passed as much time in the Midlands and the South; his first real appearance in the North was the stratagem that opened the gates of York. His men, the storm battalions of the Sunne, must have been crusty professionals of the "Frenssche warres"; a sprinkling of York retainers; and a new kind of fighter, a strictly Home Counties lad that made a business of the Roses. How else account for the fact that Edward got together two such armies in so brief a time? With Burgundian gold burning his pocket, he got all the dog-faces he needed on short term rates; while Lancaster had to depend on the old loyalty to the Rose, in the country districts of the West.

Falangtado, Falangtado, O sing the black and yellow!

"They determined to abide there the adventure that God would send them, in the quarrel they had taken in hand. And for that intent the same night they pitched themselves in a field, in a close even at the townes ende; the towne and the Abbey at theyre backs; afore them, and upon every hand of them, fowle lanes and depe dykes, and many hedges, with hylls and valleys;—a right evyl place to approche as could wel have been devised." *

Light that broods and glistens, varying, strange: brilliant yellow-green of May, sky-green of trees against a hippodrome of blue and white, bottle-green of the salmon-swift Severn, haunted green of the meadow where great blasted willows grow, fire-green of sun on cathedral glass . . . Tewkesbury.

It was the light of May fourth, it was the light of Saturday. All night that drove on through thin dark rain the Lancastrians had sentineled, huddled in their cloaks; waiting . . . Exhausted, fireless, hungry;—and over them blew memories of old desperate fields and battles long ago . . . St. Albans, ten years this Shrovetide; Wakefield, the Christmas horror; Towton, Palm Sunday, and blood gulleying amid the snow— Captain Margaret.

And like a bird flashing and singing came the memory of the Queen; round their ragged hoods and extinct fires the old dream of Margaret. But this, even they knew, in their dented iron, their scraps of leather, was the last, the last. For now they acted out a blind and bloody charade, living on irreparably Lancastrian in this murrey world of York.

The three brothers stirred before cockcrow. Richard armed: in a suit of white German armour, the gift of the Lord of Ravenstein. As at Barnet, the youngest brother of York would command the van, 4000 battle-hard soldiers. His banner was a Boar—from '*Ebor*' or York—and rampant, in signal of his own relentless nature.

Richard of Gloucester was nineteen; pale, undersized, hawk-visaged. His sudden rise had astounded England. He was incalculable. The

* 'Arrivall of King Edward' from *Chronicles of the White Rose*, p. 78.

small sickly boy, with brown sunken stare, had become a captain. More than that: Richard was a symbol of the Rose—vengeance with a sword. He never forgot that Edmund of Rutland was dead; murdered at seventeen. And the heads on Mickle Gate, rainwashed, torn by vultures —Captain Margaret's trophies.

Edward blew up his trumpets and committed his cause to fate. York's army advanced from Tredington, the night bivouac three miles from Tewkesbury, to a patch of scrub called the 'Red Piece,' just short of that evil-looking Lancastrian line. They were moving across very broken soggy country, very green and still; and for some time all they saw were the bristling hedgetops. Richard, in advance of Edward and Clarence, fanned out to the left, to cut off the Lancastrians from the Lower Lode ferry across the river Severn, now in spring freshet, with the famous 'Severn Bore' roiling.

Lancaster sprang to the alert. Round the Swan banner came the captains of the Rose: young royal Edward, the swart face of Devon, bold gallant Somerset, and the grim hunter Wenlock. Edward of Lancaster, the 'Hope of England,' was a bonny prince, splendid in his gilded breastplate, his sword-bearer, Piers Gower, beside him. Seven thousand men arrayed from the high ground—the 'Gastons'—to the marshes by the river. Somerset had selected a formidable front, 1000 yards broad, with its thorns and ditches. With his brother John Beaufort, Somerset commanded the crucial river flank where York's main blow was expected; Lord Wenlock, with the Company of the Swan in black and red, marshalled the centre, his command post at Gupshill Manor; and Thomas Courtenay, 13th Earl of Devonshire, guarded the left.

But, strong as his position was, Lancaster's Captain did not intend only to keep on the defensive—as will presently appear.

The honour of the assault was demanded by—and granted to— Richard of Gloucester. Hastings had disgraced himself at Barnet, Clarence was unreliable, Edward had to keep the whole battle in hand from his command post at Red Piece. But Richard had flared out of mist to turn Warwick's flank at Barnet and compel the black-browed Earl to snatch defeat from the jaws of victory. Now, 'Dickon' was given the job of turning Somerset.

He moved out with drum and trumpet, through the drenched green light, across the ragged fields. On the rise, Prince Edward's Company stood breathless, watching the mighty line surge toward Somerset. Now

came helmeted archers, shooting; then a horde of billmen with their
cruel hooks; last, a rank of dismounted men-at-arms carrying pole-axes
and broadswords. The victorious veterans of Barnet crossed a dip, passed
through a meadow of marigold, and swung left with trumpets ringing.

York's battalions thrust toward the river flank where a sunken wag-
gon track, joining the Gloucester road, passed in front of the Lancastrian defenses. Somerset held his fire; a sudden terrible wonder settled
over the field. With a flare of blades, the columns of the Sunne marched
stride by mortal stride across the white heart of morning. The range
fell: 150 yards, 100, 50 yards—the Boar came on.

Old men that remembered Agincourt swore softly; boys gripped their
elm hafts white-knuckled. And: the Lancastrian line exploded. Arrows
at point blank rained on Richard. The effect of a crossbolt or a cloth-
yard shaft discharged at 20 yards is the kick of a shotgun blast. Men
spun; flung into the air like marionettes. Richard's attack began to
dissolve . . . and Lancaster kept on shooting.

The soldiers of York staggered forward, blown into the fury. At the
sunken track before the hedge, the ragged line halted, the ranks crowding on one another. Richard's men began to slide forward, into a fierce
tangle of spines and creepers. The Lancastrian pikemen came to hands,
thrusting at the wretches in the ditch; long blades dripped blood.

The attack crumbled. Men shrieked in the boggy ditch or hung dying
on the thorns. Abruptly, trumpets brayed retreat. The men of the proud
bragging Boar scrambled away.

A yell went up from Lancaster. A yell that might have blown on a
wind of victory across the roiling Severn to Little Malvern Priory, 'the
poor religious place,' where Queen Margaret, with the Countess of Warwick and Lady Anne Neville, agonized time away. She was not the
Margaret of Wakefield, of St. Albans;—the laughing sobbing golden
being . . . *aye, marry, sirs, now looks he like a king!*

That black and gold Margaret, wasp of gorgeous beauty and piercing
scorn, was dead; faded now into the nervous middle-aged woman pac-
ing the Priory, hollow-eyed, the pockmarks on those pale cheeks like
seals of ruin and despair. Devoured; but not by her own exalted flamelit destiny, her ability to torment and to destroy men, but by anguish
for the safety of her son. For Margaret too remembered Edmund Earl
of Rutland; Prince Edward was but a few months older than Edmund
had been at Wakefield.

Light that flares and shimmers through a revery of green, the last
light of medieval England . . . and crimson amid catkins lie the brambled dead. Hoarse with shame, Richard brought the remnant back . . .
meantime the triumphant Somerset:

"knightly and manly advanced himself with his fellowship, somewhat
aside-hand the King's van; and, by certain paths and ways before
purveyed, and to the King's party unknown, he departed out of the
fylde, passed a lane, and came into a fayre place, or close, even before
the King, where he was embattled; and from the hyll that was in one
of the closes, he set right fiercely upon the ende of the King's battle." *

York's casual giant, sloppy in judgment as in character, had just
beheld his assault columns smashed up; now his centre was hit by a
hammer blow. Lancaster's Captain had seized advantage of the rough
and hidden ground to turn Richard's flank; he had slipped around the
furious Boar by paths previously scouted, entered an enclosed field
before Edward's position on Red Piece; and thundered down on the
Yorkist King from a small rise.

It was a brilliant stroke, the one chance Lancaster had. It deserved—
and barely missed—success.

But: the scheme depended on the coordinated attack of Wenlock and
his company, arrayed on the grassy knoll of Gupshill Manor. Wenlock
was a Warwick man and he had twice turned his coat; at St. Albans,
he had fought for Lancaster; at Towton, for York; and now he was
second-in-command of the Red Rose. But Wenlock sat his horse like
a chained Vulcan, unstirring; while time wasted like blood, in bright
irreparable drops.

The opportunity passed. Weight overcame the first shock; and Edward's forces regained balance, while Richard rallied, drawing back
his outflanked line to support his hard-pressed brother. With bitter
fighting, Somerset's men were driven back and boxed in a rude triangle
formed by the hillock, the river, and the hedges.

A fresh disaster befell. A 'plumpe' of 200 Yorkist spears lurking in
a copse a quarter-mile southwest erupted in Somerset's rear. Assailed
front and flank, the warriors of the Portcullis were caught as in the
ruinous wedge of the Lancastrians at Towton, above the dark-flowing
Cock. Steel masses closed in shooting; and the desperate line broke.
. . . "and so took to flight into the park, and into the meadow that was

* 'Arrivall' p. 80. *Vide* also: 'The Battle of Tewkesbury' by Canon William Bazeley
in Transactions of Gloucester Archaeological Society for 1903.

near, and into lanes, and dykes, where they best hoped to escape; of whom nevertheless many were distressed, taken, and slain." *

Up from the bleeding meadows came striding the Duke of Somerset, an avenging ghost risen from the wreck of his command. Somerset was bare-headed, his face black and streaked with blood. The gold-embossed cuirass was filthy. In one hand, the Duke carried an axe. He marched up to Wenlock. Words were hurled—'traitor!'—'foul knave!'—and the axe glinted.

They left him huddled in the tall grass, blood oozing from beneath his sallet; and turned as trumpets brayed. The brothers of York now stormed the May, 10,000 warriors threatening the entire front, from Swilgate Run on Devon's extreme left to Coln Brook trickling beside hedges of the right wing. The torrent of pikes was like a witch's wood moving across the morning. The archers, Sunne badges on their murrey jackets, poured a crossfire on Lancaster. And in the van, rampant to the kill, rode Richard.

Against this onslaught, Lancaster mustered scarce 4000; and these sick with defeat, the taste of death in their mouths. In the green-gold light flaunted the final banners of the Rose: the White Swan; the Gold Portcullis; the Dolphin . . . God was their witness, they were young!

But the fledgling esquires of Prince Edward, in their black and red livery, these glimpsed a pale mask loom out of the sun and their hands were oily with fear. Richard cleared the sunken road, swept aside John Beaufort's handful on the river flank. The two armoured columns of York now pincered the centre; Richard thrusting from the hedges, Edward and Clarence grinding across the fields. Along the Lancastrian line blew a wind of terror; pikes glinted as a sheet of iron thundered up the rise.

The battle dissolved into thickets of clashing steel. The grass was shining crimson and the young squires lay crumpled in the sun . . . "and it so fell in the chase of them that many were slayne in a meadow fast by the towne, and many drowned at a mill; many ranne towrds the towne; many to the church; to the Abbey; and elsewhere as best they might." **

Prince Edward was trapped in a little meadow—called 'Bloody Meadow'—beside the Avon, where a row of willows stood like great sad sentinels and rooks flapped up and down in the green still light. Edward had tried to reach the Abbey, not more than 700 yards away.

* 'Arrivall' p. 81.   ** Ibid., pp. 81–82.

But the avengers of York were determined to have him. King Edward
had offered 100 pounds annuity for life to the man who brought in the
Prince; and it was said that Richard Croft, a Herefordshire squire, who
once had been tutor to Edmund of York, captured Prince Edward.

Croft brought his prize before the King; and the King asked the
young man what he was doing in arms raising rebellion in England.
And the young man said to Edward that England was his rightful
heritage and Edward was the rebel and traitor. Whereupon, the King
"thrust him away with his glove"; and Richard, Clarence, Hastings,
and the Marquess of Dorset fell upon the Prince with daggers.*

But of this savage tale, no proof exists. It was also said that the
Prince was slain in the meadow, "whiche cryede for socoure to his
brother-in-lawe, the Duke of Clarence." **

The old meaning of succor was 'mercy'; and it was to Clarence, the
least ruthless of the brothers, that Edward appealed in the haunted
meadow where the willows grew. But Clarence, genial, life-loving, had
the fever of ambition implanted in all the children of 'Proud Cis'; and
he loved riches. Only the life of this radiant Prince, husband of Anne
Neville, stood between Clarence and the vast patrimony of Warwick.

But Clarence did not know that Richard too had designs upon the
Warwick inheritance; that he intended to wed Lady Anne himself.
Richard was not likely to rescue the rash youth. And King Edward
was rid of a menace. Like a dethroned king, a ruined Pretender is a
hostage to death. For this chestnut-curled youth, handsome, debonair,
learned, blood had rivered England—now he paid the debt.***

Seven years hence, in the red night of the Tower, Clarence would
cry for succor . . . *then came wandering by a shadow like an angel,
with bright hair dabbled in blood; and he shriek'd out aloud, 'Clarence
is come, false, fleeting, perjured Clarence, that stabb'd me in the field
by Tewkesbury. . . .'* ****

Afterward, the black monks came and begged the body for their
Abbey. Edward—forever eighteen—lies beneath the choir, where look

* Polydore Vergil, *Historia Anglica*.   ** Warworth's *Chronicle*.
*** The notion that the murder of Edward of Lancaster was an invention long after-
ward of Tudor propagandists is contradicted in the following despatch from the
Milanese Ambassador in France to Galeazzo Maria Sforza, June 2nd, 1471. 'Yester-
day his Majesty here heard with extreme sorrow, by clear and manifest news from
England, that King Edward has recently fought a battle with the Prince of Wales,
towards Wales, whither he had gone to meet him. He has not only routed the
Prince but taken and slain him, together with all the leading men with him.'
**** *King Richard the Third*, Act I, Scene 4.

down fourteen stone corbels and Rose bosses of the fan vaulting, before the greatest altar in the land, and over him glows the light of death in spring.

Ancient Tewkesbury, in a park of poplars and giant boxwood, the sun-coloured tower soaring above the green sad meadows and market village . . . during the rout, a score of Lancastrians came crying to the west portal. They were admitted to sanctuary; but hot after, killing mad, rode the fellowship of York. Bursting in, the victors blazed with swords about the fourteen Norman columns, the chantry of Lord Edward Despenser, paladin of the Black Prince, the tombs of de Clares and Despensers. Blood defiled the great altar of Purbeck marble, the rood screen like filigree of stone lace. Abbot Strensham broke into the scene, the Sacrament in his hands, warning the brothers of York of God's curse. The killers halted, blood dribbling down their sword grooves.

Edward gave his royal word.

This was Saturday noon; and it was time for dinner. Yorkist headquarters was established in Tewkesbury, a cordon thrown around the Abbey. Forty-eight hours later, sixteen sanctuary Lancastrians, including Edmund Beaufort, were induced to come forth under pledge of safe-conduct. They were seized; Richard of Gloucester, High Constable, and John Mowbray, Duke of Norfolk and Earl Marshal, held court. The sixteen were adjudged guilty of treason and sentenced to beheading. Generously, Edward waived disembowelment.

The sentence was carried out that same day.

Lancaster had been wiped out; but the inspiration and genius of the Rose knew nothing. Margaret's fortune had reached a kind of apotheosis of ruin—but all those black hours she went on waiting and praying. Not only had God abandoned her—that perhaps would have been understandable for she had much to answer for: pride, adultery, cruelty, blood—but it seemed as if the Devil himself had taken charge of her affairs. She had been forced into the Tewkesbury campaign against her judgment and intuition, all unprepared, on the heels of a torrential defeat. Everyone had argued against her, including her own son, and they had all been wrong, appallingly wrong. Though she was the daughter of the greatest exponent of chivalry of his time, Margaret never fought battles by the book of Malory; she fought with guile and subterfuge, with an acute and quite modern appreciation of getting to the right place at the right time with the heaviest battalions. So had she won Wakefield and Second St. Albans. Towton had been an old-style carnage; Captain Margaret had nothing to do with Towton.

Now: Tewkesbury.

She was not even at the field, she knew nothing of the course of events; and yet she had been forced to stake her whole career, the lives of her captains, and, most agonizing of all, the life of her own son on the outcome of this battle!

Why did Margaret allow herself to be overruled? She had waited ten years for a second chance, after Towton. She was running a thread-bare little Court in Lorraine, with some of her noble supporters going without shoes and begging from door to door; she herself had travelled in a rude wooden cart through the jeering towns of Burgundy and at collection one Sunday she had been forced to borrow from a Scottish archer who had with much pain disgorged half a groat.

She was Margaret of Anjou, one of the most fascinating women of all time; but she was also, to the hard judgment of her class and Age, a failed Queen, a suspect mother, a ruined *intriguante*. Long before, she had become a 'controversial figure'; and only other controversial figures like Mary of Gueldres were really kind to her or displayed genuine hospitality. Others, Louis of France, Philip of Burgundy, War-wick, successful politicians, used her; they did not really like her or trust her or care very much what happened to her.

And of course she knew this. She was a very intelligent woman and she knew that most of her class felt sorry for her when they did not actively dislike her. And being pitied by worldly people is almost worse than being disliked. At the summit of her career, in the winter war of 1460, she had tried to redress the balance by calling in the wild raiders of the March. Results had exceeded all expectations. These mis-erable creatures—her soldiers—had loved Margaret as the Army of Blois had loved Jeanne la Pucelle. They had given Captain Margaret two mighty triumphs and the prospect of a golden third—if she had but seized it. She did not; and the whole remainder of her life was an unsuccessful third act.

That is why Margaret agreed to—or rather, permitted—Tewkesbury. Though she knew well enough the formula for failure, she did not, it seemed, any longer know the formula for success. The young men, Edmund Beaufort, Tom Courtenay, Edward her son, might have stumbled on an answer; and she could not deny them their chance. They might never have another. She could not foresee the holocaust that one day would sweep through the House of York; and indeed, without the ruin of Lancaster, there might never have been such a swathe . . . *and now doth prosperity begin to mellow and drop into the rotten mouth of death* . . .

But whatever Margaret's fault—and grievously did she requite it—the end was most terrible.

Edward chose the most disgusting sycophant, the loudest bully: Lord Tom Stanley. Fourteen years later, Stanley would betray the House of York on the battlefield. Now, on the morning of Tuesday, May 7th, he burst like a bull into Little Malvern Priory.

"Lady Margaret!" he bellowed. "Lady Margaret!"

She came, in black and violet; gazing at this hoarse redfaced Stanley, this breathing image of the politician. Oh she was pale and quiet and proud; and her robes were like dark fallen banners.

"Lady Margaret," Stanley blared, "your bastard's dead!"

Ascension at the tower. . . .

The battle for England was over: York, a minority party, had won —thanks to Richard. His organization of betrayals, his power to strike a paralysing psychological blow, his ability as a field commander were the principal means of restoring the fat lazy Edward to the purple. And the young Constable had not hesitated to take drastic precautions against future threats.

The 'Hope of England' had been dirked in the Bloody Meadow. Thomas Courtenay Earl of Devon, his brother Walter Courtenay, their cousin Hugh Courtenay of Boconnock, and John Beaufort had fallen on the field. Edmund Beaufort, Sir John Langstrother, Lord Audeley, Sir Gervase Clifton (the Sire of the Rose) and some twelve other gentlemen had been enticed from sanctuary (as Buckingham would one day entice little Richard of York) and beheaded.*

Nor did the noble Duke of Gloucester overlook the distaff side. Lady Anne Neville, cousin to Richard, was the second wealthiest heiress in the land, her sister Isabel being the first. Neither Woodeville nor Lan-

---

* The remains of these Lancastrian leaders are interred in Tewkesbury Abbey, in the Chapel of St. James, beside the north transept. The bones of the Duke of Clarence repose in a glass case in a vault below the south ambulatory; brought here after the Duke's murder in the Tower.

castrian must have Lady Anne. Richard, in fact, intended her for himself. But when Stanley, at Little Malvern Priory, demanded Anne, she had unaccountably vanished.

Richard was distressed; but he had other, more pressing worries. The Bastard of Falconbridge, Warwick's man, was raising hell in Kent; thousands of peasants and sailors were up in arms, threatening to seize London and to restore Henry the Sixth. Richard realized that something must be done about this gaunt sad symbol of a ruined Rose; this symbol that merely by existing stirred fire and fury in York's domain.

And, as usual when a thing came into his mind, he was 'sudden.'

He was called "the Prisoner of the Tour." And on fête days and summer evenings, the people would take their children to see him, walking in the garden or sitting at a window, as they took Robin or Sue to see the lions and leopards at the King's Lyon Tower.

For this spectacle had the great merit of being free. Besides the old man had a strange magic: perhaps he really was a saint. The pale hands, the grey hollow face, the eyes dark and far-gazing; and always in a gown of sad blew or russet . . . if he should touch one of the children or even glance piteously toward one, the child might have good fortune the whole of his life.

But now—to their immense regret!—the people were denied access to the old man. He was shut up, some said in the Wakefield Tower, and permitted only to go to Vespers and matins in a small oratory on the barred second storey. The King's soldiers in blue and murrey patrolled the Tower and no one was allowed in or out unless by the King's order. The people understood that this was for the old man's guarding, for there were wicked persons who scrupled not to harm a saint.

And in this dread May, other matters intervened. For merry cursing Tom o'Falconbridge thundered at the gates with the wild lads of Kent: fire and blood in Southwark; bodies charred and split, floating in the river. And Captain Tom, that was bastard of Lord Falconbridge, a Neville, was Earl Warwick's man and had cried that he came to "rescue" the Prisoner of the Tour and put him once more on the throne.

So rumours ran like rats in moonlight, while for five days Falconbridge flared and Lord Scales and Lord Essex held the City—and from Canterbury, they said, marched the Army of Tewkesbury under the Constable, the duke of Gloucester. And Falconbridge, though having a horde of ten thousand and more, broke his camp on the south bank and withdrew into Kent; and the day after, that was Tuesday the 21st of May, Ascension Eve, the King's army entered the City.

And then what a glory of armour, of banners and horses, their bridles glinting in the sun! The iron days of Edward; and small boys pelted along the cheering streets in the army's wake. And at the fore, in an open char drawn by four black horses, sat the hooded woman, the Queen that was, old Margaret, a prisoner. They could not see her weeping, her ravaged face, the horror and madness in her eyes . . . she was a spectacle, a portent of blood, a legend of doom—and from the unpaved streets they threw mudclods until the franc archers drew their swords, for King Edward did not wish his captive hurt.

Boys and girls, wimpled matrons, sober-black clarkes, pied apprentices, they trailed after the hooded woman up to His Majesty's great Tower of London . . . and the bridge was drawn up and a steel patrol held the portcullis. It was near sunset, but little knots of excited persons hung for hours about the Tower; and they were happy in their patience, for between eleven and twelve of the clock, a cloud of mailed horsemen, cloaks billowing, swung up to the postern gate . . . it was silverdark, moonlight upon the river, and the onlookers glimpsed the pale long face and burning eyes of Richard, duke of Gloucester.

And they began to wonder, and some said this, and some said that: but no one could be certain; and after a time the moon set and night like a huge raven came down on the City, the river, the Tower . . . and they all went home, wondering.

The next day, Ascension Day—a holy fête in the Calendar for it was the day on which Our Lord, abandoning grief and death, ascended into Heaven—the brut caused a mighty stir at street corners and Crosses. For it was rumoured that in the night the old man, who had become a kind of sacred image to the people, had perished of sheer melancholy, at the news of the rout of Tewkesbury and the slaying of Prince Edward, his presumed son. And folk said the King's officers had brought the old man to St. Paul's and there he had already begun to work miracles, for his body bled on the pavement of Paul's; and after they had taken him to Blackfriars, where he had bled afresh.

Now it was a very winking time of danger and suspicion, and no man might be certain of his neighbour, so very little was said openly concerning the manner of Henry's death. But men remembered the sunken stare and burning eyes of young Gloucester, the horsemen at the postern gate, and that Falconbridge had sworn to make old Harry a king again.

And they remembered his pale hands and great pleading eyes, the loneliness and terror of his life—a tame rook his only friend—and what dread visitor in the moon's silver dust had come to him; to the Tower of Night—and wept as they remembered, for he had been their king. . . .*

Richard found her cooking and greasy, in an obscure London tavern where she had been put by the gracious foresight of her brother-in-law, the duke of Clarence, to whom she had appealed after Tewkesbury. As a cook-maid, she was probably not much help, for she had ever been buttressed by servants and knew not how to do a thing for herself. This was not her fault; but the nature of her fate.

Richard offered a return to previous status, Duchess of Gloucester, a share in the domains of her father. And though her small chain-legged suitor was suspected of complicity in her husband's death, as well as the murder of Henry the Sixth, she did not long resist. Anne was not the sort to play an heroic role; and Richard, masterful, victorious, fluent, now took the place of former dominant personalities in her life: Earl Warwick and Queen Margaret.

He gave her clothes and jewels, this Cinderella of the Roses, and prepared the nuptial couch.

But Richard's plan was not consumated without angry protest. Un-

* Proponents of York have contested Henry's murder on Ascension Eve, May 21st. The author of *The Arrivall of King Edward* maintained that Henry "perished of pure displeasure and melancholy" on May 23rd, at hearing the news of Tewkesbury. Yorkist *Notes to Hearne's Fragment* relate: 'In the same year died Henricus Sextus, formerly King, in the Tower of London and buried in the monastery of Chertsey . . . Gloucester with the first army (vanguard) invaded Kent; and was followed by the Lord King on the day after Ascension with the rest of the army, that is the 23rd of May.' Sir Clement Markham found evidence in the Rolls that Henry's servants had been paid up to May 24th, or after Gloucester had gone into Kent; but this argues only that their wages were fixed for a particular term, perhaps fortnightly, and they were paid the last full term, though their duties had ceased. Philip Commines, Dr. John Warkworth, and the London *Chronicle*, of contemporary sources, all report Henry's murder and put Richard of Gloucester at the scene. The Croyland Continuator gives the fact of murder, without accusing anyone specifically. Exhumation of Henry's bones in 1911, at Windsor, revealed that the saintly Lancastrian's skull had been bashed in.

STOP

able to prevent the union, Clarence swore that he and Isabel "should part no livelihood" to Richard and Anne; that is, would not share the heritage of Warwick. But Clarence, as ever, was living in a world of massive unreality. Richard's claim was backed by a grateful sovereign; and Richard received a substantial share of the spoils of Warwick. Further, it was brought home to Clarence that he, a perjured traitor to York, might hope for no preferment. All the honours went to Richard; after 1473, he became, as well as Constable, Admiral, Lieutenant of the North, and in effect commander of the Army. He was also certainly a member of the Privy Council.

Clarence, rejected and bitter, fell back on the issue of Edward's marriage. Presumably, both brothers and their mother Duchess Cecily had known for some time about this matter. Edward was not in fact married at all. He had been previously troth-plight to Lady Eleanor Butler, the daughter of old Talbot, Earl of Shrewsbury; such troth-plight was not a real marriage but did constitute an impediment to subsequent marriage, until formally dissolved by the Church. Now Edward, since he had never openly avowed the compact with Lady Eleanor, had not bothered about a formal dissolution.

There the matter would have rested save for two factors: Edward was a king and had married an unpopular scheming widow; and he had two intensely ambitious brothers. The possibility of a crown had not escaped the notice of the duke of Gloucester. Why should it? He was young, popular, competent, wealthy. Of the six bars to his succession in 1453, four were dead, all violently; on the other hand, the birth of Edward's sons, Edward in 1470, and Richard at Shrewsbury in 1473, and the birth of a son to Clarence in 1475, had restored three of the four original bars. Now if this tale of Edward's troth-plight were true, it might prevent the sons of Edward from succeeding. But not while Edward was alive. That was surely obvious. Edward had staked too much on the Woodeville alliance to allow the question to be raised.

But if obvious to canny Richard, it was not, unhappily for him, obvious to the duke of Clarence. He was indiscreet, hawked the secret about, allowed his views to come to the ears of Elizabeth Woodeville. It is possible that Clarence had known for some time. Lady Eleanor had died in 1466, broken-hearted at Edward's infamous conduct (he had tasted her joys on the strength of the troth-plight); and just before her death she had revealed her sorrow to Chancellor Robert Stillington, who had taken it up with Edward. But Stillington, for his pains, had been deprived of his Chancellorship and clapped in jail. He kept quiet thereafter, as long as King Edward lived.

But Clarence talked. He went on talking even with the example before him of the unfortunate Earl of Desmond who had fallen afoul of Elizabeth Woodeville and whose head now rested with the severed vertebrae in the ancestral tomb of the Fitzgeralds. Clarence was drinking, too; more heavily than ever, and his wife was sick, growing more pale and hollow every month, and his little son was ailing and none too bright. Brooding, he concluded that someone had put a "spell" upon his fortunes. When, in 1476, Isabel died, Clarence had a servant named Anckenett Tynedowe arrested and charged with the death of the duchess. Acting as prosecutor, judge, and jury, Clarence executed Anckenett Tynedowe.

This assumption of feudal justice enormously annoyed King Edward. He had early taken a personal interest in the administration of justice and had tried to halt the chaos of King Henry's reign, when great lords took over completely judicial causes in the realm. Edward was additionally irked when Clarence, after assuming the royal prerogative of administering justice, began to mix in foreign relations, as well; and opened his own negotiations with Duchess Margaret of Burgundy for the hand of Mary, her step-daughter. Such a match would make Clarence more powerful than the King. Besides, as always, a Woodeville hovered in the offing of a juicy marriage—Anthony Lord Scales, a recent widower, offering himself as bridegroom. But Duchess Margaret would have none of him.

Clarence had thus far not done anything openly treasonable; he had merely tried to behave like an independent power in King Edward's domain. But now he became involved in something ugly and obscure; with the stamp of Woodeville on it. Clarence was most probably framed; that is, two of his gentlemen were accused of something capital, in order to hit at the duke. Thomas Burdett and William Stacey, in the duke's service, were now charged with plotting the death of Richard Lord Beauchamp,* by the black arts. Beauchamp's wife was claimed to have paid the two in order to further her own adulterous schemes.

All this is most curious. Lady Beauchamp was not arrested or ques-

---

* Lord Beauchamp was Edward's Treasurer. He was also father of that Dickon Beauchamp who slammed the gates of Gloucester in Margaret's face; thereby making almost certain the ruin of Lancaster.

tioned. Lord Beauchamp was not examined. No effort was made to learn from the principals the truth of the charge. What did happen was that Burdett and Stacey were put into the clutch of the rackmaster; and he extracted, along with teeth and nails, the requisite "confession." Burdett and Stacey were sentenced to be hanged, drawn, and quartered; and the awful punishment was promptly carried out at Tyburn.

As his enemies had foreseen, Clarence was wild. It is a point in the duke's favour that he came to his end through loyalty to two poor gentlemen in his service, who were probably as innocent as he of the deadly charge against them. In these times a charge of melting leaden images was about as mortal as anything one could bring against a man. Clarence was too late to save their lives; but he was determined to clear their reputations and he rushed into the Council Chamber at Westminster with a Master William Goddard of the Grey Friars,* who, the duke asserted, had taken depositions of the condemned men which proved their innocence.

He seemed to have no idea what he was getting into. Here he was defying the King's justice, crying that they had put to death two innocent men. Edward was furious; it was the last straw. A warrant was issued for confinement of Clarence to the Tower. He was never again to be at liberty.

Richard played a wary role. He hated the Woodevilles as much as Clarence, but he had no wish to end in the Tower. He made a few guarded remarks in his brother's favour, but refused to go further. The King's blood was up; and he was determined to silence Clarence once for all. Clarence was dragged from the Tower to answer accusations in open Parliament, in January, 1478; but no one save Edward accused the duke and he, some shreds of dignity clinging at the last, after all the perjury and blood, spoke up boldly and told Edward what he thought of him—though he must have known that he was sealing his own death warrant.

Clarence was found guilty of treason and sentenced to death; but the execution of the sentence was deferred until Henry Stafford, young duke of Buckingham, moved in the Lords that the King carry out the sentence. The real motives of Buckingham and his hatred and jealousy of the House of York would be revealed only on Edward's death and the coup d'état of Richard.

Edward was going downhill. He was only forty-one; but he had over-

---

* That is, of the Friars Minor; or Third Order of Saint Francis.

indulged for years: in drink, in food, in women. It is said that he prac-
tised the Roman custom of disgorging masses of half-digested food in
order to gorge again. He was also fond of exhibiting himself, his huge
parts, publicly; and his subjects delighted in these exhibitions.* His
military campaigns, by restricting his diet and by compelling him to
arduous exercise in the open air, had preserved his health for some
years; but he had done no real campaigning since Tewkesbury and
indeed it was doubtful now whether he could get on a horse—he had
grown so unwieldy—and take any effective part.

He left more and more to Richard. The Duke of Gloucester had his
headquarters at Middleham, in Yorkshire. He presided over the Council
of the North, which waged peace along the March; and he took a
prominent role in local justice. He was forging an iron loyalty in the
North. When he came down to York, he was cordially received and put
up at the King's Manor within the grounds of the great Benedictine
Abbey of St. Mary.**

In contrast to Edward, the Duke of Gloucester was regally generous.
Men of all degree looked to the young leader for preferment. And while
he favoured his confidants, men like Percy, Lovell, Ratcliffe, who had
early taken his colours, he was equally ready to listen to petitions from
the burghers of York. In 1477, the York Corporation was greatly
plagued by royal fish-garths obstructing navigation on the Ouse. Repeated appeals to the Duchy of Lancaster and to Edward personally got
nowhere; the Corporation turned to their great and good friend, Richard of Gloucester. The Duke was gracious, obliging; he not only obtained immediate action on the fish-garths but wrote to the Corporation: "the which or any other thing that we may do to the weal of your
said City, we shall put us in our utmost devotion and good will by
God's grace, who keep you." *** Such bannered friendship was not forgot in later days when the Lord Richard was fishing in waters even more
troubled than those of the Ouse: the waters of high statecraft.

But now he lived the life of a Yorkshire gentleman, hawking on the
moors, administering his fiefs, long rides about Wensleydale, festivals

---

* Mancini.
** Substantially rebuilt by Lord Huntingdon, President of the Council of the North
   in the reign of Elizabeth I. When Richard kept his state at St. Mary's, this residence was the Abbott's princely house and was only given the title of "King's
   Manor" in the 16th Century. It is now a school for blind, but has been splendidly
   preserved and is well worth a visit.
*** Davies, York Records.

at Yule and midsummer . . . we glimpse him: small, busy, fiercely concentrated. So much to do in this apprentice time of royalty. For it must be pointed out that Edward did everything possible to prepare Richard for kingship. He knew that Richard knew about the troth-plight; yet he allowed Gloucester to become the most important officer in the realm. And in 1474 Duchess Anne was brought to bed of a son. From his birth this fragile being was pampered, idolized; to the doting father came the whisper of a royal line in the cadet House of Gloucester.

King Edward was not consciously indifferent to the welfare of his own line; indeed, he was as proud and happy a parent as could be found anywhere. But, increasingly, the problems of government and military affairs bored him. He could still put on a fine regal display, as he did in October, 1473, on the occasion of the state visit of the Sire de la Gruuthus. This Flemish lord had been a mighty help in adversity, and Edward repaid his debt handsomely. The Sire Louis was feasted at Westminster and Windsor; given a gown of pure cloth of gold; created Earl of Winchester and a knight of the Garter. Richard was present at the festivities, for he too owed the Sire Louis a debt of gratitude.

But this, the beautiful stage-play of royalty that Edward managed so well, could not compensate for failure in practical politics. For instance, the abortive expedition to France in 1475. The English nation had long lived with the dream of conquering and plundering France. No matter that this had ceased to be a practical objective, either in politics or economy, and that the vain effort to hang on in Normandy and Guyenne had been a total waste of national effort. The monarchy of England still possessed good credit with the people for war; and Edward now pro-ceeded to ruin that credit by raising a huge sum to invade France and make real the old vision of a Yorkist Agincourt. His army was far superior to the valiant "band of brothers" of Harry the Hero-King; and hopes were high that the twenty years of English defeat would be at last avenged.

But King Louis the Eleventh was in some ways the shrewdest poli-tician who ever sat upon a throne and he had accurately taken Edward's measure. Louis refused to fight; and the splendid army of Edward was unable either to force a field action or to unite with its ally, Charles the Turbulent. French gold decided the day. The leaders of the English host, from Edward down, were greased; and agreed to get out of France. Only Richard refused French bribes, thereby making a mortal foe of Louis. Too late, the Turbulent arrived: to find the Universal Spider in possession of the field and his quondam ally willing to talk of anything save war. Indeed the King of England had some wine-drenched dream of going on to Paris, not as a conqueror, but as a tourist—and one can well imagine the kind of outing he had in mind. His presumed host, Louis, poured a liberal douche of cold water on this project.

This inglorious campaign is typical of Edward's later years. His foreign policy, since he had become a pensioner of the King of France, was non-existent; he was a gross spectator on the European scene, with 50,000 crowns annually from Louis. Money that Edward shrugged off as "tribute"; a bad jest, for everyone knew that the King of England had been bought. Louis, whose policy of aid to Lancaster Edward had defeated in arms, was victorious in negotiation. For a fraction of the cost of a large-scale war, he had neutralized England; and by the simple expedient of carrying on endless talks he kept the poor old drunkard of York hanging on the hook of a grand marriage for his daughter Elizabeth: Dauphine of France. And then, when he was ready, Louis abruptly broke off the talks and married the Dauphin Charles to Margaret of Austria.

He had a crying spell almost as bad as when they told him Clarence was dead. His girl whom he loved more than anything on earth was not to have the splendid marriage; he had been tricked, made a fool of before the whole of Europe. His girl, lovely, redgold, full of fire—she was like a re-incarnation of his own wonderful youth. Youth spent, destroyed; and now his looking-glass told him the truth and all his purple might not hide it.

His drinking increased; but he had reached the point where even a small amount of liquor upset his ruined stomach and he could hardly keep anything down, even broth cooked from chicken bones. He was going to die, his physicians dared not lie to a King. And, Blessed Virgin! he was no more ready for death than the Universal Spider himself who was also dying in this spring of Eighty-three, who was utterly terrified by death, and who had summoned wizards and holy men from all over Europe, and even the sacred ampulla of Reims, in an effort to conjure a little more time out of God.

Dying at forty-one, a wreck; and even he could see the fierce bickerings that destroyed the peace of his Court, the Woodevilles more hated than ever, Hastings not speaking to Scales, Richard watching tensely from the North. What would become of his boys?

He had tried to safeguard the princes by a solemn ceremony of oath-taking and investiture, attended by his whole Council. Would this prove durable? He knew too well the history of the English monarchy to believe in the lasting effect of such rites. So much depended on Richard. Protector? The Council of Regency must decide. But Richard would play a strong role. Since Ravenspur, he had been Edward's right hand.

April, the green soft light, the rain; the old wondrous sorrow of time and April . . . and dying; the feeling of death in April, memories fading in a silver dusk, and tears . . . and again the hushed rain, the shrouding green, and leaves trembling and whispering, like voices of the dead. . . .

Oh Bess! Bess!

❖   ❖   ❖   ❖   ❖

"CC MEN, defensably Arrayed. . . ."

They buried him at Windsor in a gorgeous tomb, with Cornish Tresilian's magnificent wrought-iron gates, like black Spanish lace. And over his tester they hung his helmet, his great sword, his brigandine with plates of pure gold. In his time he had been a warrior; and England would not see his like again, so splendid and brave and life-loving.

Elizabeth Woodeville wept, with a cold iron in her bowels. Her son was now Edward the Fifth; and the ambitions of the descendants of Grafton Sheriffs had reached a dazzling climax. But there was a dangerous unknown in the Queen's calculation: Richard Duke of Gloucester. High Constable, Admiral, Earl of Carlisle, Lieutenant of the North, Gloucester must be accepted as Protector by the Council.* He had been immensely correct; his gentlemen all in black, a solemn requiem Mass at York Minster, taking the Oath to Edward the Fifth, inquiring of Queen Elizabeth what service he might render her.

Gloucester had not, the Queen noted, sworn himself in as Protector at York, as he might well have done had the dying Edward appointed his brother to the job. But all this show of fealty on Gloucester's part

---

* Kendall talks of the "all-important codicil" appointing Richard Protector. This is sheer conjecture. No one has ever seen this codicil; and no one ever will. Edward's Testament of 1475, as given in Bentley's *Excerpta Historica,* makes no mention of Richard. More and Holinshed say that Richard was appointed Protector by the Council in May; on the other hand a PR reference of April 21 mentions the "Protector" *before* the coup d'état of April 30th.

was mere display; and Queen Elizabeth wanted her boy brought up from Ludlow, on the March of Wales, with the strongest escort England could provide under the captaincy of her knightly brother, Lord Anthony. In this plan she was blocked by Hastings, who, hating all Woodevilles, had no wish to equip them with an army. The Council compromised on an escort of 2000, under Lord Anthony and Richard Grey, the Queen's younger son by her first marriage.

Meantime, the noble Duke of Gloucester was making a leisurely progress south with a few hundred followers in deepest sable. At Northampton the two companies crossed and the captains, Scales and Gloucester, dined together. Richard was awaiting the arrival of his cousin of Buckingham, with a troop of Stafford horse. Lord Scales retired; and shortly afterward Buckingham galloped into Northampton. He had set a blazing pace from London, for he bore news of the greatest import: the Woodevilles had laid a plot to murder Richard.

How Buckingham "discovered" the secret intent of the Queen has never been explained. It is evident, however, that Richard, even before hearing of Buckingham's discovery, was anxious to obtain the re-inforcement of the Stafford horse. The young King, his Chamberlain Vaughan, his brother Grey had gone on to Stony Stratford with the main body of the escort. Scales lay at Northampton. In the fell of night, the two dukes concerted a paralysing stroke at the plotters. Anthony Lord Scales was seized in his bed; Grey and Vaughan similarly taken at dawn in Stony Stratford, fourteen miles away; the leaderless escort rounded up and given the choice of the White Boar or Stafford Knot—or the oubliettes of Castle Pontefract. Most choose active service under the noble Dukes of Gloucester and Buckingham.

This masterly little coup d'état which, as Hastings himself pointed out with admiration, cost not so much as a drop of blood from a cut finger, made Richard in effect the Law of England. But outwardly the Duke was all smiles and loyalty; he had merely removed a set of murderous schemers from the young King Edward.

In London, the Council at Westminster—bullied by Will Hastings—approved Gloucester as Lord Protector; and writs were issued for a Parliament. One pressing item of business awaited the Protector and jovial Buckingham. Their treacherous enemy Elizabeth Woodeville, instead of allowing herself to be quietly captured, had most annoyingly fled into Sanctuary at Westminster, taking her five daughters and her

second son, ten-year old Richard of York. It was essential to get this
boy out of Sanctuary and into the Tower, with his brother.*

Why?

If Richard of Gloucester had never heard of the troth-plight, if he
had no designs on the throne, why did he not leave the Queen in peace,
as had her avowed enemies, the Lancastrians, in 1471? Why did Buckingham orate on the impossibility of "sanctuary children?"—the Duke's
argument being that sanctuary was only for criminals and since children could not be criminals they could not claim the right of sanctuary.
Why did Richard threaten to send soldiers to drag the boy out?

What possible difference did young Richard's presence in Sanctuary
make to the two Dukes unless they were preparing to seize the throne?
In which case, they could not leave a pretender at liberty. By the
bloodless coup of April 30th, Gloucester was the *de facto* ruler of England. His concern must now be to justify a legal right to the crown.

The Council of Regency set up by Edward the Fourth was em-
powered to issue writs in the name of Edward the Fifth; to prepare
the Coronation; to coin money; ** to carry on foreign policy; and to
summon Parliament. It had no authority to inquire into the King's title
or to name a successor to the crown. In theory, Richard the Second had
freely abdicated in favour of Henry Bolingbroke; and Edward the Second had abdicated in favour of his son, Edward the Third. Even the
turbulent barons who screwed the Magna Carta out of John had no
thought of putting Lackland off the throne.

England may have been belly-fed with the problems of a long minority; and Richard of Gloucester may have been the best man for St.
Edward's seat. But this begs the question. Whatever his qualifications,
Gloucester had no legal right. He could seal the sons of his brother in
the Tower; summon armed men to back up his own claim. There was
no force to stop him from declaring himself King, save that no Englishman not of his immediate party could possibly recognize his title.

Hence, several maneuvers now occur to establish this royal right.
Buckingham's sensitivity to plots was extraordinary; he managed to

* "Soon after the King's arrival in London, it was considered advisable to remove
him from London House to some more commodious residence. Council were
divided. Some recommended Westminster, others the Hospital of St. John at
Clerkenwell; but the Duke of Buckingham proposed the Tower . . ." Gairdner,
Life and Reign of Richard the Third.

** Hastings had the lucrative job of Master of the Mint.

"discover" another on the morning of Friday, June 13th, when the unfortunate Hastings fell afoul of the Protector. Hastings was a career man of York, who had served Edward for twenty years. He was Lord Chamberlain, Captain of Calais, and the dominant voice at the Council, next to the Protector himself. Drinking in London's by-ways, he was the first to discover that among the silver spoons and salt castles goldsmith William Shore of Lombard Street concealed a delicious little treasure—his wife Jane. Hastings passed on Jane to Edward; and then took her back to his bed on Edward's death.

Pious, strict, a fanatical reformer at heart, Gloucester could not think of Hastings and Jane Shore without revulsion. Contamination . . . Hastings had loyally served the interests of Gloucester as Protector, but could such morally corrupt men really be trusted? Apparently not. For presently the Protector learned that Hastings had resolved to stick by his oath to Edward the Fifth, no matter what might be the best interests of this realm of England.

Buckingham had sounded Hastings through William Catesby, a Northampton lawyer and confidant of the Chamberlain. Whether or not Catesby got his master out of Jane Shore's bed to discuss Richard's claim to kingship—one of history's most ill-timed conferences—Hastings gave sufficient evidence that he personally wanted no part of a Richard the Third.

On the critical morning of Friday, June 13th, Buckingham and Catesby (who had secretly come over to the Protector) were extremely busy. First: the pair negotiated a loan of 200 pounds from Thomas Ormonde and William Bullen.* They required this money to distribute among Hastings' men. For that very morning Buckingham, to his horror, had discovered yet another plot against the Protector's life. This one headed by the odd triumvirate of Hastings, Elizabeth Woodeville and Jane Shore. No matter that two of the "conspirators" were not on speaking terms; and the third was a party girl in only one sense; somehow they had got together to bewitch and shrivel up the Protector. The first Woodeville plot had been apparently straightforward murder; the second, however, made use of the black arts.

Buckingham and Catesby rushed to the Tower where the Council had begun session at nine o'clock in the great chamber of the White Tower. Richard, presiding and all unaware of the awful danger, was

* Parliament Rolls, 2nd Ricardus Tertius, Entry December 1st, 1484.

having a merry exchange with John Morton, Bishop of Ely, on the subject of strawberries.

". . . (Gloucester) My Lord of Ely, when I was last in Holborn, I saw good strawberries in your garden there: I do beseech you send for some of them. (Ely) Marry, and will, my lord, with all my heart. . . ." *

Buckingham interrupted the proceedings, called out the Protector, and privily informed him of the plot. Richard was aghast; summary justice seemed the only course. Fortunately, Buckingham had the foresight to muster an armed company and the liverymen of Lord Hastings were strangely apathetic. Returning to the Council, Richard rolled up his sleeve, revealing his withered left arm.

". . . (Gloucester) Look how I am bewitched; behold mine arm is, like a blasted sapling, withered up; And this is Edward's wife, that monstrous witch, consorted with that harlot-strumpet Shore, that by their witchcraft thus have marked me. (Hastings) If they have done this thing, my gracious lord—. (Gloucester) If! thou protector of this damned strumpet, talkest thou to me of 'ifs'? Thou art a traitor:—off with his head! Now by Saint Paul, I swear I will not dine until I see the same . . ." **

Hastings was hustled down to Tower Green; a convenient log was found; someone fetched a rusty sword—and the head of the second nobleman of the Realm was hacked off. Morton and Thomas of Rotherham, Archbishop of York, were arrested, as being also of the party of Edward the Fifth. Lord Tom Stanley suffered a head wound as he ducked under the Council table just in time.*** For all practical purposes the Regency was at an end.

Whatever were Buckingham's real motives, Richard had acted consistently with his loyalty to York. Though he had yet to convince the English, he believed as had Clarence that the sons of Edward were bastards. George of Clarence was dead and his line attainted. Who, then, represented the legitimate descent of York?

Richard. . . .

The decks were now cleared for major propaganda action. Hastings

* King Richard the Third, Act III, Scene 4.
** Ibid.
*** Shakespeare, following More and Holinshed, does not appear to have exaggerated the circumstances of Hastings' execution. Some controversy has existed as to whether Hastings was beheaded on the spot or a week later. However the Fellowship of the Whyte Boar has now come around to June 13th as the correct date.

was dead; Morton and Rotherham locked up; and Scales, Grey and Vaughan were soon to be "let blood" at Pontefract. Sir Edward Woodeville and Thomas Grey, Marquess of Dorset, the Queen's brother and son, had fled to Brittany, taking with them a substantial part of King Edward's personal treasure, although the fugitives were unsuccessful in their corollary design of swiping the royal navy, composed of canny Genoese.

On June 16th, three days after the debacle at the Tower, Elizabeth Woodeville yielded her son, little York, from Sanctuary. The boy was sent immediately to the Tower. How could she? The Queen's attitude in this, as in subsequent relations with Richard, is baffling. Despite the assurances of the venerable Bourchier, Archbishop of Canterbury, she can have had no illusions concerning Gloucester and Buckingham. She might at least have resisted to the last and compelled the Protector to commit a brutal violation of the sacred right of Sanctuary. By yielding, she smoothed the Protector's path.

His nephews under lock and key, Richard moved swiftly. He had several Councils, operating simultaneously; at Crosby Hall, his town house in Bishopsgate; at Westminster; and at the Tower. The Councils at Westminster and the Tower were official, in that they were composed of members of the Government; that at Crosby Hall consisted strictly of Richard's personal supporters. Ratcliffe, Sir Richard Ratcliffe of Derwentwater, was one of the Crosby cabal and he was now despatched on a mission to York, with a letter from the Protector requesting immediate armed aid . . . "we pray you to come unto us to London in all the diligence ye can . . . there to aid and assist us against the Queen, her blood adherent and affinitie, which have intended to murder and utterly destroy us together with our cousin the Duke of Buckingham, and the old blood royal of this realm, and as it is now openly known, by their subtle and damnable ways forecasted the same, and also the final destruction and disherison of you and all other inheritors and men of honour, as well of the north parts as other countries that belong to us (that is, men of other shires owing allegiance to Richard's personal cognizance of the Whyte Boar) . . . Given under our signet, at London, the Xth day of June. . . ." *

What was Richard afraid of? Even Buckingham, who had "discovered" two Woodeville plots, could not have discerned anything menacing in the present suppliant attitude of the Queen. The letter, it

* Davies, York Records.

is true, is dated June 10th; but it was delivered by Ratcliffe in York on Sunday, June 15th. And soldiers from the North could not possibly have reached Richard before another week had passed. The request for armed aid therefore had nothing to do with the crushing of the party of Edward the Fifth on June 13th. Richard was looking ahead; and was concerned about the effect of his next move.

For the boy Edward, his supporters dead, locked up, or in flight, was still nominally the King; and the Protector was preparing a lavish Coronation on June 22nd. Now: a propaganda bombshell exploded. On June 19th, Robert Stillington, Bishop of Bath and Wells, officially proclaimed Edward's troth-plight with Lady Eleanor Talbot, the illegality of Edward's union with Elizabeth Woodeville, and the consequent bastardy of all his children. Stillington, terrified into silence by Edward, now plays his brief part, struts and frets upon the stage, and then is heard no more.

The "uncle and Brother of Kinges"—his epistolary style of these days—professed himself astounded. Here he was, preparing his nephew's Coronation and that nephew a bastard! A Protector's lot is not an easy one and he had to contend with several disagreeable surprises recently. The knightly Anthony Lord Scales plotting murder; Hastings and Jane Shore deep in witchcraft; and now this last blow—Edward the Fifth had no right to the crown. Whom may a man trust? Happily, his cousin of Buckingham was at hand to advise. The Protector himself must take the throne. The honour and future of York—nay, of England —demanded it. The appeal was not lost on this conscientious Prince. Would the people agree? he wondered. Buckingham guaranteed that they would.

That Sunday, the lost Coronation day of the lost little King, the gay and insouciant Duke of Buckingham had rigged a performance out of doors at Paul's Cross by one of London's most rabid hellfire preachers, Dr. Ralph Shaw, brother of the Lord Mayor Edmund Shaw. His text "Bastard slips shall not take deep root," Buckingham's mouthpiece launched into a brimstone discourse: the late Edward's lewdness, his extortions, his cruelties rivaling Tiberius, and finally—his bastardy and the bastardy of his children.*

---

* Unwilling to admit that Richard, now living at the family residence of Baynard Castle, had dragged his mother's name through the mud, Kendall says that the over-zealous Buckingham had hired additional preachers to smear Duchess Cecily. But this will not wash. What preachers? Where and when did they deliver their orations?

Buckingham had arranged that Richard, who hovered in the background while this edifying show was going on, should come forward as Shaw blared his peroration: "This is the very noble prince, the special patron of knightly prowess, who, as well in all princely behavior as in lineaments and favour of his visage, representeth the very face of the noble Duke of York, his father. This is his father's own figure, this his own countenance, the very print of his visage, the sure undoubted image, the plain express likeness of the noble Duke, whose remembrance can never die while he liveth." *

The Plantagenet paragon did come forward, but, despite Shaw's lectern-shaking eulogy, was received in a kind of stunned silence. "The citizens," as Kendall says, "quietly melted away to their homes." Though he meant well, Buckingham was a tyro at this kind of demonstration. Warwick had done far better in March, 1460, when he had staged the popular rally in favour of Edward the Fourth. Buckingham tried again at London's Guildhall, the following Tuesday. Silver-tongued, he would have gone far in the modern era. But now he was in advance of his time. Other than a few liverymen of Stafford, no one cheered.

But if Richard was not to mount the throne by general acclaim, noble Buckingham need not despair. Three hundred horsemen were on their way from York, under Ratcliffe; ** while the two Dukes had several thousand men under arms, either already in the city or on their way from other shires. On June 25, Ratcliffe and his troop halted at Pontefract to oversee the execution of Scales, Grey and Vaughan. Then, joined by Percy of Northumberland, they continued what was in effect a triumphal progress toward London.

For in King Lud's City events were moving fast. During the hectic week following the heading of Hastings, the Parliament writs had been cancelled. Though it was the intent to pack the assembly with Northern men (four members, for instance, were summoned from York instead of the customary two), the Protector may have felt in these unsettled times it was best to take no chances. Now the Dukes got to-

---

* St. Thomas More, *Life and Pitiful Raigne of Edward V*. This is the correct title and subject of More's book. More and Mancini are the principal authorities for the Protectorate. Though unsympathetic to Richard, they are by no means wholesale fabricators. More, especially, lends the subject a biting mordant wit that makes Buckingham and Gloucester alive in a way no chronicler has ever done.

** "At the which day (June 16th) it was agreed that there shall go out of the City CC men, together with C men out of Aynsty . . ." *York Records*.

gether a strictly casual body, composed of Yorkist prelates and career nobles of York, and a scattering of knights of the shire. This convocation represented England, in so far as York was now the majority party; but it must not be forgot that the noble Dukes who had summoned their fellow peers spoke only on behalf of the cadet House of Gloucester—and only time might reveal whether this younger branch represented the stubborn heart of the English nation.*

This Yorkist assembly ratified the deposition of Edward the Fifth; then, prodded by Buckingham, a delegation waited on the Protector at Baynard Castle and pressed him to take the throne. The Prince was nothing loath; and in Westminster Hall, June 26th (the stone angels of Richard the Second looking down) they cried a new Richard: Ricardus Tertius, by the grace of God, King. . . .

It was wonderful. He had never known it would be so exhilarating. King; King, for weal or woe—for Aye. He paraded before the glass, in the glistening goldbraided crimson doublet and stomacher, the magnificent shroud of the purple mantle blazing with gold netts and gold pineapples and furred with long silky blanche vair. He was having a crown made, a rush order, with four golden arches and flashing sapphires and rubies.

In his joy, he forgot all about plots and betrayals. His enemies were dead or withering in Brittany. He alone was left to bustle in the world; he and his great friend the Duke of Buckingham. Already, during the brief royalty of Edward the Fifth, the Protector had showered offices on his friend: High Constable, Seneschal of Royal Castles, Chamberlain of South Wales, Supervisor subditorum suorum in Hereford and Somerset—and there were honours to follow. Nothing was too good for our cousin of Buckingham. In keeping with his exalted state, the Duke had ordered a gorgeous array, a Coronation costume: blue velvet mantle and doublet braided all over with the gold Stafford Knot.

Westminster Abbey, July the Sixth. . . .

* The House of York was the first to introduce the notion of government by popular consent to England. From the time of an overt appeal to the mob in arms through Cade's Rebellion of 1450, every important political move of York was signalized by a popular demonstration of some sort. As we have seen, Edward lost his throne in a popular election to Clarence and Warwick; then won it back, at least in the early stages, by a skilful appeal to popular sentiments. Richard probably worked harder at being a King by popular consent than any English monarch in history. It is ironical that due to the propaganda of his political foes, the Tudors, who were themselves among the worst tyrants known to England, Richard's name should have become synonymous with savage tyranny.

Never was such a Coronation seen. In the royal procession walked three Dukes (Norfolk, Suffolk, Buckingham), six Earls (Northumberland, Lincoln, Surrey, Kent, Huntingdon, Wiltshire), two Viscounts (Lovell, Lyle), Barons and assorted Bishops. As Our Dread Lord came up to the great West Portal the sun glowed through a wrack of clouds, a fire-gold light on swords and maces, lance tips, braid—the Sunne, Herald and glory of York.

Purple-shod, he passed. A smile, the wave of a glittering hand—he had not known it would be like this! Trumpets. . . .

They prayed over him, absolved him, anointed him and Anne, both naked to the waist, on back, breasts, and forehead. He took the mystical Oath; and they wedded him to his people with the gold ring of King Aethelred. Trumpets flared, a brazen lion amid the vast echoing nave; and upon his head they put the Crown. He sat above the surf-like cheers and worship, small and pale, purple-wrapped, throned in the marvelous light of time and God gleaming forever through the glass. . . .

Dieu et mon droit!

The noble Duke of Gloucester had now become Richard the Third; he held in his nervous hands life's burning jewel—a crown. And the cost had been trifling: four deaths and a few public slurs on his mother and his dead brother. True, one of the beheaded had been his good friend and loss of friends cannot but be lamented, even friends of evil diet. But he had other loving companions: John Howard, whom he had just made Duke of Norfolk (the imprisoned bastard, little Richard of York, had lost this title, too); Thomas Earl of Surrey, Howard's son; John Earl of Lincoln, his sister Elizabeth's son; and Buckingham. Above all, Buckingham.

Seldom was such an intimacy known as existed between the King and his High Constable; an intimacy, too, untainted by any hint of vice, such as had gilded the friendship of Edward the Second and Piers Gaveston, or of Richard the First and Blondel, or of Richard the Second and Robin de Vere, Earl of Oxford. Richard the Third and Henry Stafford, Duke of Buckingham, were a perfect match. Buckingham's wit, his rapier intelligence complimented the King's fiery spirit and falcon pride. Buckingham had that ability to hit off mutual foes possessed by the brilliant murdered Gason, Piers Gaveston.

Too soon, the best of friends must part; Buckingham for his ancestral

1. Richard III, King of England. An early portrait of Richard, very seldom reproduced. Probably first temporary likeness. Artist unknown.

XIV. Elizabeth of York. Effigy carved in wood from death mask of Elizabeth, 1503. Photographed by R. P. Howgrave-Graham, Assistant Keeper, Muniments, Westminster Abbey.

XV. Henry VII. Death mask in plaster, 1509. Photographed by R. P. Howgrave-Graham, Assistant Keeper, Muniments, Westminster Abbey.

castle of Brecknock on the Welsh March, King Richard for a triumphal progress. It was Buckingham's idea to relieve the King of the worry and embarrassment of the Bishop of Ely's presence by carting him off to Brecknock, where the High Constable himself would keep an eye on the frocked intriguer.

Buckingham accompanied the King as far as Gloucester; the "Shining City" of the Celts. What York memories blazoned Gloucester! Mortimer's Cross and the bleeding beautiful head of Owen Tudor; the agony of Queen Margaret, Tewkesbury and the death of the Rose; the passing of the Young King, of the youth Edward, on his royal road to darkness . . . Inspired, the two friends discoursed of York greatness. And York magnanimity; the mark of a regal spirit. What more did our friend desire? Why, there was Hereford; the estate and movables of the Earldom of Hereford. Buckingham claimed in right of his great great grand-dam, Eleanor de Bohun, daughter and heiress of Humphrey Earl of Hereford; but the other Bohun girl, Mary, had been wife to Henry Bolingbroke, the same that had murdered golden royal Richard and put a halter on England's neck: the founder of the House of Lancaster.

So Buckingham wanted Hereford? Buckingham's friend smiled that pale sardonic smile. "The Earldom of Hereford was of the inheritance of Henry the Fourth, who was also King of England—tho' by tort and Usurpation—and will you, Milord Buckingham, claim to be heir of Henry? You may then haply assume his spirits and lay claim to the Crown by the same titles." *

Our cousin was not in humour. His wit failed; conversation lagged. No more was said about Hereford; but many a time and oft, he glanced backward to that curtained char where reposed the perspiring bulk of the Bishop of Ely. . . .

Richard rode on to Worcester and Warwick. Then, Oxford. The role suited him perfectly: patron of Caxton and learning. He lodged at Magdalene and heard the scholars in disputation. One day he would found a college of his own. On to Leicester, Nottingham, and—York. Everywhere, a joyous welcome: the Mayor and Corporation in scarlet; Recorder and bailiffs in violet. Offers of money; things were going better than he had dared dream. Richard refused the offers, saying, with his happy flair for the *mot juste,* that he would "rather have the hearts of his people than their purses."

* Sir George Buck, *The Life, Reign, and Extraordinary Death of Richard the Third.*

Was such a King ever dreamed of?

"He doth content the hearts of the people where he goes best that ever did Prince," wrote Thomas Langton, Bishop of St. David's, "for many a poor man that hath suffered wrong many days have been relieved and helped by him and his commands. And in many great cities and towns were great sums of money given him which he hath refused. On my truth, I never liked the conditions of any prince so well as his. God hath sent him to us for the weal of us all."

Many a poor man!

When did the late King Edward ever relieve a poor man, except to relieve him of what little cash he had been able to secrete from the exhausting labour to keep alive? And had Edward ever been known to refuse money from any source whatever? The thing was inconceivable.

His sons Edward and Richard, mewed up in the Tower by a wary uncle, excited curiosity and compassion. Little knots of citizens were forever gathering about the Lyon Tower or the postern Gate, to the annoyance of Sir Robert Brakenbury, the Lieutenant. Whispering; waiting; they remembered Ascension Eve and the grey discrowned martyr. In early September, the boys could be seen shooting at the butts in the Tower garden.* But this public display was dangerous; no use in stirring people up, reminding them of an Edward the Fifth. They had a Richard to reign over them. "He and his brother were withdrawn into the inner apartments of the Tower proper, and day by day began to be seen more rarely behind the bars and windows, until at length they ceased to appear altogether." **

And so all the lavish care of tutors, the studies under scholarly Lord Anthony, the beautiful and pleasing accomplishments that had so delighted a doting father, all this was thrust into a dark cell. Without, the lonely boots of twilight scraped up and down. And here it was always Vespers; always the shadows and the whispers, the stone-echoing centuries. Black Will Slaughter, the Keeper; Brackenbury, the Lieutenant; Tyrell, Master of the King's Henchmen—crying, they cried a great deal and prayed a great deal, and comforted one another. Lantern-haunted, stone-echoing, in the Norman light they waited. Forever should they wait and he be King!

His finest welcome was reserved for York. Immediately on arrival,

* "The children of Kynge Edward were seen shooting and playing in the gardyn of the Tower by sundry tymes." *Great Chronicle of London.*
** Mancini.

August 31st, Richard sent to Piers Courteis, his Keeper of the Wardrobe, for suitable attire: for gorgeous robes of silk, velvet and vair; for
coat armour beaten with fine gold and for gilt spurs; for forty trumpet
banners of sarcenet; for four thousand jackets of fustian blazoned with
the Boar; for sarcenet banners of Our Lady, Saint Edward, Saint
George, and Saint Cuthbert.

Though not officially proclaimed as such, this was a kind of second
Coronation: Richard Plantagenet's consecration to the North. On Monday, September eighth, Richard, Anne, the tiny sickly Prince Edward,
wearing golden crowns, walked through leafy aisles of cheering subjects
to the Guildhall and York Minster. A glittering pageantry followed:
Richard's son was formally invested as Prince of Wales (Yorkshiremen,
here is your Prince!); given a golden wand, three ostrich feathers, and
the sword of Knighthood. The slim dark Jean of Gloucester, a King's
bastard, who had no mother, whose mother had utterly vanished, was
likewise knighted by his gracious sire. York Corporation presented the
King with 450 pounds and a golden dinner service; gifts which he accepted from his old country of the North, as a special mark of royal
favour. The ceremonies concluded in a blaze of love and mutual con-
gratulation; and they all went to see Saint Christopher's Guild put on
the Creed Play at York Minster.*

And now did Sir James Tyrell, Knight-Banneret, Master Henchman,
Tyrell of Gipping—did he post up from London with seven tall lads
in green to confer with Our Dread Lord? What did Tyrell want? The
Tyrells of the world, prim and brutal, policemen of the heart, always
on the side of some terrifying confusion known as "law and order,"
they intrude like fate. Was it confirmation of a secret command from
Buckingham—"must I be plain? I wish the bastards dead!"—or was
this coming itself a trick to reassure the unsuspecting King.

They met in the Abbot's Hall at St. Mary's, a great black-beamed
room one hundred feet long. From the crackling hearth shadows flowed
into the Hall, about the guardsmen stiff and silent, the badge of *Blaunche
Sanglier,* the tusked ferocious Boar, blazoning their doublets. A gleam
of cloth-of-gold and Richard limped into the morning, plucking at his
dagger. And Tyrell, prim, shock-shouldered, in steel and leather, whip-

---

* The York Mystery Plays have recently been revived in a splendid performance,
which is far less publicized than it deserves to be—the press and public relations
facilities being as lamentable as the show itself is rich and unique. The costuming,
lighting, and choreography are especially magnificent.

ping his gauntlet against an iron rushlight. God and Mary! and all those weeping halls of Ascension—what was it? What terror behind iceblue eyes? Richard did not pry. He had begun his reign with mercy; he forgave. Buckingham was High Constable. Buckingham was responsible for the Tower.

The word Tyrell had come to hear. He bowed; turned to mellow shotgold September. A horse was waiting. . . .

Four deaths; a few public slurs on the House of York. Surely not a lavish price—but now was brewed that devil's broth which was to change all, the death beyond death, the death that would not die. As the echo of Tyrell's boots faded in the morning, there fell the shadow of the Constable, the witty deep-revolving friend, dearest Buckingham —he would spare the King pain. He would do whatever disagreeable tasks his high office demanded, such as ridding his Dread Lord of potential sources of disaffection (how judicious and legal-sounding, that!), quietly and efficiently. He would do more. He would if called upon— and he had heard a summons!—bear the burden of monarchy himself.

Buckingham down in Brecknock, firelit conclaves with the wheezing captive Bishop, the gross body, the eyes that glared like agates at the sight of silver, and here he was—Godlike, a Warwick come down in a shower of light—unmaking his Richard, the man he adored, the King he had created, unmaking him with this frocked black mass of lies and avarice, talking in the red glow of bald disgusting Tudor . . . how could Buckingham torture himself with such men?

In reality, he was only using them. He had already anointed himself. He, Henry Stafford—Henry the Seventh . . . he would use Morton as Morton fancied he was using Buckingham and when the time came he would eliminate the whole conniving set of priestly scoundrels. Ever since he had boldly demanded the death of Clarence from Edward, he had heard the voice of God—or was it the Devil?—like a trumpet in the wind. He agreed to whatever Morton proposed because none of it mattered in the least; he hated Morton as he had never hated any man, and it not been for the political necessity, he would much like to have made Morton and Tudor guilty of murdering the sons of Edward.

But the murderer must be Richard.

He has been chosen, anointed for this role. Not by Buckingham; the noble Duke is merely an instrument. Richard the Third has been cast by the arrayed and shining conditions of his life; by his blood-heritage; by Duchess Cecily's corrupt and holy ambition; by Duke

Richard's passion for war. And not least by this very flame of the Roses, that has consumed a hundred thousand men, seared whole pages of time; the white sunhot flame of this last monarchy.

the legend of the wicked uncle. . . .

Commands streamed up from Brecknock. Knight-Banneret Sir James Tyrell was put in charge of the Tower for a single evening. He picked his own men, among them John Dighton, a priest; Black Will, the Keeper. And then in the dusk, the wind and rain of October, the sad ravens on the Green, they came to the Garden Tower . . . and the voices whispering, the echoes ringing, ringing, the fire and huge shadows; all tears exhausted, staring at the door. *Strangling is such a quiet death. . . .*

Down in Brecknock, the Duke took weapons from the wall; he called out his Welshmen. His purpose was to rid England of a tyrant; a tyrant, moreover, who had just committed a hideous crime. From hearth to hearth, the rumours leaped. The King was a murderer, a child murderer. Herod; King John . . . this was worse. A York Childermas; an October Festival of the Innocents. . . .

He flared toward Herefordshire. Henry Tudor took to the Manche with a scraggle of bought mutinous Frenchmen; Grey of Dorset and Lionel Woodeville aroused Wiltshire. They marched against tyranny, against a blood-supper of children.

While the new Herod, wrapped in the wonder of the happiest monarchy ever known in England, was on his way from York to Lincoln. But all this wonder and glory proved false as the painted hellish smile of Buckingham. Earth roared; the joyous kingdom burst into flame. From Lincoln, the King wrote to Bishop John Russell, the Chancellor, for the Great Seal. "Here, loved be God"—a postcript in his own royal hand—"is all well and truly determined for to resist the malice of him that had best cause to be true, the Duke of Buckingham, the most untrue creature living; whom, with God's grace, we shall not be long until that we will be in that parts and subdue his malice."

the most untrue creature living. . . .

Why he was raging up from Wales, plundering and rioting, a pennyweight Achilles, with a horde of blackfaced Welsh; Tudor was cruising off the coast; and the whole southwest was in chaos. Then it hit them, the worst storm of the century, a shrieking wind, torrential rain, the Severn flooding whole parishes. The rebel army was broken up; scattered to the winds of Wales. Overnight the proud and soaring Duke became a hunted fugitive, wandering with shaven head and friar's gown, muttering and dirty in this absurd and pitiful disguise, a little mad. . . .

And he the master-Judas of his time was appropriately sold for money by one of his own creatures, with whom he had taken a pleading refuge. King Richard had posted a reward of 1000 pounds for his old friend; a massive sum. He was dragged to Salisbury; and there implored an interview with Richard. What did he expect? Forgiveness? He had gone too far; he was beyond any conceivable grace this side of Heaven. To assassinate Richard? A preposterous notion.

What then did ruined Buckingham want?

On Hell's brink, he did not view the matter as others. Eloquent; too eloquent. He had always been able to talk friend or foe into almost anything. Now he wanted to talk to Richard, old comrade and mortal enemy. Perhaps he wanted to talk about the Princes; the love he had borne the King; and how much he hated John Morton and Henry Tudor. He longed to talk himself back into—not pardon—but some kind of acceptance. Life was vanishing from Buckingham; he stood alone at an appalling gate. Richard, whom he had tried to destroy, whom he had made King, linked forever in death and life, Richard would understand him. He must talk to Richard.

Richard refused to see him.

An error. For surely in the course of that terrible justification would glow some truth about the Princes; the October night, the great strangling hands, the cache of the bodies. Or it might be just this possibility that Richard himself could not confront: *the necessity of having to search for the dead*. To stir and quicken the dead; to dig up the stiff rotting bodies, the purple-black faces, the still-screaming eyes. . . . Tyrell had come to see him at York. Yet he had not known it would be like this. He had not known. . . .

Buckingham was beheaded on All Souls Day.

WHIRLING and glowing the burning disc of the Sunne monarchy; in whitehot time, he was forging a new realm. With his staff, Chancellor John Russell, Secretary John Kendall, Chamberlain Francis Lovell, confidential adviser Catesby, personal emissary Richard Ratcliffe, he drafted plans for the coming Parliament, already twice postponed.

In the Docket Book of his soul—to match the meticulous entries in

Russell's record of the reign—he had ticketed as *nolle prosequi* the case of his nephews. They had become shadowy, boys he might have known long ago in another kingdom; mostly, they came to him as voices, crying and whispering a long way off, like October leaves. And this was always at night, when he endured his first attacks of wakefulness. In the North he had slept well; but in this lavish goldcurtained chamber of Westminster he would lie awake, staring. He saw the shrouding dark, the red torchfires that flared upward in the vast halls, the guards like statues, the tapestries that appeared to move and glimmer. And then he heard the voices. A man would not think bodies burned in quick-lime, in a kitchen-hole—where had he got such a notion?—would whisper to the living. What did the voices want? He had done all that he could for them. It would do no good, solve nothing, to put Tyrell to the question. He had considered that; as he had considered everything else. But the matter was past mending.

If only the voices would understand; would allow him to sleep. Double the guards. Allow no one to pass without a permit. Somehow the voices got in; came to him; and he heard their far off sighing, that was like leaves—October leaves. . . .

His days, on the other hand, were another country. It was true, and in his own case he had known it confirmed, Night was a Kingdom; by day, he was Richard the Third; by night, he was becoming a legend, a monarch that never existed on land or sea. By day, he went about the exciting business of his first Parliament: confirmation of his royal right; benevolences; attainders; the woollen trade; books and learning, the patronage of the House of York.

William Catesby was Speaker of this Yorkist assembly; and Chancellor John Russell delivered the Speech from the Throne, in the Marcolf Chamber at Westminster, January 23rd, 1484. "We have many members in one body, and all members have not the same office" was the Chancellor's keynote; a plea for national unity. The new alignment of the nation behind the cadet House of Gloucester was signalized by the passing of the Act establishing the royal title of Richard the Third. *Titulus Regius* was in keeping with the York tradition of popular consent, Parliament itself approving the King's title. The Act also gave Richard the opportunity to record the horrendous facts of the late King Edward's career.

It was not enough to set down the invalid marriage to Lady Grey and the bastardy of Edward's heirs; royal viciousness must be pro-

claimed. Edward had been a being "delighting in adulation, and flat-
tery, and led by sensuality and concupiscence, followed the counsel of
persons insolent, vicious, and of inordinate avarice . . . the land was
ruled by self-will, and pleasure, fear and dread, all manner of equity
and law laid apart and despised, whereof ensued many inconveniences
and mischiefs, as murders, extortions and oppressions . . . so that no
man was sure of his life, land, or livelihood, nor of his wife, daughter,
or servant, every good maiden and woman standing in fear to be rav-
ished and deflowered."

The Puritan flavour—the fierce denunciations of foes as "horrible
adulterers and bawds"—was now become characteristic of the King's
public style. With the growing terror of his night-time monarchy went
a zealot's abhorrence of vice, especially sexual vice; as if the wakeful
torchlit legend of the Dark Tower were as nothing to the leprous souls
of enemies. A note already twice struck in the proclamation that set
forth the awful corruption of Hastings, the sexual depravity of Jane
Shore, and the danger to the young in having such persons about; and
in the Proclamation of Kent, issued October 23rd, against the Marquess
of Dorset who also had succumbed to Jane and was "wallowing" in
fornication.

In fact, the Proclamations would appear to say that the luscious body
of Jane Shore was the cause of all this treachery, sin and death—haunting Richard from the first. Merry melon-breasted Jane with whorls of
spungold hair; he could not bear to think of her. He had tried to destroy
the image of her in his mind by a public shame; forcing her to walk
almost naked down Cheapside to St. Paul's, carrying a lighted candle.
But he only roused sympathy for the girl. He tried to get rid of this
lovely and damned creature, who horrified him, by shutting her in
Ludgate prison. Only to have his own Solicitor-General, William
Lynom, plead for the girl's release because he desired to marry
her!

How he choked and pulled his dagger up and down in the gold-
embossed sheath, that nervous habit of his that made men uneasy (who
was he thinking of getting rid of next?); but would not give up his
new forbearance. What the letter cost him!—but he managed it and
could even dwell on the wry smile of Chancellor Russell. "We, for many
causes, would be very sorry that he should be so disposed; and pray you,
send for him in that ye goodly may exhort and stir him to the contrary.
And, if ye find him utter set for to marry her, and none other be ad-

vertised, then, if it may stand with the law of the Church, we be content. . . ."

But this hatred, this persecution of the fair Jane, was it not really
desire? Desire that inflamed him? Did he lust for the laughing wanton,
so different from his pale Anne? . . . His self-disgust was infinite. He
had to punish himself; punish his own lust. By denouncing the hideous
vice of Hastings and Dorset, he denounced himself. By flinging his
dead brother's name in the mud—a flare of virtuous outrage in the
Parliament Roll that was totally irrelevant to the question of Richard's
title—he inflicted angry wounds upon himself. The horror of lust; of
forbidden pleasure. To his shame, he had sired a bastard; but no one
should ever know the woman's name. For him, there had ever been
but one woman: his mother. In the shadows of his soul stood the Duchess, the perfection of woman. But then: this agony of shame and desire
—and the need, remembered at midnight, to still the havoc of his heart
with the knowledge of evil; the dark wrestling in a goldcurtained
prison.

He was a man of blameless life; blameless. . . .

In money matters the contrast was equally striking. King Edward,
it will be recalled, had screwed a huge sum out of his subjects for war;
and then had utilized the army thus arrayed to screw an equally huge
sum out of the Universal Spider. This tax the King, with cynical irony,
termed a "benevolence." The benevolence amounted to a fifteenth of a
man's gross income; not perhaps very alarming by comparison with
the usurious demands of the wasteful and continually warring modern
state, but highly oppressive by medieval standards.

In a magnificent gesture of largess, Richard by formal act of Parliament abolished the benevolence forever. No single action of the reign
was more popular or more productive of woe. For, a generous and
popularity-seeking Richard overlooked certain facts. The hard cash,
accumulated by Edward (he and the Turbulent, the two richest men in
Europe, were both notorious *avares*) over a period of twenty years,
had been pilfered by the Woodevilles who had skipped to Brittany.
Granted the customary tonnage and poundage for life, the King had
further reduced his slender revenues by cutting customs receipts, as a
gesture toward English traders. In effect, Parliament put an embargo on
merchant strangers, forbidding them any form of retail trade in England and excluding them altogether from the manufacture and sale of
woollen cloth.

In an emergency the feudal reliefs exacted by the King were by no means sufficient to raise and equip an army. The answer was to open up new sources of income; but it is not very easy to determine where or how, by a monarch who voluntarily gave up his taxes at the same time that he insisted on sweetening friendships with lavish gifts (the old Warwick technique of beef and ale streamlined to Richard's purposes). In the previous December the royal finances had sunk so low that Richard had sold £550 of silver plate to Edmund Shaw, former Lord Mayor, at the bargain price of 3s 4d the ounce. A little later, he began trading in wool as Edward had done. Acting as Richard's agent, Tyrell sold £3000 of wool for him on the Calais Staple.

But such devices were a mere stop-gap. If real trouble came, trouble with the French, Richard would have no money to defend the realm. His old enemy, the Universal Spider, had abruptly cut off the 50,000 crowns annual "tribute"; he had received Richard's letters and Heralds (one of them was *Blaunche Senglier*) with studied discourtesy, almost insult; while the Spider's descent in July, 1483, to an evil frightened grave loaded with images and charms ("He had deceived all Europe; now he tried to deceive God Himself") meant only that his policy was carried on by the Regent, Anne de Beaujeu. And in this very month of happy English unity, January, 1484, the Estates of France were convoked at Tours to hear a blast against the hereditary foe, the "Goddamns," by the Chancellor of Charles the Eighth, Guillaume de Rochefort.

The Chancellor began with a paean to the order, prosperity and harmony in the realm of France, in contrast to the treachery and violence of the beef-eaters over the Manche; and then went on to say: "If I wished to bring forward special proofs of your love to your Prince and the treachery of others, a whole day would not suffice. It will be enough to cite the example of the neighbouring English. Behold, I pray you, what happened in that land after the death of King Edward, how his children, already grown and noble, were put to death with impunity, and the royal crown transferred by favour of the people to their murderer."

Voices in the wind. . . .

Could any true Englishman believe such rot, the frothings of Dominic Mancini, the Dominican stooge of Guillaume de Rochefort, and of the twice-perjured Bishop John Morton? Was not the truth to be sought in those loyal faces arrayed in the Marcolf Chamber, upturned to Speaker Catesby, to Chancellor John Russell, the applause, the smiles?

Honi Soit Qui Mal Y Pense. Perhaps, like grey discrowned Henry, whose tomb at Chertsey was become the focal point of pilgrims and miracle-hunters, the boys had died of "pure displeasure and melancholy."

It may or may not have been of significance that in this happy Parliament of 1484 there was no mention at any point of the present status or the means of maintenance of the Princes in the Tower.* But Richard's own boy, frail Edward of the ostrich plumes, was amply provided for. The lords and gentry of this Parliament were asked to take an oath to young Edward as the next heir and successor of Richard the Third in a nocturnal ceremony in a basement chamber at Westminster.

It is not on record that anyone refused.

But even he, pale, dagger-plucking, limping about with sacred relics for the oath, must have known what such rites were worth. Had he not, in an almost identical stage-play sworn fealty to the son of Edward, brother and sovereign? An oath taken at the time he knew of the troth-plight to Eleanor Talbot.

But he relied not on oaths alone. Largess was one additional means. Mercy was another. For the grievous rebellion of October, Parliament's Bill of Attainder contained no more than one hundred names. And of these, fully half were allowed to purchase pardon. To be sure, a few could expect no forgiveness: Thomas Grey, Marquess of Dorset; Lionel Woodeville, Bishop of Salisbury; Sir John Cheyney, Master of the Horse under Edward; Sir William Brandon; Sir Thomas Arundell of Lanherne; Sir Thomas St. Leger, husband of Richard's elder sister Anne (the naked corpse of a previous husband, the Duke of Exeter, had been found floating in the Channel in 1471). These men constituted the hard core of treason. All but St. Leger, seized and beheaded, escaped to Brittany.

Richard had been mortal in his falcon youth; iron and velvet during his track to the throne. Once anointed, he charged his shield with the martel of mercy. Henry Percy, 4th Earl of Northumberland, notorious coat-changer, was confirmed in ancestral honours and made Warden of the North. The Stanleys of Derbyshire, supporters of Edward the Fifth, were ablaze with favours. Sir William had been made Constable of Carnarvon and Warden of Delamere; Lord Thomas had been kicked upstairs from Steward to High Constable, in succession to the late

---

* Buck claimed to have found such a reference in the Parliament Roll. But he neglected to say where and no one has been able to locate the reference.

lamented Buckingham. This policy appeared to pay off when Lord George Strange, son of Lord Thomas, took the field against Buckingham, at the head of several thousand men.

And lesser lights. William Collingbourne, gentleman usher under Edward the Fourth, was made Sheriff of Wiltshire and custodian of Duchess Cecily's property in that shire. Sir John Fogge, who had cheated Edmund Cooke, Lord Mayor of London in Edward's reign, out of a substantial piece of property, and who had married a Woodeville—Fogge was taken into favour and his wretched claim upheld. And even after he had been caught *in flagrante delicto* with the Woodevilles in October, 1483, Fogge was forgiven and turned loose.

(down in Italy, a lean black-eyed Ambassador of the Florentine Republic, a man of obscure lineage named Niccolo Machiavelli, pondered the chemistry of worldly power; and in the diamond glass of his Italian soul was forming the image of the perfect ruler: the man who was cruel in order to be kind; the man who began by ruthless elimination of his foes and went on to amity and brotherhood . . . the *Prince*)

He had a third means of binding his subjects to the new and glorious monarchy of the Sunne. For he was aware, as he demonstrated in his great final utterance before Bosworth, that his kingship stood at the end of a long tradition of mystery, protective values, faith and doom —the end of a whole world of thought and behavior. He had been reared in the age of Henry the Sixth, a Lancastrian cosmos in which God and the divine hierarchy on earth still retained its magic; however battered by war and treachery. As we have seen, Warwick and the House of York did not attempt to assert that God had dethroned Henry and created Richard of York as his Deputy. Henry of Bolingbroke had asserted this, or something like it, when he had staged the formal abdication of Richard the Second. But the House of York had turned to a new concept of popular consent. The subjects themselves expressed their preference that York should reign over them. No matter that these popular ceremonies were packed; the important element is that popular consent should have been recognized at all.

Richard was the heir of this new tradition; and every important step of his kingship is signalized by an appeal to his subjects. Thus, he— through his mouthpieces—had pleaded at Paul's Cross and London's Guildhall for his right to the throne. Thus, he had staged the most lavish and popular coronation ever known; and thus he had wedded himself to the North in what was in effect a second coronation. Thus, he in person would publicly avow his good faith toward Elizabeth Woodeville and her five daughters. Thus, to deny a policy which had become distinctly unpopular, he would again take the rostrum to state that he never had any intention of marrying his niece Elizabeth.

The policy of promoting books and printing was certainly one aspect of this appeal to popular consent. For, despite the cultural heritage of Queen Marguerite d'Anjou and despite the secular learning of the Good Duke Humphrey, the reign of Henry the Sixth was not notable for tolerance or for learned inquiry. One of the leading works of the time was the *Booke of Margery Kempe,* an outpouring of religious hysteria, which is a fearful example of the decadence of Christian mysticism. Lancastrian poets such as Thomas Occleve and John Lydegate were poets of such meagre inspiration and technique, and with such innocuous sentiments, that in a richer age they would hardly be considered poets at all, but scribblers. And of course any attempt to write a serious philosophical work such as the inquiry into Church doctrine of Reginald Pecock, Bishop of Chichester, ended up on the faggot heap. Even the sonnets of William de la Pole, Duke and Marquess of Suffolk, to the golden beauty of Marguerite d'Anjou aroused suspicion and rancor; and, far from being a point in his favour, the Duke's learned attainments contributed to his downfall.

The House of York changed all this. Up to the reign of York, most learning had been jealously locked within the Church; and meagerly provided in an alien language: Latin. Chaucer, it is true, had penned his marvelous pictures of the time in southeast English; but both Chaucer and the monarch under whom he flourished, Richard the Second, were ahead of their age; and both had to await the advent of York for restoration to their proper appreciation.

But with York what had been called, perhaps inaccurately, "the new learning" becomes a part of English life. For it was really old learning, the learning long-buried of Greece and Rome and the poetry of France and Italy, that now was spread wide through the printing art of William Caxton.* Former Governor of the Merchant Adventurers of the Netherlands, Caxton abandoned wool for literature in 1468. His earliest patron was the rich, sensual Margaret of York, who alternately bullied and

---

* Professor E. H. Harbison of Princeton has favoured me with the curious view that the invention and spread of printing had little to do with the obvious growth of secular learning. This seems to me like saying the invention of steam combustion had little to do with the rise of the modern industrial state.

coaxed Caxton into completing his translation from the French of *The Recuyell of the Histories of Troy*. Translator as well as editor and printer, Caxton was an all-around man, a Johnsonian figure in Fifteenth Century literature. Like Geoffrey Chaucer a southeast of England man, Caxton's renditions into vernacular English of this busy populous area helped establish this form as the common language.

Two elements were essential in this new dispensation: the technique —supplied by Caxton; and the political favour—liberally bestowed by the House of York.

Like his sister Margaret, King Edward—that notorious man about town—had a reverential awe of learning. He had had a good education himself, thanks to the "odious demeaning" of Richard Croft, and his reign was distinguished by the continued patronage of Caxton, who set up shop at the sign of the Red Pale in Westminster, and by his powerful ministers, Anthony Lord Scales, the most learned knight of his day, and by John Tiptoft, Earl of Worcester and Constable, who tuned his Latin sonnets to the iron brake and the Duke of Exeter's Daughter.* He was eager that his son and heir, Edward, should have similar tastes; and nothing is more pathetic than the universally attested fact of the Young King's scholarship and his beautiful eloquence contrasting with the dread factors of power politics which cast him into the Tower and deprived him of his life.

Now Caxton was shaping a mighty work, the editing and printing of Malory's compleat *Morte d'Artur*—calculated to appeal to the flair for gorgeous pageantry of the time. The *Morte d'Artur* was the first bestseller in history; a smash success over the next two centuries. A work, too, in which King Richard took the keenest interest, with his passion for the outward trappings of chivalry, as well as for the inner mysteries of the Arthurian legend: brotherhood, sorcery, and death.

Not only did Richard continue York's patronage of Caxton, but his Parliament exempted books from the embargo on imports; and foreign printers domiciled in England were encouraged to pursue their art. Where the agile and subtle mind of Richard appreciated the immense importance of the coming Golden Age, his narrow, provincial and tyrannous successors, with their axe-murders and censorship, set back the English Renaissance by at least half a century.

Parliament adjourned, *sine die,* on February 20th; received the gra-

---

* This was, apparently, a form of Iron Maiden; in which the victim was enclosed within a glowing iron mold.

cious thanks of the King, which it had well deserved, and went home. . . .

". . . (Buckingham) Ah, my lord, this Prince is not an Edward! He is not lolling on a lewd day-bed, but on his knees in meditation; not dallying with a brace of Strumpets, but meditating with two deep divines; not sleeping, to engross his idle body, but praying, to enrich his watchful soul." *

He was, indeed. He had a rendezvous with Heaven; and so concerned was he for the spiritual welfare of his subjects that shortly after his Parliament adjourned he got out a sort of pastoral letter to the clergy, exhorting a moral revival amongst the shepherds themselves; and promising that the old right of Church courts to try clerical offenders should be respected. He was not unmindful that even Bishops were not blameless; and several had so fallen on lewd and wicked ways as to betray "so good a master"—Morton of Ely, Lionel Woodeville of Salisbury, Piers Courtenay of Exeter. He spent lavishly on chantries; maintaining and enhancing the previous foundations of York: the beautiful little Lady Chapel at the Bridge of Nine Arches at Wakefield; ** the chantries of Fotheringay; his own colleges at Barnard and Middleham. His daily services, at Windsor or Westminster, were as soul-enriching as one might wish. His choir was famous. Like Gilles de Rais, he had gathered these tender thrushes from every corner of his Realm; friends sent him presents of boys, for no gift was more pleasing to the King.

Bathed in righteousness, he occupied himself in translating the corse of Henry the Sixth from Chertsey Abbey to St. George's Chapel at Windsor. Some ill-disposed persons murmured that the true reason was to keep an eye on Henry and control the working of miracles; a Lancastrian saint was in the making . . . but it seemed only proper to him to honour a martyr, even a martyr that he himself had helped along the road to sainthood.

He was equally aware of the moral necessity of putting in order his relations with Elizabeth Woodeville. In this trysting-time of reconciliation, Christ-like, he forbore to hate even Woodevilles. Since the coup d'état of April, 1483, and the overthrow of her House, Lady Grey—

---

* King Richard the Third. Act III; Scene 7.
** Still standing, astonishingly beautiful and tragic in the hideous setting of modern Wakefield. The Lady Chapel ought to be removed to a more appropriate site, truckless and in the countryside; restored and offered to the public as a late-medieval treasure.

as the ex-Queen was now commonly termed—had lain in Sanctuary
with her five daughters, closely guarded by John Nesfield, Squire of
the Body and "a man of the greatest austerities." Frightened and alone,
jealously hoarding her daughters, was not ashblonde ruined Elizabeth
Woodeville, quondam Queen of the White Rose, the very symbol of
tragedy?

His worst foes had been women—Marguerite d'Anjou, Elizabeth
Woodeville, Lady Margaret Beaufort, Jane Shore—and undeniably he
had done the most injury to women: especially those two Queens of the
Red and White Roses, both of whom he had utterly destroyed. Neither
Queen of course would have scrupled to destroy him had she been
victorious.

But he was in the forgiving vein; it remained whether Lady Grey
were equally so. For, after all, he might take away her regality, even
her marriage of twenty years; he could not obliterate her motherhood.
It was hardly to be supposed that she would consort with the murderer
of her boys.

But was he the murderer?

The truth was: the sons of Edward were not dead. Buckingham had
lied; Morton had lied; he took an oath on it. If Lady Grey and her
five daughters would come out of Sanctuary, they should see Edward
and Richard. The boys were in the Tower; close-guarded but not unhappy.*

Still, she hesitated. She recalled that when old cackling Bourchier
Episcopus of Canterbury had come pleading with her for delivery of
little Richard he had guaranteed that no harm should come to the boy.
But her son had been thrust into a dark dungeon in the Tower; and
she would not permit that to happen to her girls.

Would the King take a public oath? He would. More; he would
personally draft the terms: fair and honourable treatment; no imprisonment in the Tower or anywhere else; no ravishing or defiling, but
suitable husbands and dowries; the allowance of 700 marks yearly, now
paid quarterly through John Nesfield, was to be continued to Lady
Grey.** His advisers, Ratcliffe, Catesby, were not enthusiastic about the

---

* The suggestion has been made that Richard convinced Lady Grey of Buckingham's
guilt. Nothing is more illogical. If he could convince Lady Grey, he could convince England. He did not stand a chance with her, short of persuading her the
boys are still alive. This is the line followed in the author's novel *FIRE AND
MORNING;* and the only possible line for the King.
** An allowance that was better by 300 marks than the sum granted by Henry Tudor
to his mother-in-law in her old age at Bermondsey Abbey.

prospect of Lady Grey's return to public life, even in a highly restricted capacity. Both of them had been involved in the coup d'état; and Lady Grey had an infinite memory. They were over-ruled by Richard and the Council; for the monarchy stood to gain handsomely. The Council members—York career men and old front fighters of the Rose—did not inquire into Richard's promise and secret undertakings to Lady Grey. If it was a question of the boys, something would turn up. Something always had. Remember the Miracle of Seventy-One.

". . . if the Daughters of Elizabeth Grey, late calling herself Queen of England, to wit, Elizabeth, Cecily, Anne, Katherine, and Bridget, will come to me out of the Sanctuary of Westminster, and be guided, ruled, demeaned after me, then I shall that they be in surety of their lives and suffer no manner of hurt, by ravishing or defiling contrary to their wills, nor any of them imprison in the Tower of London or other prison; but I shall put them into honest places of good fame and them honestly and courteously shall be treated, and have all things necessary for their exhibitions and findings as my kinswomen. . . ."

By this oath, solemnly avowed in London's Guildhall before the City Corporation and a conclave of lords spiritual and temporal, Richard scored a diplomatic ten-strike. Only the previous December, on Christmas Day, Tudor had taken his bald head and lean shanks onto the high altar of the Cathedral of Rennes to pledge troth to Elizabeth Plantagenet; grafting White Rose and Red. For this result, Lady Beaufort, Abbess-faced indefatigable traitoress, had laboured as mightily as a whole covey of Stanleys; not yet were they certain that they could do better under avaricious Tudor. This Christmas troth alarmed the monarchy of the Sunne; and it was about this time that another evil rumour was set going by Morton in the fenland: Richard had threatened first to ravish and then murder his niece Elizabeth if she did not prostitute herself to his criminal lust.

But with the Reconciliation of March it was the turn of traitors in Brittany to be scared. Their union of the Roses was kicked aside like so much rubbish by the enigmatic Lady Grey. They were further discommoded by the sudden collapse of Duke Francis the Second, of the holy celtic principality of Brittany, who had at last gone mad, and the evident willingness of the *de facto* ruler Pierre Landois to make a deal for Henry Tudor's person. Francis had been dickering for years, without getting anywhere, partly because his price was too fantastic, and partly because vestiges of knighthood like old soup-stains clung to him and he did not really want to sell Tudor. But Pierre Landois, ex-tailor of Vitre, out of the glorious tradition of Olivier le Diable, *he* had no such scruples; and he speedily came to terms with Richard. Tudor was warned in the knick of time; and managed to elude his pursuers and get over the frontier. Shortly after, Francis, in a brief moment of lucidity, hanged his minister for peculations; and sent on Tudor's threadbare gentlemen to France, with apologies. From now on, the conspiracy was based on the old terrain of Lancaster and Marguerite d'Anjou: the Court of France. . . .

But this setback, while annoying, did not affect the new and solid relationship between King Richard and his former relentless foe. Elizabeth Woodeville appeared to have forgot all about uniting the Roses. Her five daughters came to Court; Elizabeth, the eldest, was maid to the Queen, to Lady Anne Neville, who was feverish, a little hysterical and strange, crying and laughing as one possessed. Folk recalled how Isabel, her sister, had been taken just this way; shutting herself in a stifling room; pale, with crimson stains on her wasted cheeks; always cold. . . .

Anne Neville had light continually about her; a brazier smoking in a curtained room. And without, the sun blazing.

So far, it seemed, Richard could not lose. Rising from success to success; but abruptly he and the House of Gloucester were dealt a mortal blow. On April ninth, at Nottingham, Richard received word that his son and heir Edward had perished at Middleham. Fled; in a single night of agony and darkness. Richard inquired what day it was; repeated the question, whitefaced and staring, they wondered if he were going mad. *April the ninth* . . . this was the *day* his brother Edward had died; this was the *day* Edward had gone, leaving Richard the Protector of his sons. Protector? Where now were those boys, those tender Princes? April; April had come again; the green and fragrant dying time, the soft rain, the green light, the rain like tears and—the whispers, the far off voices . . . and not sleeping, never sleeping, a Lord of death and April. He asked them once more, to be certain.

And they told him: *April the ninth.*

THE BURNING-GLASS OF LOVE

One aspect everyone must admire. Richard did not quit. He went on fighting to the end and died in glory. Even his worst enemies, the

chroniclers of the Tudor historical novel-writing school, had to admit
that. Richard the Second quit cold when the going got rough; stole
away from his army in the night and fled to Conway Castle, from
which he was presently lifted by Henry Bolingbroke and dragged to
London for the mock-abdication—abdicating with a knife at his throat
—and shortly afterward battered to death by Henry's belted thugs. Edward the Second also quit; and endured an even more hideous death
at Berkeley (they say his screams could be heard a quarter mile).

Richard the Third was of stronger stuff. When he lost his son, the
chief prop of his Monarchy, he did not crack. He threw himself into a
frenzy of administration: clearing out the deadwood in government
offices; reorganizing the Council of the North; appointing commercial
consuls in Europe, the first English ruler to do so. But the man who
could behead Lord Hastings before dinner was to find, like Executives
in all ages, that it was easier to strike down the leading nobleman of
the Realm than to split the hard shell of entrenched bureaucracy. The
King gave orders that one Richard Bele, a clerk in the Privy Seal, was
to be fired for malfeasance. Bele had been running a little promotion
racket in the office, accepting bribes in return for favouritism among
the under-clerks. Sad to relate, a few months later the obnoxious Bele
was still at the Privy Seal and presumably still terrorizing the under-
clerks.

The Council of the North, with headquarters at Middleham and
York, was a project especially close to Richard. He had been the first
to organize such a body, during his own lieutenancy under Edward.
Now he appointed John Earl of Lincoln, a most promising youth of
twenty-one and the son of Richard's elder sister Elizabeth Duchess of
Suffolk, his Deputy in the North and President of the Council. Lincoln
was slated for additional honours. He was created non-resident Lieutenant in Ireland, with Fitzgerald of Kildare his Deputy. And, most
significant of all, he was by this thorough innoculation with Richard's
policy, groomed as lineal heir to St. Edward's throne. Edward Earl of
Warwick, twelve-year old son of the attainted Clarence, had been made
Richard's heir; but the King very wisely had second thoughts. Warwick
was a child; and further his line had been attainted in formal Parliament.

Ireland was a focal point of York power. From the time of Duke
Richard's lieutenancy in 1440 to the judicial murder of Perkin Warbeck, the land of Brian Boru had supported not only legitimate York

heirs but even the most obvious pretenders to the glory of the Sunne, such as the baker's boy Lambert Simnel. There were reasons for this loyalty. The House of York had tried to rule through the native chieftains and the great Norman-Irish barons. Jack Cade was an Irishman and when the Duke of York landed in England in 1450, at the time of Cade's Rebellion, he brought with him an Irish army of kerns and gallo-glasses. It is not on record that either Edward or Richard visited Ireland during the kingship of either, but both continued the successful and tolerant policy of the Duke of York.

The fearful atrocities which were to turn the name of Ireland into a by-word of horror for centuries have been unjustly attributed to English policy as a whole. They were not. They began and were carried on by the deliberate cruelty and blood-madness of the Tudors, from Henry the Seventh to Gloriana. The creation of the Pale and the legend "to Hell or Connaught"; Poynings Law; the extermination of native leadership; the bestial ravages of a defenseless people—all this was perpetrated by the Tudors who, somewhat restrained in England, found no check in Ireland to the free expression of their Ottoman characteristics.

If the House of York had done nothing else worthy, its policy in Ireland would shine in an otherwise dark and bloody tradition.

Though outside the scope of this study, the question might well be posed at this point: why were the Tudors so cruel? Why did Henry the Seventh plant *agent provocateurs* among his most faithful servants to obtain evidence to kill them? * Why did Henry the Eighth go into mortal frenzies at the least opposition to his will? Why did Mary torture and slay Protestants? And Elizabeth torture and slay Catholics? The truth must be sought in the fact that the Tudors had no right whatever to the throne. Each Tudor ruler must continually assert his will in the only way a Tudor could recognize: naked physical cruelty—in order to prove to his Tudor nature and to his terrified subjects that he had a royal right.

Richard turned to another project: the College of Heralds. The Heralds were the personal representatives of the Sovereign in the field. They were often employed in embassies to foreign Courts. In the creation of new patents of nobility or the re-assignment of ancient titles, it was essential to have the Heralds' advice concerning the proper Arms.

---

* Exactly what Nikita S. Khrushchev accused the late Joseph Stalin of doing, in the famous Bill of Indictment of March, 1956.

Disputes over property rights often hinged on some aspect of heraldic interpretation. Though of such significance, these royal officers had been organized in a more or less haphazard manner, with not even a meeting-place of their own. Richard established three grades in the College: Kings-of-Arms, Heralds, Pursuivants. He gave the officers the mansion of Cold-Harbour, former town house of the Duke of Exeter, as a headquarters. Richard's Kings-at-Arms were four: Garter, Clarenceux, Norroy, Gloucester; * his Heralds were five: Windsor, Chester, York, Lancaster, Richmond; his Pursuivants were three: *Rouge-Croix,* Bluemantle, *Blaunche Senglier.*

The King's passion for Arthurian tradition was stimulated by the visit of knight-errant Nicholas von Poppelau, a wandering Silesian *ritter,* who came to Pontefract in May. The new friends got on famously. Richard commanded an excellent table and the Chapel music was magnificent. Every morning a shining Mass was performed by the Royal Choir under Gilbert Banaster, especially notable in the rendition of Pasche's *Christus Resurgens* that was written for the private chapel of Anne Duchess of Exeter.

Von Poppelau remained ten days, regaling his diminutive host with tales of warfare against Turks and Bulgarians. Richard said to the knight: "I wish that my kingdom lay upon the confines of Turkey; with my own people alone and without the help of other princes, I should like to drive away not only the Turks, but all my foes."

On parting, Richard presented von Poppelau with a golden necklace; and the wandering *ritter* remembered his host as a man "of great heart."

The King, no doubt, was thinking of how his Monarchy had been undermined, though he had no conception of the extent of the rot. A few cases came to light. Roger de Clifford, justice of the peace, was caught in communication with Tudor. His blazon sent him to the Block; no connexion of Clifford might ever be forgiven by the House of York. Will Collingbourne, Sheriff of Wilts and custodian for Duchess Cecily, had been the first to betray the Sunne, sending the man Yate to Brittany on the very day of Richard's Coronation. Collingbourne had been active with Dorset and Lionel Woodeville in the October Rebellion; when that failed, he went underground to conduct a propaganda campaign, of which a famous sample has survived: "the Cat, the

---

* GARTER: John Writh. CLARENCEUX: Thomas Holme. NORROY: John Moor. GLOUCESTER: Richard Champney.

Rat, and Lovell the Dog rule all England under the Hog." And went on to proclaim: "the Crookbackt Boar the way hath found to root our Roses from the ground." *

Richard reverted to an earlier merciless manner. Collingbourne was torn to pieces on Tower Hill.

The most potent sources of treason remained untouched: Lady Beaufort, Stanley's wife; Stanley himself; Percy of Northumberland, Warden of the North. The two last were among the principal military officers of the Realm and were in a position to destroy the King. The truth was: he did not dare break with these men. He needed their levies, since he had voluntarily given up the financial means to raise and equip a field army.

Sleepless, wire-taut, he tried to oversee personally every aspect of defense. He hurried to Scarborough in June, for a few whirlwind weeks of activity on the Yorkshire coast; provisioning ships, recruiting soldiers, sailors, artificers, even trying to regulate obscure English fisher folk in the Irish Sea. In July, he rode on to York, to issue warrants for the provisioning of Calais and of Blount's English garrison. On the 23rd, he was at Pontefract; on the 30th, at Nottingham; and on August 9, back at Westminster.** Here he occupied himself in strengthening the works of the Tower and of Westminster; he was building a new West Gate in the royal enclave. Perhaps he had some notion of a last ditch stand on the island of Westminster itself.

Richard found occasion, even in this harried hour, to issue a warrant for £5 to Johannes Forest, widow of a faithful servant of York, Miles Forest, Keeper of the Wardrobe at Barnard Castle. A man who achieved a ferocious fame in Thomas More's tale as a fellow "well-fleshed in murder aforetime" who had exercised his skill on the King's nephews; and afterward had "rotted away piecemeal" at St. Martin's Sanctuary.***

In September, the King set out once more for Nottingham, his "Castle of Care," as he now referred to it, where he had received the news of his son. Nottingham, in the centre of England, cloistered about with

* This disproves the contention that Richard was not called "Crookback" in his own day. His son was known in the North as "Little Crumplin." But, as already pointed out, Richard had no hideous deformation; and this kind of pleasantry was the poetic exaggeration of bitter foes.

** To Will Cambreshalle, Master of the barque *Elizabeth*, letters to convoy merchants and fishermen between England and Ireland. Warrants to sutlers John Papedy and Alexander Lye, issued at Scarborough. Harleian Misc. 433.

*** *Vide* Appendix: "The Wicked Uncle."

memories of Robin Hood, the wicked Sheriff and Sir Guy of Gisborne, had now become the military headquarters of Our Sovereign Lord, Richard the Third. He elaborated a system of postal relays that he had already developed between London and the North; a webbing of couriers and post houses over half England, permitting a change of horses every twenty miles and the moving of Government despatches 100 miles a day. Great beacon flares were set to kindle along the Channel coast, directly enemy ships hove into view. Bombards and small arms, barrels of "touche poudre" were issued to Governors of key castles, Carnarvon and Beaumaris in Wales, Pontefract, Alnwick and Bamborough along the Scottish March.

But, despite this essential precaution, relations with Scotland had never been better and it was not from the North the threat would come. A decisive naval victory over the Scots earlier in 1484 had brought peace offers from James the Third. Scottish commissioners arrived at Nottingham; and the remarks of one of them, Archibald Whitelaw, alluded to the English King's stature in a graceful compliment. "Nature," the envoy of James said, "never enclosed within a smaller frame so great a mind or such remarkable powers."

The holiday with Lady Grey continued. By cajoling her out of Sanctuary, Richard had given the lie to enemy rumours concerning her sons. He had created an atmosphere of confidence, however precarious, in which it was easier for Lady Grey herself to believe that the Princes still lived. The conspirators across the Manche found it necessary to set alight another rumour of foul play about this time.* A rumour which was equally unsuccessful in disturbing the new-found cordiality between the King and the woman who had been his most dangerous antagonist.

Accepting the 700 marks' yearly pension from the King, sending her daughters to Court, even, it appears, a little later discussing a royal fate for her eldest Elizabeth, Lady Grey lived on the oaths and promises of him whom in all the world she had most reason to distrust.

". . . (Lady Grey) What canst thou swear by now? (King Richard) The time to come. (Lady Grey) That thou hast wronged in the time o'er past; For I myself have many tears to wash hereafter time, for time past wrong'd by thee. . . ." **

---

* The existence of such a rumour is indicated by the remark in the Great Chronicle of London that a little before Easter, 1484, men whispered that the Princes had been put to silence.
** *King Richard the Third*. Act IV; Scene 4.

But she was neither a fool nor empty of maternal feeling. Her aim was to have removed the bar of bastardy from her children; and she was willing to accept a less than royal status for her two sons, if they could be made legitimate as the Beauforts had been legitimatized by grace of Richard the Second. And such a procedure would have been in no way a bar to the highest aspiration for her daughter Elizabeth. Everything depended on whether her sons were, as the King avowed, still living. One day, Lady Grey knew, he would have to make good on that avowal.

He knew it, too. But he was playing for time, months, even weeks. Time to establish his Monarchy beyond overthrow. Time to draw Tudor into the field and deal the traitor a crushing blow. Time to restore his own blood-line, now extinct. For awhile he had considered the possibility of a union between his niece and the present heir, John Earl of Lincoln; a plan that would effectively check-mate Henry Tudor's marital ambitions. But as the year drew to a close and the Lady Anne became ever more pale and wasted, another design formed in the King's mind. If he should soon become a widower, would not his people expect that their Sovereign give the nation an heir in the direct line?

The notion of marriage intruded gradually, not unmixed with desire. The sheer physical charm of Bess has been too little regarded; her flowering was tragically brief and was followed by a long winter of suppression and heartbreak. But in this year of 1484 the eighteen-year-old girl was a redgold princess—the more lovely and appealing because of the Bar that had been put on her. Bess had a broad brow, greenish-blue eyes, a full sensitive mouth, a mane of tawny shining hair. Her body was tall and rounded; her complexion rose and cream. She might well be the most beautiful Plantagenet since Fulke of Anjou had married dark smouldering Melusine, the Devil's Daughter.

Only the poisonous vapours of the Tudor mind could create a criminal plot out of this most natural attraction of a disillusioned lonely monarch for an exquisite being, who also happened to be his niece. Threaten her? Would a proud emotional girl need to be threatened with dangerous romance and the chance of royalty? Rather, it would be wonderful if she were not attracted: the brave and embattled King, the falcon warrior, the chevalier of Enlightenment and the new Age.

Certainly, Bess did not believe that Richard was stained with the blood-guilt of her brothers. Certainly, she accepted his promises and protestations as did her mother. But with this difference. Where Lady Grey, shrewd political operator, always left ajar the door of a second judgment, the girl Bess Plantagenet gave her heart and soul. And it may well be that the failure of this faith in Richard—a belief on which she had staked all the powerful emotional depths of her being—had as much to do with the breaking of lovely Bess as seventeen years of wedded life with Henry Tudor.

This year of 1484—the only complete year of Sunne Kingship—ended in a burst of Christmas rejoicing. Mirth that was like a shout of defiance; as if the King had heard from far off the trumpet-echo of glory, whether an echo of Monarchy or of Death.

Richard conceived a daring notion.

He appeared at Epiphany, magnificently regal, his four-arched Crown aflame with rubies and sapphires, his train a Byzantine vision of purple velvet and gold netts and gold pineapples. But it was not the King's gorgeous attire lit the whispers, the stares. It was Bess that caused the wonder. Bess, the disinherited, the bar-sinister princess of the Sunne. She was radiant in pearls and cloth-of-gold, Richard's gift—a gown exactly like that worn by the Queen, a feverish painted Anne.

Did she understand? did Anne?

Laughing . . . she laughed as loudly as anyone beneath her steeple head-dress; and went numb, while the King danced with Bess (how well he danced!) and from a little distance one might believe that Richard was dancing with his Queen—as perhaps he was. . . .

An urgent messenger broke through. He brought news from France: the Welsh ferret would invade England in the spring. Richard raised a jeweled hand; it was the best word he could have. To slake his steel in blood. Rat's blood! Abruptly he was thoughtful and sent for Tyrell. He had a mission for his Master Henchman. He needed money. And he knew but one person in Christendom who had the kind of money he required: his sister Margaret.

Tyrell set off in January of the new year, the fatal year of 1485. He was never to return to England during the lifetime of his sovereign, Richard the Third. The Embassy was a failure, despite Richard's urgent plea and the gift of a purebred Spanish hobby, a beautiful silver grey, to Margaret at Bruges. For Richard's envoy had been preceded by one John Morton, Bishop of Ely and Chancellor to the seedy make-believe Court of Henry Tudor. Morton, it seems, revealed the appalling truth concerning Richard and his nephews; he must also have reassured Margaret as to the status of her income from estates in England, should

Henry Tudor become Henry the Seventh—an assurance immediately breached once this conjectural upgrading had been astoundingly fulfilled. But, for the present, the immensely wealthy daughter of York was neutralized; and with an income of 160,000 ridders from Burgundian sources alone, Margaret contributed not a farthing to the defense of Yorkist England.*

And then too "Gentle Tyrell" himself was not above suspicion. If Buckingham's man had already become Tudor's man, as in verity he was to become after Bosworth, how easily he might have ruined his own plea on Richard's behalf by soft hints and iceblue looks! Yet if gratitude has any compulsion in this world, which we may sadly doubt, what royal largess had been lavished on this Master of Henchmen to secure his love. He had received the manors of the attainted Thomas Arundel of Lanherne, in right of Lady Tyrell, who was Anne Arundel; he had been made Steward of the Duchy of Cornwall, and Constable of Dundagell; he had been appointed Governor of the Marches of the Wales. In addition, Sir James had been entrusted with personal missions of the highest importance.

It may be that Richard, having sounded his man, had no wish to recall him to England. He was too delicate in loyalty to have at Court; and too deep in York night to alienate. He was given the job of Constable, pro tem, of the town and castle of Guisnes, in the English enclave of Calais. This appointment, nominally held by the ailing Blount Lord Mountjoy, had been promised on Mountjoy's death to Sir Ralph Hastings, brother of the beheaded Lord Hastings, in return for a payment of £666—another of those improvised transactions by which a harassed monarch endeavored to retrieve a vanishing treasury.**

Meantime, it appeared that Tyrell qualified as one of those queasy loyalties of which Thomas More spoke: "Free was he called of dispense, and somewhat above his power liberal; with large gifts he got him unstedfast friendships."

Other recipients of this liberal dispensation remained true. Francis

---

* RECEIPTS of Malines, Account Books for the years 1460–1490; Account Books of Brabant, 1467–1469; Acquit de Lille, Folio ms. 923 (the famous "wedding folio" of the marriage between Charles and Margaret). Royal Archives of Brussels. A ridder was equal to one pound, five shillings. The purchasing power of the pound was at least thirty times the present value. The income of Margaret was truly enormous.

** A provisional grant dated Feb. 24, 1484. Harleian Miscellany 433.

Viscount Lovell, boyhood companion of the King, was made Lord Chamberlain and Chief Botiller (Butler) of the Realm; to Lovell went the estate of the murdered Henry Holland Duke of Exeter, one of the ill-fated husbands of Anne Plantagenet.* Lovell survived Bosworth; but fell at Stoke, June 20, 1487, or possibly may have survived that battle as well only to perish of starvation in a walled-up room of his own manor. Sir Robert Percy, another friend from magical Warwick years, and Sir Richard Ratcliffe were created knights of the Body and served as officers of the Royal Guard in succession to Tyrell. Sir Robert Brackenbury was given a life appointment as Lieutenant of the Tower, with £100 annually and various manors in Kent, Sussex and Surrey, late belonging to Anthony Lord Scales and to Sir John Cheyney.**

Will Catesby, who had been Speaker of that highly effective Parliament, held the remunerative post of Chancellor of the Earldom of March; Catesby was also in the Privy Council as Chancellor of the Exchequer. Sir John Howard had received the dukedom of Norfolk and the office of Earl Marshal; his son Thomas was created Earl of Surrey and granted £1000 yearly during the Duke's lifetime.

These, save Catesby and Surrey, died for York. The little lawyer, so adept at trimming, was busy saving Stanley's son during that last mortal ride at Bosworth. Surrey, staunch to the end, was made captive and lived to become the most famous Tudor general of his age and victor of Flodden.

Comrades of the iron memory, these (giving the lie to More) were friends as "stedfast" as a King might wish. But his most significant fellowship was a very recent one—Lady Grey. This astonishing harmony, which no one would have dared predict a few months before, flourished amid rumours of Queen Anne's end. As spring came on, the dying woman hid within her lavish rooms. Gold-curtained, she

---

* Exeter, loyal Lancastrian, was attainted by Edward the Fourth and divorced by Edward's sister Anne. Following Tewkesbury, the ruined nobleman was hunted down and murdered; in September 1471, Exeter's naked corpse was found floating in the Channel. Edward pilfered the Exeter estate, granting a large part to Richard Grey, younger son of Queen Elizabeth Woodeville. Grey was one of those "let blood" at Pontefract in 1483; and the Exeter property fell to King Richard. It seems, however, that the miserable fate which overtook the Duke was entirely the work of Edward and Anne.

** "To the same Robert, the Keeping of the Lyons in the Toure of London; with XIVd a day for himself and 6d a day for the mete of every Lyon and Leopard." Harleian Miscellany 433.

gasped and fought for breath. It was said that she would not last the month of February, but somehow she did—and it seemed to Lady Bess that "the Queen would never die."

Ruthless nineteen. . . . Yet Lady Bess had her reasons. Intensely romantic, bright with hunger, she was in her way an adventurer of the ideal. Royalty haunted her, as other girls are haunted by pleasure or money. And with this obsessive royalty glowed a dream of love.

He was almost old enough to be her father; and in truth he was her blood-uncle. He seemed to have a touch of mortality, as well; so many about him had died. But, to romantic nineteen, a touch of death is part of love's terror and beauty; of love's burning-glass. Besides, the girl had the durability of her ash-gold mother. She possessed good survival value, a necessary asset in that phosphorescent hour. Never again would Bess know such flame and wonder; such miraculous candles as burned for her and Richard.

Now it was certainly untrue that King Richard devised the death of his wife Anne. He owed to her his castles and regiments in the North; the gold of Warwick loyalty, so precious to his kingship. He also owed to her love—a much more doubtful and troubling gift.

But a man may kill his love in various ways; with a kiss, as with a sword—or by merely not wanting her to live. This slaying, the most irreparable of all, would be the way of a man of duty; to do all; to spend all; to leave no effort untried save that essential elixir of the soul—the will to live (For we go on living, surely, because someone, somewhere, wants us to go on . . .).

The ailing Queen "languished in Weakness and Extremity of Sorrow, until she seemed rather to overtake Death, than Death, her. . . ." *

And this lonely wasting in a gold-curtained stifling room, with a sea-coal fire in the grate, and the candles burning, burning, in the mortal spring, in the last birdhaunted noon . . . and she twenty-nine and dying, upon a silken heraldic couch, limp breasts, pale hollows of her purple-shadowed face, coughing . . . and the blood upon her pillows, upon her robe, blood-flecks everywhere . . . and the thud of her heart-stroke like a cracked bell and memories that rushed up and down, wringing their hands and sobbing, in the haunted chantry of her mind.

Anne: Anne. . . .

* Vide: Sir George Buck, *Life and Extraordinary Raign of Richard the Third*.

He did everything conceivable, even importing physicians from Italy, but still Death came winking and whispering, the familiar king-at-arms of his dimming monarchy, and this time perhaps not unwelcome . . . for he was thinking of her, of the redgold radiant niece, and the temptation was dazzling; to capture forever the shrewdest foe of his past, the girl's mother; to checkmate Tudor's scheme of "uniting the Roses" by forcing his lean Welsh shanks into the girl's bed; to achieve, not least, for York's Queenship a splendid being, lusty and loving, a nest of spicery where he, York's King, might make more sons.

The odds against? He had not, it seems, reckoned this aspect. When he wished to do something—to marry, to seize the crown, to behead his opponents—he generally did it, without troubling overmuch about possible objections. For the one great advantage he had always possessed, in relation to his rivals, was the power of direct action. While other men wondered and worried, he acted; and so rare and salutory is this quality that he had a record of unbroken success up to this present year of 1485.

The girl herself, from Epiphany and her "vain changes of raiment" to Clerkenwell in April, was living in a dream. Joy flickered redly in her soul; she beckoned Death. And when Death was laggard, she wrote a letter to John Howard, Duke of Norfolk, Earl Marshal of England, beseeching him "to be a mediator for her to the King in the matter of the marriage propounded between them, who was her only joy and maker in the world, and she was his in heart and thought, withal that the better part of February was past and she feared the Queen would never die. . . ." *

A letter so cruel and beautiful that one wonders what the brickfaced Essex squire, John Howard, made of it. Pondering, brow-heavy before this perilous parchment—but either through carelessness or design the letter slipped out and the King's confidants were alerted.

They fell into a kind of panic. Their reaction is easy to fathom. The "Rat"—Sir Richard Ratcliffe of Derwentwater, Cumberland, Knight of the Body—had let the blood of the girl's uncle and brother at Pontefract

---

* Buck's *Life*. The existence of this letter has been a dragon wing of controversy. The Warbecks (Vide Appendix) and earlier schools reject it; but Gairdner, as captain of the traditionalists, favours its authenticity. The best evidence in support is the Clerkenwell oath of April, plus the genuine alarm of Tudor and Morton, who even sent an envoy to ask the daughter of Sir Walter Herbert as an alternative bride.

in June, 1483. The "Cat"—William Catesby of Ashby sur-la-Zouch, Leicester, Chancellor of the Exchequer and Privy Councillor—had betrayed his old master Lord Hastings and the faction of Edward the Fifth to the rising Sunne of Richard. And Lovell, the Dog? Francis Viscount Lovell, Chamberlain and friend, was devoted to Anne; to her who lay shivering in that stifling room where the great mothlike wings of death beat invisibly up and down.

The King perceived the mortal presence. Richard abstained from Anne's tainted bed; then gave out that his wife was not like to last beyond the mid-part of February; and, meantime, prepared as it were that the funeral baked meats should furnish forth the wedding feast. But if he stubbornly refused the terrible portents of this death, his captains were not equally unaffected.

She died in darkness, in the midst of a shining spring day, when the sun, herald and blazon of this monarchy, was totally eclipsed, the world plunged in shadow. . . .

Now he was "free"; but in truth more remote than ever from Elizabeth—for the girl's letter had got out and his captains were insisting on a formal renunciation. So: once more, solemn oaths, holy relics from the Abbey . . . King Richard stood in the Great Hall of St. John's Priory at Clerkenwell, before London's Lord Mayor and Corporation, the Knights of Malta, and other interested parties, and proclaimed in a loud voice that the notion of marrying his niece Elizabeth had never entered his mind.

This ceremony may have contented the Cat, the Rat, and the Dog. It certainly did not content the elliptical Lady Grey, mother of the renounced bride. Richard had fenced off his former enemy with promises and private understandings; their new affection was the showpiece of the Monarchy, the proof that Lady Grey's sons yet lived. He had even prevailed on her to send secretly to her last remaining son, Thomas Grey, Marquess of Dorset, in Paris to abandon Tudor and seek preferment with a generous and forgiving Richard. This the young man did subsequently attempt to do; but like most of his enterprises the escape was so badly managed that Morton's pursuing horsemen caught Dorset at Compiègne sur l'Oise, a few kilometres from Paris.

Now this affection had been sealed by Elizabeth and the old Woodeville dream of royalty. The bemused mother had accepted the man's promises concerning both her daughter and her sons. Had not prisoners of state lived years immured within the grim Norman Tower, seen by no one save the King's own officials? * If he kept his word regarding Elizabeth, would he not do so with respect to the Princes?

At one stroke he had annihilated Elizabeth's prospects; and perhaps his own. This game of time that he played had its limitations. The time purchased from Lady Grey was cancelled by the time bought from his captains by the oath of Clerkenwell. He could not have it both ways. He may well have decided wrongly; for what were the Cat, the Rat, the Dog by comparison with this massive imponderable of the "union of the Roses"—the secret dream of Englishmen everywhere? And if he now alienated Lady Grey, it was forever. He could not retrace; and the credit that he sacrificed concerning the Princes was the credit that turned the balance at Bosworth Field.

Whatever might be the sentiments of her daughter, Lady Grey was no more the avid friend. She may not have executed a volte-face; she did not require to do so. It was only necessary to intimate to certain chosen persons, among whom may be counted Christopher Urswicke and Reginald Bray, the confidential emissaries of Lady Margaret Beaufort, that no longer would she resist the marriage scheme between her daughter and Henry Tudor. This was enough to sway the Stanleys and Northumberland; for whatever was said or done hereafter by the frantic King he had not the money to defend his crown without the aid of these barons. His sister Margaret had rejected his plea; and if his own House turned him down, it was not likely his subjects would be more generous.

One aspect may be noted in passing: Richard did not altogether abandon Elizabeth. He might—one would think—have by-passed Clerkenwell and satisfied his Captains by immediately marrying off his niece. Surely the fact that he did not take this obvious method of foreclosing Tudor's hopes argues that he had not utterly relinquished his own candidacy. If he destroyed Tudor on the battlefield, the nation's mood might change; he might seal York's victory with a union of White Roses and a new and glorious dynasty of the Sunne.**

* Two examples of notable state prisoners in the early years of the century are Prince Llewellyn of Wales and King James the First of Scotland. Both were held incommunicado for several years; the rigours of James' confinement were later relaxed by Henry the Fifth.

** The marriage was by no means impossible from a papal dispensation aspect. See the remarks of N. Harris Nicolas, *Privy Purse Expenses of Elizabeth of York,* pp. xliv–xlv.

And here we perceive the mortal flaw, the fatal passion for improvisation in this limping time of monarchy. He was a man who believed in luck and, in view of his career, he had reason. He had fought life with intelligence, courage, skill—and luck. Up to this year of 1485, he had gone from triumph to triumph; abruptly, life exacted from him a long overdue payment, a bill of adjustment that at first King Richard found difficult to take seriously.

His enemies had failed so often and so catastrophically, from Warwick at Barnet to Buckingham washed away in the deluge, that Richard now undervalued his dangers. Scrawny Tudor, looking like a starved priest, and obese Morton—could such men prevail where Warwick had crashed? Even the French did not rate their protege's chances very high after the debacle of October 1483. They gave grudgingly and insufficiently to finance a second try. Yet these neo-Lancastrians had one inestimable advantage: a consistent and coherent policy. From the time that Morton took control of Tudor's affairs, the various elements of the bald young man's schemes were fused into a master-plan. Henry Tudor began to behave—not like a king, perhaps—but like someone who might one day become a king. This was Bishop Morton's work; and creating regality out of such material was not the least of the great man's achievements.

Morton's directing genius might also be discerned in the net gradually woven about King Richard. The Sunne monarch was alleged to have employed horrible threats to compel men to fight for him and to have covered England with a cloud of spies. Certainly, he would have been better off had these charges been true, as they came true in the time of his successors. But the King's intelligence reports were so inadequate that he totally failed to comprehend the extent to which his enemies had infiltrated his realm. Tudor's relations with royal deputies in Wales, especially Walter Herbert and Sir William Stanley; Lady Margaret Beaufort's negotiations with Lady Grey; the double-dealing of yet another High Constable, Lord Thomas Stanley; Richard appeared hopelessly innocent—"too childish-foolish for this world."

But, to deal plainly, the King had no choice. He had to go on trusting Lady Grey, even when it might have been evident that she had ceased to believe in him and in his assurances concerning her boys. Clerkenwell had changed the whole climate of the monarchy; and Lady Grey was resolved, one way or another, to royalize her Bess. This "busy negotiating woman" now turned to Lady Beaufort and the Stanleys;

and "in her withdrawing Chamber the conspiracy against Richard hatched" and Henry's earlier scheme of uniting the Roses revived.*

The shadow of his murdered nephews fell upon all the King's work. Not only did Lady Grey no longer accept his leanly plausible excuses, but the whole of England began to wonder about him. It is not true that he was ever universally considered guilty of the blood of his House; the Minutes Book of the York Corporation contains ample evidence to the contrary. But he moved increasingly in an atmosphere of distrust, of cringing rumour. Morton did his best; and to the Italianate tale of a poison plot involving the lonely terrified Anne was added a new and hideous accusation: the King's intent to ravish and murder Princess Elizabeth. One can imagine these whispered tales flicking in and out like serpents' tongues in the deadly uneasiness surrounding the King; after all it was true that a number of persons who had been in contact with him at one time or another had died young. . . .

In these greenlit April days, bell-haunted—he was a prey to continual anxiety.

It is said that sleep had deserted his bed; and that he must be ever wakeful, wandering vast draughty Halls where light constantly burned. What was he looking for? Probably not, as his enemies declared, searching dagger in hand for imagined assassins. It is likely that the threats to his rest were of a more subtle and profound kind. Only the merest simpleton can believe that this man achieved royalty without really knowing what he was doing or without incurring a heavy charge upon his soul. It is true that he was doing his best to liquidate that charge through penance and good works as king. But it may well be doubted that in the matter of the Princes, he would ever manage a satisfactory equation of guilt and atonement.

The memory of those two young lives, vanished into some awful and eternal Silence, continued to haunt the English nation, as much as all the blood of the Roses. How were these deaths to be paid for? For this was not only a Duncan-spot upon the blazon of York that all the sea might not wash clean, it was a stain upon the nation. Edward and Richard had been Princes of the blood-royal; they had been the sons and heirs of England. Against the lightning strokes of the Protector

* The Lord Verulam, Viscount St. Albans, better known as Sir Francis Bacon, in his *History of Henry VII*. In connection with the Lambert Simnel rising of 1487, Bacon referred to Lady Grey, "and none could hold the Book so well to prompt and instruct this Stage-Play, as she could."

and his coadjutor Buckingham, no one had lifted a hand. Obscurely, men felt that the King himself must answer. . . .

Stray voices in the wind: the mayoralty roll of the town of Lincoln for the year 1483—"This yere the kynge sons were put to silence. . . ." *

What nameless clerk had written this? Whence had he obtained his information? For this is set down, not in a monastery chronicle, but in an official record, like the York Minutes-Book. And in how many other records throughout England, records now long disappeared, might some similar entry have been found? Lincoln, one might just notice en passant was the episcopal seat of Richard's Chancellor; there, if anywhere, one might expect faith in York and disbelief in Buckingham.

With echoes of the dead ringing amid the torchflares, the blazing galleries of the soul, went certain practical obligations. For even this unspeakable tragedy was mixed with the ordinary; with unpaid bills, with gratuities for unspecified services. Honours were heaped on Sir Robert Brakenbury, the Lieutenant of the Tower; small friendly sums given to Black Will Slaughter, the Keeper. Tyrell, as we have seen, was doing very well at Calais.

Settlement of other debts was made. Richard paid a long-standing account of £200 for "victuals spended in the House of Edward pretending to be Kynge"; and he granted a general pardon to "Margaret Elyngton, widow of John, Knt., Clerk of the Hanaper of Edward IV, Edward the Bastard, and the present King. . . ." **

This winding-up of the "piteous Raign" of the boy Edward argues his death. No other references to Edward, subsequent to 1483, exist, as they would if he had survived. The single obscure allusion to a "Lord Bastard" seized on as evidence of Edward's survival has been explained as a description of Jean of Gloucester, the King's own bastard. Occasional references to Edward Earl of Warwick occur; but nothing of the Princes of York, the vanished innocents.

While in London, echoing and far off, rose the old lament of the lost child . . . *down oh down in merry Lincoln.* . . .

THE APOTHEOSIS OF YORK

In mid-June, King Richard set up military headquarters at Notting-

* Hiss, *Medieval Lincoln.*
** The first item is from Harleian 433, undated but probably occurring in 1485; the second is from the Parliament Roll, Secundo Ricardus Tertius, dated June 14, 1485.

ham Castle. From this strategic centre, he could move rapidly in any direction. Reports came in concerning Tudor's Operation Dragon. A swarm of ships was readying at Harfleur, in Normandy; the Regency of France recruited for the invasion from its jails and galleys. But a good part of the ragtail little army consisted of adventurous Normans under a Norman mercenary captain, Philibert de Shaundé. In their conical helmets with the iron nosepiece, these sturdy brothers of the sword recalled their conquering ancestors from the rock-scrabbed duchy of Normandy, who had gone forth under William the Bastard.

Tudor's sail, Richard conjectured, would make for a southern port, where the Pretender would be near his native Wales. He sent Lovell down to Southampton Water to outfit the Royal Squadron, six tall ships: *Mary of the Tower, Grace à Dieu, Nicholas, Governor, Martin Garcia, Falcon.*

Dagger-plucking, sleepless, Richard roved Nottingham. Within this fortress crag, the wicked Sheriff and Guy of Gisborne had tried to trap Robin Hood in the time of Richard Yea and Nay. Here, the she-wolf Isabelle, mother of Edward the Third, had been walled up after the bestial murder of her husband, the second Edward. Sherwood Forest crept almost to the barbican of the rock-hewed battlement.

Almost daily the harried King rode out, a hooded falcon on his wrist. In Sherwood Forest was the royal hunting lodge of Beskwood; the gold and glimmer of spring on woodland paths, the ladyslipper, the honeysuckle and the harebell—patterns of white and blue—and the sudden shining echo of the past as they loosed their falcons, the lost merry voices, the outlawed, the beautiful and the dead. . . .

Richard rode through the wood in tawny breeches and leather doublet with silver studs, pondering Lord Stanley's refusal to join the muster of royal captains. The wily Constable had pleaded the sweating sickness to his urgent master. Richard suspected a case of "sweating treachery." The other Stanley, Sir William, the Constable of Carnarvon in Wales, was as slippery as his brother. The King had taken the precaution of securing the person of George Stanley, Lord Strange, the Constable's heir, in the vain hope of compelling loyalty and good faith where none had ever existed. This was the only instance in which Richard threatened anyone, in order to force the man to fight for him.

On June 23rd, the King got out a Proclamation against "Henry Tydder calling himself Tudor Earl of Richmond" and his band of "murderers, adulterers, and extortioners." The King's declamatory style had never been better; his sense of moral outrage never more effective. It was like the old days of proclamations against Mistress Shore and her bedfellows. "Henry Tydder . . . is descended of bastard blood, both of his father's side and of his mother's side; for the said Owen the Grandfather was bastard-born; and his mother was daughter unto John Earl of Somerset, son unto Dame Katherine Swynford, and of double adultery gotten. . . ." *

The English nation was warned that Tydder and his crew threatened "the most cruel murders, slaughters, robberies and disherisons that were ever seen in Christian realm. . . ."

Yet no vast number responded to this dramatic appeal. The loyal cities of the Rose—Gloucester, Worcester, London, York—might easily have recruited and paid several thousand dependable lads. Only York seems to have taken any action. Nicholas Lancastre, the Mayor, and other members of the York Corporation directed the King's Proclamation to be cried throughout the City; and commanded the Searchers of every Guild that all freemen be mustered, "defensably arrayed," to hold themselves in readiness to obey the King's wishes. In addition, company officers were appointed to the City troop and money appropriated to pay these captains.

In 1485, the population of York was about ten thousand. The Guilds were rich and numerous; the freemen of the Merchant Adventurers only (which included quite a few of the individual trade guilds in its flourishing organization) would have amounted to several hundred armed recruits for Richard. Taking the York Corporation's July directive as a base, it appears the King might very reasonably have expected one thousand men from York.**

In fact, no more than eighty men under John Sponer, Sergeant to

* RICHARD here errs. There is no evidence that Owen was a bastard, but it is probable that he was never formally married to Katherine of Valois; and therefore Henry's father Edmund was a bastard. Also, Lady Beaufort's father was John, 1st Duke of Somerset, 1404–1444. John was grandson to John of Gaunt and Katherine Swynford and therefore not a bastard, since the Beaufort line had been legitimatized by Richard the Second. But Richard the Third's general observation that Henry was descended from bastard blood on both sides is certainly correct. The Beaufort line *was* conceived in double adultery, as both the Duchess of Lancaster and Sir Hugh Swynford were living at the time of the notorious affair between Old Gaunt and the Flemish girl, Katherine Roët, wife to Swynford.

** What I have termed the "July directive" is based on two entries in the Minutes Book of the York Corporation: for July 6 and July 8. Davies' *York Records* omits the first, that of July 6. *Vide:* original folio, Minutes Book of Corporation, year 1485, pp. 167 et passim.

the Mace, set out on August 19th to join Richard's army. And even this little company, whether of foot or horse is not certain, failed to arrive in time. Bosworth was fought without a single soldier of York. Following the July directive, to form an immediate and mighty troop for King Richard, the Corporation's policy shifted. Instructions of August 16th to the City Wardens referred to a City-wide muster for purposes of defense only; for "the weal of this Citie."

Was this shift in policy due to subsequent orders from Richard, orders secretly conveyed and unrecorded in the Minutes Book, presaging in case of need a retreat to the line of the Ouse and a "Fortress York" in the heart of the old loyalty? Some scheme of this sort might be read into the King's action of secluding at Sheriff Hutton, a half-dozen miles from York, the remaining heirs of the Sunne: John Earl of Lincoln, Edward Earl of Warwick, Elizabeth Plantagenet, the royal bastard Jean of Gloucester. Sheriff Hutton became a stone chalice that held all the last blood of York.

Or was it that, with plague raging and an invading horde stalking the land, the City Fathers hesitated to strip York, even for their idol, Richard? An attitude of caution appeared to have succeeded the heroic mood of July; eighty men was a shallow enough risk for the ardent faith of the White Rose.

Richard had another potential source of strength: the shire levies. The less than Spartan quality of this rude militia has been depicted by the Stratford Bard in a famous scene of recruiting in which Sir John Falstaff "pricks" several rogues, Bullcalf, Shadow, Mouldy, for the King's Service. This dubious fighting timber was matched by an equally uncertain allegiance. The King issued his Commissions of Array to the Shire Lieutenants, usually though not invariably the local great man. The Shire Lieutenant might or might not be devoted to the King. Percy of Northumberland was Lieutenant in Yorkshire; Lord Stanley, in Derbyshire; Sir William Stanley, in Cheshire; Sir Gilbert Talbot, on the March of Wales. By his Commissions of Array, the King in effect gave to potential traitors the legal authority to muster the forces that might be used to betray him.

On June 22nd, one day before the Proclamation, Richard had sent out under the Privy Seal the instructions to the Shire Lieutenants to array. But the actual levying and despatch of recruits to the marshalling point at Nottingham seems not to have taken place until early August—coincident with the invasion. The turncoat Lieutenants were able to maintain control of their forces right up to the eve of battle; and the King never had more than a nominal command over the levies of Derbyshire or of Yorkshire.

There remained the livery of the Boar, the personal retainers of King Richard. But the Yeomen of the Crown had been riddled with disloyalty in '83, striking proof that the Corps, recruited under King Edward, was much affected by the propaganda concerning the Princes. Richard had tried to weed out the malcontent and to organize a company of franc archers on the lines of the Guard of France, but this company, sufficient for porte duty at Westminster or the Tower, was hardly enough to turn the scale in battle.

The worst problem of all was money.

Despite his lavish façade, his gorgeous raiment, the pageantry of his public appearances, Richard disposed of far less income than had his brother Edward. But toward money, Edward had the attitude of a bourgeois avare; while Richard possessed a kingly largess. There was always something a little disgusting, a little vulgar about Edward. Perhaps his true sire *was* a Norman archer named Blayborgne, as the Turbulent liked to relate. But never did Richard give this ignoble impression.

Having given up Edward's "benevolences," having refused French gold, having cut his own customs duties by restricting foreign trade, Richard had not enough for the ordinary running expenses of the government, to say nothing of a full-dress military campaign. Already, in December of his Coronation Year, he had been driven to the extremity of pawning the royal dinner service. What would the King now require to garrison and to arm vital fortresses; to maintain a coastal watch; to field an army at least as large as that by which Hal the Hero-King had broke the heart of France at Agincourt?*

Taking as the base wage of his soldiers, a shilling a day plus keep, Richard would need between £40,000 and £50,000—even for a brief campaign. But such a sum was completely out. Not his own peers, men like Surrey and Norfolk that he himself had made, would stand for it. Interminable wrangling at the Council board resulted in a com-

---

* See, for example, warrants of January 28, Primo Ricardus Tertius, to the Constable of the Tower to deliver to one Roger Bikley eight serpentines upon carts, twenty harquebusiers with frames, one barrel of touche poudre, two barrels of serpentine poudre, 200 bows, 400 sheafs of arrows, ten gross of bow strings, 200 bills; and warrants of February 25, primo Ricardus, for provisioning Beaumaris Castle by Sir Richard Huddleston, the Constable. Harleian Miscellany 433.

promise to raise £30,000. Agents were despatched to the shires with individual promissory notes, ranging from £50 to £200, and over the fine copperplate tracery of the signature "Ricardus Rex" the pledge: "And we promise you . . . truly to recontent you thereof at Martin-mas next coming, and the residue at the Feast of St. John Baptist then next following."

In this manner some £20,000 was obtained; at best half the sum needed. England was far from poor. A nation of three million had invaded and crushed the most flourishing realm in Christendom—the Kingdom of France, with fourteen millions of inhabitants. The English had fielded splendid well-furnished armies to emblazon upon the Golden Leopards the victories of Cressy and Poitiers; of Agincourt.

Yet Richard, faced with invasion by a horde of attainted exiles and hired French and Bretons, failed to obtain sufficient credits for national defense. Certainly, by the Proclamation of June he had tried to counter the effect of having previously taken too lightly his enemies. But Richard's preachments for the weal of the Realm, his lightning bolts of morality—the echo of Proud Cis and *Hilton on Contemplation* forever droning on in the brown oriel gleam of Vespers—had lost their power to rouse men. The King's desperate resort to this forced loan had more emotional impact on his subjects' minds than the war cry of the "insatiable covetise of Henry Tydder"—a description but too accurate, yet which no Englishman had experienced at first hand.

But all Richard's Proclamations and all his oaths might not offset the terrifying silence of the Tower. . . .

Even more, he might justly remark with pride the brilliant achievement of his mercurial reign: the prosperity of the kingdom, the peace with Ireland and Scotland, the spread of learning and tolerance, the new eagerness for books, the order and honesty in the administration of the common law, from parish magistrates up to Chief Justice Ralph Hussey of the Court of King's Bench. Not a single instance of religious persecution; not a single instance of literary censorship.* He had suppressed only those who openly advocated the overthrow of his government, the simple self-protection available to any government in any age.

---

* In view of the record both of succeeding and preceding reigns, this seems to me a remarkable exhibition of tolerance. The Tudors of course were savage in their intolerance, both of religious and civil dissent, and even that paragon of knightly valor, King Hal, presided over public burnings of so-called heretics.

Was all this happy benefit to the Nation to weigh so little beside the emotional obsession with the fate of two guiltless boys, once royal, once the pride and hope of Englishmen everywhere. It seemed so. And in choosing thus, in accepting the unkingly bastard-descended Welsh Pretender, the Nation revealed paradoxically its devotion to the mystique of monarchy. A mystique now so watered down and ineffectual that one can scarcely imagine its power in former times. Though of the ancient Blood of England, King Richard had violated that mystique by his treatment of his nephews; violated it in a terrible and irreparable way. And though the actual murder might be the work of traitors, the King himself could not shed an ultimate responsibility. Even with the beloved Buckingham still alive and lethal, the King could easily have safeguarded the boys. He could have taken them on his triumphal progress to York; or he could have ringed the Tower with men sworn to die (and a King could find such men in England) before anyone obtained access to the Princes.

He did neither; and they were murdered.

Now in June, 1485, Richard awaited an invasion which those conquering guiltless monarchs of old, Edward the Third, King Hal, his own brother Edward, might have laughed to scorn. Despite the bravado of Epiphany, he could not afford to do so. For it was not the invasion itself, the beggarly and ill-assorted levies of the unheroic Tudor that he need fear; it was the spreading stain of treason within. . . .

The hardest task of all was merely to wait. In this, death's trysting time, he began wearing black, his sable journade setting off a massive gold collar of York sunnes, the slashed sleeves and open neck revealing a beautiful cloth of gold brocaded tunic over a white cambric shirt. On his head he wore a black velvet chaperon with a blazing jewel. It was mourning, perhaps; but of a rare and regal kind. And no one dared inquire whether he mourned his wife Anne, or the renounced Elizabeth—or his Kingship.

In this attire, Richard had his portrait painted; the most magically evocative portrait of any King of England. The artist was probably John Serle, "King's Painter," of the native Court School of portrait painting; a school which owed much to the genius of Andre Beauneveu of Valenciennes, whose strangely moving vision of the young Richard the Second hung in Westminster Hall.

Ricardus, rex Angliae, anno secundo . . . in black journade and cloth of gold brocade, looking out now and forever from his black and gold, the deepset gaze of pain and intelligence, the taut mouth, the sharp thrusting chin . . . and the onlooker's eye falls to the delicate, almost feminine gesture of the left thumb and index finger exquisitely pressing the gold ring about the little finger of the right hand.

A gesture not strange to Lorenzo the Magnificent, the beau ideal of the Renaissance Prince; and most characteristic of this Falcon of York, this Richard. For when he was not plucking his dagger up and down in the gold-embossed sheath, slim nervous fingers toyed with his rings, as with the throats of his enemies. He customarily wore three: a sapphire, a ruby, and a gold band—on the thumb, fourth and little finger of the right hand. . . .

In this waiting loneliness, June-haunted, when life was a glistening Sunday that went on and on, Richard received word from France. Henry Tudor had sworn anew to wed Elizabeth Plantagenet. News to bring a flash of scorn to the King's eyes, as he evoked the pale long face with the strawberry mark on the cheek, the lidded glance, the lean shanks. This image of death and guile bedded with Elizabeth? An event hardly to be dreamed of! Tudor must win his bride by the sword and this dry little Welshman was the most laughable warrior in Christendom. Tudor was twenty-nine; he had fought no battles, had no experience of arms whatever. He was a fair shot with the Welsh bow, but to stand against Richard he must be more than a rustic at the butts.

The man who as a youth of nineteen had flourished a sword bright with Lancastrian blood, who had blazed York's armies to victory, he could not believe in isolation, in defeat. Daily, he rode out; to hunt with his peregrines, to survey the coastal alert, and not least to show himself to his English, a King—still reigning and proud. Couriers galloped in with pledges of loyalty from knights and royal officials. Richard persuaded himself that he heard the Nation's voice: that a wall of steel would rise up against those "notorious bawds and adulterers"—his enemies—when they dared brave his English realm. . . .

Time and the Monarchy stood still, a long shining pause in the torrents of August; and faint, oh far off and haunting! the horns of destiny softly blowing.

All his life arrayed in this moment and round him like a flame were joy and doom. He was pale; sunken eyes glowed. He was dwelling on some burning plain, the colour of dried blood in the sunset, where memories like great birds wheeled and screamed. He, the Stranger, the marvelous Sojourner, had come home again . . . to the iron beginning, to pain and nakedness.

What death his glory had bought!

Tewkesbury's gleaming blood, spilt beside the Severn . . . the muted dagger of Ascension Eve . . . the glazed livid faces of the beheaded . . . the grate of ancient bolts and a brother's sons . . . Anne, his wife.

And yet! Some clarion of his soul still echoed. Laughter, Sunne laughter, ringing loud and clear, hallooing in the red waste of his monarchy; searing defiance and joy—and how a Falcon dies: proud and sun-crying. . . .

In silver wraithy Wales, mist-wrapped and druidic, in Pembrokeshire, at Milford Haven, Cadwallader's heir came home again, a Prince of proud old bastardy . . . Dragon unfurled, splashing ashore and crying in the Welsh tongue, the dark merlin magic. Setting sail on August 1st, Lammas Day, one of the four powerful days in the druidic calendar, he touched native ground on August 7th. Shooting forth starlike proclamations of royalty, trailing clouds of prophecy, the self-anointed Arthur began his march, in his train 2000 hired French and Bretons.

O Dragon of Cadwallader!

Ringing and singing the joyous tidings, down the hill-locked valleys, the ancient stone circles, the oak-haunted memories. Flaming upon green and white, marching, marching . . . and one after another the Castellans of the Sunne tore off the fanged Boar. As at Banbury, Clarence's men had torn off the Crimson Rose; as at Tewkesbury, Wenlock had stabbed Lancaster in the back. For he who lives by treachery and the split heart. . . . These were the names that destroyed the Sunne: Rhys ap Thomas of Carmarthen, "the Mars of Wales"; Sir Walter Herbert, Royal Deputy of South Wales; Sir William Stanley, Chamberlain of North Wales, Constable of Carnarvon, Warden of Delamere; Sir Gilbert Talbot, Lieutenant of Shropshire.

The ragged two thousand was doubled; then tripled. The Dog of Shrewsbury, the Talbot Dog, gold-collared, remembering York's old insult to Eleanor Talbot, ruined daughter of a warrior House—this Gilbert Talbot brought the entire livery of Shrewsbury, one thousand avengers of Eleanor.

Humfrey stood in a high tower, and looked into the West Countrye;

*Sir William Stanley and seaven in grene came ryding straight into the city. . . .**

And Mytton, bluff Tom Mytton, quondam Sheriff of Shropshire, bailey of Shrewsbury—had not Tom sworn the invader should enter only over his prostrate body? Now, affording to these deadly proceedings an absurd Falstaffian touch, Tom Mytton lay down in the dust of Shrewsbury's main gateway, while Henry, this sly and scrawny Arthur, scrambled over the huge belly.

Yet, it was not all magic and Banners. The army was attacked by the "sweating sickness," a mysterious plague that struck with sudden fever and delirium, then shivering and a coffin-cold rigor, then a foetid perspiration, then death—all in a few hours. The country people fled in horror from their pestilent "liberators"; but the Dragon band might take consolation in the imminent prospect of greater treacheries.

England's Richard . . . at Beskwood, on Thursday, August 11th, a panting courier leaped from the saddle to fall at the King's feet—a tale of treason and despair. Wales lost; the West Country gone; the midlands threatened. "As one news straight came huddling on another; of death and death and death. . . ."

But: must this Sunne fail? He called up his English; appointed an army rendezvous at Leicester. Under the Great Seal, the red wax of monarchy, he collected twelve thousand men; of whom four thousand were the guard of Essex, Norfolk's rally of the Whyte Lyon. The outward aspect was splendid: a vision of the last oriflamme of medieval England; of horsemen clanking into courtyards with urgent scrolls; of trumpets and marshalling and armoured lords browheavy in the lancing sun of great Halls . . . and the small limping King, the black and gold King, chaperon with the glowing ruby—he against a backdrop of blue-velvet night and winking stars, the towers of a visionary Nottingham, talking, jesting, pale and taut . . . that melodious voice, the nimble grace, the wonder and midnight royalty of it all. . . .

"Wherefore, I pray you that ye meet with me at Bury, for by the Grace of God I purpose to lie at Bury as upon Tuesday night, and that ye bring with you such company of tall men, as ye may goodly make at my cost and charge, besides that ye have promised the King, and I pray you ordain them jackets of my livery, and I shall content you at your meeting with me."

* From *The Song of the Lady Bessy;* by Humphrey Brereton, a liveryman of Lord Thomas Stanley, later the Earl of Derby.

So the Earl Marshal, Jock o' Norfolk. . . .

Richard came down from his visionary tower, the wonderful and lost kingship; led forth the Company of the Sunne, the old magnificent Banners—the Sunne-in-Splendour, the Lyon of March, the Falcon Unfettered, the Whyte Boar. Swirling sarcenet, brilliant and dawn-filled, above the plumed Captains, the men-at-arms glinting in the saddle, the slogging foot-columns.

He supped on Saturday at Leicester, at the Sign of the Whyte Boar; lay down for the last time in his state bed, brought from Windsor, with the gorgeous tester of gold and crimson, the embroidered Royal Arms, and white satin coverlet. The bed had a false bottom, crammed with gold pieces.

As Leicester morning broke hot and clear, trumpets marshalled the Rose. Down High Cross Street, across Bow Bridge over the River Soar, and along the Kirkby Mallory Road . . . marching five abreast in a train three miles long, the lads of Lincoln, of Essex and Surrey, of York and Sussex; and in their midst the King.

Flashing white armour of Tewkesbury, golden circlet on his helm, mounted on the arab war-gelding White Surrey; the royal visor was up, that Leicester might behold him—his sleepless glory, the terror and beauty in his face, the war gaze of old England, cruel and proud and lonely. . . .

A few persons remarked that the King "brake his spur" on the stone coping of Bow Bridge.

He lay that night near the village of Sutton Cheyney, twelve miles west of Leicester, where, taking his stand on the high ground, he might bar the route into the heart of his Realm. The quaking Dragon, torn between cowardice and the slavering pangs of royalty, had passed several queasy nights on the march from Wales. Secret interviews at Shrewsbury and Lichfield, where "gonnes cracked" for the Dragon, had failed to produce that overt handclasp of treason so ardently desired from Lord Tom Stanley of Derbyshire. In good season; in good season . . . but this Dragon sweated as he came.

. . . (King Richard) "Give me a bowl of wine. For I have not that alacrity of spirit nor cheer of mind that is my wont. . . ." *

Bosworth: the Eve . . . the glowing forge of summer burned dull red. Helmets and breast-plates, thigh tassets gleamed in the old red light. An occasional murmuring arose from the men around the cook-

* Richard the Third; Act V, Scene 3.

fires, a few sad jokes dying into the sunset, the immense sky like dried blood. But for the most part the soldiers were quiet; only a rattle of cups and soup bowls, the glug-glug of wine pouring. . . .

Here, on fate's final escarpment, the rock of Plantagenet; and somewhere the wind and the horror . . . he heard the mighty past, the blood-memory—ancestral voices prophesying dread. The child Arthur of Brittany, chain-whipped to bloody rags in a Rouen dungeon by King John; the glowing spit thrust into the fundament of Edward the Second; Edward the Third's deathbed; the shrieks of Richard the Second, as he was hammered by the thugs of Henry Bolingbroke. . . .

This was the real black dawn of Richard; the hour before the light. This—and the old lament of Lincoln, the lost child, the child that perhaps never was: in the night, did he hear a child cry?

The lights burn blue. . . .

He was alone; why every man is alone; naked. What—did he fear this scrawny Dragon, this shivering band across Redmore plain? Nay . . . he feared himself, the heritage of his House: Melusine-born. He who lives by treachery and the split heart. . . .

The Sunne of Bosworth . . . Ratcliffe had seen it as he came with esquires to the royal tent. The glow and ripple of banners, the snorting horses, the stir and jangle of a battle morning. His esquires armed the King. He was ghastly pale; drawn, sunken-eyed—but armed also with a kind of terrible fire, blazing within, flickering in the hollow madness of his eyes.

As the other Captains assembled, Norfolk, Surrey, Ferrers, Scroop and Dacres, Richard drew their attention with a dire prophecy. He had one of those startling moments of clarity sometimes vouchsafed to a soul in agony. The old England, the England of their childhood tears, was dead. Whoever gained the day, a new monarchy must arise, a time of terror and blood. He saw a red horizon breaking, the dread new age. He had been too kind; he intended to exterminate his foes.

He broke off in a livid silence, as deathlike as his own royal countenance. A sentry came crying for the King, with a scrap of paper found pinned to the Earl Marshal's tent . . . *Jockey of Norfolk, be not too bold; for Dickon thy Master is bought and sold.* . . .

Richard read it aloud. The thin taut mouth grew cruel; the eyes darkened. He rolled the paper into a ball, tossed it away. He had known it all before. His Realm was rotten with treachery. His glance roved the frozen Captains. Suddenly, in a sharp cutting voice, a voice tuned to the headsman's axe, he asked for Stanley and Northumberland. They had not, it seemed, come up. Pursuivants were despatched to these divisional officers with a pre-emptory command to move.

The King turned to the Order of the Day. Someone reminded Richard of breakfast, but he shrugged this off. The men would eat; but the King intended to fast before his consecration of blood. As for a field Mass, he was not in a praying mood. Nor was a Mass on the verge of battle always usual. No Mass had been said before Barnet; and none before Towton. At Tewkesbury, both sides had said a formal Mass.

With his rapid eye for terrain, the King had selected the most advantageous ground to array. He knew the country well, having hunted out of Nottingham for years. Pursuant to orders, Norfolk and Surrey had at cockcrow seized the bald crest of Ambien Hill, a four-hundred-foot elevation overlooking Redmore Plain. Ambien or *Ann Beam,* the Saxon One Tree Hill, had a gentle declivity to the southwest and a steep slope to the north. The royal van ward of four thousand Essex lads arrayed against the south, whence the Dragon assault might be expected.

The scurryers' reports were in; and Richard knew that three small armies ringed the Hill. The Dragon band of five or six thousand bedded at White Moor, about three miles south and west of the King; Stanley, the Constable, with that Griffin Claw badge on 3000 jackets, camped at Stapleton, two miles south of Ambien; while Sir William Stanley and his iron command of 2000 Cheshire dragoons in "coats red as blude" hovered to the northwest of Ambien, watching, waiting. . . .

It was now just past eight of the clock. Wrath like an eagle brooded over the plain. In this fierce hush, the royal bombardiers readied the cannonade. Iron snouts of serpentines, toads, fowlers, culverins—the ordnance of the Tower—lined the bald ridge.*

Across the broken plain fluttered the green and white tents of the invader. There were "gonnes" here as well; but failure to seize Ambien compelled the Dragon horde to abandon artillery tactics. Tudor's men had an almost impossible task: to cross the naked plain, to maneuver about a marsh at the base of Ambien slope, to climb the long southern approach of 500 yards to the ridgetop—all in full view of the mighty

---

* Kendall denies Richard any guns, but this is certainly wrong. Not only is there the plain evidence of the Parliament Roll (Vol. VI, p. 276), but stone shot have been dug up on the southern slope. It is impossible to site Tudor's artillery, although it is clear he brought guns to the field.

power of the Sunne, the mortal serpentines linked cradle to cradle, the bristling hedgerows of archers and crossbowmen.

Madness. . . .

Yet, as the mist cleared, the great banners of bright sarcenet thrust out of the morning: the Dragon of flame, the Dun Bull, the image of Saint George. In the van appeared the white hoods of Sir John Savage's company; then, the blue and silver of de Vere, Earl of Oxford, field general of the Rose; then, the Talbot Dog on black and white checky livery; and after, old greasy jacks and battered tin hats of the mercenaries . . . on they came, a ragged glinting line, a reddish cloud rising over the plain . . .

His gaze on the advancing ranks, soon to be ripped by point-blank fire, Richard glimpsed the blue and murrey Pursuivant *Blaunche Senglier* galloping over the crest. Stanley's reply! The King tensed; nearby, Catesby and Ferrers waited with Stanley's son.

At the Pursuivant's first word, he knew. Stanley intended to betray him. Three thousand men! Worse than Buckingham—betrayed on the very field of battle. Now he knew why Lady Grey had smiled so strangely that morning at Westminster, when he had said goodbye. She was preparing to kill someone; and he had not known—but it was himself.

His hand fell to his side, where customarily he wore his belted dagger. But he was in full armour. Fingers twitching emptily, he stared into the molten day. Abruptly, he gave orders to behead George Stanley. Walter, Lord Ferrers offered a protest. Richard brushed him off. Catesby led off the trembling young man. He was grey-faced. Pitiless, Richard watched them. Now by Holy Paul! he was resolved to exterminate the House of Stanley.

(What he did not foresee was the last of all his betrayals by the little lawyer Catesby, who saved Stanley's son, hoping—uselessly as it proved—for grace at Stanley's hands.)

Richard turned back to the slope, holding his breath as the long swinging line came on, sun-washed and crying . . . he was counting the moments until he loosed the cannonade. And now, he saw the Dragon horde confused and milling at the marsh, some floundering in, while officers in de Vere blue and silver whipped with flat blades at the men's legs to keep them moving.

Like curs, Richard thought. Had not Edward and he beaten John de Vere, 13th Earl of Oxford, at Barnet? True, Oxford had first broke

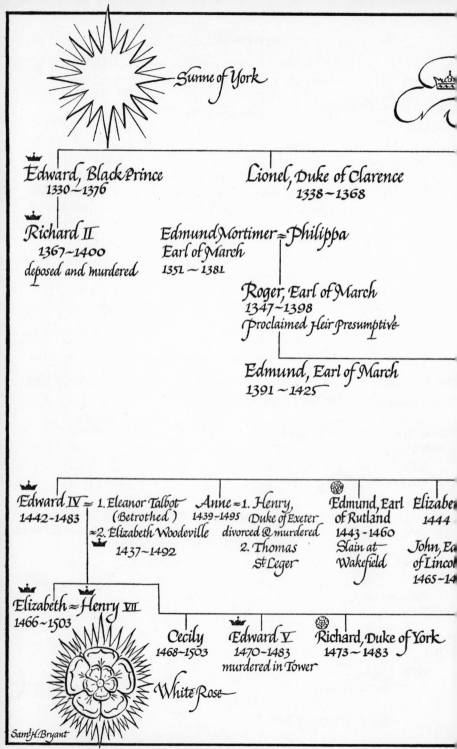

Sunne of York

Edward, Black Prince
1330~1376

Lionel, Duke of Clarence
1338~1368

Richard II
1367~1400
deposed and murdered

Edmund Mortimer ≈ Philippa
Earl of March
1351 ~ 1381

Roger, Earl of March
1347~1398
Proclaimed Heir Presumptive

Edmund, Earl of March
1391 ~ 1425

Edward IV ≈ 1. Eleanor Talbot
1442-1483   (Betrothed)
          ≈2. Elizabeth Woodeville
              1437~1492

Anne ≈1. Henry,
1439~1495 Duke of Exeter
        divorced & murdered
        2. Thomas
            St Leger

Edmund, Earl
of Rutland
1443 - 1460
Slain at
Wakefield

Elizabe
1444

John, Ea
of Lincol
1465~14

Elizabeth ≈ Henry VII
1466~1503

Cecily
1468~1503

Edward V
1470~1483
murdered in Tower

Richard, Duke of York
1473 ~ 1483

White Rose

Sam! H. Bryant

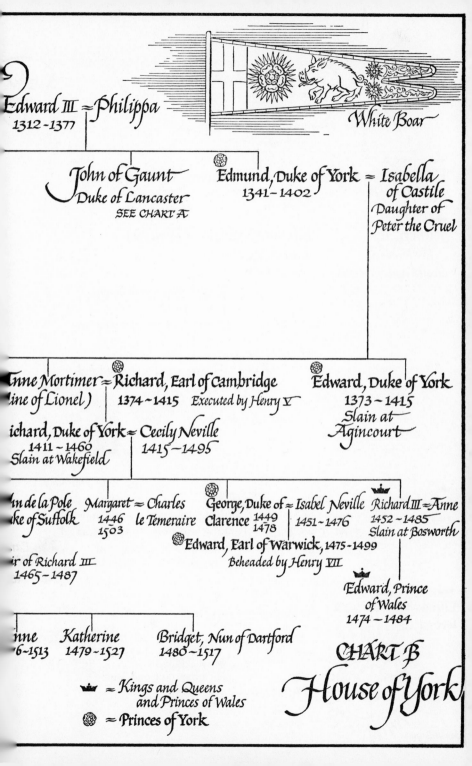

Edward III = Philippa
1312 -1377

John of Gaunt
Duke of Lancaster
SEE CHART A

Edmund, Duke of York = Isabella
1341- 1402   of Castile
                         Daughter of
                         Peter the Cruel

White Boar

Anne Mortimer = Richard, Earl of Cambridge
(line of Lionel)   1374 - 1415   Executed by Henry V

Edward, Duke of York
1373 - 1415
Slain at
Agincourt

Richard, Duke of York = Cecily Neville
1411 - 1460   1415 - 1495
Slain at Wakefield

...n de la Pole   Margaret = Charles   George, Duke of = Isabel Neville   Richard III = Anne
...ke of Suffolk   1446   le Temeraire   Clarence 1449   1451 - 1476   1452 - 1485
                   1503   1478   Slain at Bosworth

                                    Edward, Earl of Warwick, 1475 -1499
...ir of Richard III   Beheaded by Henry VII
1465 - 1487

                                                                      Edward, Prince
                                                                      of Wales
                                                                      1474 - 1484

...nne   Katherine   Bridget, Nun of Dartford
...6 -1513   1479 - 1527   1480 - 1517

                                              CHART B
                                              House of York

👑 = Kings and Queens
     and Princes of Wales
🌹 = Princes of York

Hastings with a dawn thunderbolt. But Hastings! Already rotten, with the foulness of Jane Shore. Thank God he knew evil when he saw it! Tainted; tainted. It was a dread matter to lose a friend; but leprosy of the soul was worse.

And while Oxford, captain-General of the Dragon, on his silver grey horse, with his Banner-Bearer beside him, struggled around the marsh, the King gazed upon the Radiant Star of de Vere—more and more he was haunted by Barnet!—remembering how Warwick's red-jackets had mistook the Star for York's Sunne-in-Splendour and had cut to pieces their ally . . . when was that? The question broke out of the listening summertime of the dead. Why in the lost wonder of his youth, the fires of his unspeakable glory. He looked backward, as if imploring the past . . . but his glance was turned toward Sutton Cheyney, where lay his rear ward, 3000 Northern men in leather jackets and grey fustian breeches. He listened: for the battlescream, for the old Percy cry of "Esperance!" and boots coming on the double, the Golden Shacklebolt surging in the sun and his Northerners shouting up the slope from Sutton Cheyney.

But nothing stirred.

And it came to the King that this was a visionary battle; that the real encounter was not here at all, but in Lady Grey's Withdrawing Room, in the old Norman twilight of the Tower, in his mother's chapel at Barnard Castle, she was always in sable now . . . desperately, he came back to the field.

Savage's white hoods, the blue and silver of de Vere had passed the marsh; the enemy was climbing the slope and Richard's own soldiers of the Sunne stared at the King, waiting for the command to fire. Now he loosed the bombardiers. They leaped with flaming matches to their touch-holes; the hill shook with roaring and tongues of orange and crimson flickered into the iron light. Oxford's company was gashed by stone shot and murderous chain bursts. A wind of shrieks blew toward the crest.

The King knew it was no use waiting for Percy; he ought to hit Oxford now, hit him with everything, before the Stanleys got on the move. He called over the Duke of Norfolk. No time for speeches, a few terse commands barked into the morning . . . they were going into action, the storm battalions of Essex, old front fighters of York. Drive the curs into the marsh! Richard had a reputation for lightning. The trumpets rang; all along the line men grew taut and lonely.

Norfolk's division moved out, under a barrage of arrows; and the King felt the old heart-wringing exaltation—steel and banners in the sun!—while his soldier's mind performed frantic calculations. He had committed one-half his remaining force, four thousand men, to the initial assault; while Tudor, by treachery, had more than doubled the five thousand he had brought to the field. Yet—strangely—the King's spirit, far from being overwhelmed, soared like the marvelous longing of *Christus Resurgens,* the golden choir whose voices now seemed to fill the brazen vault of heaven in unbearable joy. . . .

Oxford's men had halted, drawn together in a sudden hush. Norfolk came on briskly, steel bare . . . oh God he felt like weeping, and re-membered long ago crying at the barricade, in Warwick's tilting yard, in the green summerland of Warwick . . . he dashed away a few tears.

And now with glory and bright thunder the lines clashed at mid-slope; wrestling together, the gleaming rainlight of blood, and men crumpling in the sun. And all this time, while the spirit of the King brooded above the battle, the King's body stood beside the Royal Ban-ner giving brusque commands; feeding re-inforcements to Norfolk, sending out scurryers, marshalling his Household of knights and men-at-arms.

Oxford's line sagged, a curve that splintered and leaned dangerously toward the marsh. The King's spirit leaped; and then he heard the flare of trumpets. Miraculously, the line tightened, bent inward toward Ox-ford's Standard of the Star. Oxford had taken the King's best; and still held. And time, that thin bright flame, wasted. While Norfolk and Surrey fought on, he heard the deadly beat of rescue. Stanley . . . coming fast, with fire and steel, against the flank of Norfolk. Stanley —another traitor Constable—surging toward the Whyte Lyon.

Yet, for an instant, Norfolk and his men stood firm. Old comrades of the Sunne . . . once more the joy and wonder of his monarchy swept over the King. Why, long after, he and they would be living, paladins of the Sunne, cantering amid the great pavilions of gold and white. In him glowed a terrible majesty. He laughed; and men turned to stare. He knew what they were thinking: that he was ruined, done for . . . but it was not true.

Suddenly he was crying; crying at the barricade, the agony of his small twisted body, the sweating and the armour . . . officers rushed up. "Treason! Treason!" the King blazed, pointing at Stanley's men of Derbyshire.

Before Richard panted a pale courier. Norfolk was dead, slain by a coward arrow as man to man he dueled in the old gallant tradition with the opposing commander Oxford. Surrey was desperately beset, at the point of death or capture. Richard was silent. John Howard, Duke and Earl Marshal—a symbol. Dimly, voices came to the King urging flight. He shrugged them off. A Plantagenet of the old Blood of England did not void the field. His glance roved the waiting Household. In the horror of the sun, the light of Hell that poured out of a sky of brass, he saw his last companions. They stared at him as if he were a ghost; as indeed he was, dwelling in this immense and visionary world. Weeping and smiling—and that pleasant voice echoing forever down the sky-swept cloister of dreams—he bade his men mount.

He wanted time to stand still; to capture forever this proud beautiful moment. He was swinging down the sun, riding into magnificence. It was his flesh, his blood, demanded on the flaming altars of the Sunne. *See how my sword weeps!* . . . and he who had made other men martyrs now offered the final sacrifice: himself.

These were of the company who rode with Richard: Walter Lord Ferrers, Lord Dacres, Sir Richard Ratcliffe, Sir Robert Brakenbury (the Lieutenant of the Tower), Sir William Conyers, Sir Richard Clarendon, Sir Humphrey Stafford, Sir Gervase Clifton, the Lord of the Rose (whose sire had died for Margaret), Sir Bryan Stapleton, Sir William Parker of the Royal Standard, and five or six score knights, esquires and men-at-arms.*

Cantering over the slope, the ragged gorse and white shrunken flowers, swinging wide around the marsh and the bleeding wreck of Norfolk's command, King Richard hunted the Dragon. Scurryers had reported the enemy Standard near Shenton, 3000 yards west. The pace increased to a gallop; rhythmic thunder of war destriers . . . a band of blazing angels, visored and with a song of steel.

North of Tudor, in the flying dust, lurked the "blude coats" of Sir William Stanley, the cavalry reserve with their Standard of the Buck's Head; waiting, jesting, horses tossing great manes . . . what a chance— even for a Stanley! A double betrayal. For the redcoated dragoons saw

---

* Francis Viscount Lovell is missing. It is hardly thinkable he would have avoided this last ride; and since all the principal officers of Richard were cut down, Lovell must not have been at Bosworth. He survived to lead a revolt on behalf of Edward Earl of Warwick, culminating in the battle of Stoke, June 20th, 1487, in which York was again defeated by the Stanleys and Oxford. Lovell escaped, only to perish of starvation in a walled-up hiding place in his own manor.

the King coming, his Leopards in the burning cloud, and instantly they perceived his purpose. To let Tudor die—nothing easier for Stanley. Then to move in, slay the Boar—and proclaim a Stanley Regency. The temptation was golden.

Now at last Richard found the Dragon's end, the great flame-coloured Standard limp on a little crest, bald as Tudor himself, and a clump of unsuspecting knights. He waved on his company, bringing his lance to the ready . . . they struck with a fury, scattering standards, foot-stools, horseholders—avenging Angels, Michaels of the Sunne.

Sir John Cheyney, Cavalry Master of the Dragon, loomed out of the gorge of death. Richard's lance splintered; the huge armoured captain reeled to the dust. The King swung to confront Sir William Brandon, of the rebel Standard. His axe smote Brandon's helm; from dying fingers he plucked the insolent Dragon, shook aloft the Standard—and hurled it.

(Three hundred miles away, at Sheriff Hutton, Elizabeth Plantagenet looked up from a game of jeu de cartes with John Earl of Lincoln; over her spirit passed a dark wind; she stared, rigid . . . *wele could she wyrke by prophesye*)

Hunting Tudor with wild blade, clashing up and down the camp, and Death, bright-winged and shining at his back. But he did not hear the thunder of Stanley's dragoons; nor see the white hawthorn flowers at his feet. Nor ever know the moment when his own men began to fall, ringed by bloody coats and bloody swords.

A mace crashed on the King's pauldron, his shoulder-guard. He swayed; shook his head. An axe rang on his bascinet; he tottered . . . and about him were eager knives, flashes of steel, the swords singing in the flame . . . Richard fell bleeding. On the bascinet with its golden fleurons axes hammered, crushing the King's head; blood and brain mingled in the dust.

Above, a hawk circled in the noon. . . .

They brought the body back to Leicester and the Grey Friars Convent, naked even to the privy member, mired with blood and filth and slung across a horse's withers, the red-dark royal hair hanging down, slung like carrion before the Whyte Boar badge, "the Proud Bragging Boar" of his Pursuivant *Blaunche Senglier*. Oh terrible Absolution! Grace of blood . . . the pleasant voice, the towered nightingale, forever broke. And thus it was that, naked and bloodstained, Richard entered his visionary Kingdom.

Bald, lean, smirking, still a little grey from fright, Henry Tudor was crowned at Stoke Golding, near Bosworth; crowned Henry the Seventh with Richard's golden circlet (what royal magic lived in even his poor dented circlet!), hacked from the King's helm and plucked from a hawthorn bush. Christopher Urswicke held the silken cushion and Lord Tom Stanley settled the crown on the fringe of yellowish locks, and Bishop John Morton croaked a few remarks about peace and unity. But over the scene presided the shades of three women, three cold furies in a scene built out of woman's vengeance and irreparable royalty—Lady Margaret Beaufort, Lady Elizabeth Grey, Queen Marguerite d'Anjou. God was everywhere, triumphant; and these His handmaidens, His Acolytes of Death . . . cold, cruel and proud. . . .

In Norman twilight, London's Tower dreamed. Above the river, smoke-gold and glinting, the river that went on forever . . . October, a moment of terror; someone looked down a dim stone stair. Do you hear a sound of weeping, of tears and young voices? Do you hear a whispering at the Bolt?

BIBLIOGRAPHY

APPENDICES

INDEX

MATERIALS FOR THE STUDY OF JEANNE LA PUCELLE

CONTEMPORARY SOURCES:
The Trial of Jeanne d'Arc. With historical essay and biographical sketches by Pierre Champion. Edited and translated by W. P. Barrett. Gotham House, 1932.

The Trial of Joan of Arc. With Notes by W. S. Scott. Edited and translated by W. S. Scott from 'French Minute' of Trial for Lapse. Folio Society, 1956.

La vie et la mort de Jeanne d'Arc. Les témoignages du procès de Rehabilitation. Edited and with Notes by Regine Pernoud. Hachette, 1953.

Chronique de la Pucelle by G. Cousinot, Chancellor of the Duchy of Orléans. Paris, 1859.

Journal du siège d'Orléans by G. Cousinot. Edition P. Charpentier, Orléans, 1896.

Journal d'un bourgeois de Paris. Edition André Mary, Paris, 1929.

BIOGRAPHICAL STUDIES:
Jeanne d'Arc by Jules Michelet. Paris, 1856.

La vie de Jeanne d'Arc by Anatole France. 4 vols. Paris 1909–10.

The Maid of France by Andrew Lang. Longmans Green, 1909.

Saint Joan of Arc by Victoria Sackville-West. Doubleday Doran, 1936.

Louis duc d'Orléans by F. D. Darwin. John Murray, 1936.

Joan of Arc and the Recovery of France by Alice Buchan. Hodder & Stoughton, 1948.

Jeanne d'Arc a-t-elle brulée? by Jean Grimod. Amiot Dumont, revised 1956.

Telle fut Jeanne d'Arc by Regine Pernoud. Fasquelle, 1957.

Charles d'Orléans by Jacques Charpier. Pierre Seghers, 1958.

SPECIAL STUDIES:
Histoire du siège et la déliverance d'Orléans by P. Mantellier, Director Musée Historique, Orleans. Orleans, 1855.

La vie quotidienne au temps de Jeanne d'Arc by Marcelin Defourneaux, Hachette, 1952.

The Agincourt War by Col. Alfred H. Burne. Eyre & Spottiswoode, 1956.

MANUSCRIPT SOURCES:

Bibliothèque Municipal, Orléans. MSS 1673. French translation of Latin reports destined to Procès de Rehabilitation, with brief biography of Jeanne. End of 16th Century.

Bibliothèque Municipal, Orléans. MSS 518. 'French Minute' of Trial for lapse, with biography of Jeanne, and testimony from Procès de Rehabilitation. Drawn up by direction of Louis the Twelfth and of the Sieur de Graville, Admiral of France, in the year 1500.

Archives du département de la Loire, Orléans. Comptes de la forteresse, Registré Coté CC 654 et CC 655.

MATERIALS FOR THE STUDY OF RENÉ AND MARGUERITE D'ANJOU

CHRONICLE HISTORIES:

Chronicles of the White Rose "Manner and Guiding of the Earl of Warwick at Angers" London, 1845.

Chroniques d'Angleterre by Jehan Waurin. Edited by Mlle. Dupont. Societe de l'Histoire de France. Paris, 1859.

Oeuvres de Georges Chastellain, 8 Vols. Edited by Baron Kervyn de Lettenhove. Brussels, 1863.

CONTEMPORARY SOURCES:

Letters of Margaret of Anjou and Bishop Beckington. Camden Society, 1863.

Lettres de Louis XI. Edited by Vaesen and Charavay. Paris, 1885.

Paston Letters, 4 Vols. Edited by Dr. James Gairdner. London, 1910.

English Historical Literature in the Fifteenth Century. Edited by C. L. Kingsford. Oxford, 1913.

Calendar of Milanese State Papers, Vol. I. Edited by A. B. Hinds. London, 1912.

Le Livre des Tournois du Roi René. Edition Verve. Paris, 1946.

Le Livre du Coeur d'Amour Epris du Roi René. Edition Verve. Paris, 1949.

BIOGRAPHICAL STUDIES:

Lives of the Queens of England, Vol. I, by Agnes Strickland. London, 1864.

Marguerite d'Anjou, reine d'Angleterre by Philippe Erlanger. Edition Emile-Paul, 1932.

Life and Reign of Edward IV, 2 Vols. by Cora L. Scofield. Longmans, 1923.

La vie et les moeurs du bon Roi René by Jacques Levron. Amiot Dumont, 1953.

Warwick the Kingmaker by Paul Murray Kendall. Allen Unwin, 1958.

SPECIAL STUDIES:
The Battlefields of England by Col. Alfred H. Burne. Methuen, 1950.

The Battle of Tewkesbury by Canon William Bazeley. Transactions of the Gloucester Archaeological Society for 1903.

MANUSCRIPT SOURCES:
Recueil des pieces originals pour la guerre des Roses. Bibliothèque Nationale; Mss. fr. 4054.

Autograph letter of Margaret of Anjou to the Sieur du Bouchage. Bibliothèque Nationale; Mss. fr. 2909, folio 34.

MATERIALS FOR THE STUDY OF RICHARD III

CONTEMPORARY SOURCES:
Arrivall of King Edward (Fleetwood's Ms.) in *Chronicles of the White Rose.* The most important Yorkist chronicle by a member of the household of Edward IV. The chief source for the battles of Barnet and Tewkesbury.

Croyland Chronicle. Yorkist; but anti-Richard. Probably compiled by Piers Courtoise, Master of the Wardrobe under both Edward IV and Richard III.

Davies' *York Records.* A very excellent Northern source. Pro-Yorkist and pro-Richard.

Great Chronicle of London. Yorkist; but anti-Richard. One source for disappearance of Princes after October 1483.

Stow's *Chronicle* (1592). Not strictly contemporary; but making use of contemporary materials in a judicious way.

Warkworth's *Chronicle.* Strongly Lancastrian. The principal source for the accusation that Richard murdered Henry VI. Also that Clarence was involved in the death of Edward of the Red Rose at Tewkesbury.

TUDOR PROPAGANDA FACTORY:
History of England by Bernard Andre.

Anglica Historia by Polydore Vergil; 1534.

Hall's *Chronicle* by Edward Hall; 1542.

Holinshed's *Chronicles,* 1578.

Song of the Lady Bessy, by Humphrey Bretherton (Harl. Ms. 367, f. 89). These are works of straight Tudor propaganda, with shameless inventions, omissions, slantings. Vergil and Andre were Italians in the pay of Henry VII; Holinshed was the name of a syndicate of printers headed by Reyne Wolfe, who made no pretense at anything but sales. Bretherton was a Steward of Lord Stanley. Hall was a barrister and M. P.

EARLY BIOGRAPHICAL STUDIES:
The Usurpation of Richard the Third by Dominic Mancini. The earliest known study by an Augustinian prior, in the service of France. It is strongly anti-Richard; and is the earliest source for the slaying of the Princes of York. Latin ms. edited and translated by C. A. G. Armstrong, 1936.

The Life and Pitiful Raign of Edward V by Sir Thomas More—sometimes miscalled *Richard III,* which title belongs to a later work compiled by Printer Dick Grafton, More's son-in-law. More's work was first printed by Rastell in 1557 from a copy in More's own hand, dated 1513. Grafton edited this Latin work and added his own version of events after Buckingham's rebellion, as More breaks off with the disappearance of Edward V and Morton's conspiracy. More plus Grafton plus the Tudor Chronicles were the historical sources for Shakespeare's play *Richard the Third.* It is probable that More received his information from Cardinal Morton, Richard's bitter enemy.

STUDIES OF THE "MIDDLE PERIOD":
Richard III by Sir George Buck; 1646. The first 'revisionist' effort, by the descendant of an officer of Richard's Household. Buck reproduces the letter purported to have been written by Elizabeth Plantagenet to the Duke of Norfolk, concerning her passion for her uncle Richard. In Buck is also found the notion that Richard knew all about Edward's pre-contract with Lady Eleanor Talbot years before Edward died. Buck believed the Princes survived during Richard's reign (this was before the discovery of the Bones) and claimed to have found a specific entry in the Parliament Roll proving his belief—an entry no one else has been able to locate.

Historic Doubts by Horace Walpole; 1768. A literary 'vindication' of Richard by one of the leading cranks of the Enlightenment. Walpole had no new sources, but he was able to show by internal evidence how silly and fabricated was much of the Tudor propaganda. Walpole also ridiculed the discovery of the Bones and the version that these remains were the murdered sons of Edward.

Bosworth Field by Thomas Hutton; 2nd edition, 1813. A balanced study, presenting Richard not as a monster, but as a man molded by the cruelty of his time, and with praise for Richard as a soldier and statesman. Mainly concerned with the battle, this is the most complete source for that aspect of Richard's reign.

VICTORIANS ON RICHARD:
Richard III by Caroline Halsted; 2 vols. 1844. Highly favourable to King Richard; a work of intensive, if somewhat uncritical, scholarship, and the real foundation of the modern school of revisionists.

The Unpopular King by Alfred Legge; 1885. A two-volume apologia for Richard.

Richard III by Dr. James Gairdner; 1898. The principal exponent of the Tudor tradition, with a work solidly based on exhaustive scholarship and of great value in striking a balance on the subject of Richard, between the excesses of traditionalists and revisionists.

Richard III, his life and character by Clement Markham; 1906. Strongly pro-Richard and based on the theory that Edward's sons were murdered by Henry VII after he came to the throne.

MODERN STUDIES:
Richard III by Philip Lindsay; 1933. A collection of encomiums and tributes to Richard's memory by one of the elder generation of 'Ricardians.'

Daughter of Time by Josephine Tey; 1952. A light popular version of Richard, drawing heavily on Markham and Halsted.

Richard III by Paul Murray Kendall; 1955. A scholarly analysis, generally favourable to Richard. Too much qualification and speculative deduction for a clear portrait; and a bit fuzzy around the moral edges.

DOCUMENTARY SOURCES:
Rolls of Parliament Series, Vol. VI.

Patent Rolls of Richard III.

Letters and Papers of Richard III, edited by Dr. Gairdner; 2 vols. 1863.

Harleian Miscellany, 433. BM MSS (a docket book for Richard's reign of more than 400 folio pages, never transcribed and printed save for brief excerpts. The principal source for our knowledge of Richard as king during the epoch July 1483—July 1485. The docket book was probably compiled at the direction of John Russell, Bishop of Lincoln, and Richard's Chancellor).

A-E

JEANNE LA PUCELLE

A. L'ILLUMINÉE

THE savage and desperate scene which concluded Jeanne's life was only saved from overwhelming horror by the presence of the victim, la Pucelle herself . . . her charity, her eloquent plea for love, the poignant episode of the English soldier and the cross redeem, insofar as it may be redeemed, this frightful day.

When one considers the personality of Jeanne la Pucelle, so far from the greed and passion of most of mankind, it seems an emanation from another world, to offer a difference not only in degree but in kind. She herself claimed to be God's Daughter; and this claim has now been endorsed by the Church of Rome. But for those of us who have at best an academic interest in any gallery of official 'Saints,' many of them partly or wholly legendary, Jeanne la Pucelle remains a mystery.

The 'Voices' of Jeanne may be likened to the 'controls' of a modern medium. What are these controls; what functions do they perform? Whether calling themselves Swamis, red Indians, or beings from Mars, the controls are in reality secondary personalities of the medium. Officially, the controls act as intermediaries between the medium's trance state and those who have passed over to the "listening summertime of the dead." The controls bring to their peculiar teleceptor Uncle Rodney and Cousin Elvira and little Cuthbert who vanished one glistening June day at the age of five for rebroadcast to their surviving relatives; that is, the spirits talk to the controls and the controls relay the information via the medium to the 'sitters.'

In practise, the situation is somewhat different. The astonishingly accurate information conveyed by the medium—and seized on as evidence conclusive that Cousin Elvira and little Cuthbert are actually 'there'—is garnered telepathically by the medium from the minds of the sitters and played back via the secondary personality of the control.

Jeanne's controls assumed the guise appropriate to the age; saints and archangels. They relayed communications from the spirits of the departed (Charlemagne, Saint Louis), from Our Lady Mary, and especially from God Himself. God was by far the most frequent Communicator. French was invariably spoken by the controls; manifestations were accompanied by a glowing light and a sense of detached stillness—the trance.

Jeanne's first experience occurred at the age of thirteen. It was the summer of the year 1425, the year following the terrible defeat of Verneuil (August 17, 1424), another Agincourt. D'Alençon was captured and a splendid Franco-Scottish army destroyed. No hope for a liberated France appeared to remain.

The Voices that Jeanne heard did not at first identify themselves; only sometime after the visitation in the garden did the Voices become established as Saint Catherine and Saint Margaret and the Archangel Michael. On the first occasion, it was Michael who had come. In the beginning, the communications were simple and cautionary: Jeanne was to be a good girl, obey her parents, go to Church. Later the Voices became more imperative, the martial note was heard—"Daughter of God, go, go. Go into France and beat the English!"

From general directives, the Voices went on to a specific plan: Jeanne was to obtain help from Robert de Baudricourt, Sieur de Vaucouleurs, to visit the Dauphin and to raise the siege of Orléans. While she was on the road to Chinon, news of Jeanne reached the Bastard of Orléans, captain of the siege; he sent two gentlemen to investigate. On the morrow of her arrival, the seventeen-year-old girl played hostess at Chinon to a fascinated Jean duc d'Alençon, son-in-law of Charles duc d'Orléans. House guest at Saint Florent, the girl in the black and grey tunic was treated as a beloved friend, almost a member of the family, by Jeanne d'Orléans, who called her "Jeannette"— which no one save Hauviette had ever done. "Jeannette's" claims to leadership and her value as a morale-builder were sponsored at the Royal Council by d'Alençon and the Bastard.

It was as if the House of Orléans had been expecting Jeanne. In a sense they had. For years, they had been talking of a redeemer; and suddenly the redeemer had appeared. But: who was responsible for the Coming? If God did not choose Jeanne—by far the most direct though not necessarily the simplest explanation—who did? Her immediate family were not only indifferent to the fate of France (holding in fee simple from the Duchy of Bar), they were bitterly opposed to Jeanne getting involved in the fray. Jeanne herself wanted no guidance from priests or local leaders on the subject of her inspiration.

The possibility of a seer or prophetess in the neighborhood, like old Marie, the 'Gasque of Avignon,' cannot be overlooked. This notion had already occurred to the Bishop of Beauvais, and he made a thorough canvass for 'diabolic' influences. As the Bishop, with numerous investigators and money no object, was unable to turn up anything, it may be reasonably supposed that no such influences existed.

Yet, who communicated?

The House of Orléans created the visionary image of Orléans that pervaded the age. Louis, at the last red turning of the night; Valentine, in her black and silver chamber, *Soupir, Souci, Solitude;* the gallantry and pride of Jean the Bastard . . . All her life Jeanne la Pucelle was passionately devoted to the House of Orléans, to the point where some persons have pressed the interpretation that she was the illicit child of Louis duc d'Orléans and of Ysabeau de Bavière. No shred of evidence exists for such a theory, but Jeanne did feel mystically bound to the fortunes of Orléans. Always her most urgent concern was to collect enough prisoners in battle to ransom Charles duc d'Orléans. Her two great friends were Jean duc d'Alençon and Jean, Bastard of Orléans. Her chief military mission was the liberation of the capital of the Duchy.

It was a powerful association of inspired flame and the high, tragic and visionary destiny of the noble House of Orléans. Jeanne won her splendid victories with Orléans; alone, she accomplished little. She was both protector and protégé, the flame and the sword. At Jargeau, she saved the life of d'Alençon.

The information received from her Voices, astonishingly accurate during the active period of Jeanne's Song of Orléans, became vague and unreliable afterward.

This suggests a partial answer to the mystery. These wonderful powers were derived from an interpenetration of minds. Without that direct contact, Jeanne was a fallow instrument. Everyone noted how at times the 'marvelous girl' of Orléans was just like everyone else, and a good deal more simple than many. She was, without the active use of her power, just what would be expected from her background and lack of education.

Jeanne's power was to a real degree independent of her and she had no absolute control of it. Exactly the same phenomena have been observed in certain illiterate mediums, who do not scruple to cheat when their power fails. Jeanne of course never cheated; she was not in the game for money; she was bewildered and desolate when her illumination was cut off.

Certain emotions conceived in blood and horror, nourished in frenzies of grief, burning and broken in the lamp of life, take on an existence of their own; persist in a kind of ideal terror after the original actors have voided the scene.

In her day, Valentine of Milan, daughter of the great *condottiere,* Gian Galeazzo Visconti, had no mean reputation as a seeress. Louis duc d'Orléans was described by the Burgundian mouthpiece Jean le petit as vastly committed to necromancy, raising the spirits of the dead and enlarging their company from amongst his corporeal foes.

These accusations to justify the ferocity of that November eve in 1407, outside the Porte Barbette, were germinal in the Duke's stable of astrologers and alchemists, his passion for laboratory experiment, his orgiastic pride, which led his ruthless rival to pose as a friend of the people. And it was believed that the outraged spirit of the murdered Louis haunted his assassin, driving him from horror to horror, laying a curse on all the works of Burgundy.

Whether this be so, the image of Orléans laid a profound imprint on many persons, from simple peasants to the youngest survivors of the House. "He is fitter than any of mine to avenge his father," Valentine Visconti said of ten-year-old Jean, Bastard of Orléans.

But avenging his father meant not only the elimination of Jean sans peur—

Tanneguy du Chastel and his hatchet saw to that—but utterly frustrating the ambitions of Burgundy and of the Duchy's English allies. And thus spread abroad was the heroic dream of Orléans, this monarchy of the heart, that was to redeem France, to cast out the invader. The living members of the House, Louis' son Charles, his bastard Jean, Charles' daughter Jeanne, her husband d'Alençon—these bore the blood-image of vengeance and redemption.

And it was these persons who later acted directly on the mind and on the spirit of Jeanne la Pucelle. A great deal more subliminal communication has always taken place than most people have any idea of or would like to admit. Especially in dreams. Dreams are a very obvious inter-penetration of minds. For in sleep we share in all sorts of strange scenes, encounter with familiarity persons we have never seen before, travel backwards and forwards in time, become ourselves briefly and forever different beings.

Dreams are in fact glittering proof that such mental powers as we possess have an enormous potential, far beyond anything imagined or allowed for in society today.

Sexually, the idea has been advanced that the Voices appeared as Jeanne was approaching puberty and that her sexual and psychic life were intimately linked. This is evident as a statement of general principle. What is not acceptable is the notion that the Voices were a kind of substitute for puberty, and that Jeanne la Pucelle never became a woman.

Yet, from the sexual aspect, there is something strange about Jeanne. Any girl who speaks in a deep commanding voice, insists on wearing trousers, and goes in for masculine pastimes is going to get herself talked about. Especially if she is known to be uninterested in men, as such. Jeanne was by no means unattractive; at sixteen, her breasts were admirable, her thighs sturdy and full-fleshed. But she seemed to cool the ardent. They attributed this to her mission, rightly of course, because only a virgin might redeem the land; but the claims of the mission happened to sort very well with Jeanne's own preferences.

Vowed to chastity, she might have gone in for church work, like Saint Colette de Corbie who flourished at the same period, healing the sick and relieving the poor instead of brandishing a sword. But this would not have satisfied the profound urge to dominate in a masculine sense—the most striking way being that of war. So compelling was the instinct for man's attire —the sign of masculine leadership—that Jeanne clung to her tunic even at the risk of the stake.

It is apparent too that in the Christian tradition the repression of normal sexual drives has an effect on the development of psychical powers, as in other religious movements illumination may have a direct relation to orgiastic rites.

Just as medium and sitter combine forces to produce a phantasm, so did the subliminal mind of Jeanne la Pucelle combine with other minds to evoke Saints and Archangels and the whole patriotic-mystique that so annoyed Voltaire. Investigation of this line of approach has been hampered by the insistence on arbitrary concepts of the human personality; whole philosophies have been constructed around the idea of the indivisibility of the human ego.

Why strong psychic powers are bestowed on certain persons is obscure. Jeanne's abilities were extraordinary. She had immense telepathic gifts; her dreams were projected into the dreams of her father, notably in the instance of the dream of Jeanne going off with soldiers. At Chinon, she gave the Dauphin a Sign obtained telepathically from his own mind. Clairvoyance was revealed in the matter of the sword buried behind the altar at St. Catherine of Fierbois. Precognition, in the instance of the breast wound at Orléans and in Jeanne's capture. In addition, she possessed remarkable power of self-healing and incredible muscular and nervous control, as when she jumped from a sixty-foot tower at Beaurevoir and sustained no bodily injury.

We can pass over claims made by zealous partisans that Jeanne could raise the dead, as in the case of the baby at Lagny, or the miraculous power of healing attributed to her blessing. She herself never made any such claims. But leaving out these abilities, the assortment of powers is impressive enough.

In Lorraine's meadows and forests, the mind of Jeanne la Pucelle received the inspiration of Orléans—the impulse of the murdered Duke and of the grief-killed Valentine Visconti projected to their heirs. This inspiration was woven by Jeanne's subconscious into patterns of divine redemption. Naturally, such a manifestation would seem Godlike to the peasant girl; indeed, it is Godlike when compared to the usual level of man's existence. God does not define the sordidness and stupidity of man's life; man does that. Yet: there may exist marvelous depths of perception—*we are such stuff as dreams are made of* . . . we are, indeed.

Recently, a Professor John Butterfield, writing in an English periodical,* has endeavored to explain Jeanne's visions in terms of a tubercular lesion of the brain, as a result of tuberculosis contracted from the cows of Domremy! Professor Butterfield relies chiefly on medical studies of at least seventy-five years' vintage, set down in the hey-day of Pasteurism, when all sorts of symptoms were seized on as evidence of the ravages of bovine tuberculosis and to support the new doctrine of vaccination.

In concentrating on the Voices, the Professor ignores that these manifestations were an intimate part of a broad and wholly remarkable gift of supranormal power, including telepathy, precognition, and extraordinary control over bodily reactions. In other words, abilities very similar to those displayed by great Indian masters, Hindus and Buddhists. Of course, the Professor might prefer to explain their gifts in termes of tumours and lesions, but even in the materialistic West advanced opinion is coming around to an admission that certain persons may possess supranormal powers, without any known physical explanation. Dr. J. B. Rhine, of Duke University, has demonstrated the existence of rudimentary powers of the sort in quite ordinary persons.

The fact is that Jeanne spent little time with cows or sheep and preferred sewing and helping around the house, as she told the tribunal at Poitiers. Up to the moment of her capture, she had not known a serious illness; she was the image of radiant health; she was able to endure the rigors of Fifteenth-Cen-

* *History Today,* September 1958. "Joan of Arc: a Medical View" by John and Isobel-Ann Butterfield.

tury campaigning and the wearing of ninety-pound plate armour for twelve and fifteen hours; slept in the fields in all kinds of weather and could remain in the saddle as long as the toughest campaigner. She recovered in record time from two severe wounds, the breast wound at Orléans, the thigh wound before Paris. This is not the picture of a hopeless tubercular case, doomed to die in early youth. She was knocked flat at Jargeau by a glancing stone on the helmet and if one is going in for lesions of the brain, he might more convincingly begin with this incident. However, there is not the least evidence of any after-effects from the blow.

Professor Butterfield makes much of the fact that Jeanne's memory seems to fail and she gives vague answers at her Trial in Ordinary. He is quite correct about this; and there are two explanations. Most of the vagueness and evasion took place in April and after, when Jeanne had been worn down by the abuse of her captors; she was in a state of inconceivable torment and often simply fell back on the device of either promising to answer in three weeks or of referring the Rouen judges to her previous replies.

Another explanation is that some of these questions were downright dangerous and deliberately designed to lead Jeanne to the flames. No doubt, the Professor is not an expert on Fifteenth Century canon law or could readily put himself in the mental ambiance of a medieval inquisition on heresy. The example cited, that of Jeanne's inability to describe the clothes of her Saints and of Michael the Archangel, far from being an example of mental debility, is an acute case of shrewdness on the part of la Pucelle. To describe in detail such matters as the attire and physical aspect of angels might lead to an accusation of sorcery, of conjuring up devils in the guise of heavenly visitors. Jeanne was smart enough to know this.

It would not be surprising, in view of the treatment that she had, if Jeanne had developed some physical disorder during her captivity. Nor if, as a result of frightful food and sometimes no food at all, she had serious stomach trouble. The fact is: she never had such trouble before she experienced English hospitality. Not cows, but two English lords, Warwick and Bedford, both models of piety, were directly responsible for the breakdown of Jeanne's health.

One further point. The Professor says that one of the two physicians called in to treat Jeanne vilified her. This is inexact. No physician in England's service but tried to help Jeanne, the Professor should be glad to know. The person in question is certainly Jean d'Estivet, canon of Beauvais and of Bayeux, and Promoter or Prosecutor of the Trial, who attended one of the medical examinations and screamed filthy abuse and accused Jeanne of poisoning herself.*

* "*C'est toi, paillarde, qui as mangé de l'alose et d'autres choses qui t'ont fait du mal!*" Or: "It's you, filthy whore, who have eaten the trout and other things that have made you sick!"

B. ORDEAL OF JEANNE LA PUCELLE

No English historian has dared tackle the moral question of Jeanne's treatment by the English. Most of them get off the hook by attacking Charles and his ingratitude. I have not spared Charles; but I fail to see how the King's wretched behaviour exculpates the English. Most writers also gloss over details, relying on that desperate cry for her uncorrupted body when she heard that she was to be put into the fire. Against that cry must be set her confession to Brother Martin Ladvenu, which had to be exact, that she was violated the very night before her death. One must set also the fact that she had a complete nervous breakdown in prison; and I conceive that the criminal abuse, as well as the beatings and the starvation, began sometime in March, when it became apparent that the Bishop and his helpers were having all they could do to hold their own. Brother Martin Ladvenu testified that Jeanne revealed to him that she had been beaten and raped. Brother Ysambart de la Pierre testified that he had seen Jeanne's face covered with tears, and that she was *"defigurée et outragée"* after the horrors of a dungeon night.*

Warwick and Bedford were responsible. The brutal 'strawnecks' who abused Jeanne were merely the creatures of these English lords. What was the purpose? The purpose was to break the girl's spirit, to induce her to sign anything and everything to get away from her tormentors. Warwick appeared one evening on an inspection tour of the prison just as a rape was in progress. This was too much, even for Warwick. He fired the guards; and threatened to hang anyone else who assaulted his prize captive—a threat operative until the English had got what they wanted, a confession of error.

The tactics of Warwick and Bedford were partly successful. The Abjuration was the result of Jeanne's treatment in prison and owed little to the Bishop's arguments. And it was Jeanne's impression—in which she was correct by canon law—that if she accepted the Bishop's terms, she would be put into custody of the Church and ultimately released. Instead, the Bishop sent her directly back to the English Hell, with a sentence of perpetual confinement. She broke down; and accused the Bishop of deceiving her. No doubt he did; but what she seems not to have understood was that the English never, under any circumstances, intended to let her go. They put up with the delays and expense of the Trial in order to get a confession out of her, something on which they might base a charge of witchcraft, to destroy her influence and impair the validity of Charles' kingship. But in any case, the English always intended to kill her. She had hurt them too much.

* Proces de Rehabilitation, Edited by Regine Pernoud. The reference is evidently to the period after the Abjuration. Warwick's intervention, related by Guillaume Manchon, Recorder of the Trial in Ordinary, occurred some time before. It can hardly have been a unique occasion for such treatment. Jeanne also complained to the Bishop and to Loiseleur of "attempted" rapes. As late as the end of February, la Pucelle was still a virgin. Guillaume de la Chambre, a physician called in during Jeanne's first illness, made a superficial examination of her sexual organs and found her intact—"très fermée."

The idea—as presented in modern drama—that Warwick or other English lords ever had the slightest compassion or sympathy for Jeanne is without foundation. They hated and feared her; and Humphrey Lord Stafford actually tried to murder Jeanne with a dagger, when she was first brought to Rouen. It may be noticed, for what it is worth, that even the hatchetman of pirate Burgundy, Jean de Luxembourg, behaved toward Jeanne in a humane and civilized way by comparison with these English lords.

C. "JEANNE DE VALOIS"

CERTAIN French writers have propagated the idea that Jeanne la Pucelle was of royal blood, adultery's daughter, the child of Louis duc d'Orléans and Ysabeau de Bavière. When the flashing gallant visited his paramour that mortal Wednesday in November of 1407, Isabeau had been brought to bed with her twelfth and last *accouchement*. The Court would give out that the enfant was a boy, stillborn—baptised Phillipe and coffined in an obscure grave. But in fact the child born shortly before the debonair lover rode out to that rendezvous with red-chaperoned Raoul d'Anquetonville had been a girl—called Jeanne. And this child of adultery and blood would be hidden away, like Oedipus, amongst the shepherds of Lorraine; watched over by her simple guardians until the moment when her royalty would be revealed and she herself chosen by Heaven to redeem the *vert sombre*.

The legend is tempting; indeed, it would make a novel. But, as for history, it rests on no proof of any kind. The most recent proponent, M. Jean Grimod,* builds his case on Jeanne's ready assumption of high estate and the bond between la Pucelle and the House of Orléans. He cites Jeanne's wearing of the colours of Orléans; her resolve to liberate Charles duc d'Orléans; her greeting to d'Alençon at Chinon, "The more of the royal blood are together, the better it will be."—as if she meant to include herself with d'Alençon and Charles; her passion for fine clothes and blooded stallions; Comte Jean d'Armagnac heading his letter on the Popes, 'My dear lady'; Jeanne calling herself 'la Pucelle d'Orléans.' All this indicates that Jeanne was a proud intensely dedicated girl, well aware of her own unique value, and with a fervent attachment to the House of Orléans—generally recognized as the fount of opposition to the machinations of English and Burgundians. But there is no evidence for a blood-tie between Jeanne and Orléans.

Presumably, Jeanne was born on Epiphany (January 6th), 1412, almost five years after the murder of Louis duc d'Orléans. Hauviette, at the Trial of Rehabilitation, put Jeanne's birth in 1408 or 1407. But Jeanne's own testimony at Rouen gave her age as nineteen and, as we know, the Bishop of Beauvais checked every statement on the spot in Domremy. It is more likely that Hauviette was in error than Jeanne.

However, M. Grimod suggests that Jeanne deliberately gave her age incorrectly; and that she and the Bishop were in cahoots to conceal her true

* *Jeanne d'Arc a-t-elle été brulée?* Amiot-Dumont, Paris, 1956.

lineage. All this mysterious by-play, these celestial Fifth Amendments, "I have not leave to answer" and "That is not in your Trial," were part of a secret understanding to save Jeanne from the stake. For M. Grimod has seized on the legend of royalty to support his main thesis: that Jeanne escaped the flames.

The Bishop worked hand-in-glove with Bedford and Warwick to rescue Jeanne from the University of Paris, bent on hounding the girl to her doom. Bedford was influenced by his gentle Duchess Anne; Warwick, 'the King-maker,' was ambitious to play a political role between French and English; the ignorant masses were deceived by the burning of a masked woman. The real Jeanne escaped by means of a secret passage from her tower prison leading to a vault with a trap door opening into Bedford's own mansion in Rouen.*

Jeanne lay low for five years; she turned up in Lorraine, in 1436, after the Treaty of Arras between France and Burgundy, a secret codicil of which provided for her release. At first, the stranger called herself 'Claude' and spoke obscurely of recent wrongs and troubles. Very soon, people began saying this was Jeanne la Pucelle, risen phoenix-like, Jeanne come home again! 'Claude' did not deny it; there were tearful reunions.

The good news spread. The city of Orléans heard of the return of its de-liverer. So, presumably, did d'Alençon and the Bastard, but they took no part in this comedy. Jeanne's brothers, Pierre and Jean, showed no reticence. They demanded—and got—extensive sums from the City for services in connection with 'la Pucelle.' Orléans records for the period reveal that in August 1436, 'Jehan du Lys' received a cash present of twelve livres tournois; he claimed that the King had ordered he be compensated for an outlay of 100 francs (having been five days on the road with letters from Jeanne), of which he had received but twenty and had already spent fourteen. At the same time, the City issued warrants to purveyors of wine and poultry, reimbursing them for supplying the table of Jehan du Lys. The City Herald, Coeur de lys, also came in for his share of compensation, as he had acted as courier between Orléans and Luxembourg, Jeanne's present abode. It is recorded that Coeur de lys had "a great thirst"—*ung grant soif*—when he refreshed himself at the City's expense.**

Despite the correspondence with 'Jeanne la Pucelle,' the City of Orléans continued to celebrate every eighth of May a commemorative mass for the soul of Jeanne la Pucelle. In June of 1436, there took place a marriage be-tween 'Jeanne' and Robert III des Armoises, of Arlon in Luxembourg.

For three years nothing further was heard of Pucelles. England's military comeback was well advanced; and Talbot staged a whirlwind campaign in

---

* An escape worthy of Edmond Dantes, the hero of Alexander Dumas' novel *The Count of Monte Cristo*, who was walled up in the Chateau d'If, in the harbour of Marseilles.
** Comptes de forteresse de la ville d'Orléans pour l'année 1436; numero 654, folio 34 *et sequitur*. The Heralds of the Duchy were 'Ortie' and 'Valois'; that of the City, 'Coeur de lys' and 'Orléans.'

Normandy in the winter of 1437, with three major victories that opened the road to Paris. A peace conference at Calais in July of 1439 failed; and both sides prepared for a renewal of the struggle. Then in 1439 another Pucelle appeared, sponsored by Gilles de Rais, besieging Le Mans in Normandy. The Dark Prince had embarked on his satanic course and his Pucelle was, appropriately, lit by an evil glow. She was often drunk, lay with soldiers, the foulest oaths were as a familiar greeting on her lips. Her behaviour was too much for Charles; he summoned the Pucelle of Le Mans, exposed and jailed her.*

To forestall other Pucelles of the sort and to invigorate the fight against the English, it was essential to find a more presentable candidate. Jeanne des Armoises was available. She could be counted on not to disgrace the legend. To be sure, the resemblance was superficial. Jeanne des Armoises was a pleasant girl, of attractive manners, with no more *mystique* than any other girl of good county stock. But she would do well enough for a fête or a masque, perhaps not notably different from that put on today in Orléans on May eighth, when a local girl is rigged out in armour and rides a horse through the streets. The Lord of Darkness himself had composed and staged a glittering 'mystère' on the subject of la Pucelle; but as the offering of Gilles de Rais was one of the most colossal productions in history, it is probable that in August 1439 something more modest was attempted.

'Jeanne la Pucelle' was once more amongst her Orléanais. Enthusiasm was tremendous—for a few days. Obviously, Isabelle Romée, Pierre and Jehan du Lys, the Lord Mayor and Council, Jacques Boucher, Jeanne's host ten years before, Jacques de Chabannes, old-comrade-in-arms, the last man off the boulevard at Compiègne, now persuaded to lend his valour to this comedy —they *knew*.**

For the *peuple,* the line between reality and play-acting was never very clear. At Mystery plays, the fiends evoked a literal belief; Hell gaped and smoked, flames leaped forth; the infernal machine that cranked out doom was terrifyingly real. After all, every day of their lives this *peuple* was taught that a plate of wafers and a cup of wine was changed into the flesh and blood of Christ, by the consecration of the Host.

It cannot have been so difficult to accept a resurrected Pucelle in the person of Jeanne des Armoises. City records *** indicate more than a month of wining and dining, from the end of July to the beginning of September; with doubtless a beneficial effect on future campaigns against 'the great Achilles of the field' and his tailed henchmen. Nevertheless, something seems to have gone amiss at the end, perhaps an unseemly scuffle among the wine-heated, somebody suddenly shouting in the midst of the dignitaries and the speeches, "But the Emperor has nothing on!" Jeanne des Armoises slipped quietly out of

* M. Grimod rightly distinguishes between the Pucelle of Le Mans and Jeanne des Armoises; but in my own view, they were both imposters.
** "to the said Jacques Leprestre for XII pintes and choppine of wine carried to the said Jehan Hatte at the price of X deniers parisis the pint given and presented to Messire Jacques de Chabannes this 7th day (of August) *au matin*. For this, X sols, five deniers parisis." *Comptes de forteresse;* numero 655, folio 54.
*** *opus cit.* folios 53, 56, 74.

town in early September, having collected 210 francs plus 'expenses'; and nothing more was ever heard of her. The brothers du Lys received handsome honorariums and the freedom of the city. With their mother, Isabelle, they were now in the substantial bourgeois bracket.

There were no more re-appearances in Orléans, but Pucelles popped up in other places. There was the Pucelle of Cologne who gained her first victory over her old mother whom she knocked flat with a blow of her fist in a family *discussion;* she was last seen leading a 'crusade' across the Rhine into the long-suffering land of Germany. There was the Pucelle of Saumur, who spent considerable time in jail in that city as a result of a family quarrel. There was the Pucelle of France, a sea champion, who with the aid of a Catholic squadron routed the Protestants of La Rochelle. (This Pucelle may be entirely mythical, as the reference to her is plainly from the religious wars of the 16th Century.)

But certainly, M. Grimod is right to select Jeanne des Armoises. The entries taken from the account books of Orléans are interesting. I have personally checked every entry quoted and as far as I can see, M. Grimod has not misrepresented the evidence. Considered apart, the record of Orléans seems to support M. Grimod. Nor is it a question of cooking the accounts; the parchment folios, in a splendid state of preservation, are the original minute books of the Council and no one has tampered with the entries.

Writing in 1884, an Editor of the Accounts of Orléans said in part: "It appears that this lady of Armoises, *sans Bonté,* false Pucelle, fearing to be exposed, departed furtively from Orléans, after having been entertained by the Orléanais, and given a present in money of 210 francs, which would be worth today 2000 francs.*

"It appears also that this lady of Armoises, the better to hide her deceit and more easily to mislead the good inhabitants of Orléans, had led with her in this city from the country of Lorraine Isabeau, mother of the true Pucelle, and her two brothers Jean and Pierre du Lys, which proves our opinion. It is the presence of these three persons in Orléans at this time, the historical notices that we have found in the archives of the city, and in a manuscript of the public library which carry textually: 'Year 1439. Isabeau, mother of Jehanne d'Arc, Jehan du Lys and Pierre du Lys, her brothers, came to live in Orléans and would live there through the generosity of the duc d'Orléans and the inhabitants of that city. . . .' " **

The rest of M. Grimod's case is legend or supposition. Evidence as to the return of 'Claude' and her metamorphosis into Jeanne la Pucelle comes from the *Chronique de Lorraine,* a curious collection of local fables put together in the 16th Century and quite unreliable. With regard to proceedings at Rouen, quotations from the *Journal of the Bourgeois of Paris,* by a writer

* Ten times only seems like a most conservative calculation. The medieval franc was worth slightly less than the pound, 15 or 16 shillings. To obtain an equivalent value for today, the reader would require to multiply the pound by at least 30, giving 6000 pounds. A rather handsome gift for a month of personal appearances!
** *Recherches historique sur les comptes d'Orléans.* A manuscript by Lottin, père; Bibliothèque Municipale, Orléans numero 587–588.

who never saw Jeanne and was repeating Parisien gossip are of little weight beside the documentation of the two Trials.

M. Grimod's theory that the English saved Jeanne is preposterous. He knows nothing of English sources; for Jeanne, he quotes Polydore Vergil, Caxton, and even Shakespeare! He talks of 'Falstaff' instead of Sir John Fastolf; and mixes up Richard Beauchamp, 5th Earl of Warwick, with his great son-in-law, Richard Neville, 7th Earl and 'Kingmaker.' He calls Nicholas Loiseleur 'Pierre'; and misquotes completely the substance of Pierre Cusquel's testimony concerning Rouen.* More serious is the rejection of the massive documentation of both the Rouen and Paris Trials. The fact that there were numerous eye-witness accounts of Jeanne's death, and especially three long and detailed descriptions by Jean Massieu, Martin Ladvenu, and Ysambart de la Pierre, who were with Jeanne to the end, is passed over. M. Grimod has not specifically denied these accounts; he has simply ignored them. Denial would mean that these Church witnesses committed perjury in a most solemn affair—the rehabilitation of Jeanne la Pucelle.

From 1431 to 1455, a period of twenty-four years, not a single person who had been at Rouen came forward to assert of his own knowledge that Jeanne had not perished in the flames.**

When Jean Brehal, Inquisitor General of France, reopened the case in April 1452, at the behest of King Charles the Very Victorious, he did so with positive knowledge that Jeanne la Pucelle had been burned at the stake as a heretic and that she was not or had not been living in Luxembourg, a well-to-do county matron, the mother of two sons. Such a conclusion makes idiocy of the whole proceeding. For one of the major purposes of this Trial of 1455 was to wipe out the awful stain on Jeanne's memory—and on the kingship of Charles—as a result of the execution for heresy in 1431. If the Bishop of Beauvais and the English had in fact refused to put Jeanne into the fire, it would scarcely have been necessary to hold a Trial of Rehabilitation at all.

The fête at Orléans served a national end and helped the family of Jeanne to a significant personal gain. But it is unthinkable that if Jeanne la Pucelle had returned from the dead, no mention of this would have been made at the Trial of 1455.

She did not return.

* By lifting a sentence out of context, he makes Pierre Cusquel cast doubt on Jeanne's execution. But a perusal of a fair sample of testimony indicates beyond question that Cusquel knew Jeanne had been burned. In fact, Cusquel appears to be the authority for the famous cry, "We are lost, for it is a good and holy person we have burned!"—said to have been uttered by Jean Tressard, Secretary to the King of England.

** Two minor points. Jeanne, at her execution, was not masked, but wore a paper mitre cap usual for heretics about to be burned. This cap certainly did not cover the face. The absence of a formal condemnation by the secular arm may seem shocking to the Latin mind, but it was not uncommon in the period. The Bishop had pronounced his sentence of expulsion, which in the brutal lexicon of the age meant death by fire; and the English, as witnesses relate, were not in a waiting mood.

D. SHAKESPEARE AND JEANNE LA PUCELLE

As M. Jean Grimod quotes wholly out of text a few lines from Shakespeare's *King Henry the Sixth,* Part I, as evidence for Jeanne's royalty, it might be interesting to know what that 'tiger's heart wrapped in a player's hide,' and 'the only Shake-scene in the country' really thought of Jeanne la Pucelle. For there can be little doubt that what Shakespeare thought of Jeanne is much closer to English opinion of the time than anything set down by Messrs. Jean Anouilh, Maxwell Anderson, and Bernard Shaw.

After an opening scene in which Jeanne appears favourably as the Virgin Redeemer, guns of nationalism are unmuzzled and the Redeemer begins to resemble more and more the unfortunate Pucelle of Le Mans . . . (Jeanne) "I prithee, give me leave to curse awhile." Toward the end, she is summoning Fiends, offering her blood on which she is "wont to feed you"; then vowing to "lop off a member" of her body for delectation of her familiars; then promising her whole body; and finally her soul—to obtain the victory.

At the last, captured, in chains, Jeanne is led before Warwick and Richard Duke of York. To fend off death, she begins to make wild revelations . . . (Jeanne) "Not me begotten of a shepherd swain, but issu'd from the progeny of kings . . ." Warwick is not convinced. "Spare no faggots, let there be enow: place barrels of pitch upon the fatal stake."

Jeanne shrieks that she is with child; she names various possibilities, Charles, d'Alençon, Regnier—anyone that might strike a merciful chord. All useless. She is taken away and Richard of York pronounces her epitaph: "Break thou in pieces and consume to ashes, thou foul accursed minister of hell!" *

This 'atrocious rot' is not only unworthy of Shakespeare, it is unworthy of anyone. Authorship is in dispute. Professor Tucker Brooke feels that George Peele, a notorious jingoist, originally wrote the play, with Shakespeare revising. Internal evidence indicates Shakespeare's hand in certain scenes; and he did allow the whole play to be published and performed over his name. Shakespeare, in 1592, was aiming for the pit; and the fierce nationalism of this *Henry the Sixth* was best calculated to titillate the Englishman of the Golden Age. Nationalistic hatred and the wildest lies—what brought Mary of Scotland to the block three years before—were the common change of men.

Yet: what a pity! that the author and the perfect subject should be forever divided by the insane picket of nationalism. For beyond any other on earth, Jeanne belonged to Shakespeare. Her marvelous eloquence, her poetry and tears, her wonder—this was Shakespeare.

---

* *Henry the Sixth,* Part One, Act V; Scene 4. The Yale Shakespeare: edited by Tucker Brooke. Compare Queen Margaret's denunciation of Richard of Gloucester. "Have not to do with him, beware of him; sin, death, and Hell have set their marks on him, and all their ministers attend on him." *Richard the Third,* Act I; Scene 3.

E. DRAMATIC PORTRAYAL OF JEANNE

THE present writer has seen the following dramatic portrayals of Jeanne: Falconetti in the Carl Dreyer film *The Passion of Jeanne d'Arc;* Ingrid Bergman in the Hollywood film *Jeanne d'Arc;* Katherine Cornell and Siobhan McKenna in Bernard Shaw's play *Saint Joan;* Luise Rainer in Maxwell Anderson's play *Joan of Lorraine;* Dorothy Tutin, Suzanne Flon, and Julie Harris in Jean Anouilh's play *The Lark.*

The role of Jeanne is a tremendous challenge; and this is a very imposing array of actresses over the past thirty years. But of all these interpreters, none comes close to Falconetti—fine and sensitive as the others are. Falconetti had the advantage of a superlative director, Carl Dreyer; but more than that, Falconetti looked like Jeanne, she had the rare quality of tragic illumination associated with la Pucelle. It has been said that this Italian actress, with the ability to convey the whole of Jeanne in a nuance of facial expression, was so moved by her own portrayal that she never did anything of note afterward. Whether this is true, I do not know; but I can understand that it might well be true. The name of Falconetti is linked with Jeanne—and with no other role. Without, seemingly, any make-up at all, with cropped hair, without even the assistance of her voice (for this was a silent film, made in 1928), Falconetti has made Jeanne live. If, for example, one thinks of the pity and wonder of Jeanne, then Falconetti has done this better than anyone.

Aspects of the Dreyer film are not above reproach. Jeanne is too passive, she is weeping almost constantly, she launches few of the verbal shafts recorded in the Trial documents. This is characteristic of Dreyer, all black and white, and his chief interpreters overwhelmed by the evil of the world. Yet the marvel of Jeanne comes through.

One believes in Falconetti, this is the significant difference; the other portrayals, especially that of Ingrid Bergman—a very splendid actress—are most likeable and appealing; but one could not for a moment imagine any of them as inspired by God. And this, after all, is essentially what we demand from this role. Superficially, it looks not too difficult, there is so much documentation; in practise, it is probably the most crucial challenge any actress may ever face. I pass over the effort of the Iowa school girl, Jean Seberg.

In the future—a word to the wise—one might say to any young actress: if you really perform this role as it should be performed, you may well unfit yourself for any other serious interpretation. If you do not, is it worth the doing?

F. THE STRICKEN LUTE

THE Universal Spider was the evil genius of Margaret's last years. It was he who persuaded the Angevine princess into the incongruous alliance with Warwick; who arranged the marriage between Anne Neville and Edward of Lancaster; who financed Margaret's return to England in 1471. Louis' project may appear more fanciful than it was, because it failed so catastrophically with death and ruin to all concerned, yet the venture was inherently fated and contained the basic political contradictions of its own doom. The Lancastrian Restoration of 1470–71 seemed to fail due to weather hazards, the mist at Barnet, the Channel storm that delayed Margaret; but this was only part of the tale—and the lesser part.

Why did Warwick lose control of London (where he was much more popular than Edward of York); and why was he forced into a battle that he might with profit have avoided until all his forces had rallied? Solely as a result of Clarence's treachery at Banbury. But Clarence had betrayed his great father-in-law because the weak and jealous Duke felt Warwick had already betrayed *him*.

And on the face of it, Clarence would appear to have been right.

Undoubtedly, Warwick at first intended to supplant Edward with George of Clarence; thus he, through his daughter Isabel, would sire a line of kings. But Louis, at the last moment, rushed in with another proposition: an alliance between Margaret and Warwick, the fatal union of Red Rose and White, with the Succession secured to Margaret's son, Edward of Lancaster. Warwick would still sire a line of kings through his younger daughter Anne, while the noble Duke of Clarence would be fobbed off with a lieutenantcy amid the bogs of Ireland!

Louis was much too astute a politician not to perceive that one proposition cancelled out the other; that supplanting George by his young brother-in-law was an open invitation to treachery and the destruction of the alliance. If Louis had only let them alone, Warwick and Clarence together would have had an excellent chance against the dethroned Edward.

But that would have left Margaret and her son in Lorraine, with reversionary rights to Anjou, Maine, Lorraine, Bar, and Provence—territories upon which the Universal Spider maintained a cold and lavish eye. If mother and son could only be got out and involved again in English woes, there was always the chance the heir of Anjou might be killed; or, if he survived, he would probably be so busy in England, he would have little time for France.

It is inescapable that when Louis promoted this alliance between Margaret and Warwick, he was thinking primarily not of England, but of France.*

The Universal Spider did little fighting himself; it was his policy to embroil friend and foe, out of which something might be got for France. He has been much praised by French historians for his triumphs of statecraft rather than blood; but they might consider that the Spider was indirectly the cause

---

* It may be objected to this theory of Louis' real motives that at the time other heirs of Anjou were not lacking, John of Calabria and his son Nicholas in the direct male line, the collateral branch of Charles of Maine, and the children of Yolande and Ferry de Vaudemont, the heirs of Lorraine and Bar. But two things may be said. The claims of the House of Anjou were vast enough to give something to each surviving heir. The claim of Edward of Lancaster was in some sense superior to that of anyone else; for Edward represented not only his mother's right, but the old claim of the Plantagenets to Anjou, Maine, and Guyenne.

of as much horror, grief, and blood as if he had spent his whole life campaigning.

In the Lancastrian Restoration, the Spider's real aims, far from being
defeated, were all too successful. The heir of Anjou was slain on the field;
Warwick himself went down at Barnet; and the politically weakest con-
testant—and from Louis' point of view, the most malleable—Edward of
York, was left in possession of the English throne.

Margaret of Anjou had bitter years to lament that she had listened to
her wily cousin of France. From the first instant of captivity at Little Malvern
Priory, she had shrieked against York (Hastings: "My hair doth stand on
end to hear her curses"); pelted with mud, the frenzied woman had been
led in Edward's triumphal chariot train and incarcerated in the Tower the
very Ascension Eve of Henry's murder. Abandoned to stone and night,
Margaret of Anjou called on her legendary ancestress Melusine; invoked
the Devil's daughter to strike down the House of York.

René who, within a few weeks of these tragic events of 1471, would lose
his only surviving son John of Calabria, his son-in-law Ferry of Vaudemont,
and a natural (and very beloved) daughter Blanche of Anjou, wrote to
the grief-maddened Margaret: "My child, may God help thee with his counsels! for rarely is the aid of man offered in such reverse of fortune. When
you can spare a thought from your own sufferings, think of mine; they
are terrible, my daughter, yet would I console thee."

René had always possessed a more resilient nature than Margaret; his
masques and 'disguisings' continued up to the end. Death itself inspired the
King's brush and he painted *Le Roi Mort,* a skeleton wearing a golden
crown and bearing in each bony claw the sceptre and the orb; a mortuary
tableau for Rene's gorgeous tomb in the Cathedral at Angers, then under
construction by the Flemish artist Coppin Delft. There had always been
something theatrical about René's misfortune; like all artists, he mined his
sufferings for inspiration. His agony was that of Coeur d'Amour, immediately
translated into perfume and poetry, whole islands of groaning knights.

But the poor old gallant, now nearing seventy, was really sick; and it
was no one's fault save his own if people found it hard to take his illness
seriously. He had prostate trouble, was on a strict regime, had been virtually
impotent for years. Carried about in a litter or set down in his Provençal
garden of jasmin and lilac, René's chief delight was the company of Marguerite of Lorraine, daughter of Yolande and Ferry de Vaudemont.

Perhaps this young Marguerite recalled to René that radiant girl sent
to England long desolate years ago. But her, or what was said to be her,
the old King seldom saw. She depressed him too much. For of what she
had been, he found hardly a trace.

Oh it was bitter—in his old age and ruin.

Her eyes, he could not forget her eyes. Louis of France had ransomed
her for 50,000 crowns in 1475, at the Treaty of Brétigny; and she had come
home. During the intervening years, Margaret had been Edward's prisoner,
shunted from the Tower to Windsor Castle and finally to the manor of
Wallingford in Oxfordshire. The plight of her former Lady of the Rose had

touched even the frigid heart of Elizabeth Woodeville and she had persuaded her lord to release Margaret to the custody of her oldest and dearest friend, Alice Chaucer, dowager Duchess of Suffolk, at Wallingford, and to furnish eight marks weekly for the Queen's support—no mean feat on Elizabeth's part, all things considered.

"I, Margaret, formerly married in the realm of England . . ." began the articles of renunciation extorted by Edward, before giving Margaret her freedom. Surrendering all claims in England, she had become just a simple immigrant from over the Manche; and a deportee from the realm of the White Rose. But the High and Mighty Princess Margaret, oh she had gone, vanished with that golden dancing child, the flame and shadow.

"Why Margaret," the Duchess of Bourbon had once said to her, "I have never heard nor read of a noblewoman so blameless, who has suffered so. A princess who, without having committed notorious crimes, has been reduced so low as not to possess a foot of land or a house, nor yet money of silver or copper, unless borrowed, to purchase the common necessities of life." *

Even before Tewkesbury, she had attained a kind of uniqueness in disaster which fascinated her contemporaries. But then her troubles, however they appeared to the Duchess, had been bearable. What difference did it make what kind of dress she had as long as she was arrayed in the gold and scarlet of life?

Now she was dead; but they had not come to bury her. "Richard, where art thou, thou art not here? murder is thy alms-deed; petitioners for blood thou ne'er putt'st back." ** So indeed might she have cried at Tewkesbury, staggering from one brother to another, pleading for the poignard. But they were more cruel; they let her live.

Her father gave Margaret into the charge of an elderly castellan, Francis Vignolles; and she spent her last years at the castle of Damprierre, near Saumur, companioned only by the faithful Katherine Vaus. She subsisted on an annual allowance of 6000 livres from the King of France; paid grudgingly and seldom on time. One would have thought that as there was no danger of the ruined woman contracting alliances or of leaving descendants other than Grief and Tragedy, Louis might have let her in peace with what remained of her once-glorious patrimony. But the Universal Spider preferred a giltedged proposition. For her ransom of 50,000 crowns and her modest allowance, Margaret was forced to sign away her reversionary rights in Anjou, Maine, Lorraine, Bar, and Provence.

Anjou, the Spider had already seized, alleging as an excuse King René's threat to will his domain to Charles the Turbulent. It was openly bruited that a little time previously the Spider had helped from earthly woe the last direct heir of Anjou in the male line. And even the easy-going Edward the Fourth could not stomach, it seems, the emissaries of his eight-legged patron . . . "Item, the King came to this town (London) on Wednesday; as for the French ambassade that is here, they came not in the King's presence by

* Chastellain, Georges, *Oeuvres.*
** *King Henry the Sixth,* Part Three, Act V, Scene VI.

likelihood, for men say that the chief of them is he that poisoned the Duke of Berry and the Duke of Calabria." *

Bar and Lorraine were out of the Spider's grasp; for an active (and un-poisoned) male heir survived in René the Second, son of Yolande and Ferry de Vaudemont; an heir moreover who had proved his title with the sword, for René's legions, fighting under the historic barred Cross of Lorraine, had destroyed the House of Burgundy at Nancy, January 1477. In a last effort to stake a claim, Louis egged Margaret into a futile quarrel with her sister Yolande over the reversionary right to Lorraine. But the only result was to cut off Margaret from this remaining source of solace, her Lorraine relatives.

Provence, the Spider entrapped as soon as King René died, at Aix, in July 1480. Master of five languages, artist, poet, chevalier of the Ideal, titular ruler of glorious realms, the Good King René had at his death scarcely a square foot of land that he might call his own.** Yet, René possessed the hearts of his people, what Richard the Third, then trembling on greatness, would say he valued above any treasure. "Never prince," wrote Bourdigne of the dead King, "so much loved his subjects as he loved his; and was better loved and regarded than he was by them."

René bequeathed Margaret one thousand gold crowns and an annuity of 2000 livres, but, as the accounts of Anjou had been sequestered by the Spider, there was difficulty about paying any of the Good King's bequests. Margaret was destitute; and she wrote to the former treasurer of René, now serving Louis . . . *"Je me vous recommande tant que je puis. Le Roy a fait savoir à sa ville d'Angiers que le Roy de Sicille, Monseigneur mon père, etoit alle à Dieu. Je lui en escritz affin qu'il lui plaise prendre mon pauvre fait en ce qui me peut et doit appartenir, en ses mains pour en faire son bon vouloir et plaisir, et toujours m'avoir en sa bonne grace et amour, en laquelle je vous prie que me veuillez toujours entretenir. Et à Dieu, Monsieur du Boucage, qui vous donne ce que vous désirez. Escript en Reculée-les-Angers, le premier jour d'aoust."* ***

To this piteous appeal, there seems to have been no reply. Such a letter recalls by contrast letters written in days of pride and wrath, and one especially

---

* *Paston Letters,* CCCXLVIII. The Duke of Berry was Charles de Valois, younger brother of Louis, whom the Spider had devoured in this manner, as he had earlier devoured his father Charles the Victorious. The Duke of Calabria was Nicholas, son of John, a young man of twenty-five, in perfect health, who had died suddenly in 1473. It was said that a marriage project between Nicholas and Marie de Bourgogne galvanized Louis into action.

** RENÉ was fluent in French, Italian, Catalan, Provençal, Latin.

*** "I recommend me to you as much as I can. The King has made known to his city of Angers that the King of Sicily, the lord my father, had gone to God. I am writing to him that it please him to take in hand my poor affair in that which can and must belong to me, to do his good will and pleasure, and always to have me in his good grace and love, for which I do beseech you to ever wish me well. And (commend me) to God, Monsieur de Boucage, who gives you what you desire. Written at Reculée-les-Angers, the first day of August."

to her cousin of France, whose regal tone at a time of ruin impressed even him and that he read to his Council with the comment, "See how proudly she writes!"

Margaret lived on, secluded, cries ringing and echoing in the broken donjon of the past. She thought of her dead—there was little else to think about—and implored the English to give back the body of Edward her son. But no one, any more, attended to her pleadings; and all she might keep of Edward was that green haunted meadow where the willows grew. . . .

Her blood poisoned by anguish, Margaret fell victim to a psychosomatic skin ailment, a dry scaly withering of her once-golden beauty. Overnight, she became hideous. Only her eyes remained, ravaged and terrible, glowing with a sunken fire.

Did she suspect, then, what wonder and doom she had made, how her life would be exalted to a legend? It may be. . . . She is said to have deposed a secret testament, setting forth in words of flame her unconquerable claims on destiny. But of this document, if indeed it exist, no public view has ever been had.*

Margaret did not know the satisfaction of the fulfillment of her curse. When, on a day of brass, August 25, 1482, the desolate Queen of the Rose died, six princes of York flourished; within three years five were dead, three by violence, and a sixth was never to emerge from his Tower cell.

She was only fifty-two; but she had lived ages of splendour and grief, ages of death. She had looked horror in the face . . . . Now might the Duchess of Bourbon say there had been no story like hers.

Margaret's body was said to have been interred in the tomb of René and Isabella, in the Cathedral of St. Maurice at Angers, but nothing marks the resting-place. The King of France, who was Margaret's heir and executor, considered a tomb or even a small commemorative plaque for his cousin as mere extravagance. He was more concerned with the fate of his dogs. He had, it seems, in a convulsion of generosity, given the poor woman a few dogs to help her pass the time. Directly he heard of her death, he wrote to Madame de Montsereau: "I am sending to you my equerry, Jean de Chasteaudreux, to bring me all the dogs you have had from the late Queen of England. You know she has made me her heir, and that this is all I shall get; also, it is what I love best. I pray you not to keep any back, for you would

---

* As described to the writer by Yvonne d'Anjou, younger daughter of René comte d'Anjou, who claimed to have seen the testament. Requests to view this evidence have been unavailing. I am indebted to M. René de Segrais for an analysis of d'Anjou lines, subsequent to the 15th Century. The d'Anjou of Bois-Nantier, of Norman chivalric origin, were Seigneurs de Briqueville, en Normandie; becoming extinct about 1821. Another family, the de Falcoz, was invested with the baronnie d'Anjou, in Dauphiné, by royal patent in 1681. Alexandre de Falcoz then became the first comte d'Anjou, a title transmitted through male and female to the present. The family de Falcoz had nothing to do with the Valois d'Anjou; and indeed their title stems from Dauphiné. Their arms are a silver falcon on azure. M. de Segrais found no other d'Anjou lines.

displease me severely; but if you know of anyone who has any of them, tell Chasteaudreux." *

this is all I shall get . . . Louis was too modest. He and the Crown did much better than a few dogs out of Margaret's ruin. Anjou, Maine, Provence were annexed outright; claims were established to Bar and Lorraine.

Margaret of Anjou, like those other flamelit shadows on the cave of time, Jeanne la Pucelle and Richard Plantagenet, vanishes without the least tablet; but, like them, the princess of Anjou has built of her memory a more enduring wonder than the mightiest marble.

G. "THE WICKED UNCLE"

RICHARD is like a glass that gives back the image of the beholder. The Markhamists (after Sir Clement Markham, author of *Richard the Third*) saw in Richard the reflection of sentimental Nineteenth Century virtues. A jolly professional uncle, Richard presided over a Dickensian household of prattlers, including three nephews who might be presumed to have anticipated him on the throne had not their titles been clouded. The villain of the piece was bald conniving Ralph Nickleby Tudor, who not only stole Richard's royal heritage but deprived the great and good King of his reputation as well.

Josephine Tey was the publicity girl of this Markhamist school and did more to popularize Richard in her book *Daughter of Time* than any other single writer. Stubbornly, however, the evidence to support the intriguing design of a secret murder of the Princes by Henry Tudor in 1486 refused to come to light. The two meagre bits quoted from the docket book of Richard's reign, Harleian Ms. 433, by Markham are ambiguous and may be held to refer to other royal children in the King's household, his own bastard, John of Gloucester, for instance. But the coup de grâce to Markham's theory was delivered by the appearance in 1936 of Armstrong's edition of Dominic Mancini. In his contemporary account of Richard's Protectorate, Mancini explicitly set forth that the Princes of York were killed shortly after Richard's accession.

There was also the massive fact that the Princes never appeared publicly after September 1483; but all good Markhamists asserted that there had been in fact numerous appearances—if one only interpreted the record correctly.

Another school, an off-shoot of the Markhamists, might be termed the Warbecks, after Perkin Warbeck. The Princes are said to have escaped by water from the Tower; to have shipped to Burgundy and Duchess Margaret. Edward either fell—or was pushed—overboard; but Richard Duke of York survived to become the Pretender Perkin Warbeck. The Warbecks also believe that Sir James Tyrell may have aided Bishop John Morton in rigging the escape, perhaps even hiding the boys for a time in his mansion on the Thames.

* *Lettres de Louis XI;* edited by Vaesen and Charavay. Letter of August 12, 1482. This does not conform to the death date, given in the DNB, and elsewhere, for Margaret.

Morton's purpose, it seems, was to frighten Henry Tudor with the spectre of a legitimate Pretender; perhaps even to switch over to Warbeck's claim, in case Tudor failed, died, or proved unmanageable.

Perkin Warbeck has been exposed by Dr. James Gairdner in his work, *Richard the Third;* and by a modern Belgian writer, Jean-Didier Chastelain, in *L'Imposture de Perkin Warbeck*. The Pretender was Jewish, the son of a boatman of Tournai in Flanders; and was exploited by Margaret of York, James the Fourth of Scotland (who gave Perkin his cousin Katherine Gordon in marriage), and Emperor Maximilian for their own political ends.

Hugh Ross Williamson,* a man not overly enamoured of facts, began life as an uncompromising Markhamist; he later switched to a rather curious variant of Warbeckism: Perkin was the bastard son of Margaret of York and the Bishop of Cambrai. Williamson clung to this notion until it was pointed out to him by the Fellowship of the Whyte Boar that Charles the Turbulent was very much alive in 1473, the supposed date of the Pretender's birth, and would scarcely have remained supine during this clerical invasion of his household. Williamson then shifted to orthodox Warbeckism; and is now a spokesman for that point of view.

The Fellowship of the Whyte Boar has said: "we are faced with two irreconcilable facts: Perkin Warbeck or the supposed bones of the Princes in Westminster Abbey." **

True. But, while it is not necessary to believe in *these* bones to disbelieve in Warbeckism, such belief does eliminate all question of Perkin as Richard the Fourth. The bones, now contained within an urn reposing in the tomb of Elizabeth the First, were discovered in the reign of Charles the Second, July 1673. The site of the discovery, 'metely deep' in the foundation of an outer staircase on the south side of the White Tower, could not have been the original burial place. This staircase site took days, even weeks, to prepare; and is far from being the hasty hole of a few hours' preparation described by Thomas More in his masterly *Life and Pitiful Raign of Edward the Fifth*.

The bodies may have been thrown originally into a kitchen-hole of the Tower. For the Bones found in the leaden chest contained not a scrap of

---

* See *Historical Whodunit* by Hugh Ross Williamson.

** From an "Historical Note" by Miss Isolde Wigram, Hon. Secretary of the Fellowship of the Whyte Boar, and distributed with the program for "The Sun of York"—a Fellowship-backed play on Richard authored by O. and I. Wigram, produced at the Royal Court Theatre in London in October 1955. In correspondence with the writer, Miss Wigram has elaborated a twist to the Warbeck legend that not even Williamson had thought of: Perkin Warbeck and Richard of York both existed! Perkin masqueraded as Richard and Richard masqueraded as Perkin, like the Prince and the Pauper in Mark Twain's tale. And when you imagined you were exposing Perkin Warbeck pretending to be Richard of York, you were actually unmasking Richard of York pretending to be Perkin Warbeck! This is a situation for the pen of James Thurber. *Wigram-Leary Correspondence,* letters of Feb. 22nd and April 12th, 1957, from Isolde Wigram; my letter of Feb. 27th, 1957.

cloth, not a button; and mingled with the human remains were various animal bones—a chicken, duck, ox.

The presence of these animal bones has also been explained as of much later origin. After the discovery in 1673, the Bones remained for some months in the keeping of the Master of Ordnance at the Tower, before finding a temporary interment in the vault of the Duke of Albemarle. The Master exhibited the Bones to various friends, even loaning out a shank here and a tibia there. So reduced had his collection become that he found it necessary to piece out the remainder with bones from his own pot. Considering the spirit of Restoration times and the Merry Monarch, this may well be as good an explanation as any.

Who reburied the Bones? Henry Tudor, then Henry the Seventh, reburied them. But why, having cached the remains of the real Claimant, did Henry fear Perkin Warbeck? He feared him, because Warbeck was backed by powerful interests hostile to Henry and because Henry's title to the throne was so insecure. Further, it is not known at what point Henry discovered and buried the Bones. His two chief threats, Perkin Warbeck and the pathetic Edward Earl of Warwick (whose intelligence and character had been ruined by his captivity; could not, they say, "tell a goose from a capon.") had been executed in 1499; but it is conceivable that Henry did not dig up the Bones until the alleged 'confession' of Sir James Tyrell, in May 1502. Giving as an excuse Tyrell's aid to a refugee Plantagenet, Edmund Earl of Suffolk, Henry had the Constable of Guisnes arrested and grilled. In the course of the grilling, Henry announced, Tyrell gasped out the hideous tale of the Princes—the story which Thomas More set down almost verbatim and which Shakespeare has immortalized in his play *Richard the Third*.

Conceivable, but not likely. Tyrell, who deserted Richard before Bosworth, was Tudor's man. Henry Stafford, Duke of Buckingham and ally of Tudor, employed Tyrell to murder the Princes in October 1483; and used their disappearance as a rallying cry against Richard. Buckingham had a diabolic quality; he was far cleverer than anyone realized.*

It is probable that Henry knew all about Tyrell; including the secret hiding-place of the bodies. The fact that Tyrell had committed an atrocious crime would not have prevented Henry from making use of him. Indeed, such background information would have equipped Henry with a useful hold. Even if Tyrell had not 'talked' before 1502, there was also John Dighton, living wretchedly on Henry's gratitude at Calais and "much pointed at" as the man with the inside story.

Who was this John Dighton. He seems to have been briefly a chaplain in the Tower, later granted the living of Fulbeck by Henry the Seventh on condition that he reside outside England. Dighton was a Fifteenth Century remittance man. Dighton was certainly not Tyrell's 'horsekeeper'—as More makes him out. According to Dick Grafton, the Continuator of More,

---

* I suggested an imaginative solution to the murder in my recent novel *Fire and Morning*, with Buckingham the evil genius of the House of York. Paul Murray Kendall was far from being the first to suggest a deadly role for Buckingham; Alfred O. Legge in *The Unpopular King*, published in 1885, brought forth the idea.

Dighton died "in great misery" at Calais. This may well be exact, as he was subsisting on the bounty of a notorious *avare*. His role in history was that of the go-between, the man who was present at the stowing away of the bodies of the murdered Princes and who carried the glad tidings to Henry Tudor. And in a pinch Dighton was always available; the man "who speaketh best for the King"—that is, the man who was able to vouch for the demise of the real Claimant and for the identity of the murderer, Sir James Tyrell.

If this be true, why did not Henry Tudor publicly dig up the Bones in 1485 and proclaim Richard's guilt. This has been the argument of Richard's ardent defenders—'Ricardians,' as they call themselves. But it is a disingenuous argument. It postulates that either Richard or Henry was the actual murderer and if Richard was guilty his enemy had everything to gain by a public demonstration. If no such demonstration took place, Tudor must be guilty.

However, both Richard and Henry were tarred with the brush. Richard, because Buckingham had been his principal officer and the man responsible for the Tower. Henry, because Buckingham was secretly a part of the Tudor frame-up and rebellion. Tyrell's sudden trip to York in September 1483, during the gorgeous festivities of Richard's northern 'Coronation,' may have been an intent to sound the royal will with regard to "those bastards in the Tower." Tyrell was canny; he would never have got himself out on a limb. The Princes were an embarrassment; yet that Richard would devise such a murder is repugnant to the character of the man, his exacting conscience, his hitherto exemplary devotion to the House of York.

It was only essential that Tyrell be assured Buckingham had the confidence of King Richard and that if Buckingham wished to make his own dispositions regarding the safe-keeping of the bastards of York, Richard was agreeable. In such situations, while murder is, as Kendall points out, implicit in the lot of a dethroned monarch, no one ever talks of violence; and sometimes the ruined god may hang on for years like Henry the Sixth; and sometimes he may go out quite quickly, like Richard the Second.

In the case of the Princes, Richard might afford to let the boys live; Buckingham and Tudor could not. For if the Princes were an embarrassment to Richard, they were a fatal obstacle to the ambitions of this precious pair. Neither Buckingham nor Tudor could hope to get anywhere as long as the sons of Edward survived. The Princes must sleep in Abraham's bosom before ever Tudor set sail from Brittany.

By 1485, Tudor preferred to hush up the crime rather than to examine witnesses (he had at least two) publicly. Equally, there was no incentive for him to display the bodies. Even if he had not actually participated in the murder, the Duke of Buckingham had been his ally and Buckingham had in charge the Princes before the rebellion of October 1483.

Henry did put out an explanation sometime after Tyrell had been executed in 1502. But he did this when the trail was cold and when it seemed essential that Ferdinand King of Aragon be reassured as to Henry's title, in order to consent to the marriage of his daughter Katherine to Henry Duke of York. Katherine had already been married to Henry's older son Arthur, who had died suddenly in April 1502. It would seem that something had happened between the first marriage and the plans for the second to render an explanation of the Princes both essential and possible.

For one thing, Perkin Warbeck had appeared on the scene and while Ferdinand had investigated Perkin's claim and had satisfied himself that Perkin was a fake, a new cloud had gathered about Henry's title. Then in February 1503, Henry's own wife, Elizabeth of York, had died in childbirth in the Tower. Men were not so forgetful but they recalled that Elizabeth had been a not unwilling candidate for Richard's bed back in 1485. Even Henry would have hesitated, while Elizabeth was alive, to accuse his Queen of wishing to marry the murderer of her brothers. Finally, Henry was helped along by the death in 1502 of his great tormentor, Margaret of York, Duchess of Burgundy.

'Juno,' as the Lord Verulam calls her, had vexed Henry for years by raising up one Pretender after another. "Hee began again to be haunted with spirits, by the Magick and curious arts of the Lady Margaret, who raised up the ghost of Richard Duke of York, to walk and vex the King." This, in 1492. And 'hee' had never a moment's peace while this energetic and wily daughter of York endured.

On the assumption that Margaret refused aid to Richard because she believed him guilty of the murder, it must be conceded that she personally had no faith in her Pretender Warbeck. But she was interested in overturning Henry and in getting back the income from her lands in England of which Henry had deprived her. Now at last Margaret was dead, unable to conjure up new Pretenders or to gainsay any tale that Henry chose to put out.

Kendall, in his biography *Richard the Third,* suggests that Richard was able to persuade Elizabeth Woodeville of Buckingham's guilt; and for this reason the ravaged Queen recalled to England her last son Thomas Grey, Marquess of Dorset, and was prepared to bestow on Richard her daughter Elizabeth. This seems highly improbable. Once admit the boys had vanished (which Richard never did) and it would be impossible for him to clear himself with anyone, least of all with his old enemy Elizabeth Woodeville. It was, on the other hand, at least possible for Richard to deny access to the captives on one pretext or another over a period of time. Elizabeth herself was immured in sanctuary up until March 1484; and could not in any case have seen her sons. From March 1484 to Easter 1485, Richard played for time; the inconsistency of the King's conduct in wishing to marry her daughter while declaring the girl's brothers bastards seems not to have given pause to Elizabeth Woodeville.

An alternative explanation for this curious attitude on Elizabeth's part may well exist: she was playing a double game with Richard. In April 1483, the Queen had been outfoxed by Gloucester and Buckingham, with the result that her son Edward lost his throne—and his life. Vengeance became the cherished companion of the Queen. In October 1483, Elizabeth's kindred had been among the most active, arguing that she at least had no illusions about Richard, whatever her notions concerning Buckingham and Tudor. Indeed, the most cogent reason she had for preferring Tudor was that he had promised to marry Elizabeth of York and make her Queen, a reason hardly supportable if at that time Elizabeth's brothers were still alive. In March 1484, Elizabeth Woodeville emerged from sanctuary. Why not? She could do more harm to Richard by renewed freedom of movement. She appeared to cooperate in the recall of her son Dorset and in the marriage project with her daughter Elizabeth and the new-made widower, the girl's uncle Richard. But both these schemes failed dramatically and irreparably; and in such a way as not to cast blame upon Elizabeth Woodeville. Dorset's failure looked as if Master Marquess were not really trying; and afterward, he was not punished by Tudor but only left behind at the time of the invasion. The marriage project was nipped by Richard's captains, who had been led to think that vengeance would be exacted from them by the new Queen for the blood of her beheaded relatives. Who gave the captains this idea? Surely the woman, the prospective Queen's gilthaired mother, who had engineered the destruction of Clarence and the Earl of Desmond, was capable of stirring panic in those ruthless hearts: 'The Cat, the Rat, and Lovell the Dog.'

By the time Tudor got around to his second try, Elizabeth Woodeville was ready. By a deal with Margaret Beaufort she agreed to match her daughter Elizabeth with Margaret's son Henry. Equally important, she made her attitude clear to the Stanleys, Lord Tom and Sir William, who would destroy Richard on the field of battle. By these actions, Elizabeth Woodeville sought to avenge her murdered sons. It must then have been a frightful revelation when she discovered, too late, that her bald new son-in-law, Henry Tudor, was as guilty as anyone. How, precisely, she discovered this, no one knows; no doubt her suspicions were aroused when Henry refused to look for the bodies and tried to hush up the whole affair. By 1486, Elizabeth was prepared to underwrite a new program of vengeance, this time against the *quondam* avenger himself: the Lambert Simnel rising, in which a scullion was coached to impersonate the imprisoned son of Clarence, the only living legitimate Plantagenet in direct male line, Edward Earl of Warwick. Lambert Simnel failed; and Elizabeth was shut in Bermondsey nunnery by her son-in-law. By this time, surely, she had reached the stage of Margaret of Anjou—hating on an exalted level.

Such an analysis argues a formidable duplicity and a great power of will. But the career of Elizabeth Woodeville proves that she possessed those qualities. And, assuming a consistency of conduct on the part of this crafty dangerous woman would go far to explain the most baffling aspect of the Princes: Elizabeth Woodeville's rapprochement with Richard.

Elizabeth Woodeville's attitude in 1486 is also testimony to the guilt of Henry Tudor. By 1502, Henry felt the need to get rid of the question of the Princes, which had haunted his reign as much as Richard's. Characteristically, he began with a judicial murder: that of his faithful servant Sir James Tyrell, Captain of Guisnes.* Sometime after, he put out the bogus 'confession' by Tyrell.

* HENRY himself recognized that his treatment of Tyrell had been a frame-up. In April 1507, he reversed Tyrell's attainder and restored young Tyrell to grace. This may suggest that Tyrell had not been involved in the murder of the Princes

Henry had known all along about the murder. He could scarcely tell every-thing; but he could suggest the general outline. His own connexion must be carefully screened.

More's story had to be rigged in several essentials. The date of the murder had to be altered, from October to July, blinking the fact that the victims had been publicly seen in late August or early September. The murder would thus appear a cause of Buckingham's rebellion, rather than a result—as it actually was. A few phony accomplices had to be got up: John Green, Miles Forest, John Dighton. The reburial had to occur almost immediately, the next night, when Richard would have been responsible. The actual reburial took place in Henry's reign. More's tale must then be made to fit the chosen hiding place ten feet deep in the foundation stone of the outer staircase on the south face of the White Tower. Many persons have found this approximate confirmation (in 1673) of More's story one hundred and fifty years earlier quite remarkable. It is remarkable if one assumes that the reburial took place during Richard's reign; less so, if the tale-bearer himself performed the interment.

The question remains: are these Bones in fact the bones of the sons of Edward? The opening of the funerary urn on July 6, 1933—Richard's Corona-tion Day—afforded evidence that these were the bones of two children aged about ten and thirteen. Aside from the comment of the Archdeacon of West-minster that the unusually deep bone sockets of the eyes might have been caused by excessive weeping (!), little could be said concerning the circum-stances of death. The late Professor William Wright, leading pathologist and past president of the British Anatomical Society, suggested that a large stain on the atlas (the first cervical vertebra, which supports the head) of the elder child might have been due to a massive suffusion of blood as a result of violent death by suffocation—but this conclusion has been bitterly disputed by Ri-cardians, who have represented the Bones as being 'foundation sacrifices' dating from some remote period of the Tower's history. Professor Wright's other conclusion, that these were the remains of two male children, has been equally attacked. Dr. Northcroft, a past president of the British Dental As-sociation, contributed the dental findings: that is, the principal evidence for the age of the two children, and the fact that the elder had suffered from severe dental caries and from inflammation of the gums. Neither Professor Wright nor Dr. Northcroft could offer a definite opinion as to the approximate antiq-uity of the Bones.*

Re-examination of the contents of the urn would serve little purpose un-

---

at all. We have only Henry's word that he was. But if Tyrell was not directly involved, he undoubtedly knew the real story—and Henry found it convenient to get rid of him on a trumped-up charge.

* Vide: Tanner and Wright, "Recent Investigations Concerning the Princes in the Tower" *Archaeologia*, LXXXIV. Philip Lindsay, *The Bones in Westminster Abbey* (1934). In a letter to the writer dated Feb. 23, 1956, Mr. Lawrence Tanner ex-presses himself as completely satisfied with the conclusions of the experts made twenty-three years previously.

less some scientific procedure exists for determining the antiquity of these Bones—a key question in the controversy. For if the Bones could be proved to date from the Fifteenth Century, the argument in favour of the remains being those of the Princes of York would be virtually clinched.

Just as the circumstances of the actual murder have been shrouded, so these Bones have become part of the controversy; the most fascinating historical mystery in England. The Lord Verulam speaks of Henry's passion for "shewing things by Pieces and Dark Lights" and his ability to "muffle" a question. Morton was equally adept and the handling of the murder of Edward's sons was their joint masterpiece—so compassed about with half-truths and off-trail scents that it will probably never be wholly resolved. But it ought to be clear that Henry was in up to his neck; and was the ally of the real murderer, Henry Stafford, Duke of Buckingham.

Richard's guilt was that of the man who allows a dread deed to occur. Tyrell's visit to York in 1483 may have had reference to the Princes; or it may not. Sir James was shrewd; but not shrewd enough to outlive Henry Tudor. What is incontrovertible is that Richard himself placed his nephews, entrusted to him by his dying brother Edward, in Buckingham's mortal grip; and he allowed the Duke full sway over the 'seely children.' It was that bitter, that irreparable guilt for which he lost his crown; for which, on Bosworth's ruined field, he proclaimed: "yet have I with strict penance and salt tears expiated the same offense, which abominable crime I do require you of friendship as clearly to forget, as I do daily to deplore and lament. . . ."

INDEX

Alençon, Jean duc d', 63-64, 67, 82, 328, 335, 339.
Angers, Citadel of, 14, 118.
Anjou, Marguerite d' (1429–1482), xxiii, xxvii, 121, 123-126, 133, 136, 138, 141, 150, 158-159, 167-168, 171-173, 196-199, 233-235, 237, 241-243, 316, 340-346.
Anjou, René or Regnier, xxvii, 70, 80, 115-123, 152-153, 339, 342.
Anjou, Yolande d', 121, 152, 341n, 344.
Anquetonville, Raoul, xxn, 334.
Aragon, Yolande of, 14, 24, 32.
Arc, Jacques d', 5, 70.
Arc, Jeanne d', *See* Jeanne La Pucelle.
Armagnac, Jean IV, Comte, 76, 334.
Armoises, Jeanne des, 335-337.
Arras, Treaty of, 335.
Aulon, Jean d', 48, 52, 57-58, 82, 86.

Bacon, Sir Francis, 294-295, 295n, 353.
Bâle, Council of, 97, 97n, 100.
Baretti, Bartolomeo, 84-86.
Barnet, Battle of, April 14, 1471, *See* Richard III.
Baudricourt, Robert de, 5, 10, 328.
Bavière, Ysabeau de (1370–1435), xix, 6, 328, 334.
Beauchamp, Sir Richard, 234.
Beaufort, Henry, Cardinal, xx, xxii, 101-102, 107, 109, 121, 124, 127-131, 145, 157-158, 164.
       John, 146, 236, 243.
       Lady Margaret, 278-279, 284, 294.
       See also Somerset, Dukes of.
Beaugency, 64-65.
Beaumont, John, Viscount, 129, 163.
Beaupère, Jean le, 90-92, 108.
Bedford, Anne, Duchess of (1402–1430), 13, 71, 335.
       John, Duke of (1385–1435),

xxiv, 13, 71-72, 88, 218, 332-333, 335.
Blaunche Senglier, 265, 272, 283.
"Bloody Friday," June 13, 1483, 256-257.
Blore Heath, Battle of, 162, 165.
Boniface VIII, Pope, 92n.
Bosch, Hieronymus, xvii, xxix, 78, 151.
Bosworth, Battle of, August 22, 1485, *See* Richard III.
Boucher, Catherine, 47-48.
       Jacques, 47, 336.
Bourbon, Charles de, Comte de Clermont, 27, 80, 84.
Brackenbury, Sir Robert, 264, 289, 289n, 296, 314.
Brandon, Sir William, 273, 315.
Bray, Dr. Reginald, xxii, 293.
Bretigny, Treaty of, 1475, 342.
Brézé, Pierre de, 123, 161, 232.
Buck, Sir George, 290, 291.
Buckingham, Dukes of:
       Humphrey Stafford, 1st Duke, 141, 158, 159.
       Henry Stafford, 2nd Duke, (1454–1483), 218, 249, 254-257, 259-263, 266-268, 302, 348-349, 353.
Burgundy, Anthony, Grand Bastard of, 216-217, 217n.
Burgundy, Dukes of:
       Charles le Témeraire (1433–1477), xxvi, 217, 222-223, 225.
       Jean sans peur (1371–1419), xix-xx, 12, 239.
       Philippe le bon (1396–1467), 43-44, 77-78, 85-86, 120.
Burgundy, Isabella, Duchess of, 77, 83-84, 222.
       Margaret, Duchess of, *See* York, Margaret of.

Cade, Jack, 135-144, 169, 192.
Calabria, John of, 341n, 342.

353

Calabria, John of (*continued*)
Nicholas of, 341n, 344n.
Catesby, William (the "Cat"), 256-257, 268-269, 278-279, 289, 292, 309.
Cauchon, Pierre, Bishop of Beauvais, xxvi, 17, 88-101, 104-105, 110, 328, 333, 335.
Caxton, William, xxi, xxix, 275-276, 338.
Charité, La, 82-83.
Charles II (Duke of Lorraine), 21, 115-118.
VI ("Le Fou") (1368-1422), xix, 25, 150.
VII (1402-1461), xix, xxvi, 23-27, 86-87, 333, 336, 338-339.
VIII (1470-1498), 272.
Charolais, Charles, Count of, *See* Burgundy, Dukes of, Charles le Témeraire.
Charlton, Thomas, 140, 142.
Chartres, Regnault de, Archbishop of Reims, xxv, 68, 75, 86.
Chasteaudreux, Jean de, 345-346.
Chaucer, Alice, *See* Suffolk, Alice, Duchess of.
Chertsey, 273, 277.
Chester, Earl of, *See* Lancaster, Edward, Prince of.
Cheyney, Sir John, 273, 289, 315.
Chronique de Lorraine, 337.
Clarence, George, Duke of, xxvn, 207, 217, 223-225, 227, 239-240, 246-249, 340-346, 351.
"Claude," *See* Jeanne la Pucelle.
Clifford, John, 9th Lord, 170-172, 186-188, 192-193.
Clifton, Sir Gervase ("Sire de la Rose"), 232, 243.
Coeur-de-lys, 334-338.
College of Heralds, 282-283.
Collingbourne, Will, 274, 283-284.
Compiegne, 74, 76, 81, 92n, 336.
Conyers, Sir John, 220, 314.
Courcelles, Thomas de, 17, 98-100, 108.
Coutes, Louis des, 54, 57.
Crofts, Sir Richard, 206-207, 240.

Derby, Lord Tom Stanley, Earl of, 243, 273-274, 284, 294, 299, 305, 305n, 308, 316, 351.
Dighton, John, 348-349, 352.
Domremy, 5-8, 15-16, 18, 33, 334.

Dorset, Thomas Grey, Marquess of, 218-219, 258, 270, 273, 283, 292.
Dumay, Alison, 116, 119, 152.
Dunois, Comte, *See,* Orléans, Jean, Bastard of.

Ecclesia Unam Sanctam (Papal Bull), 92. *See also* Boniface VIII, Pope.
"Edward the Bastard," *See* Edward V.
Edward I, ("Longshanks"), xxiv, xxviii.
Edward II (1284-1326), 281.
Edward IV (1442-1483), xviii, xxiii-xxiv, 169, 171, 177, 191-192, 198, 218-219, 221n, 225-226, 233-234, 236, 238, 249-253, 253n.
Edward V (1470-1483), xxvn, 222, 253, 259, 263-264, 264n, 300, 302.
Edward, Prince of Wales (1474-1484), 265, 273, 280, 346-353.
Estivet, Jean d', Canon of Beauvais, 17, 93, 101-102, 107, 332.
Eton, 128, 130, 149.
Exeter, Anne, Duchess of, 217n, 225, 273, 289, 289n.
Henry Holland, Duke of, 289, 289n.

Falconbridge, Tom, Bastard of, 244.
Lord William, 193, 197.
Fastolf, Sir John, 11, 64-65, 140, 338.
Fellowship of the Whyte Boar, 315, 346-353.
Ferrers, Walter, Lord, 309, 314.
Ferrybridge, 192, 196, 196n.
Fierbois, 23, 42.
Flavy, Guillaume de, 84-86.
"Flemish School" of painters, xxix, 78, 342.
Formigny, Battle of, 131.
Forrest, Miles, 284, 343, 352.
Fotheringay, Castle of, 132, 204, 208.
Francis II, Duke of Brittany, 279-280.
Fulford, Sir Baldwin, 174, 191.

Garden of Earthly Pleasures, xvii, xxix.
Gaucourt, Raoul de, 53, 73.
Glansdale, Sir William, 43, 47, 58.
Gloucester, Eleanor, Duchess of, xvii, 126, 126n, 129.
Humphrey, Good Duke of, xxii, xxvn, 124-126, 129-130, 141, 145.

Richard, Duke of, *See* Richard III.

Gloucester, "Shining City," 234, 263.

Gough, Matthew, 64-65, 143-144.

Greenwich, Palace of, 125, 159.

Grey, Lady Elizabeth, *See* Woodville, Elizabeth.

Sir John, 107, 107n.

Sir John, of Groby, 107n, 148, 174, 218.

Hall, Davy, 169, 171.

Harcourt, Christopher, 61-62, 73.

Hastings, William, Lord, 228-230, 254, 255n, 256-257, 260, 270.

Hauviette, 4, 7, 334.

Henry IV (1367–1413), xxii.

V (1387–1422), xxii, xxiv, 13, 300, 303.

VI (1422–1471), xxii-xxiii, xxvn, xxviii, 11-12, 74, 96n, 127-130, 130, 138, 141, 146-151, 155, 157-160, 162, 164-166, 179, 189, 196, 199, 244-246.

James IV of Scotland, 347.

Jargeau, 62-64.

Jean le Bombardier, 50, 52.

Jean le bon Roi de France (1319–1364), 50n.

of Gloucester, 265, 296, 299.

Jeanne la Pucelle (1412–1431), xxvi, 3-7, 9-10, 15-16, 27-31, 33-42, 44-45, 47-49, 52-59, 62-71, 79-81, 84-103, 109-112, 115-118, 327-334, 339-340.

"John Amende-alle," *See* Cade, Jack.

Kemp, John, 139, 141, 155-156, 159.

King's College, Cambridge, 128, 130.

Kyriel, Sir Thomas, 131, 185n, 189-190.

Ladvenu, Brother Martin, 103, 106, 109-110, 112, 332-333, 338.

Lancaster, Edward, Prince of (1453–1471), xxvn, 146-152, 157, 165-166, 174, 176-177, 189, 199, 236, 239, 241, 340-346.

John of Gaunt, Duke of, 298n.

Nicholas, Mayor of York, 298.

Lancastrian Restoration, 340-346.

Lannoy, Hughes de, 73-74, 83.

Laval, Guy de, 62-63.

Laxart, Durand, 9-10, 18-19, 22, 70.

Lincoln, John de la Pole, Earl of, 262, 281, 299.

Little Malvern Priory, 237, 342.

Loiseleur, Nicholas, Canon of Rouen, 17, 97, 108-109, 333n, 338.

Lollards, xxi, xxiin.

Lorraine, 176, 185.

Lorraine, Isabella of, 119, 152.

Louis III, d'Anjou, 119-120.

XI ("Universal Spider") (1423–1483), 251-252, 272, 340-346.

XII, 31.

Lovelace, Harry, 137, 188.

Lovell, Francis (the "Dog"), 268, 288-289, 292, 297.

Ludlow Castle, 163, 207.

Luxembourg, Demoiselle of, 88, 91.

Jean (Comte de Ligny), 73, 334.

Lyonnel, 86.

Lys, Jean du, 47n, 335-337.

Jeanne, *See* Jeanne la Pucelle.

Pierre, 86, 335-337.

Maistre, Jean le, 89, 107, 110.

Malory, Sir Thomas, xvii-xviii, xxiii.

Manchon, Guillaume, 98, 333n.

March, Edward, Earl of, *See* Edward IV.

Marie, "Gasque of Avignon," 30, 328.

Mary of Gueldres, Queen of Scotland, 148, 167.

Massieu, Brother Jean, 102-106, 110-111, 338.

Maurice, Master Pierre, 98-99, 108.

Midi, Nicholas, Canon of Rouen, 107-109.

Moleyns, Adam, Lord Privy Seal, 131, 159, 189.

More, Sir Thomas, 288, 347.

Morte d'Artur, See Malory, Sir Thomas.

Mortimer, Alice, 131, 141n.

Mortimer's Cross, Battle of, xxiii, 178.

"Mortimer, Sir John," *See* Cade, Jack.

Morton, John, Bishop of Ely, xxii, 257, 263, 266-268, 287-288, 294-295, 316, 346-353.

Neville, Anne (1456–1485), 221, 237, 243-244, 265, 280, 289-292, 302, 304, 340-341.

Neville, Anne (*continued*)
  Cecil, Duchess of York ("Proud
    Cis"), *See,* York, Cecily, Duchess of.
  Isabel, 224, 248, 340-346.
  John, Marquess of Montague,
    180, 220, 226, 231-232.
Norfolk, Dukes of:
  John Mowbray, 3rd Duke, 134,
    156, 156n, 198, 241.
  John Howard, 6th Duke, 262,
    289, 291, 305-314.
Northampton, Battle of, 163, 165.
Northumberland, Earls of:
      Henry Percy, 2nd Earl
    (1394-1455), 159, 198.
      Henry Percy, 4th Earl
  (-1488), 260, 262, 273, 299,
    308.
Nottingham ("Castle of Care"), 284,
  296-297.

Orléans, City of, 38-39, 42, 335.
Orléans, Dukes of:
    Louis (1380-1407), xix, 329-
      330, 334.
    Charles (1391-1465), 330,
      334, 337.
Orléans, Jean, Bastard of, 25-26, 44-45,
  47, 50, 53, 53n, 54, 57-58, 87n, 328-
  330, 335.
    Jeanne d', 328, 330.
Ormonde, James Butler, 4th Earl of,
  147, 147n, 159, 178, 196.
Oxford, John de Vere, 13th Earl of, 222,
  225-226, 229-230, 309-312.

Pacquerel, Father Jean, 41, 54-55.
Pierre, Brother Ysambart de la, 98, 333,
  338.
Poitiers, 35-37, 331.
Poppelau, Nicholas von, 206, 283.
Pontefract, Castle, 170, 254.

Rais, Gilles de, xvii, xx-xxi, xxvi, 40-41,
  118-119, 336.
Ratcliffe, Sir Richard (the "Rat"), 259-
  260, 278-279, 289, 291-292, 307-
  314.
Rempston, Sir Thomas, 39, 64.
Richard, Brother, 69-70.

Richard II (1367-1400), xviii, xxvn, 281.
  III (1452-1485), xxviii-xxix,
    203-206, 211-215, 224-225, 230-231,
    233-241, 244-247, 250-251, 253-259,
    262-280, 284-298, 301-316, 346-363.
Richemont, Artus de, 24, 65-66.
Rivers, Anthony Woodville, Lord, 216-
  218, 244, 248, 254.
Robin of Redesdale, *See* Conyers, Sir
  John.
Rochelle, Catherine de la, 81-83.
Rouen, 111, 334-338.
Royal Succession Act, 1470, 222.
Russell, John, Bishop of Lincoln, 268-
  269.
Ruthyn, Lord Grey de, 134, 163, 197.
Rutland, Edmund, Earl of, 172.

St. Albans, 1st Battle of, May 22, 1455,
  158-160.
St. Albans, 2nd Battle of, February 19,
  1461, *See* Anjou, Marguerite d'.
St. Florent, 34-35.
Salisbury, Richard, Earl of, 160, 162,
  169.
      Thomas   Montague,   Lord,
    42-43.
Say, (Sir) James Fiennes, Lord, 141-142,
  159.
Scales, Anthony, Lord, *See* Rivers, An-
  thony, Lord.
      Thomas, Lord, 64, 107, 143.
Sendal Castle, 170-171.
Shakespeare, William, 339.
Shore, Jane, 219, 256, 270-271, 312.
Shrewsbury, John, Earl of, 148-149, 336.
Simnel, Lambert, xxix, 351.
Somerset, Dukes of:
      John, 1st Duke (1404-1444),
    126, 133.
      Edmund, 2nd Duke (1405-
    1455), 124, 129-131, 133, 136, 139,
    146, 148, 150, 154, 158-159.
      Henry Beaufort, 3rd Duke
    (1434-1464), 146-148, 160, 176,
    193.
      Edmund Beaufort, 4th Duke
    (1438-1471), 146, 232, 234, 236,
    238, 239, 241.
Sorel, Agnes, 60, 80, 87n, 147, 154.
Southwark, Borough of, 139, 149n, 244.
Stafford, Humphrey, Lord, 67, 139, 314.

Stanley, George, Lord Strange, 274, 297, 309.

Stanley, Sir Thomas, 129, 163.
    Sir William, 273, 294, 297, 307-315, 351.

Stillington, Robert, Bishop of Bath and Wells, 247-248, 259.

"Strawnecks," 96, 100, 105, 105n, 107, 333.

Suffolk, Alice, Duchess of, 128, 134, 343.
    Elizabeth, Duchess of, 217n, 225.

Suffolk, Dukes of:
    John de la Pole, 186, 262.
    William de la Pole, 43, 62-64, 121-123, 125, 130-131, 133, 136, 138, 159.

Surrey, Thomas, Earl of, 262, 289.

Talbot, Gilbert, 299, 304-305.
    Lady Eleanor, 247-248, 259, 304.

Tanneguy du Chastel, 79, 330.

Tewkesbury, Battle of, May 4, 1471, See Richard III.

Tourelles, Les, 42-43, 49, 55-59.

Towton, Battle of, Palm Sunday, March 29, 1461, See Anjou, Marguerite d'.

Trémoïlle, Georges de la, 24-26, 33-34, 65, 69, 73-75, 82-83, 85-86, 92

Tresham, William, 131-132, 134, 139.

Trollope, Sir Andrew, 163, 169-171, 196, 198-199.

Troyes, Treaty of, 1420, 69, 78.

Tudor, Henry, Earl of Richmond, 266-268, 279, 282, 293-294, 301-303, 316, 346-353.
    Owen, 178, 263, 289n.

Tyler, Wat, 137, 140, 190.

Tynedowe, Anckenett, 248.

Tyrell, Sir James, 264-267, 272, 287-288, 348-351, 351n.

Urswicke, Christopher, xxii, 293, 315.

Valois, Katherine de, 13, 124.

Vaucouleurs, Sire de, See Baudricourt, Robert de.

Vaudemont, Ferry de, 341n, 342, 344.

Verneuil, Battle of, August 17, 1424, 328.

Verulam, Lord, See Bacon, Sir Francis.

Vignolles, Etienne de, 5, 41, 47.

Villiers de l'isle Adam, 69, 80.

Villon, François, xviii, 153.

Visconti, Bonne, 60-61.
    Valentine, Duchesse d'Orléans, 12, 25, 33, 45, 328-329.

Wainflete, William, Bishop of Winchester, 144.

Wakefield, Lady Chapel, 277, 277n.

Warbeck, Perkin ("Richard IV"), xxix, 346, 348-350.

Warwick, Anne Beauchamp, Countess of, 237.

Warwick, Earls of:
    Richard Beauchamp, 3rd Earl, 106-107, 111, 332, 335, 338-339.
    Richard Neville, 7th Earl ("Kingmaker") (1428–1471), xxi, 147, 158, 161, 166, 177, 179, 184-189, 197, 208-210, 219-225, 227-232, 338, 340-346.
    Edward Plantagenet, 8th Earl, xxvn, 299, 348.

Wenlock, Sir John, 160, 190, 232-233, 236, 238-239, 304.

Whethamstede, Abbot John, 185, 188.

Wiltshire, Earl of, See Ormonde, James Butler, 4th Earl of.

Woodeville, Elizabeth (1428–1495), 174, 222, 253, 256, 277-279, 280, 285-287, 292-295, 302, 312, 343, 350-351.
    Edward, 218-219, 258.

Woodeville, Lionel, Bishop of Salisbury, 273, 277, 283.

Worcester, John Tiptoft, Earl of, xxi, 221-222.

Xantrailles, Poton de, 40, 43.

York, Anne of, See Exeter, Duchess of.
    Cecily, Duchess of ("Proud Cis"), 132, 149-150, 156, 158, 169, 177, 178n, 301.
    City of, 173-176, 226, 250, 250n, 264-265, 265n, 298-299.

York, Dukes of:
    Edward, 2nd Duke (1373–1415), 132.
    Richard, 3rd Duke, xxvn, 126, 134, 136, 141, 154, 156-158, 163, 165-166, 172, 339.

York, Dukes of (*continued*)

    Edward, 4th Duke, *See* Edward IV.

    Richard, 5th Duke (1472–1483), xxvn, 247, 255, 258, 264, 264n, 346-353.

York, Elizabeth of (1466–1503), 252, 279-280, 286-287, 299.

    Elizabeth of, *See* Suffolk, Duchess of.

    Margaret of, xxviii-xxix, 217, 287-288, 346, 350.

DATE DUE

PRINTED IN U.S.A.